ARCHITECTURE AND
IDEOLOGY IN
EARLY MEDIEVAL SPAIN

ARCHITECTURE AND IDEOLOGY IN EARLY MEDIEVAL SPAIN

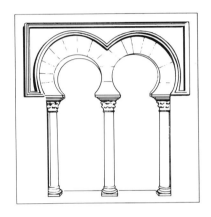

Jerrilynn D. Dodds

THE PENNSYLVANIA STATE UNIVERSITY PRESS
University Park, Pennsylvania

Publication of this book has been aided by a grant from The Program for Cultural Cooperation Between Spain's Ministry of Culture and United States' Universities.

Publication of this book has been aided by a grant from the Millard Meiss Publication Fund of the College Art Association.

$$\boxed{\textbf{MM}}$$

Library of Congress Cataloging-in-Publication Data
Dodds, Jerrilynn D.
    Architecture and ideology in early medieval Spain / Jerrilynn D. Dodds.
       p.   cm.
    Bibliography: p.
    Includes index.
    ISBN 0-271-00671-4 (cloth). — ISBN 0-271-01325-7 (pbk.)
    I. Architecture—Spain. 2. Architecture, Medieval—Spain. 3. Architecture and society—Spain.
I. Title
NA1303.D63   1989
720'.946'09021—dc20

88-43437

Second printing, 1994

It is the policy of The Pennsylvania State University Press to use acid-free paper for the first printing of all clothbound books. Publications on uncoated stock satisfy the minimum requirements of American National Standard for Information Sciences—Permanence of Paper for Printed Library Materials, ANSI Z39.48-1984.

Contents

List of Illustrations

Illustration Sources

Figures

All Plans executed by Charles A. Gifford.

Figure 8 is by Theodor Hauschild from Schlunk and Hauschild, *Die Denkmäler der frühchristlichen und westgotischen Zeit*, Mainz, 1978, and Figure 30 by Christian Ewert, "Die Moschee am Bāb al-Mardūm in Toledo—ein 'Kopie' der Moschee von Córdoba," *MM* 18 (1977). They are used here with the kind permission of Professors Hauschild and Ewert.

Figures 1, 2, 3, 4, 5, 6, 9, 10, and 11 are after those in Schlunk and Hauschild, *Die Denkmäler der frühchristlichen und westgotischen Zeit*, Mainz, 1978, with the permission of Professor Hauschild and Verlag Philipp Von Zabern.

Figures 7 and 24 are after the plans of Luis Caballero Zoreda with the kind permission of Professor Caballero. Figure 12 is after José Menéndez Pidal; Figure 13 is courtesy of Editorial León Sánchez Cuesta; Figures 14 and 15 are after plans that appear in Heitz, *L'Architecture carolingienne*, Paris, 1980, with the permission of Editions Picard; Figure 16 is after the plan from L. Grodecki, *L'Architecture ottonienne*, Paris, 1958, with permission of Armand Colin; Figures 17 and 19 are after those published in Lampérez, *Historia de la arquitectura cristiana española*, vol. 1, Madrid, 1930, with corrections by the author; Figure 23 is after Manuel Núñez in *Arquitectura prerrománica*, Madrid, 1978; Figures 18, 21, 22, 26, 27, and 28 are after Gómez-Moreno in *Iglesias Mozárabes*, Madrid, 1919, and Granada, 1975, some with corrections by the author; Figure 25 is after that published in Fontaine, *L'Art préroman hispanique*, vol. 2, 1977; Figure 17, with the permission of Editions Zodiaque, including corrections by the author; Figures 29, 31, and 32 are after Christian Ewert in *Forschungen zur almohadischen Moschee, Lieferung 1: Vorstufen. Hierarchische Gliederungen westislamischer Betsäle des 8 bis 11 Jahrhunderts: Die Hauptmoscheen von Qairawān und Córdoba und ihr Bannkreis*, Mainz, 1981, and "Die Moschee am Bāb al-Mardūm in Toledo—ein 'Kopie' der Moschee von Córdoba," *MM* 18 (1977), with the kind permission of Professor Ewert.

Plates

Plates 1, 14, 21, 36, 51, 62, 65, and 70 courtesy of Editions Zodiaque. Plates 2 and 63 are courtesy of Verlag Max Hirmer; Plate 4 courtesy of Verlag Philipp Von Zabern; Plate 15 appears with thanks to Professor John Williams; Plate 23 courtesy of Foto Marburg; Plates 24–26 and 30 courtesy of Editorial León Sánchez Cuesta; and Plate 27 courtesy of Dumbarton Oaks. Plate 28 is from F. Wirth, *Römische Wandmalerei*, Berlin, 1934; Plate 29 appears with permission of the Soprintendenza Archeologica of Ostia; Plate 31 courtesy of Editions Gallimard; Plate 32 appears with thanks to Professor Lawrence Nees; Plate 60 courtesy of the Morgan Library; Plates 66 and 73 courtesy of Centro de Estudios Históricos of the Consejo Superior de Investigaciones Científicas in Madrid, and Plate 81 is by P. Witte, courtesy of the Deutsches Archäologisches Institut in Madrid with thanks to Professor Christian Ewert.

All other plates are by Jerrilynn D. Dodds and Charles A. Gifford.

Acknowledgments

This book has been in the making for a long time, and the list of those I ought to thank is absurdly long. In many ways, even this condensed version seems more formidable than the book that follows it for the care and generosity of those colleagues and friends whose names appear so briefly.

Fieldwork in Spain and North Africa and preliminary documentation were accomplished with a Fellowship for Independent Research from the National Endowment for the Humanities, and I twice received additional funding for travel from the Columbia University Council for Research in the Humanities and Social Sciences. I was able to complete writing upon receiving the Hettleman Prize at Columbia. I am grateful indeed for this financial support.

Professors Thomas Glick, Oleg Grabar, and David Simon read and commented upon the entire manuscript, and Professors Terry Allen, Herbert Kessler, Lawrence Nees, and Roger Reynolds offered extremely valuable comments concerning individual chapters. I owe these colleagues in particular warm thanks for their important and humane guidance. Naturally none of those acknowledged here can be held accountable for what I have written in these pages. But to the extent that there is any evidence here of an energetic interest in the unveiling of a social subconscious by means of the analysis of art, it is probably owed to the extraordinary teaching, remembered now for over a decade, of Oleg Grabar.

Those who have offered specific comments concerning some part of the material discussed here (without necessarily having consulted the manuscript) are many. I wish to thank in particular Professors Richard Bulliet, Vicente Cantarino, David Freedberg, Thomas Lyman, Marvin Trachtenberg, Karl Werckmeister, John Williams, and my dear, lamented friend, the late Professor Noureddine Mezoughi. Finally, my notes attest to the extent to which this study is indebted to the scholarship of my colleagues in Spanish Medieval Art and History, without which it would have been virtually impossible.

I am indebted to Professor Duane Carpenter for his generous scrutiny of my Latin translations, and to Professor Wayne Finke for editing the Spanish text and notes. Ahmad El-Dallal took much time and care in editing the Arabic transliterations, and this work is indebted to Tayeb El-Hibri for several elegant translations from Arabic and other excellent counsel. Valuable materials and both practical and spiritual help were generously supplied by Professors Edson Armi, Isidro Bango, Luis Caballero, Rafael Cómez, Christian Ewert, Jacques Fontaine, Sima Godfrey, Rona Goffen,

Rosa Guerriero Golay, Theodor Hauschild, Peter Klein, Tom Mathews, Charles McClendon, Mirelle Mentré, Serafín Moralejo, Sabine Noack, Joseph O'Callaghan, Milagros Rivera, Sonia Simon, Brooks and Whitney Stoddard, Kenneth Wolf, and Juan Zozaya, as well as Enrique Asensio, Suse Childs, Gregory Diamant, Mari José Lobo, Elena Quevedo, Christina Viereck, Frère Christophe of Sainte-Marie de la Pierre-qui-Vire, and especially my dear friends and colleagues Professors Leila Kinney and Edward Sullivan.

There are probably none to whom I am so indebted for the endless practical work this manuscript required as that battery of latter-day martyrs—the highly intelligent, good-humored, and incredibly hard-working scholars (known also as Research Assistants) who have worked on this project over the years: Ethan Carr, Raquel Da Rosa, María Fernández, Janice Mann, Rachel Maskowitz, Tom O'Connor, Irina Oryshkevich, Jenny Shaffer, Adrienne Shirley, Janice Vrana, and in particular my good friend Max Alexander.

I am enormously grateful as well for my editor, Philip Winsor, a gentleman and a scholar who has cared attentively for this manuscript and its author in the final phases of writing and production, and to Cherene Holland, Janet Dietz, and Steven Kress for time and attention lavished on its text and illustrations.

In a sense this book began long ago with my first travels, with that thrill that occurs as one confronts oneself in the mirror of a divergent culture. I wish to thank my parents for the value they place on learning and the gifts of travel, and the opportunities they gave me to repeat those experiences again and again, to fashion and refashion dreams around them. Finally, my husband, Charlie Gifford, though he has never read this manuscript, is more important to it than any other person I could name. He left his own work to be my partner in fieldwork and to produce all of the plans and many of the photographs reproduced here. But more important, his unquestioning, unflinching embrace of every definition of parenthood has been the single most contributory factor to the appearance of this manuscript during our lifetimes. I treasure such autonomy buoyed by such support more than I can say.

Abbreviations

AEArq	*Archivo Español de Arqueología*
AEArte	*Archivo Español de Arte*
AEArteArq	*Archivo Español de Arte y Arqueología*
AH	*Ars Hispaniae*, Madrid, vol. 2 (1947), and vol. 3 (1951)
BRAH	*Boletín de la Real Academia de Historia*
BSCE	*Boletín de la Sociedad Castellana de Excursiones*
BSEE	*Boletín de la Sociedad Española de Excursiones*
BSAAV	*Boletín del Seminario de Arte y Arqueología,* University of Valladolid
DACL	F. Cabrol and H. Leclerq, *Dictionnaire d'archéologie et de liturgie,* Paris, 1935
ES	*España Sagrada*, ed. E. Flórez et al., Madrid, 1747–1918
MGH	*Monumenta Germaniae Historica*, Munich, 1939–75
MM	*Madrider Mitteilungen*
PL	*Patrologia cursus completus*, series latina, ed. J.-P. Migne
Spoleto	*Settimane di studio del Centro italiano di studi sull'alto medioevo,* Spoleto

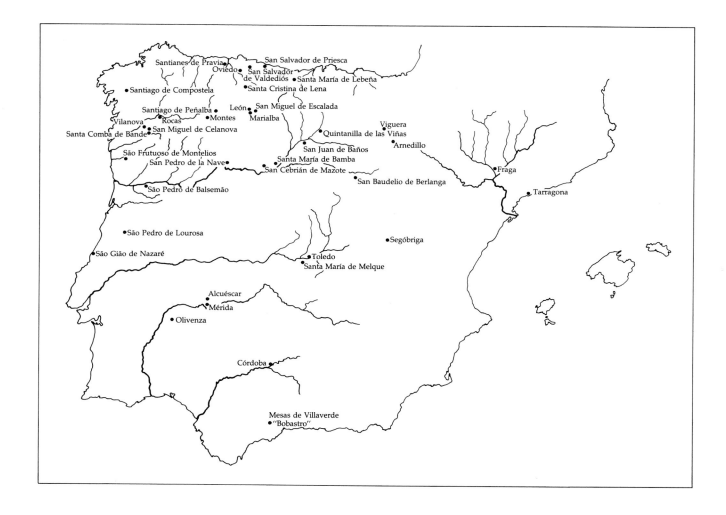

Introduction

What do we care about your otherwise unknown authors: a Eugene, an Ildefonse, a Julian. . . . If they are really the authors of your liturgy it's not surprising that God delivered you to the infidels as punishment!
—Alcuin at Aachen to Elipandus, Bishop of Toledo[1]

Anything is possible in Spain.
—Erwin Panofsky[2]

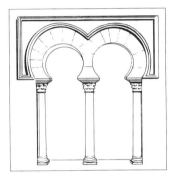

The Iberian Peninsula dangles from the high mountain chain that links it to Europe, poised ambivalently a few kilometers from a North Africa it will never touch. It weds only the sea—inhabits the Mediterranean in fact with an authority that must explain in part its integration as one of the most Roman of the provinces of the Roman Empire. But as power slipped from the grasp of Rome, with the rise of Europe came the gradual, permeable seclusion of Spain, a condition that has continued almost uninterrupted—politically and intellectually—from the sixth century until recent times. It is the fear of that which is separate and unknown perhaps that spawns the condescension of Alcuin (exasperated) and Panofsky (lighthearted), the sure knowledge that the historical and cultural issue of Spain will not easily fit intellectual paradigms fashioned for the rest of Europe.

In the chapters that follow I hope to reveal something of that experience which sets Spain apart from the rest of Europe, through an understanding of the symbols, formal ideals, and unconscious attitudes encased in early medieval buildings of the Iberian Peninsula, those destined for both Christian and Muslim worship. These essays focus on the formation of cultural identity through the confrontation of diverse and changing indigenous populations with those perceived by them to be outsiders—in particular the Visigoths from the fifth through the eighth century, and Arab and Berber Muslims from the eighth to the fifteenth century—and also on the changing cultures of those invasive groups as their identities become embroiled with that of the peninsula. I should say from the start that in exploring the relationship of architecture to ideology I do not mean to limit my inquiry to the conscious gestures of patrons; I also use architecture at times as a passageway to certain collective assumptions, exploring the ways that formal solutions become the unconscious repositories of ideological struggle. In this concern these studies both challenge parts of an anguished tradition of historiographical thought and try to toddle in the footsteps of some distinguished mavericks.[3]

It is well known that the Middle Ages figure as the most stimulating and vibrant battleground for Spain's view of its contemporary self, a fact Russell blandly accepts as "an inevitable result of the ceaseless reminders . . . that Spain's noblest historical role had already been staged between 711 and 1492."[4] Whether or not one accepts this judgment, it must be received as the acknowledged position of Spanish historians of the past three generations, who plunged themselves into a dramatic and enigmatic time to try to understand—or perhaps explain away—what Gómez-Moreno called "our modern inferiority" to northern European countries.[5] One scholar, at the end of a chapter on Visigothic Spain, puts it in the following way: "I believe quite simply that only in the full consciousness of what we have been, can we raise ourself to a higher destiny—if we really desire to improve that destiny."[6]

At stake is the search for something that is immutable or at least unique in the Spanish identity, a perilous goal sought most significantly by two venerable contemporary scholars: Américo Castro and Claudio Sánchez-Albornoz.[7] Castro began their famous polemic with the publication, in 1948, of *España en su historia*, a volume which suggested that the Spanish national character only formed as a result of the interaction of "three casts": Christians, Muslims, and Jews. Sánchez-Albornoz replied with the cyclopean work *España: Un enigma histórico*, which held that the "Spanish temperament" existed even in pre-Roman times, and was such a strong force that it impressed itself repeatedly on invaders. Sánchez-Albornoz refused to accept the impact of any Semitic culture—Muslim or Jewish—on the *homo hispanus*.[8]

Thomas Glick has shown the extent to which the two scholars' works reflect notions of cultural evolution characteristic of the intellectual generation to which each belongs: Sánchez-Albornoz's reflects "moderate Catholic evolutionism of the late 19th century" in which "the biological model is explicit, but decidedly anti-evolutionary" because it accepted change only above the level of species, of which the nation was the cultural analogue. Castro, in contrast, took a Hegelian position on social evolution, which allowed a wider latitude for social change.[9] Thus Sánchez-Albornoz's immutable and ancient national personality faced Castro's changing Christian culture, one transformed profoundly since Hispano-Roman times through "convivencia" with people of Islamic and Jewish cultures.

The work of Sánchez-Albornoz is swamped in political and racial prejudices that completely shroud his view of Spanish history; he is, in less theoretical studies, more exacting and objective.[10] Castro's essay is certainly more useful for its supposition that Spanish Christian culture evolved both through imitation of Muslim and Jewish institutions, but in resistance to those strong cultural forces as well.

But Castro, like Sánchez-Albornoz, sought ultimately an elusive goal—a national personality—that cannot be demonstrated or even disproved with the techniques of their craft.[11] And yet that same goal has in many ways shaped the study of medieval Spain, even that of medieval Spanish art, born in the beginning of this century. Nearly every scholar to discuss architecture of the Visigothic period, for instance, seems to find repose in the notion that those oligarchic rulers of the Iberian Peninsula confronted an architectural tradition fully formed, one to which they could add nothing, however strong their political presence.[12] The survival of that idea in Asturian studies has been so insistent that the thesis of a prototype from the Visigothic period for the church of San Julián de los Prados—one that retained the imprint of this pre-Visigothic personality— survived rather startling evidence to the contrary.[13]

Such scholarly tensions surrounding arts seen not only as political but ethnic as well are evident in the works of the finest and most venerable scholars. Struggling with the desire to bring something unique to the overwhelmingly francophilic study of the architecture of the early Middle Ages, Gómez-Moreno represented Mozarabic architecture as the vehicle of transmission of Islamic influences to northern Europe. He was able to mitigate the impact of Islam by suggesting that Islamic art in Spain was, after all, Hispanic first, an idea that appears prominently in Sánchez-Albornoz's later work, when that historian was faced with an example of incontrovertible Islamic influence.[14] The discomfort with the presence of Islamic form in Hispanic art has continued to the present: Camón Aznar very recently reduced the same buildings to a relentless continuation of an immutable series of architectural forms, hardly changed since Visigothic times, suggesting an artistic temperament unmoved by the presence of Islam.[15] That discomfort seems at times to have overtaken the actual discipline of Spanish Islamic architecture, a subject until recently so remote from the study of Spanish Christian architecture that one would imagine it to inhabit a separate peninsula.[16]

General studies of the Christian architecture of the early medieval period written outside Spain tend to treat the monuments of the peninsula as exotic marginal foils to the creations of Frankish and Ottonian monarchs. The justification lies in the refusal of Spanish medieval churches to prepare the way for Romanesque, to serve that deterministic and geocentric view of medieval architecture as an evolutive juggernaut lumbering toward Gothic. The process of exclusion is facilitated by exercising a scholarly habit of thinking that still sees many relationships between divergent cultures and their arts in terms of influence. The word "influence" functions in these circumstances as an appendage of the word "power," and in the early medieval period its use to describe the exchange of artistic forms literally creates an unequal relationship between the parties involved, one in which the donor culture is— actually or in memory—more sophisticated and politically powerful than a passive or insipid receiver culture (which has in reality actively chosen the new form). This passivity, this assumed permeability to the art of another discipline (Islamic art), then becomes the justification for the marginalization of the early medieval art of the Iberian Peninsula: its failure to resist the seduction of the other.[17]

This book has as its premise the assumption that—far from receiving influence passively—cultures react creatively when confronted with one another, and that such encounters help to form a group's attitude toward its art and itself.[18] In a sense these essays address the traditional problem of how a Spanish experience might be defined, but not by counting or discounting motifs borrowed and incorporated into one or another artistic canon. Instead, by examining the process of that creation which grows out of confrontation, I hope to discover some of those new ideas that are peculiar to Spain, those which are only dislodged because of the presence of another culture experienced as alien.

The chapters that follow are separate studies, specific in focus and different in scope, but they proceed chronologically and build upon one another in a number of ways. Each explores a problem characteristic of the four broad scholarly subjects associated with early medieval Spain: chapter 1 addresses the problems of church building in a divided society under Visigothic rule; chapter 2 aims to unravel the process of creation of a new visual identity for the Christian kingdom that survived the Muslim invasion; Christian strategies for cultural survival while living under Muslim rule form the focus of chapter 3; and chapter 4 probes the mining, by a powerful and vibrant Islamic culture, of a subjugated Christian one, for a new rhetorical language.

Though this volume must in no way be considered a survey or introduction to the architecture of early medieval Spain, it does concern a good number of the most well-known monuments of the period. In particular I hope to demonstrate through them that the terms of artistic reaction to cultural confrontation were numerous and varied. Some of these transformations in architecture and its decoration occurred through imitation of the products of another culture, but many were reactive: formal or typological choices that energetically evaded identification with an invasive or indigenous culture, but that were, at the same time, clearly stimulated by the other's presence.

The Iberian Peninsula enjoyed a singular and somewhat insular experience in the early Middle Ages, both by the contrivance of geography and social and political history. Since much of its history is one of ethnic diversity—in particular of the supplantation of rulers by wave after wave of outsiders who often enjoyed political and socioeconomic positions superior to that of the changing indigenous population—interaction between the groups became highly conscious and structured.[19] These general conditions create a unique opportunity for tracing threads of continuity and change, and for ferreting hints of the attitudes of divergent cultures toward each other's artistic production. At times these attitudes take the form of a conscious statement by a patron or craftsman, but at times they are hidden in a reflex of craft or patronage, or in the subconscious transformation of a structure or idea. In each of these instances I hope to be able to show the manner in which a building reflects, reveals, and plays on the notion of a building tradition as a way of working through political and social tension. My arguments share as a starting point the premise—one by no means exhausted in these pages—that no part of a building, no matter how ensconced in technical habit, can be said to be without social meaning.

Within the course of this study an important part of my argument is to be found in the notes: that is, the archaeology, dating, documentation, and bibliography for many of the monuments discussed, as well as the sources and protagonists for many historical issues. I also use a number of terms throughout that require definition. On the whole, I call buildings of the mid-sixth through the beginning of the eighth century "architecture of the Visigothic period," or "constructed under Visigothic rule," because of the difficulties associated with naming the buildings directly for the minority ruling class of those centuries. The eighth- to tenth-century churches of Asturias I call "Asturian" and horseshoe-arched buildings of the tenth century "Mozarabic" for reasons discussed at length in chapter 3. I refer to the Muslim inhabitants of al-Andalus more often than not as "Islamic," primarily because this very general term is the only one capable of embracing the Arab, Berber, and Muwallad population to which I wish to refer. The word "type" refers to a plan or general building massing that is recognizable when repeated in simple, broad terms. When I speak of "style," I always have James Ackerman's words in mind. I mean it to be thought of as "an accepted vocabulary of elements . . . and a syntax by which these elements are composed" to form "a class of related solutions to a problem—or responses to a challenge."[20]

Arabic names and words have been transliterated, with the exception of words that have entered the English language or those common in art-historical studies, such as mosque, mihrab, and Koran. I also use the English equivalent for place names. To create plural forms of Arabic terms and names, I have added an *s* to the singular form to avoid the confusing transformations of transliterated names and terms that would result.

I am aware that I take an enormous liberty in using the place name Spain interchangeably with the Iberian Peninsula in the course of these pages. I use both terms geographically to indicate the peninsula—as Arab writers did—for the sake of simplicity (and syntax), knowing full well that the peninsula to which I refer contained, at the very least, a Spain, a Portugal, a Catalonia, and an Islamic entity, known as al-Andalus.[21]

1
Visigoths and Romans and Some Problems Concerning Their Architecture

I. Architecture and the Visigothic Rule

Of all the lands which stretch from the West to India, you are the most beautiful, O Spain, sacred and ever-blessed mother of leaders and of nations. By right you are the leader of all provinces, from whom not only the West but also the East obtains its light. . . .

Thus rich in foster-sons and in gems and in purple cloth, likewise fertile in rulers and in the riches of Empire, you are both opulent in adorning leaders and blessed in producing them. Thus rightly did golden Rome, the head of nations, once desire you, and although the same Romulean virtue, first victorious, betrothed you to itself, at last, nevertheless, the most flourishing nation of the Goths after many victories in the world eagerly captured and loved you, and enjoys you up to the present amid royal insignia and abundant wealth, secure in the felicity of empire.

—*Isidore of Seville*, De Laude Hispaniae[1]

The land that would be the theater for a seven-century struggle between Muslims and Christians was, a century before the Islamic invasion, already shot through with the same tensions that would distinguish it under Islamic occupation. Repeated invasions, cultural diversity, foreign rule, exchange and resistance: none of the events or concerns that pervades the study of the Iberian Peninsula during its years of Muslim rule was new to that land when it was first seized by Islamic forces in 711. That state of struggle between an indigenous people and a powerful foreign rule had already characterized much of the history of the Visigothic and Hispano-Roman peoples. Even in Isidore's strident nationalistic song, we hear the feeble tones of the compromise of a Hispano-Roman population too rich in "foster sons," often insecure, and so far from the unity and felicity of "empire."

To speak indeed of Visigothic Spain is to refer to the oligarchic rule of eight million indigenous Hispano-Romans by a governing class composed of perhaps few more than 200,000 Visigoths.[2] This condition was firmly established by the mid-sixth century, when the Visigoths made Toledo their capital, following a century of military consolidation throughout the peninsula, which included the conquest of the Suevi in the northwest of the peninsula by 585. A dual system of government was established in which indigenous inhabitants of each province were judged by a Hispano-Roman governor under Roman law, while a Visigothic duke or count—who also held some jurisdiction over the Hispano-Roman population—would primarily concern himself with the administration of the Visigothic population.

This legal separation, which was not fruitful to Visigothic rule, was finally broken by Leovigild (568–586), a visionary and energetic ruler who sought nothing less than the consolidation and unification of the Iberian Peninsula under a charismatic Visigothic kingship. He began the creation of a centralized state of a sort that had never existed before on the Iberian Peninsula, reestablishing control over enormous areas of land that had been lost, subduing Basques and Suevi, even chasing the vestiges of Byzantine troops from Spain's southeastern shores.[3] Leovigild created and developed two royal urban centers. He revised the ancient code of laws, applying them to Romans as well as Goths, and was the first of the Visigothic kings to mint his own coins, with his own image and inscription, in imitation of the Byzantines; and he was the first to use costume, ceremony, and setting to create a royal image.[4] Leovigild thus created the *Regnum Gothorum*: a myth of Visigothic kingship that long survived the rule of the Goths.[5]

The pomp and force of Leovigild's rule cloaked, however, deep social and religious tension, for the Visigoths were then an Arian minority in a land where orthodox Catholicism had become the banner of Hispano-Roman resistance to a brutish oligarchy. The force of the Church, leading sectors of an enormous indigenous population and its aristocracy, was great enough to thwart Leovigild's attempts at converting the Catholic majority to Arianism, and it was probably an understanding of the strength of its numbers and leadership that finally led his son, Reccared (586–601), to convert to Catholicism.

There is a tendency, especially among art historians, to see the conversion of Reccared in 589 as the genesis of a period of ethnic and political assimilation, and indeed that seems to be what Isidore wishes us to believe as well.[6] But recent scholarship cautions us against this notion,[7] suggesting instead that the conversion— and the abolition of separate Roman law which followed in 652—intensified the deep stratification of Hispano-Roman and Visigothic society, submitting the local, indigenous population to Visigothic law and thus increasing the economic and political power of the Goths.[8] The centralized Visigothic ruling class thus had more control, while the local, indigenous populations were deprived of their hearth of resistance and legal protection. Economic and social distinctions became greater, as the Catholic Hispano-Roman indigenous population was subjected to the ruling class in a relationship that Glick sees as being close to a feudal model.[9]

So the apparent cohesiveness of the rule of late sixth- and seventh-century Spain in the Visigothic period—that hysterical unity protested in Isidore's *De Laude*—seems to have been a calculated fiction. Rather, the personalities of power, learning, and sophistication of an old and established Hispano-Roman church hierarchy now saw their interests, for better or worse, grafted onto those of the Visigothic ruling class. Thus when Isidore, in his *History of the Goths, Vandals and Suevi,* declares, "Certainly the Gothic race is very ancient . . . no people in the whole world so distressed the Roman Empire,"[10] he is openly flattering the ruling class he had been vehemently resisting only a generation before. The generation had certainly not produced a fusion of peoples and cultures; only an uneasy truce.[11]

That truce was of enormous value, however, for the moment of prosperity and accord it generated served to nurture a cultural revival of considerable scale and depth, one to which we are indebted for most of the monuments and texts discussed in this chapter. Indeed, it is the career of Isidore that provides us with the most resonant testimony of a rich and textured restoration of Antique learning.[12] This conscious custodianship of Roman culture found some of its catalysts in North Africa.[13] But the glee with which Isidore speaks of the Gothic race "distressing" the Roman Empire suggests as well an exteriorization of the memory and idea of Rome; a sense of historical separateness kindled by the creation of the new *Regnum,* which might well have fostered interest in the consolidation of the past.

The royal Visigothic version of this same revival seems to have been divergent, and historically confused. References to Rome on the part of the monarchy were manifest in rather crude symbols of sovereignty stolen from Byzantium, the contemporary Roman Empire. The imitation of Byzantine coins, royal vestments, and court protocol constituted the typological pillage of the symbolic power of a vital and living enemy. One is indeed tempted to suggest that the subtleties of Isidore's work might have been lost upon Leovigild or Reccared, who saw more meaning in the gaudy potency of a living power than in the mute wisdom of a Rome they had conquered long ago. Be that as it may, one thing seems certain: that the values and priorities of Spain's indigenous and ruling populations were never totally fused, not even in moments of domestic peace, the moments of richest artistic and architectural accomplishment. The newly imposed political unity was strung tense and taut between the interests of a cultured Hispano-Roman population and the authority of a formidable military aristocracy.

A predominant theme in scholarship that grew from these myths of fusion has for some time sought to force the history of the architecture traditionally called Visigothic into the mold of a paradigm borrowed from political history.[14] Many of the observations growing from this tradition are valuable. But when a historical paradigm is too general or prejudicial, there is a tendency not to exploit the monuments themselves as documents of importance, but to treat them merely as visual footnotes to an already codified notion of the past. This has been the case, I believe, with certain influential works treating the great architectural monuments of the seventh and eighth centuries in Spain.[15]

The vision of the past at issue concerns the extent to which the personality of modern Spain was formed by the seven-century presence of Islam on its shores. This tradition of thought is a natural issue of the polemic between Claudio Sánchez-Albornoz and Américo Castro,[16] and though the controversy is somewhat outworn in historical circles, its concerns have had, until very recently, a potent place in determining the questions asked by art historians of medieval Spain. If Spain could be shown to have existed as a cohesive nation before the advent of Islam on the peninsula, then Sánchez-Albornoz's view of a Spanish personality innocent of any profound Islamic influence becomes a more accessible one.

The terms of this polemic put an intellectual stranglehold on the interpretation of the monuments built during the years of religious concordance between Visigoths and Hispano-Romans, in spite of many fine art-historical studies that have been applied to them. The significance of the formal dispositions of these monuments has then often been reduced to the reaffirmation of an interested vision of the past. For more often than not, the greatest monuments of the Visigothic period—buildings constructed from the late sixth through the early eighth centuries—are seen as the product of the social and political fusion of Roman and Visigoth: the creation of Spain's first coherent nation, one, then, that produces Spain's first national art.[17]

It is difficult to consider a building so poignant and resonant as Santa María de Quintanilla de las Viñas primarily as the handmaiden of a theory bound to the nervous historicism of early twentieth-century Spain. But that is precisely what happens when Palol introduces his study of Quintanilla and its contemporaries under the following rubric:

> THE LAST EPOCH—the Isidorian phase of peace and ethnic and religious fusion, of political identification between the Visigothic military state and the Hispano-Roman church—this is also the reason for the appearance of a sole [único] art in which, in architecture and sculpture, the earlier Hispano-Roman trend has a full and graceful evolution and development.[18]

Palol's formal conclusions might well hold true: the architecture of the late sixth through the early eighth centuries does indeed constitute a cohesive stylistic group, and I have no doubt that its building tradition grew from an existing Hispano-Roman one as Palol and Schlunk suggest.[19] But there is a breach in the method of nearly every art historian to treat this topic, between the careful and specific identification of the architecture's formal parentage and the vague assumption that the resulting style is the offspring of the fusion of two cohabiting cultures. Thus Palol endorses the notion of an art of national unity, though he makes a clear point (he calls it "mi posición romanista": "my Romanist's position") of the total lack of Visigothic impact. For Palol the Visigothic contribution to this new art of national cohesion was nothing more than a strong political rule: a secure context in which the indigenous Hispano-Roman population could continue the ongoing job of making culture, inspired by a new Hispanic national identification.[20] He sees in fact in the period beginning with the conversion of Reccared the "intellectual and social predominance of the Hispano-Roman group over the Visigothic military minority, and the strong tutelage of the Visigothic state by the Hispano-Roman church."[21]

The theory in itself—loosed from larger nationalistic implications—is not a bad one: the Visigoths indeed provided a centralized state, while it is widely acknowledged that the Hispano-Roman population was the source of culture and learning. The Visigoths were historically not builders, and the Hispano-Romans certainly were. And everyone seems ready to confer upon the Visigoths the full credit for the early stages of the flourishing of metalwork and minor arts since these arts are more appropriate to their culture. But as a comment on a rich and original new architectural style, it is too pat, and serves too easily a racial ideal: that Spaniards as a nation were not only formed before the advent of Islam on the peninsula, but that their culture is essentially the continuation of Western Roman culture. Twentieth-century Spaniards become, then, the last Romans. Palol very nearly says this himself: "What we have to do with here is a process of personalization, or nationalization, which was growing ever stronger and more complete with every passing year. Can we also claim it as the last offshoot, in the West, of the great art of Rome?"[22] Schlunk seconds the idea in similar terms: "The sun of the ancient world, before being extinguished forever, seems to have thrown a last ray on this outpost of the west which is Spain. But the fact is that this ray of sunlight of the ancient world did not pass through any Germanic filter; one can well say that, as far as art is concerned, the Goths in Spain bequeathed us nothing."[23]

Thus scholarship concerning Spanish architecture of the late sixth through the early eighth centuries tends to hold two important notions in a fragile tension: (1) that those buildings constitute a new monumental art of national unity, which reflects the fusion of Hispano-Roman and Visigothic peoples, and (2) that though this style is both new and cohesive, it is the uninterrupted continuation of an indigenous Roman tradition of building and design that enjoys very little or no contribution from the Visigothic part of society.[24]

The methodological leap that allows for the reconciliation of these assumptions occurs at the most basic level of interpretation. For in understanding correctly that the few and powerful Visigoths were not themselves involved in the physical act of construction, scholars have been slow to consider their probable impact—as patrons themselves or as significant catalysts for reaction and change in architecture and the society that it serves. Palol's observations concerning the cultural and intellectual superiority of the Hispano-Roman population provide the context for this assumption. Only Camps Cazorla acknowledges that certain ornamentation of seventh-century churches might reflect Visigothic taste, a recognition made possible perhaps as the extension of the tendency to relegate the Visigoths to the world of jewelry and applied ornament.[25] Schlunk, Fontaine, Palol, and even Camps Cazorla all make relatively decisive statements that deny the possibility of any formal impact that might be attributable to the Visigothic presence on the peninsula, largely on the basis of the long-standing Hispano-Roman tradition of building, and the likelihood that the Visigoths "were not themselves . . . a nation of builders and architects."[26]

The insistence is on formal and technological influence as the prerequisite to any argument for Visigothic impact on the bold flow of Roman Christian culture on the Iberian Peninsula. This approach, to my mind, excludes two avenues of inquiry that, while more speculative, are necessary to follow if one wishes to create a picture of the relationship between two cultures that reflects the true complexity of their bond. One is the conceivable intervention of Visigoths as patrons of buildings, and the other concerns the unconscious effect the Visigoths might have had on the needs of patrons from the Hispano-Roman church simply by virtue of their political and social presence. The first issue I shall mention only in passing, and the second will be discussed at greater length in the second section of this chapter.

The question of the intervention of Visigoths as patrons of church architecture is a difficult one, and the evidence does not provide a satisfying sense of closure as regards any particular monument, including those mentioned here. The issue is nevertheless well worth a bit of scrutiny, if only for the richness of the picture it reveals of the conceptual framework of Visigothic patronage in general, and of the use these oligarchic rulers made of visual imagery.

There is ample documentation for the Visigoth as church patron. Count Gudiliuva, for instance, a Visigothic magnate, built three churches near Guadix at his own expense with workers who were his servants by birth (Vernuli).[27] The Hispano-Roman church learned quite early to exploit the Visigothic rulers' need for physical testimony to their power and authority. The Visigothic duke Jalla, persuaded by the church hierarchy of Mérida, undertook a major public building campaign in an act that Orlandis feels "was not without a certain political intention, for he had to promote the prestige of the dominant in the eyes of the Hispano-Roman population."[28] There was, at least in the time of Leovigild, a royal workshop for the construction of an entire city: Reccopolis, and at least one standing church, San Juan de Baños, was built by king Recceswinth.[29]

The sort of mark the patron's hand might have left in each of these cases is difficult to determine. Of those buildings just mentioned, only San Juan de Baños survives, but in its remote and rural setting it is difficult to imagine a strong intervening hand from the king. Nevertheless, Schlunk sees in it forms originating in Ravenna, which he feels must reflect developments in court.[30] A more conscientious reflection of the preoccupations of the Visigothic court in Toledo might be found, however, in the church of São Frutuoso de Montelios.

Built by the saint himself to serve as his own funerary chapel, São Frutuoso has survived a number of unfortunate restorations.[31] The plan, proportions, and skin of the monument are relatively good indications of its original form, however, and they present us with a building that, in massing and typology, resembles no other church so much as the so-called mausoleum of Galla Placidia in Ravenna (Pls. 1 and 2).[32] I do not believe Galla Placidia to be the immediate prototype, but it places the locus of interest once again in Ravenna, perhaps as the reflection of developments in the eastern Roman Empire. In particular, São Frutuoso's interior triple-arched screens, and the five cupolas that cover its cross plan, suggest the contemplation of Justinianic monuments, perhaps, as has been suggested, a lost funerary chapel that followed the plan and vaulting pattern of the church of the Holy Apostles or Saint John at Ephesus (Pl. 3, Fig. 1).[33]

That São Frutuoso is constructed in a fine, local ashlar masonry tradition, totally divergent from the brick tradition in which the type was conceived, only verifies that its builders were indigenous, likely members of the largely Hispano-Roman building force identified by scholars.[34] It is then to the hand of its saintly patron that we must look for the surprising reference encased in its plan. Saint Fructuosus was a noble of Visigothic family, who used his great inheritance for the enrichment of monasteries. He planned a pilgrimage to "the Orient," but was called instead by the king (probably Chindaswinth) to Toledo. The monarch, fearing "lest such a shining light should withdraw from Spain," sought to keep him from his voyage.

It was after his stay at court that Fructuosus settled in Galicia; first Dumium, and then Braga, where he built São Frutuoso.[35]

The chapel of São Frutuoso can in this context be explained as the reflection of a preoccupation with Eastern or perhaps Justinianic forms seen by Fructuosus at the Visigothic royal court. The genesis of such an association at court might be traced to the reign of Leovigild, who is known to have copied Byzantine court ceremonial, and to have minted his own coins after Byzantine models, in which he appears in the dress of Byzantine kings. He even founded a royal city—Reccopolis—which in its most characteristic visual forms has been shown to follow Byzantine models. The monarch's true force lay indeed in the creation of such material royal institutions; of a royal image that defied the pretentions of a dissenting orthodox church.[36]

I would suggest that under Leovigild, certain Byzantine forms, in coinage, ceremonial, and perhaps even architecture, became emblematic of royal ideology, and that this association survived his reign as part of a general concept of Visigothic monarchy. There is ample numismatic evidence that kings of the seventh century did not simply follow Leovigild's model but refreshed their contacts with Byzantine forms, applying to the most contemporary models for their own coins those forceful instruments of royal ideology.[37] Faced with an ancient culture, and severely limited in their numbers, the Visigothic rulers surely quarried Byzantine symbolic imagery in order to create a visual idea of nationhood. It was part of the military and political idea of the Visigothic state described by D'Abadal, a "work of imposition and superposition" in which can be found the explanation for the myth of unified Visigothic nationhood.[38]

Given the startlingly cosmopolitan nature of the chapel of São Frutuoso, its patron's contacts and recent visit to the capital, might it not signal a parallel link between ideology and form in the architecture of the capital?

Such a link would have fueled the rivalry—one in which churches and the act of building them played a significant role—documented in the *Vitas Sanctorum Patrum Emeretensium* between the *Urbs Regia* and strong independent cities like Mérida, whose rich and powerful bishops resisted royal authority in the name of orthodoxy.[39] But, like the resilient Byzantinism of Visigothic rulers' images on coins, such architectural references would over time maintain a steady identity only with kingly power, their mobile potency directed at any undermining force.[40]

As a Visigothic noble and a great churchman, Fructuosus embodied, in his patronage and his charge, the infiltration of the Visigothic nobility into the upper levels of the power structure of the Hispano-Roman church. Although this infiltration was conceived in general as part of the struggles for power between Visigothic state and Hispano-Roman church, we cannot be sure of Fructuosus's political position, only of his close ties to the court and firsthand visual knowledge of the capital.[41] It is difficult to say, then, on which level this copy functioned in São Frutuoso itself; whether it was simply emblematic of a taste that could be associated with the center of power and a certain level of erudition, or if it might symbolically have represented, in its tight specificity, the extension of the royal arm in Galicia. Our understanding of the patron, however, supports either solution and does not necessarily depend on the meaning of the Eastern forms embraced in its direct prototype.

The discussion of the patronage of Visigoths is perilous, in particular as regards speculation concerning vanished monuments, but it is nevertheless important. The inquiries it prompts serve to remind us at the very least of the extent to which those rulers were active as creators of a visual world that supported their political and social needs. Their apparent abdication of stonecutting must in no way be mistaken for passivity toward a visual language of forms.

More transcendent, however, than the intentional gestures of patrons are the unconscious waves of change that occur inevitably when divergent cultures meet. Apart from São Frutuoso, conscious, symbolic imitation makes its way very little into the surviving seventh- and eighth-century architecture of the Iberian Peninsula. In the large number of existing churches—those presumably created for the large part for and by the Hispano-Roman clergy—the assimilated resonance of Byzantine plan and vaulting types can be found, but recognizable forms that might bear specific, symbolic meanings do not become a term of difference, struggle, or identification.[42] It is rather in the slow, almost imperceptible developments of architectural forms and space over time that can be read a deeper social and political reaction to the tensions of sharing a peninsula.

II. Ritual and Resistance in the Hispano-Roman Tradition

By the fifth century Rome had ceased to provide the Iberian Peninsula with new architectural forms; the great workshops closed and the construction of churches and their ornamentation was left to indigenous workshops. These rose to the occasion with a robust continuation of traditional architecture, enriched with frequent typological and decorative reflections of the style and planning of North Africa.[43] The church was the vanguard of culture and the defender of tradition. Its centers—the south, and coastal capitals—became consequently the focus of artistic production.

None of these earliest Spanish churches remains standing, but excavations reveal a good deal concerning the enduring traditions they initiated. The end of the fourth century saw in fact most of the major Christian plan types that would appear in Spain over the next five centuries. Thus the three-aisled basilica appears in the church dedicated to Saint Fructuosus and his deacons (a different saint from the Visigoth Fructuosus, whose tomb lies near Braga) in the early Christian necropolis of Tarragona.[44] A spacious single-nave basilica at Marialba (Fig. 2) has been excavated by Theodor Hauschild, who has also revealed through a reconstruction the single-nave two-level martyrium at La Alberca.[45] At La Cocosa, a centrally planned cross-shaped martyrium can be traced in foundations revealing a horseshoe-shaped apse encased in a rectangular masonry block.[46]

The horseshoe-shaped apse is not limited in this early period to La Cocosa but appeared in the fourth century at Marialba as well. It is a form the ancientness of which is well established on the Iberian Peninsula, one exploited both in Early Christian monuments and those built later under Visigothic rule.[47] At Marialba the apse entrance is a tightened section of an ever-closing circle; the narrow opening checks and gathers the swelling form of the space beyond. It is probably to the elegance and spaciousness of the nearly completed circle that is owed the Spanish Early Christian interest in the horseshoe arch, however, rather than to its partitioning qualities.[48] For most of what we know about the rest of these early churches suggests an openness of space and visual accessibility to the altar that distinguish them from later counterparts on the Iberian Peninsula. Particularly significant in this respect is Schlunk's observation that the faithful could approach the altar at the Early Christian church of Santa María de Tarrasa. Indeed, no chancel barriers are securely established in churches of this early period.[49] The horseshoe shape in plan distinguishes, then, a series of buildings of simple, open, and continuous space.

Descendants of these same *ateliers* continued like traditions of building through the fifth and early sixth centuries: the years of Visigothic incursion, and finally settling, in Spain. Experience suggests that the first Arian churches, lost today, might not have differed greatly from their Orthodox counterparts.[50] It seems likely, at this early date, that most constructions outside the capital would be caught in the web of an established program of building, which the small group of precariously poised military rulers had little time to unravel or challenge. But the spatial formulas embraced by the Hispano-Roman community itself seem to have begun, in this moment of profound social and political change, a slow and deliberate process of transformation.[51] They began to evolve within their own tradition, through the careful choice of models from conventional sources; but few of the changes that resulted can be viewed without reference to the presence in Spain of an alien and heretical aristocracy.

An extraordinary monument of the beginning of the sixth century reflects the delicate transformations of this moment.[52] The basilica of Segóbriga was constructed in a bold ashlar masonry that links it with the famous traditions of the seventh and early eighth centuries. It possessed three aisles separated by formidable arcades of ten columns each (Pl. 4).[53] The vestiges of the east end known to us through excavation drawings are those of a large transverse crypt; the church indeed appears to have served as the funerary basilica of the bishops of Segóbriga.[54] Its spaces must have formed dark and cavernous parodies of higher structures presumably reached by means of staircases from the nave.[55] The crypt's form is nevertheless fascinating: instead of opening directly onto the apse, the nave abutted this long funereal transept, the massive walls of which yielded a constricted crossing and narrow partitioned chambers to the north and south. The eastern wall of the crossing was punctured with a slightly stilted horseshoe arch on low jambs, inaugurating a passage through a thick wall to the sanctuary beyond. That narrow tunnel became, then, the contracted entrance to a ballooning horseshoe-shaped apse. The apse with its two burials crowned a vaulted crypt which must have supported a raised chancel and apse that mirrored its forms.[56]

Segóbriga introduces two startling new concerns to the study of early Spanish architecture. The first is an early indication of the use of the horseshoe arch in elevation, a form which, because it inscribes more of a circle than a semicircular arch, partitions its opening slightly by drawing the jambs forward to diminish vision and suggest the inhibition of passage. The second is the introduction of a crossing, an architectural transition between the nave and the sanctuary.[57] Though at Segóbriga we can only be sure of a crypt—and so a funereal, and not liturgical, crossing—the appearance of the form is not isolated, nor is it limited to crypts in this period. Indeed it is not long before one finds nascent crossings at the church of Villa Fortunatus near Fraga and San Pedro de Mérida, both datable to the sixth century (Fig. 3).[58]

To this development must belong the appearance of chancel barriers, firmly documented in Spain at the churches of Aljezares (second half of the sixth century), and Bobalá-Serós (first half of the sixth century) and clearly associated with the development of the crossing at San Pedro de Mérida and Fraga.[59] These carved stone plaques, held in place by similarly decorated pillars, were the first significant expression of a swelling importance of the clergy, attended by a physical and psychological distance between clergy and laity during Mass. The east ends of churches were expanding; becoming more spacious and more intricate to accommodate the clergy and to establish for them a hierarchically defined space apart. Though Syrian, North African, and Mediterranean prototypes for these barriers and crossings were consulted and at times copied, the introduction of those forms, and the profound transformations they created in the setting for the liturgy, cannot be dismissed only as a gesture of empty mimicry on the part of building workshops. These changes are bound to the various models from which they were appropriated, neither by conscious, symbolic borrowing nor simply as the vague resonance of admiration for the architecture and culture of another land.[60] The blocking of the sanctuary from the nave is a liturgical gesture that seizes Visigothic architecture of the next one hundred and fifty years with a fierceness that can only indicate its vital relevance to the church and its evolving liturgy.

This taste for partitioned and divided space which evolved in the sixth century would lie at the center of an aesthetic that would bind the buildings of the seventh and eighth centuries—those traditionally called Visigothic[61]—to one another. In massing, the articulation of walls, and the sculpting of space, Spanish churches of the Visigothic period share a common approach; a common means of answering certain formal questions that distinguish them from their contemporaries in Europe and the Mediterranean, and that dissociate them from any stylistic and typological ancestors.

The churches of the Visigothic period that remain standing today are both centrally planned and basilical. The former are without exception cruciform, but none can be associated as closely with specific Eastern prototypes as could São Frutuoso de Montelios.[62] They share, nevertheless, many of the same basic formal values—bound as they are by a common tradition of construction—in particular from the exterior. At San Pedro de la Nave (Pl. 5)[63] and Santa Comba de Bande,[64] clear and simple massing visually segregates the different vessels of the cross plan and its sacristies. The only deception occurs in the exterior of San Pedro de la Nave (and originally at Santa Comba as well),[65] where a vaulted room, without any reasonable access, surmounts the apse, allowing it to appear taller and more integrated with the general massing of the monument from without. Within, the space is only evident by means of a window that gives onto the crossing; thus the apse, while grand from without, is small and cavernous in the church's interior (Pl. 6). Despite a number of intriguing and romantic suggestions for the function of this space, I must support the most prosaic: that it serves a tradition of construction that valued grand and integrated exterior massing,[66] but a more intimate and enclosed interior space.

Indeed, the simplicity and geometry of the exteriors of these early medieval monuments are softened and complicated in many ways within, as an elaborate and complex design defies the neat clarity of the churches' exteriors. At Santa Comba de Bande the apse appears today at the end of a progression of horseshoe arches that visually enframe one another, telescoping down to the sanctuary entrance itself (Pl. 7). The crossing arms were bathed in darkness, as was the choir, before the destruction of the southern sacristy, whose door today is the source of inappropriately abundant light. Interior lighting was carefully rationed. Only two of the windows that illuminate Santa Comba today served that function initially; that which surmounts the apse was probably originally blind, opening onto an empty room like that over the apse at San Pedro de la Nave.[67] Thus light would spring from the crossing, with its large clerestory windows, but the choir beyond remained in shadow. Only a small window piercing the thick wall of the tiny, remote apse created a blade of light that might serve as a beacon in that shadowy obscurity, still leaving the periphery of the apse visually inaccessible and the choir spaces in a vague darkness.

The divisions of space suggested here by the alternation of light and dark are those emphasized by the architecture as well: the crossing, the choir, and the apse are separated by horseshoe arches that partition each space, punctuating the divisions between them, marking the transition from one to another. This is a formal preoccupation valued to a high degree in the apse entrance, where the shape and size of the apse are indistinguishable through the reduced and partitioned opening. The same concern is augmented in particular through the use of the horseshoe arch, the jambs and springers of which jut into the space of the apse entrance, shaping that space to its distinctive profile.

These are the same divisions delineated by Santa Comba's lost chancel screens (Fig. 5).[68] Scars on the walls suggest that four spaces were set apart from one another: the apse, the choir flanked by its diminutive sacristies, the crossing, and the nave arm. The screens that separated each space were 1.4 meters high, enough to impede to some extent a view of the apse entrance and the altar it contained. They not only effected physical separation, but made the glimpses of the seat of the liturgy's mysteries more awkward to attain. The visual isolation was not complete, however, and the dramatic alternation of light and dark spaces was surely meant in its deep contrasts to dramatize the presentation of the apse: more mysterious and remote but at the same time more intriguing.

An almost identical arrangement exists at San Pedro de la Nave. There, the light of three windows illuminates the apse, which appears only as a brilliant, negative shape inscribed by its horseshoe opening. It is enframed by the deep shadow of the choir, an obscure zone locked in place by the horseshoe arches of the crossing, which in turn announce a new division, a pillar of illuminated space. Here too the original chancels divided the spaces already drawn in elevation and light, the third choir embracing perhaps more of the nave at San Pedro, which is long and pillared in the basilical manner (Fig. 4).

The segmentation of Santa Comba de Bande and San Pedro de la Nave into terse little pockets of space must be the witness of the contraction of Spanish architecture to serve the divisions required by liturgy.[69] Spanish churches of the seventh and early eighth centuries confirm, and serve in their complex and unique elevations, concerns in planning that were initially seen in the first years of the sixth century, when crossings and chancel screens were first documented on the peninsula.

The same must be true of the four standing basilicas that are known to us from the seventh and eighth centuries. Unfortunately only two preserve their naves intact, and all but one (São Gião de Nazaré) leave unanswered significant questions concerning reconstruction.[70] Though the basilicas show the same concerns in the division and segmentation of space, a good deal of variety can be discerned in the solutions offered for the planning of their naves. A single nave at São Gião de Nazaré is closed off from the side aisles that serve as sacristies (Fig. 8). At San Juan de Baños the nave is defined by arcades of horseshoe arches on columns that support a clerestory above, leaving side aisles bathed in shadow behind them (Pl. 8). The naves and side aisles of both São Gião and San Juan are wooden-roofed, but there is evidence that the lost side aisles of Quintanilla de las Viñas carried low groin vaults that must have intensified their obscurity (Fig. 10).[71] The supports of the nave of Quintanilla are lost; they might have been columnar, as at San Juan de Baños (Fig. 6), or pillared, as in the nave arm of San Pedro de la Nave. It seems most likely, however, that the nave would have featured an arcade of horseshoe arches.

The division of choir and apse space was also important in basilicas, though necessarily achieved through different means than in the centrally planned structures. At San Juan de Baños the original relationship between the nave and east end has been destroyed, but some sort of crossing was formed through the creation of the sacristy arms, and it may have been reinforced by the chancel we know to have been used there originally. One possibility for the reconstruction of Baños has emerged in the recently discovered church of Santa Lucía de El Trampal, Alcuéscar, brought to light by Caballero (Fig. 7). Three boxlike apses sit on a totally separate transept, one partitioned laterally by six transverse horseshoe arches. Chancel barriers mark the apse openings, the transept entry, and a passage that separates the nave from the sanctuary area. It is an interesting plan that offers solutions of reconstruction for two other standing basilicas as well.[72]

The most complete basilica offers the most brutal solution: at São Gião de Nazaré a single nave is separated from its tripartite choir by a masonry wall, pierced only by a narrow door and two windows (Fig. 8, Pl. 9). The sacristies that traditionally flank the choir in cruciform churches seem here to be squeezed alongside the fully enclosed nave, to which they offer no access. Instead, they communicate by constricted doors to the side compartments of the choir.

The sanctuary of São Gião would only have been visible to someone standing in the nave in fleeting glimpses; the purpose of the partitioning wall is clearly not only to separate those in the choir and apse from those in the nave, but to control the visual experience of the latter as well.

At the basilica of Quintanilla de las Viñas we are presented with hints of yet another variation; a single-apsed church with a separate choir, from which there is narrow access to twin sacristies. Here the nave entrance to the choir is lost, but the side aisle doors are so narrow as to defy practical use (Pl. 10). The size and placement of the chancels at Quintanilla are unknown.

Fragmentary remains also retain the suggestion of such divisions between nave and east end. Excavations of the sixth-century church "Of the Miracles" in the amphitheater of Tarragona reveal the central nave of a three-aisled columnar basilica crowned with a horseshoe-shaped apse, which may have been separated from the nave by chancel barriers in the second nave bay (Fig. 9).[73]

And even when little is known of the shape of the choir, the apse entrance and its distinctive horseshoe silhouette retains a hint of the same spatial and formal preoccupations. At São Pedro de Balsemão a robust horseshoe arch on a rustic impost (etched and linear on the nave surface, but plastic and swelling as it meets the arch's intrados) marked the center of a wide apse wall (Pl. 11). The continuation of the impost molding marks the extent to which that wall must have partitioned the now-lost apse; and the elegant curve of the arch, with its converging springers, was thus the frame through which a limited glimpse of the altar and its mysteries was attained.

The majority of these buildings are constructed in an indigenous ashlar technique, in general like that employed at São Frutuoso de Montelios. Stones are laid at times in fine straight courses as at Quintanilla, San Pedro, and São Frutuoso. At Santa Comba de Bande, however, stones are fit together like pieces of a cyclopean puzzle, in which the tedium of regularity is fought through the carving out of the corner of an occasional block to fit it in a more complex manner with the next. This one variation in an otherwise quite restrained style enlivens the wall and gives it a movement and interest analogous to that offered at São Frutuoso by its blind arcade, or the exterior of Quintanilla in the delicate bas-reliefs that bind its east end like a garland. It is such a contrast, created this time through irregularity of a very subtle sort, that generates interest in the careful ashlar of San Pedro de la Nave. Here, as at Bande, slight variations in a regular coursed wall succeed in energizing it, especially through the introduction of tiny twin lanceted windows, placed with little regard to the courses of the masonry from which they are carved (Pl. 12). The diminutive horseshoe arches, the colonnette and its bulging entasis, and the complex curvilinear design of its capital all act as a subtle foil to the geometry and precision of the rest of the wall fabric.

I take the time to outline this because such details of craft reveal a lively and autonomous masonry tradition whose role in the larger spatial development outlined above ought to be explored. These fine points of decoration—this interest in a complexity that challenges the expectation of simplicity and regularity, in a surprise bit of disjuncture or contrast—are the echoes of grander interior strategies concerned with exclusion and disclosure that are being worked through over time by these same masons in conjunction with the churchmen who were their immediate patrons. Though it is to these patrons that we owe the introduction of chancel barriers and the disposition for interior planning that segregated and privileged the spaces defined by them, certain highly significant decisions concerning the interior appearance of churches constructed under Visigothic rule—the placement of windows and lighting, for instance, or the use of the blind room over the apse to regulate its interior and exterior effect—must have evolved over generations of interaction between patron and mason. It is from this collaboration—not just in the simpler decisions concerning a basic type of plan and elevation or the organization of spaces—that the drama of churches constructed in the Visigothic period grows: the chiarascuro that presents the eastern light of the apse at San Pedro de la Nave as if it were a framed image of the altar, or the perforated screen at São Gião that separated one from, but still allowed teasing glimpses of, the liturgical rites within the choir.

These same mutual goals, at once conscious (the segregation of apse, choir, and nave) and unconscious (the formal values that embrace and quicken these divisions), are thus served in the decoration of seventh- and eighth-century churches as well. Nowhere was the force of sculpture used to such effect as at Quintanilla de las Viñas (Pls. 13 and 14).[74] There, the faithful in the nave must have been able to glimpse the apse entrance, for its appearance is as dramatic and symbolic as that at San Pedro de la Nave. The boldness of the form of its triumphal arch, its sharp and radical cutting into the space of its own opening; the rich and impertinent reliefs of the carved voussoirs and imposts, etched in deep contrast of light and shadow, to which is added the most minute plastic values (the ropelike hair of the Virgin, or the bulging belly of a rinceau-framed partridge); the slender freestanding columns that barely brush the jambs behind them—all these works enframe the apse entrance with such unrestrained drama that one yearns to be able to step back into the now-blocked and destroyed nave to gauge its effect: to be beguiled by this stage set as one was meant to be 1,200 years ago.

The stage of a church from the Visigothic period was its choir, and it guarded in its most remote precinct the apse and its altar, illuminated through an eastern window by the rising sun. Enframed by a horseshoe arch darkened by the obscurity of the choir, the apse as viewed from the nave presented a remote but almost pictorial symbol of the arisen Christ. The appearance of the altar in brilliant light behind the deep keyhole silhouette of its enframing arch recalls many images indeed of the enthroned Christ in Spanish manuscripts of the tenth century.

Such mystery and drama is deeply rooted in the practice and taste of Spanish sculptors and masons; but the traditions in which these formal practices evolved were nurtured under the patronage of a strong and vital church, one that underwent significant changes in the very years this architectural style, and the masonry tradition associated with it, was developing. It is to the history of that church, and in particular to its liturgy, that we must finally turn, then, for an understanding of the seclusion and division that so marks Spanish church building of the seventh and early eighth centuries.

The last half of the sixth century witnessed a period of crucial development not only for Spanish architecture but for liturgy as well. The rite is traditionally called Mozarabic, both for those Spaniards who identified so strongly with it when its survival was threatened in the eleventh century and because to call it Visigothic for the period of its birth would create a confusing association with Arian rulers. It is in fact one of the group of Gallican liturgies, and as such shares common points of structure with the early liturgies of France and northern Italy. The Mozarabic rite was almost fully developed by the end of the sixth century, though it continued expanding until the Muslim invasion in 711.[75] In particular, it underwent changes in the sixth and seventh centuries that distinguish it from other Gallican liturgies and reveal its dynamic bond with a growing and changing church. The architecture that serves it during these same years does so with a responsiveness and sensitivity that speak directly to the liturgy's authority and significance for the society under Visigothic rule.

Of particular interest for the developments followed in this study is the Mass of the Faithful. The liturgical texts offer little evidence of movement during the Mass of the Faithful, except for the administration of Communion itself.[76] Indeed at churches like São Gião de Nazaré and San Pedro de la Nave, separate choir entrances suggest that the celebration of the Mass of the Faithful at these sites was quite contained in the area to the east of the first chancel barrier. The existence of eastern flanking chambers supports this notion.[77] It is known that the laity approached the choir to receive Communion, and that the end of the rite was marked by that sacrament. We would know little else of the relationship of the Mozarabic liturgy to the architectural space that harbored it were it not for the councils of the Spanish church and the church buildings themselves. In legislative action that sought to change and defend the liturgy, we find a fascinating and sensitive document of the evolving concerns of the church. In particular, in the second half of the sixth century there appears a preoccupation with the physical separation of clergy and laity during the rite.

The first Council of Braga (561) describes in its thirteenth canon the manner in which Communion was to be taken. It was decided that "the laity were not permitted to enter into the sanctuary of the altar to receive communion, neither men nor women, but only the clergy, in confirmation with the old rules." The rule of separation is repeated again in the Fourth Council of Toledo (633), which states that the following order and placement ought to be observed in the administration of communion: ". . . the bishop and the celebrant before the altar, the clergy in the choir, and the people outside of the choir."[78]

The means by which these divisions were expressed in architecture of the Visigothic period are diverse. Chancels with *solea* in the Syrian or Byzantine manner were noted by Schlunk and Maloney at Casa Herrera and Torre de Palma.[79] Another early and quite common symptom of the practice must be the low chancel barriers that begin to appear in the transitional churches of the sixth century: Bobalá-Serós, and San Pedro de Mérida, for instance.[80] It is indeed not until the mid-sixth century that barriers are consistently used to separate the clergy from the laity. These continue in the more complex and developed buildings of the seventh and early eighth centuries: fragments of a low chancel were discovered at San Juan de Baños, and Segóbriga also possessed one by the seventh century. The chancel at Santa Comba de Bande must have been similar to these, but half again as tall: while some earlier barriers measure about a meter in height, traces of those at Bande indicate chancels of 1.4 or 1.5 meters.[81] At São Gião de Nazaré, Schlunk recognized an extreme reaction to the Fourth Council of Toledo: the nave of the church is separated from the choir by a solid wall, pierced only by a door and thin windows (Pl. 9). The meagerness of the openings and their general shape ally them with what is known of the relationship of choir to basilical arm in the side aisles of Quintanilla de las Viñas (Pl. 10).[82] To this disposition might be added another, which is found in the most conservative of later buildings. In the ninth-century church of Santa Cristina de Lena and in San

Miguel de Escalada, of the beginning of the tenth century, a high screen of three arches blocks the choir from the nave (Pls. 37 and 38).[83] Both screens had low chancel plaques at their base, suggesting a form not unlike the Early Christian and Byzantine templon with its low parapet and epistyle or architrave.[84] But in these later Spanish examples can also be found provision for curtains which, when drawn, would cloak the choir as physically as the wall at São Gião. No such evidence survives, however, from the Visigothic period.[85] Perhaps a forerunner of this architectural solution can be seen at Valdecebadar near Olivenza, where central piers held arcades, the means by which two choirs were separated from an apse and a western arm.[86]

Each of these various types of barriers succeeds in segregating the choir from the nave. Whether or not the solution of Lena and Escalada existed during Visigothic rule, the churches of the Visigothic period demonstrate a wide variety of strategies for sheltering the altar in the apse, and for separating the choir by yet another barrier from the nave.

Not only were the divisions between choir and nave issues of first importance in the sixth-century councils, but divisions among the clergy were as well. The thirty-ninth canon of the Fourth Council of Toledo contains an admonishment to deacons who "become so presumptuous as to put themselves above the priests and try to put themselves ahead of them in the first choir, leaving the priests to the second choir: thus, in order that they should realize that the priests are superior to them, [the priests] should belong in one choir and they in the other."[87] The division of the choir into parts is evident in most mature churches of the Visigothic period. At San Pedro de la Nave a first choir, in front of the altar, projects farther east than the second choir, which probably included the entire crossing (and not the projecting arms, which are separate rooms).[88] A similar disposition existed at Santa Comba de Bande (which had no projecting arms) and San Pedro de la Mata, which has been reconstructed with three sets of chancel screens defining the three liturgical spaces.[89] Another solution to the problem of clerical division must be implied in basilical churches like San Juan de Baños, where the original location of the chancel barriers is unknown.[90] The disposition of the architectural spaces suggests that the portion of the nave set aside for the clergy must have been in the east, near the projection of the lateral arms. The first choir would be before the altar, in the continuation of the central nave, while the second would be divided in the spaces to either side. Such a division is suggested at Alcuéscar, and is amply documented in Mozarabic and Asturian churches of the ninth and tenth centuries, monuments serving the same liturgy: a possible rendering of these groups can be found in the painting of Aaron in the Tabernacle from the León bible of 960 (Pl. 15).[91] Perhaps the most poignant literary witness of these same divisions is a document perhaps of the eleventh century that is believed to describe the Mozarabic office of the cathedral of Toledo:

> They sang in sacred choirs in the triple sanctuary: one of these choirs sang while the other intoned a response, and the third praised with a *Gloria* the trinitary God; in unison, after the *Gloria* they chanted an *antiphone*: that is how the sanctuaries radiated the chants of the saints. One choir was near the altar, another near the *pulpitum*, another, finally, resonated in the temple a melodious echo . . .[92]

The preoccupations with hierarchy and division that have been our focus were of particular concern to the Hispano-Roman church during the sixth century: they appear in a council preceding the conversion of Reccared and, in particular, in the Fourth Council of Toledo, the one immediately following his conversion. Though they refer at times to practices which are older, the customs they prescribe are not mentioned in actual liturgical texts, nor is there any evidence—documentary or architectural—of their having enjoyed any widespread use before the sixth century. In particular, the total sequestration of the nave at São Gião testifies to a radical concealment of the choir, a permanent architectural expression of divisions articulated more gently, in less permanent materials in other, often earlier monuments. We see in monuments of the seventh and early eighth centuries, not only chancel barriers of various heights and levels of concealment, but a sympathy in diverse aspects of church design for the same issues of segregation and division, in all the surviving churches of the Iberian Peninsula. These are reflections of the same shared concerns that were distinguished as new and noteworthy at the churches at Villa Fortunatus, Bobalá-Serós, and Segóbriga. These transitional churches of the sixth century both precede and are the contemporaries of the councils that enforce their spatial peculiarities, but the concerns they reflect clearly survive—even grow—in the seventh and eighth centuries.

The low chancel barrier, the high chancel screen, and the separating wall are all known in contexts outside of the Iberian Peninsula. From Gaul, Syria, or North Africa must have come, at various times, typological models for a number of those adopted in sixth- and seventh-century Spain.[93] But the models are so dispersed, and the examples in Spain so ubiquitous and yet at the same time varied, that the notion of mimicry as a primary force in the adoption of this spatial configuration is out of the question.

Schlunk saw the primary motive for the change in plan as liturgical, relating to the importance of the polyphonic chant in monastic foundations.[94] This explanation, while certainly significant for the establishment of the three-part choir, does not explain the stridency with which the choir is consistently sequestered from the nave, or the visual remoteness and mystery of the altar itself.[95] These are particularly important issues, for they address the passion and creativity with which these barriers to the choir were taken up on the Iberian Peninsula. Their consistent use in Spain, the insistence in the church councils on the divisions they sustain, and the architectural reinforcement of the whole notion of partition and segmentation in the style of the monuments they serve reveal their enormous significance to the church. While it appears only as an occasional point of interest in other parts of Europe and the Mediterranean, the issue of division, sequestration, and partition is, by contrast, a vital central theme in the experience of the liturgy and the space in which it is enacted in nearly every monument on the Iberian Peninsula for two hundred and fifty years.

The use and development of chancel barriers in architecture of the Visigothic period responded to an urgent and timely need. With the monumentality of dividing screens, and even with lower chancel barriers came the distancing of the choir, and at times the obscuring, during the holiest parts of the Mass, of the sacraments celebrated there. It comes as little surprise to learn that from the sixth century on, the orthodox church of the Iberian Peninsula seems to be actively engaged in turning in upon itself; in jealously guarding its prestige and mysteries.

I believe that another reflection of this interest in hierarchy and division, secrecy and mystery, can be found in developments in the text of the liturgy that date from the second half of the sixth through the seventh centuries: the same moments as the councils consulted in this discussion. Díaz y Díaz sees in the "literary elaboration" of these liturgical texts some pedagogy, but for the most part "a rarity of popular participation" in a liturgy that must have been intended uniquely for other clergy; must indeed have diminished the understanding of the faithful "as the complexity, obscurity and elaboration of the formula increased."[96]

In particular, the studies of Jungmann are of significance here, for he has found that the evolving prayer type of the Visigothic liturgy "shows to a high degree the influence of the battle against Arianism."[97] Jungmann saw in changes associated with the development of the "Trinity mystery" the seeds of a separation of the laity from the sacraments, a removal of the celebrant from the community, which had a profound impact on the history of the Catholic liturgy.[98] He showed that the Spanish church of the sixth and seventh centuries was engaged in delicate alteration of the Mass—in reassessing its prayers in particular—to the end of avoiding any ambiguity between orthodox beliefs and those of the Arians. The church hesitated, for instance, to use the doxology *Gloria Patri per Filium in Spiritu Sancto* because the Arians employed it as an expression of their conviction that the Son was inferior to the Father. Gradually abandoned also was the notion in the liturgy of the mediatorship of Christ. Instead, prayers were emphasized that focused on consubstantiality.[99] Other scholars have noted with Jungmann that prayers are often addressed indifferently to the Son or the Father; they sometimes begin with an address to one and close evoking the other.[100] Similar concerns resulted in the prominence of the Trinity and Trinitarian professions of faith, which Díaz y Díaz also acknowledges as "a theological sketch for the fight against the Arian church."[101]

The most frequently cited of these liturgical novelties is the introduction of the creed, perhaps because it is represented in the Third Council of Toledo as having been adopted at the insistence of King Reccared on the occasion of his conversion.[102] Its appropriation is indeed significant, especially in view of the historical moment in which it occurs. When the canon states that the creed must be "proclaimed by the people in a clear voice" so that they might be purified to receive Communion, it is no longer only a distinction from Arian practice which is sought, but a defiant reminder of the Orthodox victory over that heresy—an effective use of propaganda possible because the Hispano-Roman church controlled the liturgy, perhaps the most powerful media of dissemination of the Middle Ages.[103] The association of the converted king's name and authority with this liturgical change, and with the general condemnation of the heresy, signals its importance to what Jungmann calls the church's "defensive position" against Arianism and the authority associated with it.

It is possible that a similar kind of imprint was left on the Mass through greater emphasis given to the *Benedicte* around the time of Reccared's conversion, a prominence that yields an even less shrouded victory cry of the Hispano-Roman church against heretical authority. The evocation of the story of the three youths thrown into the fiery furnace for not worshipping Nebuchadnezzar could convey not only a spiritual but a political message, for the story culminates in the Bible not only in their deliverance but in the subsequent conversion of their ruthless king.[104] The importance of this prayer to the Hispano-Roman church of the second half of the sixth century finds a witness in a curiously forceful reference in the Fourth Council of Toledo. Though liturgical texts restrict the use of the *Benedicte* to the feast of St. James and the first Sunday in Lent, the council's fourteenth canon orders "that this hymn be sung in all of the masses of all of the churches of Spain and Gallia, with loss of communion for anyone who shows disrespect to its ancient use."[105] Described by the canon as the song "that celebrated the diffusion of the Catholic church throughout the whole world," the story of the three "children" can be seen as a celebration of the triumph of the church over another, heretical king. Its importance to the council that immediately follows the one in which Reccared's conversion was announced is thus significant.

The defensive tactics of the Catholic church against Arianism continued during and after the conversion of Reccared. This occurred in part because the church was anxious to educate a confused and torn populace. Indeed more frontal assaults on Arianism occurred in sermons delivered in these same architectural spaces.[106] Perhaps this posture grew at the same moment as the vicious attacks against Arianism launched by Severius and Leander, gestures Collins sees as aimed at stopping an Arian "intellectual offensive" which promised to produce "defections from the Catholic ranks."[107] Intrinsic to these liturgical concerns, however, are also the strategies of a battle waged not only against a heresy but against the power and authority held by the once heretical class.[108] The spiritual battle became in some ways the outward expression of a larger social and political one that continued long after the conversion of the Visigothic monarch. Church leaders were anxious to buttress their position against that authority associated with Arianism; to confirm their own accession. It is further by no means surprising that this battle continued after the Visigoths' conversion. Since the conversion, and abolition of separate Roman law that followed, the power of Hispano-Roman churchmen had slowly been subverted by Visigothic princes who now had pretensions to spiritual as well as temporal authority.[109]

What I would like to suggest is that successive closing off of the choirs of churches built under Visigothic domination might emerge as an expression of this same defensive battle. I see these developments as the product of a gradual, largely unconscious desire on the part of the churchmen who used and built churches to reassert, in the permanent and monumental architectural language provided by builders, divisions that must first have appeared only through the intervention of chancels and other church furniture.[110] It is an architectural and spatial consideration that probably began to affect peninsular churches as early as the end of the fifth century, a time when the oppression of the new Arian rulers must have been felt. The development of crossings and the consistent use of chancel barriers are amply documented by the first half of the sixth century, decades that would end with the persecution of orthodox Catholics by Leovigild. Indeed, the development of a segmented architectural plan, one composed of discrete compartments partitioned in elevation, coincides chronologically with the Hispano-Roman church's confrontation with the

Arian hegemony, and precedes the textual testimony to the same defensive stance.

The physical and at times visual separation of the clergy complemented the conceptual separation noted by Jungmann. It also had the effect of enhancing the clergy's position, of rendering them more formidable. The obscuring of parts of the sacraments in secrecy increased the authority of the clergy as arbitrators between a gradually excluded laity and their Lord; a role of mediatorship denied Christ in the need to associate him with the Father, to shield him from the separateness and humanity of Arian belief. The distancing of the choir from the populace served simultaneously a conscious spiritual motive and an unconscious temporal one: it shrouded Christ in a mystery that intensified his remoteness and thus served the cause of his oneness with the Almighty, placing him far above the creature of Arian belief. When glimpsed, the sanctuary was revealed from behind the dark choir like an apparition bathed in a mysterious light; it was unique, remote, and unapproachable. At the same time the choir's autonomy worked with the spiritual stance of the monks to increase their authority as mediators by asserting their exclusivity, and their closeness to sacraments bathed in remoteness as well.[111]

In its battle against the Arian kings, the Hispano-Roman church thus reexamined its liturgy, organized its hierarchy and forces, and recoiled into an ever more entrenched position of liturgical isolation. The mysterious, enclosed spaces of its churches thus present us with a sort of spiritual fortress, one in which massive walls and enclosed, partitioned spaces defended an imperiled cult and lent authority to a threatened clergy. It must be this struggle that lends to Spanish architecture of the sixth through the early eighth centuries its uniqueness, and also its coherence and cohesiveness. It is indeed a national architecture, as so many of its historians proclaim, but it is far from a document of national unity. It rather contains in its terse pockets of space the testimony of an unresolved struggle for authority between tenuously reconciled, cohabiting foes.

2

San Julián de los Prados

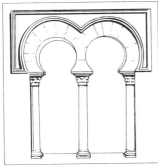

Three generations after the Muslim invasion of the Iberian Peninsula, the only hope for a Christian Spain was the tiny and rather scruffy mountain kingdom of Asturias. There an aristocracy that Gabriel Jackson has described as "wealthy cattle barons who doubled as guerrilla war captains"[1] ruled an indigenous population to which had been added the refuse of a shockingly rapid and decisive war: Christian refugees from the south. This embryonic nation was insular in nature; struggling for its own survival and faced with a foe of vastly superior powers, it had yet to ally itself with other Christian powers, and was too geographically remote to be annexed by them, as Catalonia eventually was.

The kingdom of Asturias had, of course, no Christian counterpart in the south. During almost the entire eighth century, Islam knew a troubled but uncontested rule in the territories south of the Duero river. But Islamic Spain—al-Andalus— harbored a large number of Christians, and these Mozarabs, as they came to be called, formed a number of cohesive communities within the context of the Muslim state. It is difficult to say by what cultural and social threads the first inhabitants of the kingdom of Asturias might have been bound to the Mozarabs of al-Andalus. But it seems clear that such communication and shared experience as might have existed between the inhabitants of Asturias and al-Andalus were quickly obscured by their radically divergent social and political experience in the course of the eighth century. The nature of these diverse experiences and the history of their creation are worth looking into, for in them lie valuable tools for the analysis of the monumental documents that are the focus of this study.

The invasion of Spain initiated in 711 by Tariq and his predominantly Berber army swept the ancient and urban south in two years, occupying Toledo by 713–714.[2] Deprived of their capital—the one place in which a Visigothic king might legitimately be anointed—the last hope of a cohesive defense on the part of the Visigothic kingdom was lost.[3] The invasion eventually embraced nearly the entire peninsula, as well as an impressive amount of France: the *Chronicle of Moissac* recounts that Nîmes fell to Islamic armies, who then followed the Rhône and Saône rivers to sack Autun in 725.[4]

It was probably internal unrest, however, rather than the dread of Christian forces, that called those conquering armies back into Spain. It struck in the form of civil wars involving the Berbers, who had been the backbone of the initially victorious army. Because many of them were the force by which remote northern regions such as Galicia were held, their perpetual disaffection loosened Islamic hold on the

Christian populations to the north, and so it is probably to the internal strife of eighth-century al-Andalus that is owed the formation of the Christian kingdoms.[5]

At the time of its birth the kingdom of Asturias was part of a northern zone centered on a rudimentary and unspecialized herding economy that had resisted romanization in late Imperial times.[6] Although it has been determined that a number of settlements existed before the invasion, Asturias is rarely mentioned in early sources, and there is no evidence even of an episcopal see before the eighth century.[7] The foundation of the Kingdom of Asturias certainly marked the first political force in the north. Even then the development of its culture was not spontaneous. The vestiges of the great learned men of the Visigothic church remained where they always had been—in the southern half of the peninsula, some of them attempting to maintain a church hierarchy under Muslim domination, some gathering strength in the opposition to that rule. The church was once again the center of a Christian community but one that no longer knew secular rulers of its own faith. The view taken by these southern ecclesiastics of the Christian kingdoms to the north would remain for some time that of a provincial backwater. No other document bears witness to this attitude better than the letter of Elipandus, archbishop of Toledo, to Beatus, monk of the Asturian monastery of Liébana in 783. In an argument to which we will have substantial recourse later in this chapter, Elipandus declares in exasperation that "never has anyone heard of one from Liébana giving lessons to one from Toledo."[8] Iberian Christian culture was still cradled in the Hispano-Roman church; indeed, it was still to the archbishopric of Toledo, the great Visigothic capital now gripped in a tumultuous Muslim rule, that all Spanish Christians were obliged to look for ecclesiastical authority.

How did this Christian nucleus conceive of itself, suddenly so distanced from its traditional center of power, isolated and yet unchallenged? What we know of the first Asturian architecture belies the cultural and historical dependency of its earliest monarchs on their Visigothic past. The first notice of building after the conquest survived until recently in the commemorative stone of a church founded by a King Favila and his wife Froliuba in 737, the first year of their reign, at Cangas de Onís. It is significant both as the document of a royal foundation in the first *de facto* capital of the realm, and further as the work of the son of Pelayo, the founder of the Asturian monarchy. The inscription speaks of a church dedicated to the Holy cross and built "manifesting symbolically the sign of the Holy cross," a design quite easily fit within the group of buildings constructed under Visigothic rule that were discussed in chapter 1.[9] Indeed, if any other typology had been developed in the two short and tumultuous decades that had passed since the Islamic invasion, it would have been quite a startling achievement.[10]

The first clear view offered us of both building practice and plan type is another royal foundation: Santianes de Pravia, built by King Silo (774–783) in the new home of the Asturian court.[11] Asturian Santianes emerges from considerable restoration and rebuilding as a three-aisled basilica with a single apse and a tripartite crossing (Fig. 12). The aisles were originally separated from the nave by arcades of two arches supported by square piers with beveled corners, while engaged columns supported a diaphragm arch that served to partition the crossing into three parts, both in plan and elevation.[12] A tower, or higher central space, topped the center bay of the crossing.[13]

The plan type and division of interior space of Santianes de Pravia followed in many ways the tradition of the buildings constructed under Visigothic rule. It is a basilica with short and wide proportions, crowned by a tripartite crossing, the spaces of which were divided by arches falling on engaged columns. Santianes thus belongs to the same family of architectural interpretations of the liturgy as San Pedro de la Nave. The central bay of the crossing was higher, permitting the establishment of a hierarchy of spaces like that which characterized much of the Visigothic building of the eighth century, as at San Pedro, or Santa Comba de Bande.

Santianes's plan and elevation, however, are in many ways quite different from those of churches of the Visigothic period, and they evolved from a number of forces. The basilica of Visigothic tradition in some ways must also respond to local typological variants, possibly tempered by outside influences. Such must be the explanation for Santianes's semicircular apse and western burial pantheon. In construction technique Santianes certainly diverges radically from the buildings of the Visigothic period in the *Meseta*, to which it has been typologically compared. It is constructed primarily of rubblework, which at times commands a certain horizontal order, quoined by ashlar headers and stretchers. The style is strongly reminiscent of that used in the nearby Roman baths of Campo Valdés (Gijón), one that reflects a continuous indigenous tradition of construction. Santianes exhibits certain refinements in keeping with this convention of construction: original portions of the interior, for instance, retain a covering of stucco painted red.

What emerges, then, is a church that in terms of space and proportion reflects the tradition called Visigothic, and yet is of a thin-walled type of construction: rubblework covered by a smooth coat of stucco and painted. The stonecutter's art appears at Pravia, but miserably rationed: some chancel pilasters decorated in the sharply beveled style of the Visigothic period, and, more interesting for our purposes here, a series of simple windows of one or two horseshoe arches (Pl. 16). Once again, these windows present a familiar type, but in a sharp, smooth, and flat style unfamiliar in prototypes executed under Visigothic rule. As with the planning of Santianes, the sculpture shows either a local variant of a traditional style, or the continuation, in an indigenous and more impoverished construction technique, of the style of church building practiced before the invasion in the central and southern portions of the peninsula.

Such is the murky formal background for the monumental constructions of Alfonso II "El Casto" (791–842). To some extent our fascination with these austere edifices can be attributed to the figure cut by their patron. For Alfonso II is hailed as the first leader of the Reconquest, whose military prowess won the first serious battles against Asturias's Islamic foe at Lutos and Lisbon, and whose diplomatic and political talents established the first relations between Asturias and other parts of the Christian world. Alfonso can thus be credited with the transformation of the Asturian monarchy from a rural, provincial capital into a more complex and cosmopolitan court with international concerns.[14]

But Alfonso "The Chaste" is also the monarch with whom nearly every student of medieval Spain has engaged in a scholarly frontier romance, one that centers on the identity and personality of the first Christian nation to emerge from the peninsula after the conquest. For those in whose interest it is to see a Spanish personality fully formed by the time of the Muslim conquest, the stakes for this scholarly fascination are high, for what better way to divine those aspects of Spain's Hispano-Roman and Visigothic past that survived the invasion than through this callow nation of Christian survivors.

At the heart of the matter is a seductive passage from the chronicle of Albelda, one probably conceived and written in the last quarter of the ninth century.[15]

Speaking of a revolt in which Alfonso II is dethroned, the Chronicle of Albelda tells how he was restored to his throne in Oviedo. It then immediately relates the building of his three churches in that city: San Salvador, Santa María, and San Tirso were decorated with great care, all "with arches and marble columns, gold and silver." There are two interpretations proposed for the intriguing passage that follows. One analysis implies a translation that might read: "He decorated [them] with diverse pictures, similar to the royal palace. All in the order of the Goths just as it was in Toledo . . . ," while a recent critical text and translation interprets it in the following manner: "He decorated them with diverse pictures; and all the ceremony of the Goths, just as it had been in Toledo, he completely restored in Oviedo, in the church as well as in the palace."[16] The text appears in the following form:

> Iste XI regni anno, per tirannidem regno expulsus monasterio Abelanie est retrusus. Inde a quodam Teudane uel aliis fidelibus reductus regnique Ouetao est culmine restitutus. Iste in Ouetao templum sancti Salbatoris cum XII apostolis ex silice et calce mire fabricauit aulamque sanctae Marie cum tribus altaribus hedificauit. Baselicam quoque sancti Tirsi miro hedificio cum multis angulis fundamentauit; omnesque has Domini domos cum arcis atque columnis marmoreis auro argentoque diligentur ornauit, simulque cum regiis palatiis, picturis diuersis decorauit; omnemque Gotorum ordinem, sicuti Toleto fuerat, tam in eclesia quam palatio in Ouetao cuncta statuit.[17]

By his translation, it would seem that Moralejo interprets palace and church ceremonial as having been revived. Menéndez Pidal believed the text to mean that Alfonso reinstituted a Visigothic palace organization at court.[18] Sánchez-Albornoz, finding no evidence to support a Visigothic structure at court (and seeing, on the contrary, Carolingian influence there), suggests that the "order of the Goths, just as it was in Toledo" can be found in Alfonso II's concern with establishing a Christian capital with an episcopal see and church council, in imitation of the Visigothic capital in Toledo.[19] Finally, Schlunk offered the influential theory that the document gave a literal account of the models used in the building of Alfonso II's church of San Julián de los Prados; that Alfonso II sought literally to reproduce a Toledan church of the Visigothic period in his new capital in Asturias.[20]

The questions posed by this document and the scholarship surrounding it are complex, and we will return to them as part of our discussion of Alfonso II's patronage, but three issues that it evokes are worth mentioning from the beginning. The first is that, as early as the end of the ninth or beginning of the tenth century—perhaps three-quarters of a century after Alfonso II's death—medieval Spanish Christians were already concerned with the issue of the survival of a Christian hegemonic identity, and this time they are happy to identify themselves with the Visigoths as representatives of Christian peninsular rule. The second is that the document's account corresponds to our historical understanding of Alfonso II's reign in a general sense, for he was certainly engaged in creating a capital that would function administratively as Toledo had in the previous century, and if it is true that he aimed to hold church councils there, he might certainly be seen as harboring a desire for power over ecclesiastical concerns similar to that enjoyed by Visigothic monarchs.[21] But I would stop considerably short of embracing the notion of a visual world created in imitation of Toledo, or of any suggestion that Alfonso II wished to re-create the ancient capital rather than simply to usurp its ancient authority. The reasons for this tell a story of their own, one that will fill most of the pages that follow. They have to do with the visual character of the buildings of Alfonso II's patronage, and Alfonso's relationship with the feisty and animate Toledo of his own day.

The third concern evoked by the document has to do with its reliability and applicability to the reign of Alfonso II. There is some reason to suspect this tempting allusion to Alfonso's patronage in general. The work is almost certainly an official chronicle written for Alfonso III, a monarch credited by Menéndez Pidal with the rebirth of Spanish historiography.[22] The chronicle's own representation of history is, further, one that seeks to establish a spurious continuity between the Visigothic empire and the Asturian monarchy, an interest in that time before the Islamic invasion when Christians ruled all of Spain. The chapter treating Alfonso and all Asturian kings is indeed entitled *Ordo Gothorum Obetensium Regum*. This insistence on conscious historical linkage is typical of the reign of Alfonso III, who is known to have been concerned with establishing a documented continuity between the Visigoths and his later reign, a strategy that might have been suggested to him by one of the number of Mozarabic clerics with whom he surrounded himself at court. It is not, by contrast, one typical of any materials or texts dating from Alfonso II's reign.[23]

The writers of the Chronicle of Albelda saw in Alfonso II's capital in Oviedo a significant political creation; they might even have known that he sought to create a center that would function in the Christian kingdoms to the north as Toledo had under the Visigoths. It seems quite probable, however, that the comments that might be construed as equating a conscious historicizing character to Alfonso II's urban buildings reflect the political and artistic tastes of its writers—and their own association of history and building.[24] For the extent to which they represent the aims of Alfonso II himself, we have the buildings as documents.

With Alfonso II's reign, Asturian monuments of significant size and planning begin to emerge; they are the first major Christian urban enterprise since the invasion, and the earliest significant architectural center of any period to survive in Asturias.

Most survive in Alfonso II's new capital of Oviedo, lamentably in fragmentary states. Oviedo had earlier been the site of a monastery founded in 781, and possibly the focus of some development at the time of Fruela I, Alfonso's father.[25] But it was Alfonso II who first made of this convergence of roads and valleys a capital city, one characterized by a substantial, organized campaign of building and public works.[26]

Alfonso's city was surrounded by walls and enriched by its monarch with aqueducts, courts, *triclinea*, palaces, baths, and storehouses.[27] At the heart of this new urban fabric lay a palace, composed of a long, narrow edifice embracing a two-story entrance framed by towers, of which part of the northernmost example is preserved today.[28] The palace was flanked by a gallery supported by an arcade, a Roman scheme that might well have been incorporated into an indigenous secular tradition of building. The palace facade might originally have suggested, in its plan and reconstruction, a city gate or triumphal arch whose towers embrace a two-story bay, but once again, the vestiges are too restricted and generic to interpret.[29]

Still standing is the Cámara Santa, a palatine chapel attached to one of the palace facade towers, though postdating the facade.[30] It introduces us to the workshop techniques that are repeated in each of the buildings of Alfonso II's patronage that survive: its walls are composed of frame-and-fill construction with the fill stones chipped into regular, oblong forms, and they still retain the thin wall buttresses that are distinctive of work executed under Alfonso. A two-story structure composed of superimposed naves, the Cámara Santa was accessible only by a door in the upper level that communicated with one of the palace towers (Pl. 17). Of the original work that survives, the crypt has suffered the least restoration. Dedicated to Santa Leocadia, it is a wide, low space covered by a brick barrel vault that rests on a socle about two and a half meters high.[31] The Cámara Santa was probably intended for burials from the beginning; two sarcophagi of ninth-century date are found there today.[32]

The Cámara Santa belongs to a typology easily identifiable on the peninsula. It has long been identified as emerging from the tradition of Roman funerary monuments with two floors, the top serving as cult chapel and the bottom as sepulchre. It thus inherited the form and meaning of such buildings as the funerary monument at Marusinac, though the Spanish prototype of the Paleochristian mausoleum of La Alberca points to an indigenous tradition.[33] It is further a type we can now be fairly sure was continued in Visigothic times, for the Early Christian church at Lugo has emerged recently as an intriguing possible prototype, and the "crypt" of San Antolín at Palencia is probably the bottom floor of such a martyrium, built perhaps, as tradition suggests, to hold the relics brought there by King Wamba in the seventh century.[34]

Less is known of the three churches that adorned Oviedo's center. San Salvador, dedicated in 812 to the Savior and the twelve apostles, was originally the foundation of Fruela, Alfonso's father, partially destroyed at least in Muslim raids of 794.[35] San Salvador was destroyed again in the fourteenth century, so we are left with only documentary testimony of its twelve altars, and its construction in stone by an architect named Tioda, on whom several precarious theories have been balanced.[36]

The church of Santa María is often mentioned in conjunction with San Salvador; it lay nearby, to the north of the cathedral and the palace complex.[37] Though it was destroyed in the seventeenth century, written accounts in this case yield some evidence. Santa María is known to have possessed a royal pantheon like Pravia,[38] and the Chronicle of Alfonso III (Ovetense) describes three altars. This seems to be a description of a three-part east end, an unusual form for the Iberian Peninsula before this time.[39] Our one clue concerning elevation is Ambrosio de Morales's observation in the sixteenth century that the arches of Santa María recalled those of Bamba and Hornija: "The entire fabric of the three chapels is of the (visi)gothic type, and even more so the three entry arches, quite similar to those at San Román de Hornija and Bamba, where the Visigothic kings were buried. . . . Only the three chapels are vaulted, and all the rest is covered with a bad tile and wooden roof."[40] This must mean that Santa María possessed a horseshoe-arched arcade, a motif that would bind the foundation with Visigothic elevations of the Visigothic period.

Santa María presents us with an odd combination of innovation—in the tri-apsed east end—and tradition in its horseshoe-arched elevation and vaulted apses. This monument, adorned as Morales tells us, with rich marble columns—perhaps those mentioned in the Albelda passage—was a key one in Alfonso II's plan for Oviedo, for as a royal pantheon it constituted the fitting monumental complement to the royal capital with its allusions to legitimacy and continuity.

The last of the Oviedo foundations to be discussed, San Tirso, has received the most attention from scholars because of the survival of the eastern wall of its central apse (Pl. 18).[41] This royal foundation to the west of the palace precinct was constructed in an identical tradition to the Cámara Santa: small oblong stones are set in courses in heavy mortar and quoined in neat ashlar blocks forming headers and stretchers. As in Alfonso's latest foundation, San Julián de los Prados, the top quoining block projects to become a roll corbel, which supports the eaves of the roof, and the apse featured a three-arched window. The San Tirso window is unusual, however, for it is inscribed in an *alfiz*, a molding that enframes the arches in a rectangle.

Long considered an Islamic import to the north, a scholarly tradition saw the advent of the *alfiz* in Asturias impossible before the Mozarabic immigrations of the tenth century. For this reason Schlunk called this *alfiz* a restoration of the tenth century. The discovery of another example from the reign of Alfonso II, however, confirms the originality of San Tirso's window, while allowing for a wider latitude of dates and meanings for this unobtrusive molding, which enframes an arch or series of arches.[42] I believe that the *alfiz*, as it appears here, is a variant of an indigenous form, one that might readily be seen as having developed from the twin-arched windows so characteristic of building in the Visigothic period. When both arches are cut from one block of ashlar, as in a window from the Visigothic period now in the Museo Provincial in Mérida (Pl. 19), or in the Asturian window at Santianes, they are unified and enframed. It is the same effect that is accomplished through the use of the *alfiz* in the small stone and brick tradition in which San Tirso is built.

What survives of Alfonso's building in Oviedo yields an eclectic formal message. There is substantial indication of a royal atelier, building in a consistent frame-and-fill technique of stone and large brick, using buttresses, lintels, and relieving arches. A two-leveled palatine chapel recalls a type used in the Early Christian and Visigothic periods, and at least one of the buildings included horseshoe arches, suggesting a traditional elevation, reminiscent of building before the invasion. But new and unusual forms appear in plan as well, in particular the tri-apsed east end and the western pantheon, part of the Asturian tradition since the building of the church at Santianes de Pravia.

Alfonso II's atelier created a royal precinct, including a number of ecclesiastical foundations, among which was a royal pantheon. We can see in the great number and concentration of monuments constructed under his patronage a purposeful use of building to create an urban center. The foundation of churches and a palace constituted a physical part of the new Christian capital conceived by Alfonso. Indeed patronage was one of the ways that the monarch seemed to be carving a new identity for the only Christian kingdom to survive the Islamic domination of the peninsula.

I. The Architecture of San Julián

Later in date is the most striking and best-preserved monument of Alfonso II's patronage.[43] San Julián de los Prados (or Santullano as it is also called) was the palatine chapel of Alfonso's suburban residence (Fig. 13, Pls. 20–22).[44] A western entrance originally opened into a porch, and then into San Julián's ample wooden-roofed nave, while a tribune in the northern transept provided a commanding second-story view of the transept below (Pl. 21).[45] The church itself is a simple three-aisled pier-type basilica composed of open, clearly defined spaces: a short, wide nave with side aisles, a transept and its northern portico,[46] and an east end of three rectangular barrel-vaulted apses. The vaulting and all of the arches are semicircular. At thirty-nine by twenty-five meters, it is the largest pre-Romanesque church in Spain.

Santullano's interior reveals a vast space, the monumentality of which is augmented in effect by the spatial communication between the church's different parts. The triumphal arch is tall and wide; it opens onto the transept, giving an idea of its vastness and revealing the barrel-vaulted apses beyond. The central apse continues the sense of openness and monumentality, for it is fully as wide as the triumphal arch itself. The continuous transept is in turn more impressive, topping the nave by nearly two meters; all three apses float on it, defying alignment with nave or side aisle. The transept in turn meets the nave but is not penetrated to form a crossing; the transept is an independent and formidable vessel in its own right.

The technique in which San Julián was constructed fits it within the broad building tradition remarked at Santianes de Pravia, and more specifically with the buildings of Alfonso II's patronage in Oviedo (Pl. 22). Walls are fashioned of quoined ragstone, to which is added large Roman-style brick in the arches and windows. Relieving arches are employed over linteled doors. The fabric of the walls is compact, and the roughly cut oblong stones follow fairly regular courses set in overflowing beds of heavy mortar. It is the indigenous technique of a thin-walled construction inherited from a Roman construction tradition and refined in the ambitious building campaign undertaken by Alfonso.[47] There is some evidence that parts of this construction at least were covered by a painted plaster layer, as occur in the Roman monuments of Lugo.[48] As at Santa María in Oviedo, *spolia* were used in the form of reused capitals and marble columns, here, in the apse entrance, the most honored location.[49] The building technique in all seems well suited to the planning of San Julián: frame-and-fill walls provide a delicate envelope for the vast and simple space of Santullano's interior. There, only the members of support (piers, or columns) are cut stone; the walls are covered with stucco, and with a group of extraordinary paintings, to which we shall return presently.

Much of what we see at San Julián de los Prados, then, diverges from the traditions of architectural design developed in the Visigothic period. The seventh- and eighth-century buildings discussed in chapter 1 were characterized by enclosed spaces partitioned from one another by diaphragm horseshoe arches, a disposition dependent on a square crossing or separate transept arms. Spaces, and the arches that defined transitions between them, telescoped down to a single apse. It was purposely sheltered, kept remote and exclusive. Only the plan of the choir of Quintanilla de las Viñas can recall in form that of San Julián, but in elevation it becomes clear that the precinct was too small to divide; the effect is totally divergent from the vast transept interior of Santullano.[50] The lighting of churches built under Visigothic rule was rationed and selective, and used to augment the inaccessibility and separateness of each pocket of space. It was a style that garnered strength from exposed, cut stone walls broken by selective bands of textured ornament. How far this seems from the monumental, open interior of San Julián de los Prados, with its continuous transept and three wide apses opening onto it by means of semicircular arches—the total absence in fact of any horseshoe arch. Further, while the technique of construction and treatment of the wall surface employed at Santullano allies it with the royal foundation at Pravia, important aspects of the elevation and treatment of space and scale of San Julián provide a contrast for those of the earlier church, which still seems tied to principles of division of space that recall those of the Visigothic period. Indeed, we can agree with Núñez, who remarks that the lack of impact of architecture from the Visigothic period on the architecture of Alfonso II is surprising.[51]

At San Julián de los Prados, then, a formal divergence in appearance—in its plan, elevation type, and interior space—is rendered more poignant by the fact that it is constructed in the same general tradition of construction as Pravia, a monument steeped in the older tradition of spatial planning. For this reason it seems to me, as it has to others, that the large, open spaces and continuous transept that so distinguish San Julián de los Prados from its predecessors relate it to the Early Christian Renaissance in Carolingian church building described by Krautheimer.[52]

In both general characteristics and details, Santullano exhibits affinities with the Carolingian movement. Like Saint Peter's itself, Santullano's continuous transept is a grand, uninterrupted space into which the nave does not intrude. The bare outer walls, straight inner surfaces, and brilliantly lit nave also relate it to Late Antique churches. Prados might be even more closely related, however, to a Carolingian building like Fulda (791–819) (Fig. 14), or Seligenstadt (830–834) (Fig. 15), which combines the continuous transept with a basilical plan that, like Santullano, includes rectangular piers.[53]

Indeed, on the whole, San Julián seems to be dependent less on Roman models than on examples of the Carolingian revival in the north. Though no Carolingian basilica with a continuous transept survives in elevation, a Salian church of the same plan and reflecting the impact of Fulda can provide us with a striking comparison.[54] At the basilica at Hersfeld (after 1037), as at San Julián, a large-scale central apse opens straight onto the transept (Fig. 16, Pl. 23). The transepts and naves of Santullano and Hersfeld are independent, open, and voluminous, defined by thin walls and simple piers. They create the effect of an "uncomplicated contrast between nave and transept," which Krautheimer describes as characteristic of the Carolingian tradition.[55]

In addition to these broad, recognizable references to Late Antique or Carolingian architecture, there is evidence of more detailed Carolingian influence at San Julián de los Prados. The wall arches that decorate the central apse, for instance, have northern precedents, as does the tri-apsed east end.[56] But of greater importance is a detail new to Spain both by virtue of its placement and function: the second-floor tribune that terminates the north transept. From the exterior, this addition to the nave takes the form of a deep portico, an element relatively familiar to Spanish architecture when it appears to the west.[57] However, its placement off the north transept, and its second-floor gallery with a view into the transept's vast space, distinguishes it from any development in the indigenous tradition. It is thought that the king might have watched the service in the crossing below from the vantage point of such a tribune.[58] A connection with the tribune at Aachen, though unvoiced in this scholarship, seems quite probable. However, I believe one can go much further in interpreting the importance of San Julián's tribune. Not only does the tribune recall— in its second-floor placement and its association with a royal palatine chapel—the function of one at Aachen, but it mirrors in position the tribunes of Fulda's transept, establishing deeper links between the Carolingian and Asturian buildings. For at Fulda, footing walls discovered near the transept ends are believed to have formed the foundation for arches that supported tribunes.[59] Such a tribune still survives in the early eleventh-century church of Saint Michael at Hildesheim. Once again, the general function and typology of a form—the tribune—has been adopted in the Asturian monument, but it has been expressed in a divergent, indigenous language of construction.[60]

Indeed, the most important similarities with the architecture of the north occur in the appearance of San Julián, rather than in details of decoration or craft. Thus it retains the stocky proportions in plan and the square apse exteriors—and interiors—that are common in Spanish building since Visigothic times without obscuring the meaning of the signifying motifs. One can see this in the execution of the transept: unlike the Roman and Carolingian monuments to which it has been compared, the continuous transept at San Julián does not project beyond the width of the nave and exceeds it in height by two meters. Yet it appears, both from the interior and exterior, as an autonomous space, an impressive separate vessel at right angles to the nave, much as it must have at Fulda and Saint Peter's. But San Julián de los Prados must have dazzled those who saw it even more for the simplest link of all of those that bind these monuments together: its unprecedented size. It is the largest pre-Romanesque church in Spain, one united to Fulda and other Carolingian buildings through the vast spaces and simple monumentality of which Hubert spoke when he described the grandeur of Carolingian architecture: "The secret," he said, "is to combine great spaces with simpler forms."[61]

I would like to suggest that at San Julián de los Prados, indigenous masons constructed a building much different from those built in Spain before Alfonso's time. San Julián would seem to represent an interpretation of the appearance and broad typology of a Carolingian church as it was ordered by a patron. And there is good reason to believe that Alfonso II, San Julián's patron, would be concerned with just such northern models for the design of his palatine chapel. For Santullano's evocation of Carolingian forms might well stem directly from Alfonso II's relationship with Charlemagne, an interchange that marked a new epoch in Asturian diplomacy.[62]

In 797, Alfonso II sent embassies to Charlemagne, and it is known that envoys from Charlemagne's court were sent to Oviedo in the same year. In 798, Asturian ambassadors arrived once again at Aachen, this time laden with trophies of war and Muslim slaves for the emperor.[63] The visits were reciprocated, and in addition, such important personalities as Jonas of Orleans made the journey to Alfonso's court.[64] The embassies to Charlemagne marked the first international communication exercised by an Asturian monarch, and there is evidence that their impact was felt in areas other than diplomacy. Scholars are debating Carolingian influence in the largely Visigothic legal system of Alfonso's rule, in his economic policy, and possibly in details of court organization as well.[65] And Charlemagne took a particular interest in the Asturian king. Einhard, in his life of the emperor, makes special mention of him, recounting that "Alfonso II, king of Asturias and Galicia, became so close a friend that, when he had occasion to send letters or messengers to Charlemagne, he ordered that he should always be called the king's own man."[66] A document of the terms of that intimacy can be found in the paintings of San Julián.

II. The Paintings of San Julián and the Problem of Asturian Aniconism

There are even more intriguing suggestions of the relationship between Charlemagne and Alfonso II in the extensive program of paintings that covers San Julián's interior. The paintings can be grouped into four categories (Pls. 24–26): classical ornamental designs of octagons and lozenges adorn the apse vaults and side aisles; *trompe l'oeil* architectural motifs cover the apses, nave arcades, and lower walls; a continuous frieze of architecture in illusionistic perspective forms a register between the arcade and the clerestory; and a series of large panels representing single buildings alternate with simple representations of drapery at the clerestory level. Roughly the same registers are maintained in the transept, except that the upper levels are smaller, to the profit of the middle ones, a variation possible since their height is not dictated there by the size of the clerestory windows. Many of the representations are clearly in the tradition of *opus sectile* imitations, though it is unclear if the artists themselves were aware of this.

The paintings are devoid of human figures. The only recognizable symbol is the jeweled cross, which appears four times in the composition: on the east and west walls of the transept, and on the east and west nave terminations. The program has been identified by the late Helmut Schlunk, rightly, I believe, as the Holy Jerusalem. In more recent studies, he urged in addition that the use of motifs typical of the sort found in Late Antique palaces carried secular, palatine implications at San Julián, an idea developed by Barral i Altet.[67] In both cases, Schlunk suggests Santullano's paintings to be a representation of the architecture of the celestial city like that at Santa Pudenziana in Rome, but one without the figures of Christ and the Apostles. Instead, the crosses of the transept and nave represent the True Cross, a symbol that also evokes, without figural representation, Christ's resurrection and ascension.[68]

The repetitive ornamental designs and the architectural motifs of the lower walls find their prototypes in Spanish paintings of Late Antique tradition like those of Santa Eulalia de Bóveda, and isolated architectural motifs from various Late Antique programs can also be discovered at San Julián.[69] However, nothing of the scale, subject, or monumentality of the paintings of Santullano's upper nave and transept walls can be found on the Iberian Peninsula, in particular if one juxtaposes the program's size and opulence with its lack of figures of any sort.[70] Such a divergence from Spanish tradition, both in architectural and decorative practice, poses a direct challenge to the scholarly tradition that persists in searching for an indigenous prototype for San Julián, hoping to reconcile the palatine chapel more intimately with the passage from the Chronicle of Albelda quoted at the beginning of this chapter.

It is of course not clear how the late ninth-century Christians who wrote the chronicles intended us to understand the "Gotorum ordinem," whether as a reflection of political aspirations, bureaucratic organization, court and church ceremony, or artistic reference. The last suggestion might be seen on one hand in terms of the large-scale act of patronage that constituted the founding of Oviedo; the simple existence of its churches and palaces could constitute a significant fact in the parallel created by the chronicle's authors between Toledo and Oviedo. However, Schlunk's understanding of the passage, which spoke of the "order of the visigoths" in close association with paintings in churches "similar to the royal palace," assumed a considerably more constricted interpretation. Schlunk took this to mean that the painting program of San Julián de los Prados must have followed a lost prototype from the Visigothic capital in Toledo.

Simply from the point of view of the document, this premise must be questioned. There are not only the strong interests of the chronicle's authors discussed earlier, concerns distanced by at least two generations and divergent political concerns. One must also consider that the passage speaks of Alfonso's urban churches and palace and not San Julián, which was outside of Oviedo, a fact that calls into question its direct relationship to Santullano. Indeed, the reference to an "order of the visigoths" does not appear in any of the documents that mention San Julián, even those shown to be related to the Albelda.[71] The history of the chronicle casts at least enough doubt on such an interpretation of Alfonso II's patronage to open the study of San Julián de los Prados and its paintings to other influences than those strictly indigenous—especially when indigenous forms yield so little fruit. It was indeed the consideration of an extra-Iberian influence that enabled us to understand the new and impressive forms of the architecture of Santullano, and it is to that same tradition we turn now for an understanding of its paintings.

Schlunk noted the Late Antique style and imagery of the paintings at San Julián de los Prados, relating them to both eastern and western sources, of which the *opus sectile* panel of the Hagia Sophia and the rather romantic reconstructions of Smugliwicz of the paintings of the *domus aurea* of Nero are but two examples (Pls. 27 and 28).[72] I would add to these an *opus sectile* panel from the Corporation House at Ostia, where an illusionistic frieze recalls in particular the upper sections of San Julián (Pl. 29).[73] Schlunk has more recently supposed the style to be derived from a desire on Alfonso's part to evoke nonspecific royal imagery, suggesting that in Western art illusionistic perspectives of architecture carry imperial connotations. On one level I agree, but I would go much further in interpreting these images and find a key to their meaning in formal parentage. Like Barral i Altet, I see the paintings as evidence of Alfonso's contacts with the outside world, in particular with the Carolingian empire.[74] For once again a most striking similarity can be seen between San Julián de los Prados and in particular the Carolingian interpretations of such Late Antique forms and their meaning. It occurs on one hand at a fairly detailed, unconscious level: a painted column and capital at San Julián, for instance. The painted support answers an actual structural arch with a painted capital: a lively, linear abstraction of the Corinthian order that reflects indigenous sculptural developments (Pl. 30).[75] We see the same ideas at work concerning the relationship of media and the transformation of forms in the later paintings at Saint Germain d'Auxerre, where a painting of a capital—one which reflects in the same manner the classicizing ornament of the monument itself—receives a structural arch by means of an actual sculptured abacus (Pl. 31).[76]

The parallels, however, are stronger in more complex iconographical representations. The paintings of San Julián de los Prados and the miniatures of the Gospel of Saint Médard of Soissons, for instance, share characteristics that bind both works within a late imperial artistic tradition (Pl. 32).[77] The miniature depicting the adoration of the Lamb from the Gospel Book, like the painting of San Julián, represents the Holy Jerusalem, but here with special concern for the authority of the four Gospels.[78] Both include a frieze of buildings in illusionistic perspective, and in each case there is a complexity and subtlety in the number of spatial planes represented; in the relationship between the columns, the drapery, and the buildings themselves. In each work Late Antique models are schematized and abstracted: the construction of new images with Christian meanings from diverse older parts is accomplished in remarkably similar ways. Do we see here simply a case of two unconnected traditions that are attracted to like models, or a betrothal of Carolingian and Asturian craft and intention?

The treatment of the iconographic notion of Celestial Jerusalem in other Carolingian works provides a clue, in particular as it links apocalyptic with imperial imagery. The palatine chapel at Aachen illustrates this dual theme. Charlemagne's throne in the second-floor gallery placed him symbolically between earth and the Celestial Jerusalem, above his subjects and below the image, represented in the dome, of the apocalyptic Christ acclaimed by the twenty-four elders. Thus, the celestial scene can be seen to mirror the action below, the earthly acclamation of the emperor by his people.[79]

The association of Christ with emperor is further reinforced by the relation of Charlemagne's throne to the Savior's altar. The church of San Julián de los Prados, with its second-floor gallery, emphasizes similar parallels between king and Savior.

Just as Charlemagne appeared in the same lofty region reserved for Christ's altar, Alfonso II, seated in his royal tribune, was at an elevated level like the image of the True Cross; and the cross, like the king's alcove, was enframed by a painted arch.

In each building a ruler, in consolidating allusions to imperial Rome and the Heavenly Jerusalem, associated himself and his sovereignty with Christ and the eternal reign. Such ideological proximity suggests that Alfonso II, in the paintings of San Julián de los Prados, referred to the same thematic preoccupations manifest at Aachen, and further presented a carefully calculated image of himself as a ruler of Christian Spain. In this sense the Soissons Gospel miniature is of special interest, for its iconography is closely linked to that of Aachen.[80] Perhaps the paintings of San Julián de los Prados glorify the Asturian ruler not only by allusion to imperial Rome and appeal to divine authority but also, more significantly, by direct reference to the greatness of a contemporary empire—by reference to the *dernier cri* of cultural achievement—by a conscious imitation of the ideas behind the art of Charlemagne's court.

Despite these parallels, the paintings can be said to be in another way uniquely Spanish: in their lack of figures. But in what way can an aniconic program be said to be characteristically Spanish? The primary justification for such a claim has traditionally been founded in the 36th Canon of the Council of Elvira, which took place around the year 300.[81] The canon reacts to a specific fourth-century concern with outright idolatry, as evidenced by the council's first canons, both of which condemn the worshipping of idols.[82] Significantly, although canons condemning idolatry are repeated again in the Twelfth Council of Toledo (681) and the Sixteenth Council of Toledo (693), neither of these councils features accompanying canons that speak of paintings in churches.[83] Three centuries after the initial Council of Elvira, there was clearly little risk of confusion between pagan idolatry and images in churches. And even if the best-known building tradition from the Visigothic period followed a custom of building that excluded wall painting,[84] the richness and vitality of figural architectural sculpture of the seventh and eighth centuries bear witness that the Council of Elvira had drifted into a continent's subconscious. It would be difficult indeed to suggest a conscious or articulated suspicion toward monumental figural representation by the seventh century in the shadow of the capitals of San Pedro de la Nave, the pillar from San Salvador de Mérida, or in particular the reliefs of Christ and Mary at Quintanilla de las Viñas, even though an aniconic tendency in illumination has been suggested.[85]

Thus the art of the Visigothic period provides a palpable challenge to the Council of Elvira as a historical key for the interpretation of a work estranged from it by half a millennium like San Julián, or for the characterization at that later date of a national attitude toward art. Indeed it is an anomalist quality to San Julián's paintings that cautions us from interpreting them as the product of an ongoing tradition of monumental art that rejects figural representation, for there is no plausible prototype for them on the Iberian Peninsula before Alfonso II's time.[86] I suggest that their insistent aniconic nature springs instead from the specific theological and cultural context of San Julián's construction, a moment both transient and unique in the history of early medieval Spain. The appearance at this moment of such an extensive and apparently innovative program might be seen as the product of Alfonso II's intense opposition to the Adoptionist heresy, an idea initially proposed to me by Ann DeForest.[87] The sense of this link is that it answers the bold declaration of the monument, both in its reflection of Carolingian typology and in its unusual rejection of figures. For it was a controversy that linked the interests of Alfonso II with Charlemagne, and as Alfonso's opposition to the heresy would require the de-emphasizing of Christ's humanity, it might also have triggered a highly conservative attitude toward images.[88]

The Adoptionist controversy first grew from disputes between Elipandus, bishop of Toledo, and one Migetius, a fanatic partisan of the Roman church. He was one of two sent on a mission aimed ultimately at the reform of the Spanish church, a rare and pointed example of papal intervention on the Iberian Peninsula in the years after the Islamic invasion—intervention believed by one scholar to be initiated by the Franks.[89] Their discussions revealed an "archaic theology" on the part of the Mozarabic churchmen, who called Christ the Son of God only according to his divine nature, but as regards his manhood, referred to him as God's adopted son.[90]

The issue would not perhaps have attained the drama and proportion it ultimately did had it not attracted the attention of two Asturian churchmen, Beatus of Liébana, author of the well-known commentary on the apocalypse, and Etherius, a priest who would eventually become the bishop of Osma under Alfonso II.[91] These two joined forces in a written campaign aimed at discrediting Elipandus. To Beatus and Etherius, Adoptionism constituted a revival of the Arian heresy, denying the existence of the Trinity and emphasizing Christ's human aspects. If Christ were regarded, according to the Adoptionist doctrine, as God's adopted son, he was therefore not one with God.[92] Their letter, by most accounts brutish and propagandistic—"in which moderation was not one of the dominating qualities," Amann tells us[93]—was the brunt of Elipandus's searing appraisal of the Asturians' education mentioned earlier.[94] This theological venture was surely meant to distance the two Asturians from the Mozarabic church and ally them with Rome. It is a significant stance, for at that moment the Mozarabic church of Toledo still had ecclesiastical jurisdiction over that of the growing kingdom of Asturias. Elipandus must have been aware of this, for in his response to the Asturians he bristles with the ancient authority of his see: ". . . all the world knows that Toledo has shown since the beginning of the faith with the sanctity of its doctrines, and has never fallen in error. And now a cretinous sheep tries to teach us doctrine."[95]

The Asturians used the Adoptionist controversy to weaken ties with the Mozarabic church, whose authority was rooted in its Visigothic past. That the battle reached its height during the reign of Alfonso II is not surprising; intrinsic to his desire to create a new royal and ecclesiastical capital must have been the notion of replacement of usurped Toledo in the hands of the infidel and the scarcely less alien Mozarabic church.[96] Thus it was probably in the interest of some sort of ecclesiastical autonomy that, as one scholar put it, "the Franks were dragged into the conflict by the Asturians."[97] Charlemagne, intent on codifying his role as a defender of orthodoxy throughout the Christian world, was eager to participate.

Barrau-Dihigo believed the Adoptionist controversy provided the motive for the first contacts between the Carolingians and Asturians.[98] The attitudes of Beatus and Etherius were seconded by Basilicos, a favorite of Alfonso II and his ambassador to Charlemagne.[99] The decisive events occurred during Alfonso II's rule, particularly in 792, when Felix of Urgel, who had taken up the defense of the Adoptionists, was summoned by Charlemagne to Regensburg to disavow his beliefs and when Pope Hadrian officially condemned the heresy. It is further quite possible that delegates from Asturias were present at a rehearing at the Council of Frankfurt in 794, called at the insistence of Adoptionist Spanish bishops (who included, indeed, all the Mozarabic bishops with the exception of one).[100] The dispute was of continued interest to both nations in the last years of the eighth century, while Beatus and Alcuin corresponded on the subject, until 799, when Charlemagne presided over a council at Aachen at which Felix finally recanted and asked his diocese to do the same. By 800, the Franks had control of Felix's see at Urgel.

The culmination of events for the Asturians surely occurred in the years before 812, by which time Alfonso had established a bishopric at Oviedo, where he probably held a church council of the sort that is liberally documented in Toledo during the height of the Visigothic period.[101] In establishing a bishopric in his new capital and in particular by holding a council there, Alfonso II effectively announced the supplantation of Visigothic Toledo with the royal city of his mountain kingdom. Thus a new autonomy for the Asturians was achieved through a struggle in which the authority of a strong Frankish ally and the papacy were substituted for the weakening arm of the Mozarabic church in Toledo.[102] Such were the deeper bases of contention of a conflict for which Adoptionism was the articulated expression, and the justification.

The nonfigural nature of the paintings of San Julián de los Prados can be seen as a symptom of the Asturian political stance against Adoptionism. Just as Beatus and Etherius conceived of Christ as a totally divine being whose humanity was subsidiary, so the Santullano paintings avoid depicting it. Rather, the representation of Christ is limited to the portrayal of the Cross. It is possible that Adoptionism was also associated by some with Anthropomorphism, a belief that ascribed human characteristics and limitations to God.[103] Here was a theological doctrine that, in rendering God finite and palpable, invited a metaphor with images, and intensified the associations between images and their likeness with all that was human and frail.

I think, however, that the initial idea of responding to the theological and political challenge of Adoptionism with an aniconic painting program sprang from contact with the Carolingian court, for it was at that time full of concern for the controversy concerning images. The impact of the same sort of attitude voiced in the *Libri Carolini* can be seen here;[104] the impact of a work that, like Charlemagne's councils concerning Adoptionism, illustrates that monarch's need to extend his power by means of involving himself and his court in issues of doctrine outside the limits of his rule.[105]

The argument must be made, nevertheless, that there is little evidence for the impact of the aniconic attitude of the *Libri Carolini* in the monumental art of the Carolingian lands in which it was composed.[106] Though Charlemagne himself authorized this moderate, official written position on the image controversy, his court was clearly an important center for the production of lavish figural art.[107] It is indeed primarily at Germigny des Prés, the private chapel of Theodulf—that prominent member of the Carolingian court who identifies himself as a "Goth" or Spaniard— that there survives an apparent witness of those ideas in a monumental program: the famous mosaic depiction of the Ark of the Covenant.[108] Theodulf has recently emerged in fact as the actual author of the *Libri Carolini*, and further links between Hispanic literary tradition and the rejection of figural representation have been established.[109]

The issue deserves some sorting. On one hand, a traditional acquaintance in Spain with the idea of aniconism must be distinguished from the highly charged political issue of iconoclasm as it was debated at the Carolingian court. At the same time, however, that Spanish attitude must be explored as the fertile ground for the artistic expression of an idea little heeded in practice in the Carolingian empire.

Spain's receptivity to such a radical attitude concerning figural representation as that which appears in a monumental context at San Julián cannot in itself be explained by the long-abandoned canon of the Council of Elvira. The struggle which produced that legislation might have occupied the remote cultural memory of a land engaged in a new conflict that also found in the rejection of figural representation a religious and political position. Spanish Christians of the eighth and ninth centuries were particularly aware of the arguments against the use of images in religious art, not so much because of the early abandoned canon from the Council of Elvira but also because those notions were continuously reinforced by their Muslim neighbors to the south. For while Islam can hardly be seen as the formal or conceptual force behind the paintings at Santullano, still a familiarity with the ideas behind aniconism in religious art, and firsthand knowledge of their implementation, might be seen as having survived, in part, through the presence of that culture in Spain. In their search for a language of forms that might respond to a specific didactic need—that of de-emphasizing Christ's humanity—the Asturians can, in this specific case, be seen as adopting the posture of aniconism as part of the stimulus diffusion of a practice stridently enforced in Islamic Spain.[110]

With the formation of a new Asturian diplomacy came the restructuring of certain ideas about art, not only in the adoption of certain symbols and metaphors used by the Carolingians, but more significantly in a receptivity to the concept that meaning can be conveyed through the withdrawal of figures. The acknowledged, immediate catalyst for this stance cannot be Islam, however, so the conscious creation of these images by patron and artist must be seen as the unusual and specific response to a cultural and political moment—one that draws from the interests and attitudes of both Carolingian and Asturian rulers. Spanish self-consciousness concerning images must have found its voice in the recent Carolingian preoccupation with the Iconoclastic controversy. Indeed, not only does the author of the *Libri Carolini* argue against the veneration of images, but he declares that it is impossible to produce a "vero imago" of Christ, and speaks in favor of revealed signs like the Cross, which he considers preferable;[111] and it is the Cross that is in fact the only recognizable symbol—the substitution for Christ—in Santullano's paintings.

Significantly, such concerns surrounding images were rendered prominent through the courtly connections established around the Adoptionist controversy. Indeed the two issues—images and Adoptionism—share a political and intellectual context. Thus Theodulf was the author not only of the *Libri Carolini* but also of *De Spiritu Sancto*, an anti-Adoptionist discourse written, like the *Libri Carolini*, at the request of Charlemagne.[112] Jonas of Orleans, who visited the Asturian court in 799, would much later write a work concerned with the cult of images, in which he mentions Adoptionists encountered in Spain.[113] A political connection, however, is most strikingly established by Freeman, who has shown that the Adoptionist controversy and the early history of the *Libri Carolini* were politically intertwined. A preliminary document to the *Libri Carolini* was taken to Rome in 792 on a trip the main purpose of which was the delivery of the Adoptionist Felix to the pope. Both issues—the image controversy with its challenge from Byzantium, and Adoptionism with its defiant Mozarabic bishops—addressed for Charlemagne the problem of the universal authority of the church in Rome. This is made clear by the *Libri Carolini* themselves, which make actual reference to those concerns shared with the fight against Adoptionism in questioning the right of councils of bishops (implying both those of Nicea and Toledo) to claim universality when they do not keep with the tenets of faith.[114]

There is also a certain theological interdependency between the causes. Alcuin, the court member most intimately associated with the Adoptionist controversy, had a hand in the composition of the conclusions of Theodulf's *Libri Carolini*.[115] Further, a main concern of Alcuin in combating the heresy centered on the relationship between Christ's humanity and man's salvation. According to his interpretation, man can be the recipient of salvation because he is made in God's image.[116] The biblical citation on which he based this notion is Genesis 1:26: "Faciamus hominem ad imaginem et similitudinem nostram," one Heil believes must already have enjoyed a high degree of importance in the controversy concerning images. Indeed, this very wording appears in Ambrosian and Augustinian citations from the *Libri Carolini*: "Quod non adorandas imagines peretineat, quod scriptum est: creavit Deus hominem ad imaginem et similitudinem suam," and "Quae sit differentia imaginis et similitudinis sive aequalitatis."[117]

Such ideas were dislodged in the last decades of the eighth century and the first years of the ninth century, creating an intellectual dynamic felt on both sides of the Pyrenees. The year that saw Felix of Urgel condemned for his Adoptionist beliefs, 792, falls within those during which the *Libri Carolini* were written (790–794). Indeed, the same Council of Frankfurt which condemned Adoptionism a second time (and at which Ewig feels there might have been delegates from Asturias)[118] addressed the issue of images as well. Any who witnessed or read the proceedings of that council would have known that it also condemned the *adoratio* of images. Iconoclasm gave form, and Adoptionism meaning, to a concern more familiar perhaps to Spaniards than to the denizens of the Carolingian empire.

Ambassadors and churchmen who traveled north in these years of heated theological debate must have conveyed reports of what they heard and saw to their monarch in the language of typology, iconography, and metaphor. On the basis of these, Alfonso II directed his own masons and artists to construct San Julián de los Prados. San Julián might well have been built in the first decades following this exchange, hard upon the completion of Charlemagne's palace chapel at Aachen. Its specific date has commonly depended on its exclusion from an important document of Alfonso II: the "Testament of Alfonso II" of 812, the monarch's public dedication of buildings, property, servants, ornaments, and a good deal more to the church of San Salvador, the future seat of Oviedo's bishop.[119] Because it is not numbered among the ecclesiastical foundations made over to San Salvador, San Julián is considered to have been constructed between that date and 842, when the monarch died. It is a difficult question. On one hand, I do not think the document offers definitive evidence of a post-812 date. It is possible that San Julián was not included because it was a palatine chapel of Alfonso, or because it lay outside Oviedo. It is also tempting to consider the later date, however, in what emerges as a fascinating historical moment near the middle of Alfonso II's reign. One can account for the decade that would separate the building from the events surrounding the Adoptionist controversy and the strong Carolingian contacts that ensued, I think, with a halt or delay in construction caused by Alfonso II's imprisonment in the monastery of Abelania by rival factions between the years 802 and 808. Sánchez-Albornoz sees the Cross of the Angels (808) as an offering made in thanks for the monarch's liberation from that captivity, and finds in the donation to San Salvador in 812 the strong memory of that painful time.[120] Such a challenge to the monarch's authority might indeed have served to intensify the persistent appeal of the events that informed San Julián's planning and decoration.

San Julián's construction can be seen as a monumental expression of the establishment of an episcopal see in a royal capital and convening of a church council, which are generally believed to have taken place in the reconstruction of palatine and ecclesiastical life that followed the monarch's release. The chapel is replete with metaphors linking divine and secular authority, all artistic themes learned during intensive contact with the Carolingians in the last decade of the ninth century, themes that had particular meaning for a monarch returning to power. Only now would Alfonso II be able to celebrate the theological and political fruits of the battle against Adoptionism, using the message of the *Libri Carolini*: to create a monumental and visual symbol of Oviedo's fusion with powers of international orthodoxy and its own authority.

In a fascinating discussion of Alfonso's aniconism that follows a different course than this one, Bango Torviso makes a sensitive reading of the testament of 812, which binds this moment of his career with the rejection of images and, I would argue, with the concerns of Adoptionism as well. Alfonso addresses God as "hidden God"; "invisible God" in another copy. Further on he calls on God "who is in Jerusalem"; "in Celestial Jerusalem," the later copy echos.[121] The conflation of the notion of Celestial Jerusalem with an "invisible God," a concept that seems consciously to undercut any hint of anthropomorphism, so clearly mirrors the program at Santullano with its triumphal architecture, and yet its veiled panels and mute cross, that we can see in this historical moment the powerful personal involvement of Alfonso II in the issues that would appear in his palatine chapel.

Thus resistance to Adoptionism can be seen to have been the catalyst for a royal, aniconic program in the very land that spawned the heresy. The formal language and imperial iconography of the program were borrowed from a much-admired foreign source, and cleansed of figures or living things in response to the particular resistance Alfonso II wished to show to Adoptionism: a resistance calculated to call into question the authority of the Mozarabic church in Toledo.

Consequently we can see that, much more than simply a statement against Adoptionism, the paintings of San Julián de los Prados record for us a radical change in Asturian political diplomacy. Adoptionism became the terms in fact by which an intense struggle for power was articulated: the Mozarabic church on one hand used it to point up its own isolation and separation from Rome, while Alfonso, by opposing Adoptionism, sought to ally the Asturians with forces of orthodoxy, authority, and legitimacy. In conceiving his battle against the Adoptionists, Alfonso II rejected the religious authority of Toledo, the city that had been the religious as well as temporal center of the Visigothic kingdom. Instead, for a moment, his attention and his admiration were centered on an alliance with Charlemagne and Pope Hadrian against the southern Iberian Christians. It is just the first of a number of symbolic political gestures that the northern Spanish kingdoms would make in their struggle for military and psychological reconquest of the peninsula.

This visual alliance with Carolingian forms and the conscious and didactic suppression of images were part of the creation by Alfonso II of a new identity for the Asturian nation, one as enmeshed with the notion of separateness from Mozarabic Christians as from the Muslims of al-Andalus—peoples to whom it was, nevertheless, inextricably bound.

3
Bearing Witness

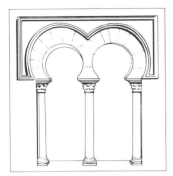

On 16 September 893, Alfonso III, king of Asturias (and distant cousin of Alfonso II) consecrated a royal church at his place of retirement near Villaviciosa. In many ways San Salvador de Valdediós presents an image of what Asturian building had become in the years since Alfonso II's death (Fig. 17, Pls. 33 and 34.) A narthex opens onto a simple three-aisled basilica, the most arresting feature of which is a grand barrel-vaulted nave of robust piers and semicircular arches. The space defined by that vault and the clear, wide plane of wall that falls below it flow continuously to the small barrel-vaulted apse, whose broad, triple-arched window illuminates it with diffused light, assuring its visual interpenetration with the well-lit nave. Only a set of low chancel barriers originally interrupted its course.[1]

Diminutive arched windows feature the only horseshoe arches in the building, cut according to a tradition now 200 years old (Pl. 35). The walls of the nave were surely covered with paintings such as those that now survive only in fragments on San Salvador's vaults and arch intrados. Their vine scrolls and geometric patterns immediately evoke a classical parentage, and they emerge in scholarship as the rigid echo of an art of monumental painting that saw its apogee in Spain in the reign of Alfonso II.[2]

The same formulas appear more than twenty years later in Asturias: a far more common wooden-roofed variant of Valdediós can be found at San Salvador de Priesca, where a wide apse opening reveals a blind-arched arcade like that which first appeared at San Julián de los Prados, combined with the same austere piers and classicizing wall painting (Pl. 36).[3]

What is extraordinary is that just to the south of the kingdom of Asturias a strikingly different style of basilica was being constructed. Alfonso III was the benefactor of the monastery of San Miguel de Escalada, where a new three-aisled church was built in 913 in the reign of his son García.[4] There the wooden roof is carried on the slender shafts of columns by means of horseshoe arches, which cut a sharp profile against the basilica's darkened side aisles (Fig. 18, Pls. 37–41). Most startling, however, is the way in which the choir is introduced at San Miguel: for there, a screen of three frail arches about half the height of the nave vessel itself partition the view of the apses and the bay preceding them. The screen was originally fitted with chancel barriers and answered by diaphragm arches in the side aisles, which complete the physical separation of the choir from the nave.[5] The apse is gained through a horseshoe arch, and is horseshoe-shaped in plan as well. Its interior is thus obscured behind a reduced opening, visible from the nave only by means of the light of a tiny window defined against the interior's formless darkness.

Common terminology has already provided for the potent differences between Valdediós and Escalada: Valdediós and Priesca are Asturian buildings, while Escalada belongs to a group of horseshoe-arched monuments most often called Mozarabic, after the new group of patrons whose dramatic immigration from al-Andalus heralded this new style in the north. Though both are found to varying degrees throughout the territories of Asturias, León, and Galicia, they are consistently distinguishable. We cannot rely upon the notion of different traditions of building to account for these differences, however much they seem to lie in the realm of style—the definition of volumes, the form of arches, patterns of illumination—and embrace decisions we are accustomed to consider the domain of workshop practice. For though the Asturian buildings are probably not constructed by precisely the same masons as San Miguel, there is striking evidence that Escalada was built by indigenous masons schooled in the very same tradition as those who worked at San Salvador de Valdediós. Both San Miguel and San Salvador are constructed in a frame-and-fill technique. Ashlar blocks quoin the corners of rubblework walls. There is a tendency in both monuments to course the fill informally in its thick mortar bed, but in neither monument is the wall fabric as large or regular as in buildings of the patronage of Alfonso II. At times, on smaller wall surfaces, larger stones available for fill are grouped around the quoining blocks, recalling bits of ashlar wall.

To this general practice can be added more detailed habits of work and taste. Both monuments use brick liberally in the upper walls in order to lighten them. In each a sawtooth course announced the transition between exterior wall and roof gable. Cymas are uncommon, and masons at both monuments reused older Asturian Corinthian capitals. The columns receiving the apse arches are adossed, only tangent to the wall, while the capitals that crown them are engaged.[6]

These are all details of construction techniques characteristic of most Asturian building. Only in the careful ashlar construction of the horseshoe-arched arcade and the arches of the apse entrances do we see the intervention of techniques unknown in Asturian buildings. This combination of the new with the continuous and indigenous plunges us deep into the problem of determining how a Mozarabic architecture might be defined.

Gómez-Moreno, Mozarabic art's eloquent first chronicler, believed the architectural style to be unified by characteristics that reflected the culture and traditions of Mozarabs, Christians who lived under Islamic domination.[7] Thus, churches built in al-Andalus under Islamic rule, as well as those built in the northern kingdoms both by Mozarabic immigrants and those influenced by them, were embraced by his wide definition.[8] It was an architecture "without uniformities, without repetitions."[9] Though he knew the term Mozarabic meant "arabized" at the time of its earliest use, he did not confuse the medieval Arabic adjective—which originally, as we shall see, referred to a far more limited group than are now called Mozarab—with the modern usage of the term, which defines a historical ethnic group: indigenous Christians living under Islamic domination. Thus, though he believed much Mozarabic architecture to be profoundly influenced by Islamic architecture, he did not see Islamic impact as a necessary justification for calling a building Mozarabic:

it was a term which implied the whole range of cultural experience that the Mozarabs embraced.

I believe, with Gómez-Moreno, that the architecture of the Mozarabs and those buildings that reflect their influence ought to be considered with as few preconceptions as possible concerning what might be an appropriate "Mozarabic" artistic attitude. The most prevalent and deterministic notion to be confronted is that a Mozarabic architecture must itself be "arabized."

The most recent reflection of such an assumption occurs in the work of Camón Aznar, who made a plea in the 1970s for renaming the group of buildings traditionally called Mozarabic.[10] Declaring that "transfusions of Califal influence" in these churches are much less influential than "traditional and contemporary Christian" characteristics, he calls them "Repopulation Architecture": the continuation of Asturian building in a new frontier area.[11] In support of this argument, he cites many of the details of construction that bind those churches traditionally called Mozarabic to Asturian building. Camón Aznar's insistence that the presence of indigenous masons excludes Escalada and Mazote from the Mozarabic fold—wherein he only admits buildings constructed within actual Islamic borders—grows from his assumption that Islamic influence and Andalusian construction techniques must be present in a building tradition called Mozarabic.

Camón Aznar is of course correct in his observation that the buildings constructed to serve the repopulation are primarily the work of northern masons. The presence, however, of Asturian construction—and thus of local masons—hardly accounts for the formal wedge driven between buildings like Valdediós and Escalada by virtue of their wildly divergent typology and aesthetic. Preferable among those who speak for the notion of an Architecture of Repopulation is Bango Torviso: "During the 10th century," he contends, "an architecture developed in Christian Spain that was still Asturian in many ways, but which had evolved through the sight of old buildings of the Visigothic period, of Islamic and Carolingian elements, and a change in mentality in confronting a new political and economic situation."[12] He acknowledges the change in these new churches, the fact that in appearance and experience they defy any theory of seamless continuity. But Bango Torviso finds the term Mozarabic, which links the immigrant monks to the architectural style, "of little significance." The architectural experience they introduce seems to me to be so distinct, however, that it demands much more of an appraisal of the circumstances that led masons to so change old habits of typology and style in buildings like Escalada. Such an appraisal necessarily includes an understanding of the Mozarabs as patrons.

At Valdediós, barrel vault and broad painted wall embrace a single vessel that flows clearly and directly into the apse. The exigencies of liturgy that demand separation of the choir by means of chancel barriers find little reflection in that space. Escalada's horseshoe-arched space, in contrast, is partitioned and segmented, its choir obscured by screening, diaphragming, and rationed light. The key to the divergent qualities of Escalada and many later buildings constructed in the kingdom of León must lie primarily in the patronage of the first of these new constructions, as Gómez-Moreno suggested at the beginning of the century. No document attests to its importance more than the famous inscription composed by Escalada's own patrons:

This place, of old dedicated in honor of the archangel Michel and built with a little building, after falling into pieces, lay long in ruin until Abbot Alfonso, coming with his brethren from Córdoba his fatherland, built up the ruined house in the time of the powerful and serene prince Alfonso. The number of monks increasing, this temple was built with admirable work, enlarged in every part from its foundations. The work was finished in twelve months, not by imperial imposition or oppression of the people, but by the insistent vigilance of Abbot Alfonso and the brethren, when García already held the scepter of the realm with Queen Mumadona in (913) and consecrated by Bishop Genedius on November 13.[13]

The Mozarabs' dedication reveals a conscious national identification for the immigrant patrons: they call themselves Cordobans, and name that city as their *patria*. They show indeed in this, their second church in the north, a keen interest in history, both their own and the history of the site on which they have built. Surely it is to such a consciously perceived difference in *patria* that the formal divergence in taste charted here is due. It must be to such new patrons that we can ascribe the invigoration of the Asturian tradition of building at the time of the repopulation, one which can appropriately retain the term "Mozarabic" for the immigrant patrons to whom we owe its introduction.

The dedication also offers guidance concerning the way the new style was brought about. It speaks of a church constructed very quickly: in twelve months, "not by imperial imposition or oppression of the people, but by the insistent vigilance of Abbot Alfonso and his brethren . . ." This passage declares, with a certain relish, the extent of the Mozarabs' independence on this northern frontier. But the monks' insistence that they do not oppress the "vulgi" identifies that group as being primarily responsible for the labor of building.[14] The monks of Escalada are boasting of their constant and minute attention to the construction of the building, perhaps even of some limited participation. But as an understanding of Escalada's fabric revealed, that attentiveness was applied to a building constructed primarily by local labor.[15]

The abrupt change in taste that erupted in northern church building with the Mozarabic immigration, one that involved the intervention of patrons in an established formal and technical tradition of building, would ally a new style with a meaning understandable both to Mozarabs from the south and Asturians in the north. Both technical access to this divergent formal system and the meaning that accompanied it were supplied through models recognizable both to northern and southern Christians.

Escalada's nave appears to be a direct copy of a church built in the Visigothic period, so careful a copy in technique and form in fact that it is perplexing that the idea has not emerged more explicitly in art-historical literature before.[16] Its nave is almost interchangeable with that of San Juan de Baños—though Baños is not necessarily the actual model—in all details of design except the clerestory window form and of course actual dimensions (Figs. 6, 18; Pls. 8, 38). The horseshoe arches of the nave arcade and apse openings at Escalada are of the same proportion as many constructed in the Visigothic period, and for the most part are similar in construction, as are the orders and aspects of the plan and division of space.[17]

The construction and appearance of the arches of Escalada reveal the care with which a model from the Visigothic period was consulted to orchestrate its nave. The appearance of the Baños arches, their size relative to the clerestory and the nave wall, their sharp profile cutting into the dark shadow of the side aisles, all are aspects of a type of planning and design that is repeated with remarkable care at San Miguel. At San Juan de Baños, horseshoe arches that surpass the semicircle by one-third of their radius fall on columns through the intermediary of Corinthian-type capitals. Escalada's are remarkably similar, exceeding the semicircle from one-third to one-half the radius, the larger proportions still within the range commonly found in buildings from the period of Visigothic rule.[18] In both naves the arches are constructed identically, with a springer composed of two stones, and voussoirs beginning at about half the height of the arch are assembled radially, according to the custom of the Visigothic period (Pls. 8 and 41).

Also following construction traditions developed under Visigothic rule, the intrados at springer level of all wall arches from both Escalada and Baños line up with the jamb, and the monuments coincide in imposts that jut slightly into the opening. There is much more in the wall and crossing arches of the east end of Escalada that suggests the close consultation of a model from the Visigothic period, and some divergences as well, hinting at the timid introduction of new construction techniques that do not, however, disrupt the broad appearance and profile of an arch copied from an older monument. For instance, the voussoirs of the side apse entrances at Escalada are placed radially, as in the Baños entrance arch, but the central apse and some of the crossing arches are uncentered, a trait that would later be associated with Islamic building tradition (Pls. 42–44).[19] The extrados of the Baños entrance arch and the Escalada side apse openings are typical of construction of the Visigothic period: vertical at the springers, parallel to the supports, and in both monuments of the Visigothic and Mozarabic periods the arch bows horizontally, so its opening is slightly wider than the jamb opening. The central apse entrance at Escalada follows a different pattern, however, its opening aligning with the receiving column, and its extrados curving into the support.[20]

A good deal of the impression made by Escalada's interior grows from the impact of the horseshoe-arched arcade and the arches of the east end. But most other aspects of the design and planning of the Mozarabic monument are found in churches built under Visigothic rule as well. San Miguel's horseshoe-shaped apse, while not found at Baños, occurred at the sixth- or seventh-century church in Tarragona's amphitheater, São Frutuoso de Montelios, Segóbriga, and in enough earlier foundations antedating the Muslim invasion to suggest that it too belongs to a prototype from the Visigothic period (Figs. 1 and 9, Pl. 4).[21] And the tripartite choir and segregated east end defined by San Miguel's screen and barriers reflect the same ardent codification of liturgical divisions into an enclosed, protected choir that we earlier found to be intrinsic to buildings constructed under Visigothic rule.[22] Escalada is embraced by a Visigothic spirit in style, typology, and liturgical space: it is as if that historical paradigm, in this first Mozarabic building of the repopulation, left no room for significant Islamic impact. While this is not the case for many later churches of Mozarabic patronage or influence, there is good reason when speaking of Escalada to question the widespread belief that "the Christian Mozarabic communities . . . finally refused Islam without refusing Islamic art."[23]

When I speak of rejecting Islamic art, or ignoring it (the two negative alternatives available to Cordoban patrons who, we presume, could not avoid making some note of it when in their *patria*), I imply an attitude formed concerning formal elements or systems that were visually prominent or easily accessible. This is a separate issue from any technical details of construction that might have penetrated the craft of the Asturian atelier that built the church, when those details have no significant visual impact on the building's interior.[24] We have seen, for instance, that Escalada possesses a few arches with uncentered voussoirs, and one with an extrados that remains concentric at the springers. Though the uncentered arch has not yet appeared in Islamic construction of the ninth century, we can probably safely say that these details reflect the tenuous infiltration of techniques of construction under development in Islamic Spain.[25] Such details of construction do not, however, have a direct bearing on the appearance of Escalada's interior; indeed one has to look very hard to understand what the fuss is all about. Islamic horseshoe arches of this period can inscribe the same or larger proportion of a circle in relationship to those built under Visigothic rule. Their voussoirs, above the springers, are more often than not laid radially before the mid-tenth century, once again like prototypes from the Visigothic period. What is important to recognize for our purposes here is that none of Escalada's horseshoe arches—radial or uncentered, with a straight or curving springer extrados—resembles the trademark brand of Islamic arch that characterized Muslim architecture in al-Andalus at this time.[26] The Islamic arches are in general constructed so that the springers jut more insistently into the arch space. They are rendered particularly distinctive by means of several technical characteristics present here but not found at Escalada, details significant in forming the aesthetic character of the Spanish Islamic horseshoe arch: habits of building wedded to a new and recognizably Islamic arch form. Enormous springers, for instance, completely out of proportion with the rest of the voussoirs, are often cut in *tas-de-charge* for the entire lower two-thirds of the arch. In doors, such as the one built by Abd ʿAllah between 888 and 912 at the Great Mosque of Córdoba (Pl. 45), the effect is strikingly different from the apse entrances at Escalada. Even if one divests it of later additions (gothic tracery and geometric decoration), the Cordoban arch's different structural parts have an assertive decorative function—one emphasized by polychromy, an arcuated lintel, and alternating stone and brick voussoirs—completely alien to the Mozarabic examples. It is these aspects of design finally that prevail over the popular radial measurements in determining what is Islamic or Visigothic about the appearance of a horseshoe arch. The door of Saint Stephen at Córdoba (855–856) is a case in point (Pl. 46). It has a basic horseshoe proportion close to its forerunners from the Visigothic period (=1/2R), but in no way can it be confused with the arches at Baños or Escalada: it is transformed by its high springers, its delicate voussoirs transformed by spiny vegetal relief, and its texture and decoration.

The lower of the two superposed arcades of the earliest sections of the Mosque interior invites a more felicitous comparison with the Escalada arcade and chancel screen, with which it shares more attenuated columns and daintier arch thickness than Baños (Pl. 47). Part of that affinity surely derives from the use of *spolia* of the Roman and Visigothic periods at Córdoba, a practice that regulates the capital proportion, abacus size, and thus, to some extent, the shape of the springer.[27] But even if we were to disregard those conditions, to extract that single arch at Córdoba from its multistoried context—not to mention the mental scrubbing we must give it to erase its red and white alternating voussoirs—in order to compare it to Escalada is to miss the point entirely. The aspects we must will away to see parallels between the monuments embody the very concerns that make the mosque's arcade Islamic, that were meant to be noticed first, and that separate it from its own certain but obscured heritage in the Visigothic period, a heritage cherished by the builders of Mozarabic churches. It is finally this hypothetical stripping away of the Islamic character of the mosques' arches that reveals to us the heart and soul of the Mozarabic ones.

Most other aspects of Escalada's construction and design are indigenous. The cupola-shaped groined vaults have prototypes in monuments built under Byzantine and Visigothic rule, and the compound piers and adossed columns belong to Asturian tradition.[28] Details of construction found in Córdoba are not unknown: the exterior roll corbels find closer prototypes in Islamic building (though their parentage is also seen by some as a development of the Visigothic period). The decoration of the chancel barriers is extremely close to carved relief of the Visigothic period, but a single motif has been singled out and associated with Islamic tradition.[29] It is not in pieces, however, that this building is best considered. It is in the experience of its interior, in the segmented space and cool horseshoe profile of its arcade, that we see a new taste promoted by the conscious choice of new patrons who sought to create, with the workers available to them, a church that looked "Visigothic."

Since a building tradition of the Visigothic period lies behind Asturian architecture as well as Islamic and Mozarabic building, that notion of consciousness must also be tested against a possible survival of forms from the Visigothic period in the Asturian style. Santa Cristina de Lena, by consensus the most Visigothic of Asturian buildings, provides us with the best control (Fig. 19, Pl. 48).[30] Santa Cristina's conservatism is planted firmly by scholars in two major aspects of its design: the tiny cruciform plan, recalling the description of the lost church of Santa Cruz at Cangas de Onís,[31] and the high altar screen, which allies its interior space with that of churches constructed under Visigothic rule, like São Gião, and Mozarabic ones, like San Miguel de Escalada. Indeed, both of these elements speak for an exceptional conservatism in an Asturian monument; no other church like it in plan or division of liturgical space survives in the north from the time of the invasion until the repopulation in the tenth century. And yet it is very far from a copy of a monument of the Visigothic period, showing no interest in the forms that shape the style of a building like Baños or San Pedro de la Nave. The articulation and decoration of Lena's elevation is overwhelmingly Ramiran in style. Its raised semicircular arches, blind arcades, flat, trapezoidal capitals covered with archaic figural reliefs, and the continuation of that texture to some columns, striated with a sweeping rope pattern, all bear witness to the importance of a local style and its meaning, and an ambivalence to the kind of stylistic detail that might show a conscious relationship to buildings associated with the Visigothic rule, such as that we have begun to trace at Escalada. Further, Lena provides no Asturian prototype or intermediary for the striking reintroduction to northern architecture of voussoired horseshoe arches received by columns, the elegant and important link between the naves of Escalada and San Juan de Baños.

Lena, however, provides an exception to what had become, since the time of Alfonso II, an Asturian rule of liturgical spatial design. Its designers rejected the continuous space and low chancel barrier used at San Julián de los Prados and continued later at Valdediós, Nora, and Priesca, for the high altar screen which created a more conservative liturgical space.[32] There is a consensus among scholars that the screen is a later addition, one Gómez-Moreno calls a "Mozarabismo," but it has been suggested that the church might originally have had another screen, of indeterminate height, replaced by this one in the tenth century.[33] Whether Lena possessed a high altar screen in an original, conservative liturgical gesture or received it with the more general, fashionable revival of the high screen under Mozarabic influence, its mere appearance is significant. Lena's unusual high altar screen puts into relief the absence of the form in every other Asturian building that survives and—more important— the rejection of the segmented, partitioned crossing spaces that reinforced such separations, tall and short, in buildings of the Visigothic period. Its appearance, too, on raised semicircular arches illuminates the differences between authentic Asturian conservatism and Mozarabic patrons' interest in buildings from the Visigothic period.

So although the use of the "Mozarabic" liturgy is a constant for Asturian and Mozarabic buildings and those built under Visigothic rule, it seems likely that Mozarabic monasteries in the south had conserved more extensive visual and architectural separation of clergy and laity than that which had survived in any of the architectural developments of the previous 200 years in Asturias. It is an attitude to be read as much in the architectural spaces that support the divisions drawn by chancels as by the size of the barriers themselves, which varied.[34] The Mozarabs' powerless position in al-Andalus might indeed have provided a similar experience of embattled persecution to that which had first engendered that entrenched liturgical space hundreds of years before. Fontaine explores the same tendency in the liturgy from a literary point of view, examining the ways in which persecution, then exile, increases the Mozarabs' sense of personal and "national" identification with their rite, and Millet-Gérard has found military metaphors in those parts of the liturgy dating after the invasion, suggesting that the siege mentality of the sixth century was renewed in different terms in the ninth and tenth centuries.[35]

The question of a Mozarabic liturgical space is an important one, for it addresses the extent to which the monks' interest in a building style of the Visigothic period is an evocation of the past, as opposed to a nostalgia for an environment for worship they might have left behind in al-Andalus. The distinction in fact between a Mozarabic conservatism in taste and a possible conscious, historical revival at Escalada is never a clear one, except insofar as we know Escalada was built in a recognizable historical style unfamiliar to the indigenous masons who participated in its construction, a style only understandable if requested specifically by its new group of patrons. As we shall see, these two attitudes toward church building reflect two views of the Mozarabs' own mangled past: one real and one ideal, and their authors were compelled to reconcile them in literature and art.

It should be clear by now that I associate many of the artistic concerns present in Escalada with other northern buildings commonly called Mozarabic: both those of Mozarabic patronage and those constructed under the influence of Mozarabs and their churches. Though no other is quite as uncomplicated in its Visigothicism as Escalada, the same self-conscious conservatism in patrons' taste (as distinct from Camón Aznar's notion of Asturian conservatism in workshop practice) manifest in attention to models from the Visigothic period both in typology and style occurs in a number of buildings constructed during the first two generations of the tenth century in Spain's Christian kingdoms. The most important of these expands our understanding of the possible relationship between mason and patron in this tenacious and poignant style. At San Cebrián de Mazote, also the foundation of monks from Córdoba, an identical tradition of construction as that used at Escalada produced a monumental basilica of horseshoe arches, tripartite choir, and horseshoe-shaped apses and apse openings (Fig. 20, Pls. 49 and 50).[36] It features the same specific and peculiar details of construction that ally it with the Asturian building tradition. On the nave window jambs, however, are carved the names of some of the monks, even bolder insistence of the kind of "instante vigilancia" described in the Escalada inscription: Lupo dcs; Arias Forti fecit; Zaddon fet; Endura diagono; Ivanes kelrici; Monio memoria; Ermanvald sum; Frtr Agila prsbiter, and others.[37] This extraordinary testimony, unprecedented in Spain, and unprecedented to my knowledge in medieval architecture of any period for the number of signatures included, can mean one of several things. It might indicate—but not necessarily—that certain of the Mozarabic monks at Mazote actually knew the craft of stone-cutting and helped local masons, teaching them to copy the horseshoe arches of local buildings that had survived from the seventh and eighth centuries, and to dress stones in the cool, refined manner of the voussoirs of Mozarabic buildings. Whether or not the monks themselves participated in the actual construction—and I think it unlikely that so many would have been trained as stonecutters—the signatures surely indicate a particularly strong and potent attachment to the idea of building, and to the personal involvement of each of the monks in the endeavor. Either solution presents us with a notion of patronage that is intense, engaged, and conscious; one in which the personal, publicly acknowledged participation of members of the community was very important.

Following constructions like Escalada, building of the tenth-century repopulation begins to exhibit a new concern with forms typical of the Visigothic period. Not only foundations of Mozarab patrons but those of uncertain patronage, as well as several built for indigenous churchmen, spread these new formal concerns to the far ends of the Christian kingdoms. A basilica at Lourosa in Portugal, dated 912 by inscription, possessed a screen like that at Escalada, and horseshoe arches that extend one-third of their radius beyond a semicircle, as at Baños (Fig. 21, Pl. 51).[38] At Santiago de Peñalba a third monastery founded by Saint Gennadius was graced with a cruciform church divided into the same sequence of high and low compartments, alternately lit and obscured, that we have come to think of as emblematic of the years of Visigothic rule on the Iberian Peninsula, in churches like Santa Comba de Bande (Fig. 22, Pl. 52).[39] In each, construction techniques and influences that do not derive from seventh- and eighth-century models vary. But all of these churches—Escalada, Lourosa, Mazote, Peñalba, and the examples from the Visigothic period at Bande and San Pedro de la Nave, those of the tenth century and those built before 711—are bound to one another by a particular means of distinguishing the apse entrance: in each case a column with a Corinthian capital bears a horseshoe arch, which enframes a tiny window.

These particular examples are significant ones, for they not only signal, in the first half of the tenth century, careful attention to the entire ensemble of elements that give a church constructed under Visigothic rule its particular potency and character, but also show that character as it emerges from different basic building types from the Visigothic period—centrally planned as well as basilical. The types are very different but are bound together in concept, for being the recognizable vestiges of the Visigothic rule, and in style, for answering certain formal problems in a way characteristic of the seventh and eighth centuries through the use of the horseshoe arch, the creation of pockets of space, of divisions, and the rationing of light. The spirit of this tenth-century architectural movement is found in smaller chapels as well, as they continue either in an emblematic way the sophisticated style formed at Escalada, Mazote, and Peñalba, or in the consultation of other models of the Visigothic period. At San Miguel de Celanova the partitioning of space, juxtaposition of different volumes, and use of light and dark mark an understanding of this style, and at Santa María de Vilanova, a small rectangular chapel retains a horseshoe-shaped apse in a rectangular block with adossed columns at the apse entrance—a smaller, emblematic gesture (Fig. 23, Pl. 53).[40] Even in rupestral churches like San Pedro de Rocas or the rock-cut chapels of Laño we find, carved from the side of mountains, the same division of space. And in the tiny chapel at Viguera, an entire wall divides the nave from the apse, much as it had at São Gião de Nazaré in Visigothic times (Pls. 9 and 54).[41]

Such a nostalgia for the Visigothic period, while not widely considered in architecture, has been recognized in other areas of Mozarabic culture. The Mozarabs' aspiration for the authority and influence of their church was often expressed in terms of a desire for a Visigothic renewal. We know they copied, annotated, and collected texts from the Visigothic period and even their "absurdly archaic vocabulary" is thought by some to be "deliberately evocative of a lost (Visigothic) past."[42] What is fascinating is that the conscious historical content of Mozarabic architecture has long been obscured because these buildings have instead been pressed into service as one of the national instruments by which the painful battle of Spain's isolation from Europe is once again fought. In a discipline where the study of the Middle Ages has long been dominated by French monuments, Focillion threw down the gauntlet many years ago when he called Mozarabic architecture "the Romanesque art of Islam," segregating it from—and subjugating it to—European medieval art and disenfranchising it from the arts of Christian Spain as well.[43] That challenge was recently taken up by one scholar, who wields Spain's tenth-century architecture, in all the potency of its mere survival, as a challenge to a Frenchman's vision of those forms worthy of study, a vision regulated by their contribution to a Romanesque architecture that was yet to be:

I decided to write this article when moved by the reading of Louis Grodecki's book *The Year 1000*, a work which affirms in its preface: "The object
of the present volume is not to illustrate the history of that century, but rather
to bring to light the artistic tendencies which can reveal development of real
and lasting phenomena in the *vie des formes*." Nevertheless, after having ana-
lysed a series of European monuments of which perhaps a wall, a window
or a column was all that was left, Grodecki ignored completely the architectural solutions of the Spanish masters of the 10th-century.[44]

Grodecki had touched a tender spot for Spanish scholars, for in conceiving of the
year 1000 only in terms of the origins of Romanesque art, he was able to dismiss
Spanish tenth-century monuments out of hand.[45]

The idea of a connection between Spain's tenth-century architecture and Romanesque has a long history in a Spanish tradition of scholarship, which for some
time tried to demonstrate its significance within a structure constructed to serve
French national interests. It was first argued by Mozarabic architecture's wise apolo-
gist, Manuel Gómez-Moreno, who, as early as 1919, put the matter quite bluntly:

> One has to be concerned that, especially outside of Spain, our whole
> chronology for these [Mozarabic] buildings will be rejected, repeating the feel-
> ings of at least Enlart and Marignan, that is, that in Spain there is no Christian
> art before French Romanesque, or if there is something it lacks in value and
> importance, except for accidents. . . . Although the injustice of it is painful,
> we are accustomed to seeing that which is Spanish disdained on the terms
> of our modern inferiority.[46]

From this struggle must have sprung Gómez-Moreno's insistence that the significance of Mozarabic churches must lie in transmitting to European architecture a
quality that only Spain could give. In a later essay, discussing the Mozarabic monasteries of Asturias, he declares them to be:

> . . . transition between Carolingian and Romanesque and independent of both,
> representing a purely Spanish initiative, the branch of Andalucía with certain
> peculiarities that separate it as well from our Islamic past.[47]

The Iberian Peninsula's contact with Islam becomes the unique quality that only
Spain can contribute to the development of a European style, but this is diffused,
Christianized through the medium of non-Islamic architectural styles: Mozarabic
and Asturian. Though Gómez-Moreno calls the Islamic architecture of the Iberian
Peninsula "andalucismo" and "lo arabizado nuestro," he still must temper its importance to this process, so that Spain's contribution can finally be a national, Christian
one, which takes advantage of the richness of Islamic culture without depending
too extensively on that dark, exotic power. Camón Aznar goes farther: in asserting
that the tenth-century buildings of northern Spain have no Islamic influence, he
declares they cannot be called Mozarabic at all, and thus links them more firmly
with a Roman and Christian tradition, making them more desirable in the battle

for belonging and importance in the European world.[48] As effective soldiers, these buildings must serve a universal cause; no insular, historical issues here. Spain's tenth-century architecture must provide a link that would prove its participation in, even its centrality to, the formation of a grand European art.

Certainly not all of Spain's scholars of early medieval architecture insist on this interpretation, but it has been influential enough to infiltrate quite a few art-historical surveys, and so naturally affects the way Mozarabic buildings are initially studied; the first questions asked about them. A case in point is Jiménez Placer's *Historia del arte español*:

> What cannot be emphasized enough is that those who assert for Spain an essential participation in the genesis of Romanesque—chief among these the master of Spanish historiography, Manuel Gómez-Moreno—base their work on incontrovertible evidence. That is, fundamentally, the fact that Spain possesses the most current and progressive architecture of the European West in the Middle Ages: the stylistic combination of Asturian and Mozarabic, indisputable precedents of Romanesque architecture.[49]

French scholars whose work centered on Spain championed the same cause as well, as if to defend the importance of their subject in terms offered by their own national disciplinary structure, one that saw Romanesque as a kind of formal goal by which the importance of previous styles was gauged. Gailliard indeed called Mozarabic architecture "the richest field of experience for pre-Romanesque art."[50] The very links they propose remind us, however, that the actual ties between Spain's tenth-century architecture (before the Catalonian buildings discussed in Puig i Cadafalch's *Le premier art roman*) and Romanesque are dubious, as is the significance of Islamic forms to the formation of Romanesque architectural style.[51] But most important, these are issues that can have had no meaning for Abbot Alfonso and his monks when they built San Miguel de Escalada in 913, or to any of those who built or experienced the horseshoe-arched buildings I will call Mozarabic here. So dislodging this study as far as possible from the search for links with a place or a future style, the significance of these buildings will be sought in the motives of their patrons. I believe that the consistent pattern in which Mozarabic monastic patrons order indigenous masons to build in a style previously unremarked by them, by means of the careful consultation of different types of models from the Visigothic period, indicates a conscious motivation, one shared by diverse monasteries of Mozarabic immigrants settled in different corners of the Christian kingdoms. It is the meaning of this formal and historical gesture that I hope to discover in a consideration of the Mozarabs' cultural, social, and political experience before leaving al-Andalus.

I. Christians and Building in al-Andalus

The Islamic invasions of the eighth century, which resulted in the creation of the kingdom of Asturias, had a deeply divergent impact upon the Christians of the rich cities of the south, those for whom fate had reserved the destiny of living among their conquerors. In the eighth century the specific terms under which this cohabitation existed were unstable and varied; it was not until the strong, central rule of the first Umayyad prince of al-Andalus, ʿAbd al-Raḥmān I (756–788), that a coherent legal and social status for Christians seems to have emerged.[52] But from the very beginning certain fundamental Muslim beliefs governed the treatment of the Visigothic populace by the first waves of invaders. Christians and Jews were of course *dhimmīs*, "protected peoples" or "People of the Book," and as such accepted individual protection, autonomy as a group, and certain freedoms in exchange for exclusion from participation in political power.[53]

The early treaty between ʿAbd al-ʿAzīz (the son of Mūsā, one of the original conquerors) and the Visigoth Theodomirus provides us with a view of the concrete working of this system during the first years of military incursion. On behalf of seven cities in eastern Spain, Theodomirus agreed in 713 to accept the protection of Allah and the prophet Muḥammad in return for the promise that his subjects would not be killed or their goods appropriated, and that their religion would not be harmed and their churches and cult objects not burned. Theodomirus retained the right to rule as long as he upheld the treaty, refused to protect the enemies of ʿAbd al-ʿAzīz, and paid with his subjects a tribute of gold and other goods.[54] It is a treaty, however, for the capitulation of a rural province; we will have to search farther afield for one that addresses more mixed, urban societies like Córdoba or Toledo.

By the third quarter of the eighth century, ʿAbd al-Raḥmān I's rule had created in al-Andalus a coherent political body. A more complex structure of social, economic, and legal relationships between Muslims and Christians had developed, one that nevertheless reflected the same system established under treaties like that of Theodomirus. The intent of the *dhimma* system was, as Glick has shown, "to ensure that the religious groups were kept separate, distinct, and apart from one another, lest the dominant religion suffer contamination from the subordinate ones."[55] Thus Christians, or Mozarabs as they are also called, and Jews alike were ruled by their own religious and traditional civil laws (as long as no Muslim was involved in the case as plaintiff or defendant) and chose the judges of their own courts. The "People of the Book" in turn paid a relatively high poll tax (the *jizya*), which served as an inducement to the abandonment of their socially autonomous group for conversion to Islam. Certain regulations of social structure complemented this arrangement. Christian men were not permitted to marry Muslim women, thus placing a Muslim in a subservient position to a Christian, and risking her apostasy and that of her children. Muslim men, on the other hand, could marry Christian women, undermining Christian numbers by the same principle.[56]

This system, which seems at first glance to be a liberal, protective accommodation for the Christians to whom it applied, harbored a complex psychological dilemma for those on whom it was imposed. For as a pact, it invited the Mozarabs to agree to moderate safety and well-being in conscious exchange for political, social, and religious subservience. For our purposes here, the visual and stylistic symptoms of this compromise are central.

The earliest treaty to survive between Muslim conquerors and subjugated Christians was probably composed in the eighth century, perhaps as a pattern treaty.[57]

Sometimes called the "Covenant of ʿUmar," the pact can be seen as a prototype of those, both surviving and lost, used a century later in Spain. Encased in its terse, direct language, it contains a clear indication of the power and meaning of visual culture to the separation of conqueror and conquered. Among the first of the pledges the Christian community makes is to promise "not to construct new monasteries, churches or hermitages either in the city or outside of town; nor to restore those which are ruined, nor those which are found in the Muslim neighborhoods."[58] No impediment to the practice of religion is posed, but the suppression of monuments that might serve as witness to the vivacity and potency of Christianity is of the first importance to the Muslim conquerors. The short document continues to discuss conversion and secrecy, and then proceeds with this extraordinary passage. The Christians pledge "not to imitate [the Muslims'] dress or shoes . . . not to wear rings with Arabic inscriptions . . . to shave their faces and to conserve as far as possible their own manner of dress, to use belts on the waist," and yet, at the same time, "not to put the cross on our churches, nor to exhibit in public places neither the cross nor sacred books." More than half of the entire document involves visual signs of the ethnicity and religiosity of the conquered; in fact, these issues are given extraordinary prominence. They are intermingled in the text with such potent issues as, for instance, the prohibition of owning a Muslim slave. The concessions Christians made to the Muslims were first to curb the visual expression of the potency of their religion (constructing churches and showing the sign of the cross) and, second, to avoid at all cost any confusion in dress and presentation between themselves and the Muslims. It was a separation of course that was to be read in terms not only of religious but also of political exclusion. To be Christian or Jew was to be excluded from the main currents of political and economic power, and so both their dress and the intensity, the strictly diminished power of their public presence, were consciously regulated signs of that impotence.

One Mozarabic text indirectly affirms that regulations concerning dress existed in al-Andalus and had an impact on Christians there. Leovigildus's *De habitu clericorum* had as one of its stated goals the instilling of pride in clerics concerning their own dress,[59] an indication perhaps that the strictures and limitations associated with it might have given clerics' garb repressive associations.

Churches in particular were recognized by Muslims as practical and symbolic witness of cultural life and presence. In the first years of conquest, a number of churches that occupied the center of urban spaces were replaced with mosques. Santa Rufina in Seville was converted into a mosque by ʿAbd al-ʿAzīz, and one tradition claims that San Vicente in Córdoba was divided into two to accommodate a mosque, before it was dedicated entirely to Muslim use and its Christian congregation sent to the suburbs. This is similar to the tradition that speaks of the appropriation of the Christian precinct on which the Great Mosque of Damascus was built by the Caliph al-Walīd between 706 and 715.[60] Such random textual references combine with the treaties to suggest a strong Muslim consciousness concerning the importance of religious buildings in public spaces, and a policy aimed at the co-opting of long-standing urban centers previously characterized by churches, sometimes along with their pious associations.[61]

Many of the churches protected or purchased from, or destroyed by, Muslim conquerors were of course constructed in the Visigothic period. None survives in the south to this day, but a number of them are known to have survived the invasion. Texts mention half a dozen in Córdoba and at least nine in the suburbs.[62] The *spolia* from the Visigothic period incorporated into the Great Mosque of Córdoba suggest that the inhabitants of the important southern cities of the seventh and eighth centuries possessed an architecture consonant with the works from central and northern Spain that survive.[63] It is not clear, however, to what extent the Christians of al-Andalus were permitted to build churches after the invasion—if they were held to the strict prohibition from church building of early Islamic pacts. When the church of San Vincente was purchased from Cordoban Christians in 785 by ʿAbd al-Raḥmān I, they were—according to a later account—given special permission to repair churches outside the city walls that had been destroyed during the invasion. Later, in the ninth century, two monasteries—Tábanos and Peñamelaria—were built by pious Mozarabic families outside the walls.[64] Church building was clearly an activity prohibited in principle, but the stricture could be overridden in extraordinary cases, and its enforcement varied with city politics.

The two surviving monuments that are often attributed to Christian patrons under Muslim rule have long obstinately disdained to shed light on this argument. They are Santa María de Melque and a ruin identified by some as the church of Bobastro.

Santa María de Melque was constructed in the fertile lands surrounding Toledo, the *de facto* frontier of Islamic and Christian lands. Whatever the official border, Toledo remained the northernmost Muslim city on the peninsula, and a vast no-man's-land stretched to the north before a changing Christian frontier was reached. The city itself possesses a number of simple, elegant basilicas with horseshoe-arched arcades that have tempted scholars who searched for a Mozarabic architecture there. They are clearly Mudéjar, however, executed in the late eleventh or twelfth centuries after Toledo fell once again into Christian hands. Their conservatism in design, like slightly affected cousins of Escalada, haunts us nevertheless with the idea that the potent historicism of the horseshoe-arched arcade had seized eleventh-century Toledo, its message more meaningful to the reconquered capital of the Visigothic state than the Romanesque style that held most other Spanish Christian lands in its cosmopolitan embrace.[65]

The situation is different for Santa María. With one significant exception, scholarship dates Melque to the mid-eighth or ninth century, when revolts in Toledo and the widely varying autonomy of its Christian population suggest that strictures impeding church construction might not have been enforced in the countryside.[66] There is indeed some evidence to suggest that the construction of Christian sacred buildings was an issue only keenly felt in the cities in general.

Melque is breathtaking for its monumentality, and yet memories of its size and breadth are less tenacious than the extraordinary beauty of its virtuoso horseshoe-arched construction (Fig. 24, Pls. 56 and 57). It is a robust church of a cross plan with lateral chambers to either side of the eastern arm. Its apse, which projects from that arm, is horseshoe-shaped, inscribed in a rectangular mass of masonry. Santa María is entirely vaulted, with horseshoe-shaped barrels—somewhat raised—in the arms and an ample cupola, constructed in rings, at the crossing. The experience of Santa María's interior space was once tempered by two chancel barriers at the apse entrance and the beginning of the eastern arm of the crossing, the latter at least 3.12 meters high. Melque thus possessed a high chancel screen of the sort we know at São Gião de Nazaré and San Miguel de Escalada.[67]

The most potent force of the building, however, is derived from its masonry, which is composed of enormous ashlar blocks fitted carefully without mortar, always with softened, rounded edges and corners so that the uneven courses seem to flow together.[68] This combines with the wildly divergent heights of the exterior courses—from nearly a meter high at the bottom to 15 centimeters at the top—to produce a wall that seems at times to be in movement, to be growing. The same burgeoning aesthetic has been applied like a yeast to the voussoirs of the windows at Santa María, whose asymmetric and uneven extrados struggle to break the tyranny of the wall around them (Pl. 57).

It is not hard to see in Melque—in its plan, elevation, spatial arrangements, and fitted ashlar masonry tradition—a direct connection with traditions of planning and building of the Visigothic period.[69] The connection is so compelling that extensive study has been dedicated to an attempt to demonstrate that Melque was built under Visigothic rule.[70] The issue seems, in the case of Melque, somewhat contrived. Whether Melque was constructed before or after 711 or 714, it represents in every imaginable way the preoccupations of the seventh- and eighth-century style, spatial planning, and fine, long-standing masonry tradition. The small breaks in symmetry that added life to the cool Visigothic wall at San Pedro de la Nave are, at Santa María de Melque, now impious organic irregularities that threaten the order and calm of the massive building exterior. It is the continuation of an existing tradition, constructed either before 714, and unaware of the divergent artistic expression of Muslim rule, or after 714, and stridently impervious to that invasive visual force.

The threads that bind Melque to the Visigothic period are quite different from those strung between that historical moment and San Miguel de Escalada. For though both buildings adhere to the architectural style preceding the invasion in plan, typology, liturgical division of space, and even arch form, they are divided in their tradition of construction. We know now that the thin-walled frame-and-fill construction technique at Escalada belongs to the Asturian-Leonese tradition. This means that Escalada, for all of its attention to the appearance and experience of a basilica of the Visigothic period, is not a direct outgrowth of that tradition, does not reflect some automatic repetition on the part of monastic masons of their tradition of building before their northward immigration.

Melque suggests, however, the possibility of a direct continuation of pre-invasion building practice in the southern countryside: in the center of al-Andalus. Such a construction might have been one mentioned by Muslim chroniclers of Ibn Ḥafṣūn, the tenth-century renegade. Ibn Ḥafṣūn led a rebellion of the Muwallads, or descendents of converted Muslims (his father was a Christian, so Ibn Ḥafṣūn must himself have been a convert to Islam), a revolt and eventual retreat to Christianity that shook al-Andalus. Islamic historians relate that at a moment when an army from Córdoba threatened the outskirts of his military stronghold, he left it in order to keep them from doing damage to a church his father had built.[71] As the existence of the church and its construction are not remarked upon with any surprise by its Muslim chroniclers, some tradition of building in the countryside seems likely.

Ibn Ḥafṣūn's name has been connected with a final building in the south, or more properly a vestigial building. It is the ruin of an unfinished rock-cut basilica in the dry hills of the Mesas de Villaverde, which I will take the liberty of calling Villaverde here. Its secluded site near a ruined "fortress" and its mysterious space inscribed by crude, incomplete keyhole-arch forms prompted early scholars to associate the church of the Mesas de Villaverde with Ibn Ḥafṣūn's stronghold of Bobastro (Fig. 25, Pls. 58 and 59).[72] More recent scholarship, in particular the work of Vallve, demonstrates that texts suggest a much different location for the renegade's stronghold, and we are thus left with an intriguing monument of the Middle Ages, with very little context to support its interpretation.[73]

It is also clear, however, that the church at Mesas de Villaverde was planned to serve the "Mozarabic" liturgy, the same liturgy used in Visigothic times. The plan and elevation effect a radical separation of nave from choir and choir from apse. The choir is tripartite and the entrance to it is impeded by partitioning of space, and by means of chancel barriers as well. The documents associating this development with Visigothic liturgical requirements—in particular the three-part choir and the drastic nature of the divisions—have of course already been discussed.[74] Liturgically, Villaverde would work like a tripartite version of São Gião de Nazaré, a basilica of a scale that does not survive from earlier dates but which surely existed. Villaverde is also a rock-cut church, however, one that surely belonged to a monastic community like those that flourished throughout the peninsula both in Visigothic times and after the invasion, communities that lived in relative seclusion in the hills, worshipping in sanctuaries carved from mountainsides or caves.[75] Like these other examples, Villaverde's divisions and lateral spaces are particularly closed down and cavelike, and this is a general impression augmented by its unfinished condition.[76]

My motive in emphasizing that which is traditional in the planning and elevation of Villaverde and Melque is not to suggest that they were built before the invasion but to show that, as the only possible vestiges of church building in al-Andalus after the Islamic invasion, they would show a predictable continuity with the strong style that had flourished under a previous political regime. And with good reason, for the secretive, enclosed spaces of basilicas of the Visigothic period and centrally planned churches were equally appropriate to the dilemma of a church caught in the grasp of an infidel rule as they were to one engaged in a struggle with a heretical rule.[77]

If the monuments that survive outside an urban context only tease us with possible interpretations concerning the status of church building in the first centuries after the Islamic invasion of the peninsula, texts of the ninth century provide evidence of the kind of despotic control that would be consonant with an urban policy close to that outlined in the "Covenant of ʿUmar," but one of only occasional enforcement. The Mozarab Saint Eulogius, in his *Memoriale Sanctorum*, complains at one point that the emir Muḥammad ordered the destruction of churches recently constructed and any additions that had been made to the basilicas during the years of

Arab rule. Muḥammad had retroactively implemented the very terms outlined in the "Covenant," strictures that, it would seem, had not been enforced in recent times.[78] Some of these repairs or additions seem to have been halfhearted, "crudely fashioned in the time of the Arabs" (rudi formatione), as if executed hastily, or with a certain fatalistic attitude concerning their survival.[79] Gómez-Moreno supports this notion, adding that the rudeness of inscriptions from this period suggests a truncated tradition.[80]

The destruction of churches became, in fact, a primary complaint of Christian clerics living under Muslim rule in al-Andalus. Eulogius mentions this issue four times in the Memoriale, as often as he complains of taxation. His discussion of the churches destroyed under Muḥammad I occurs in Book III, which is entitled, in fact, "On the Destruction of the Basilicas." The book further contains an allusion to the demolishing of the monastery of Tábanos by the same monarch.[81] In Book I the destruction of churches is listed with taxation and the dishonoring of priests as one of the three major provocations of the Muslims toward Christians.[82] He finally contrasts the contemporary conflicts concerning Christian monuments with the past, when the Christian faith was "radiant in wonderfully constructed basilicas."[83] The same author proceeds, in his Apologeticus Martyrum, to characterize a particularly violent phase of Christian persecution strictly in terms of the destruction of churches, declaring that church vaults, basilica towers, and even bell towers were overthrown.[84]

A sense of the importance of the issue was shared by Eulogius's learned contemporaries as well. The distinguished Mozarabic author Paul Albar of Córdoba complained in his Indiculus Luminosus that the Christians' churches were destroyed daily, and their sacred buildings pulled to the ground.[85] More important perhaps than the actual laws that might have been in place in the ninth century is the attitude of both Christian and Muslim toward the act of church building. Clearly it was a sensitive one, imbued with a far different meaning than the practical canonical and iconographical concerns that prevail in a uniquely Christian state. Church buildings became a sign of religious and political power, and their destruction by the Muslim state was a reminder of the contractual subordination of the Christians as dhimmīs.

The Islamic sensitivity to the monumental and visual signs of cultural and religious identity and their periodic suppression and destruction of church buildings must have supersensitized the already significant act of church building for Andalusian Christians. For Eulogius, Albar, and probably others as well, the building and destruction of churches had become one of the terms upon which their political and social struggle with Islam was articulated. They began to see, as the Muslims long had, that their constricted visual world might first act as a practical tool for the survival of a religion and way of life and, second, as the palpable symbol of their resistance to the very complacency they had contracted.

Mazote's odd monastic signatures must be considered in this light.[86] The act of church building might have been imbued with importance, even become a symbolic act, for those Cordoban Mozarabs who left al-Andalus and traveled north to resettle. The right to build had taken on meaning as regarded the Mozarabs' breadth of religious expression and their political and social power as a group.

II. Texts of the Martyr Movement

Though the church of Toledo had remained the center of Latin culture for the Iberian Peninsula in the eighth century, by the ninth century, Latin literature in al-Andalus was being issued from Córdoba.[87] Thus Eulogius and Albar were by no means common Mozarabs. They belonged to an intellectual élite centered in the churches and monasteries of Córdoba (though Albar was, as exception, a layman), a small kernel of the wider Mozarabic population. From this group sprang the great political resistance of the ninth century, one that found its heart in the Cordoban monasteries which were the center of resistance to Islamic culture.[88] This is the movement that would culminate in the mid-ninth century with the beheading of more than fifty Mozarabs by Muslim authorities. The martyrdoms, and the social and political discourse surrounding them, are of great importance for our understanding of the patronage of the Mozarabs of the kingdom of Asturias-León; for as discontented Cordobans, the monks of Abbot Alfonso at Escalada shared a monastic heritage of rage and resistance with their eloquent and passionate predecessors.

The complaints of Cordoban Christians were centered not only on the destruction of their places of worship. The autonomy granted them as *dhimmīs* carried with it countless small limitations to their effectiveness and potency in society. Some of these have been mentioned already: extra taxation and strictures in dress and behavior that prohibited Mozarabs from being confused with Muslims. To the legislation controlling marriage between Christians and Muslims might be added other laws aimed at augmenting Muslim prestige and numbers: the children of mixed marriages, for instance, were required to be raised as Muslims, and conversion to Islam was of course encouraged, while apostasy to Christianity was punishable by death.

To the Muslims, conquerors and converts, went most public offices, nearly all positions of prestige or value. "Although under special and always temporary conditions, Christians and Jews did attain considerable political power," Glick tells us, "the only way to achieve substantial upward mobility in the society at large was to convert to Islam."[89] Gone were the days when the church was the universal arbiter of justice. A bishop might be the head of Cordoban Christians, for example, but he was impotent to speak in any case involving a Muslim; these were sent to a state judge. In this and most other ways, the church was excluded from moving, changing, or making an impact on a society it had once, in many ways, dominated. Churchmen lost the economic, social, and political privileges they had had in the Hispano-Roman and even Visigothic periods. It must have seemed a cruel reversal of the position of the church before the invasion when an ancient ecclesiastical hierarchy, defensive but defiant, stood at the front of a large Hispano-Roman population and obtained the conversion of their heretical rulers.

Other strictures had a more subtle but equally frustrating effect on the church and its influence. Eulogius, a leader in the church and a martyr, and Paul Albar, a great secular defender of the church, both spill a good amount of ink defending their right to preach.[90] "And what persecution," Albar declares, "could be greater, what more severe kind of suppression can be expected when one cannot speak by mouth in public what with right reason he believes in his heart?"[91] "We have become oh fellows (if you deserve the title) of our faith," he remarks later, "dumb dogs, unable to bark."[92] Connected to these are other concerns about the curbing of less obvious rhetorical expressions of faith. These may have been considered, with the building and repair of churches, another means of suppressing Christianity's public, rhetorical expressions of faith, those that might be interpreted propagandistically. We find them most explicitly spelled out in the "Covenant of ʿUmar": "... crosses will not be put on our churches, neither crosses nor sacred books will be exhibited in Muslim public places, church bells will be rung without clamour, prayers will not be recited out loud in the presence of a Muslim, nor will palm leaves or images be held in processions, nor will funerals be celebrated with noise and lit candles in Muslim streets nor in the market."[93] In addition, a curious passage from Paul Albar attests to the power and meaning of at least one of these prohibited acts, that of raucous bell ringing. Indeed, his words suggest the appropriateness of any ringing at all to be a matter of discussion in Muslim Córdoba: "But when they hear the sign of the basilica, that is, the sound of ringing bronze, which is struck to bring together the assembly of the church at all the canonical hours, mouthing their derision and contempt, moving their heads, they wail out repeatedly unspeakable things; and they attack and deride with curses both sexes, all ages and the whole flock of Christ the Lord."[94] The weight of strictures against public expressions of faith and perhaps a hint of their relationship to building are summarized in a passage from Eulogius:

> ... the divine tabernacles are abandoned to a desolate solitude, the spider weaves her thread in the temples, silence reigns over all. Priests and ministers are disseminated here and there, because "the stones of the sanctuary have been dispersed about the public square" [Jerome, Lamentations, 4:1]; the hymns and celestial singing, reduced to silence in the assemblies of the faithful, are replaced in the hidden corners of the prisons by the murmured recitation of the sacred psalms. The chorister does not raise his voice to sing among the people, the priest no longer brings incense to the altar, because the enemy has slain the shepherd and provoked dispersion in the catholic flock.[95]

Studies concerning conversion offer a glimpse at the extent to which these policies limiting the power and rhetorical expression of the church were effective. During the early ninth century, just before Eulogius and Paul Albar wrote, Christians still outnumbered the Arabs, Berbers, and Muwallads of al-Andalus by a ratio of seven to three.

By the middle of the century the curve had started a precipitous rise, and conversions began to increase rapidly, heading for an explosive period of conversion in the first half of the tenth century, and culminating, in 1100, with a Muslim majority.[96] Further, even in the ninth century, Mozarabs—those Christians who remained unconverted—already formed substantial minorities in the cities, where both the meaning and enforcement of Islamic policies were most strongly felt.[97]

That such conversions were the result of a loss of prestige in the church and its culture is part of a story vividly told by Paul Albar himself. In a famous passage of his *Indiculus Luminosus*, he complains bitterly of the cachet of Arabic culture for young Christians:

> The Christians love to read the poems and romances of the Arabs; they study the Arab theologians and philosophers, not to refute them but to form a correct and elegant Arabic. Where is the layman who now reads the Latin commentaries on the Holy Scriptures, or who studies the Gospels, prophets or apostles? Alas! all talented young Christians read and study with enthusiasm the Arab books; they gather immense libraries at great expense; they despise the Christian literature as unworthy of attention. They have forgotten their own language. For every one who can write a letter in Latin to a friend, there are a thousand who can express themselves in Arabic with elegance, and write better poems in this language than the Arabs themselves.[98]

In fact, Vicente Cantarino has charted two groups of Christians in al-Andalus: those who were conciliatory, who showed an inclination to Arabize, to embrace all of the social and cultural rewards that implied, and those who resisted.[99] According to Cantarino, it was originally to the former that the term "Mozarabic" was first applied by the resistant Christians of al-Andalus, as a means of identifying them as "Arabized" or collaborators.[100] Those who resisted and derided their fellows were found, predictably, primarily in the church, but just as there were laymen like Paul Albar who joined their ranks, there were church leaders who collaborated as well, particularly those who were called upon to mediate between Christian and Muslim authority. Thus Paul Albar complains of a great fissure in the church, citing Bishop Reccafred, who "fell upon churches and clergy like a violent whirlwind and threw as many priests as he could into jail."[101] Even more anguishing for defiant church members were those who coped with Muslim rule by means of denial, passivity, or dissimulation.[102] And worst of all, the majority was turning to Islam in a landslide of conversions. Al-Khushānī's account of Comes, who converted so that he could be appointed to a high palace post, is only one of what must have been many cases.[103]

The resistant Mozarabs of Córdoba saw as their only recourse from this muted autonomy a violently rhetorical kind of civil disobedience, one that would restore to the church at least its voice; its physical and verbal presence in the urban landscape of Córdoba.[104] So it was that Perfectus, a priest of good education, was tricked into admitting to a group of Muslims that he held Muḥammad and all Muslims to be unpure, an opinion he repeated, after some hesitation, before Muslim authorities. For this he was imprisoned, and sentenced to decapitation, a fate he met, according to Eulogius, with the following speech:

> "I have cursed, and do curse your prophet, a man of demons, a magician, an adulterer and a liar. As I have testified, I now testify. I proclaim the profanations of your sect to be the inventions of the devil. And I bear witness that you too will suffer punishment in the eternal torments of darkness with your leader."[105]

Subsequent martyrs, as if caught by his valiant testimony, actually sought the opportunity to make such fatal declarations, and to obtain their own deaths. Isaac, the next martyr, returned the trickery that elicited Perfectus's first declaration. A monk from a fine family, skilled in Arabic, he went before the *qāḍī*, pretending he was a candidate for conversion to Islam. But as the tenets of that faith were explained to him, he abused it and Muḥammad as well. When the *qāḍī*, unaccustomed to such proclamations, asked if he were mad or drunk, Isaac replied: "I am not drunk with wine nor afflicted with any sickness, but, burning with the zeal of justice, with which I am sure your prophet and yourselves are unfamiliar, I have shown you the truth; if for this raging death is to be the result, willingly will I accept it; calmly undergo it, and not move my head from its stroke."[106]

In all, more than fifty Mozarabs openly sought decapitation by testifying to the errors of Islam and Muḥammad, and to the eternal reign of Christ. Eulogius tells each of their stories separately, reveling in temptations overcome and authority defied. There are the sons of wealthy families like Isaac, who spoke Arabic and had excellent contacts with the government, and secret Christians: the children of Muslim fathers and Christian mothers who ought to have been raised as Muslims, declare their faith openly, and face death. There were apostates as well, Muwallads probably, who publicly forsook the faith to which their ancestors had converted, to face a sure death. The executions were accomplished to the extreme discomfiture of both Muslim authorities and that part of the church that was trying to live in harmony with them (indeed all the Mozarabic bishops, with the exception of Saul of Córdoba, were opposed to the voluntary martyrdoms).[107] For the voluntary martyrs gained a powerful public platform from which to expound their faith.

As reported by Eulogius, the speeches of both Perfectus and Isaac contain language and statements of deed that indicate the extent to which strident public professions of faith were the soul of the voluntary martyr movement. This theme of bearing witness is at the center of all the literature of Eulogius and Albar, works that seek to justify and explain the motives of the voluntary martyrs. Fontaine has revealed its importance, identifying the public act of confession with a reanimated study of Antique works by the Mozarabic authors, in particular works of the third and fourth centuries that celebrated the lives of voluntary martyrs of the early church.[108] The analogy not only provided a defense for the martyrs, who were criticized by church officials for their purposeful defiance and willful march to death, but a paradigm for the expression of a struggle too long sublimated by the Mozarabs. According to the Antique model, a voluntary martyr was provoking combat with Satan himself; his blood was shed as a soldier of Christ. They were *Miles Christi*, but their combat was a battle with words, in a rhetorical war.[109]

Voluntary martyrdom was the only possible form of public testimony.[110] Bearing witness was, for the Mozarabic martyrs of Córdoba and their apologists, a much-needed means of battling an overwhelming, untouchable enemy. Fontaine notes that the Mozarabic literature contains an aggressiveness which far surpasses that of the Antique models that inspire it.[111] It also provides an identification between the Muslims and Satan, an answer to those Christians who collaborated with the oppressor and defended its policies. The style of battle was uniquely suited to the most onerous terms of the oppression for Cordoban Mozarabs: the suppression of speaking, acting, or showing their faith publicly; of any rhetorical religious expression; and of the building of new churches.

The prominent place given to the destruction of churches in these same texts suggests indeed that sacred building had become, through its careful control by Muslim authorities, one important term of the battle for public testimony of faith: a means of bearing witness. We might on one level see in the choice of models from the Visigothic period for the churches of Mozarabic immigrants in the north a survival of the dialogue concerning building in Christian texts; a memory, or rebuilding, of those churches that had been torn down by Muḥammad I, and most important, witness to the triumph of the persecuted church. I believe the gesture to be that, and something even more specific as well. For we have good reason to believe that the Mozarabs of Córdoba knew well that the churches in which they worshipped were constructed under Visigothic rule, and that they had a concrete notion of the historical implications of that knowledge.

In the same texts in which Eulogius and Albar complain of life under Muslim rule, those authors speak of churches and church building in a consciously historical manner. In the already-cited passage from the *Memoriale Sanctorum*, in which Eulogius mourns the destruction of basilicas by Muḥammad I, he complains specifically that they even pulled down the pinnacles of churches built more than "three hundred years" earlier, "in peaceful and industrious times by our fathers."[112] The importance of that earlier "time," which falls in the reign of the Visigoths, is a significant theme in his works. In order to place Muḥammad in context for his readers, Eulogius begins his lively account of the life of the prophet in the following manner:

> The heresiarch Muḥammad arose in the time of the Emperor Heraclius in the seventh year of his reign, Era 656. At this time Isidore, Bishop of Seville, was outstanding in Catholic doctrine, and Sisebut held the royal throne in Toledo. In the city of Iliturgi the church of St. Euphrasius was built on his tomb. In Toledo also the church of St. Leocadia, a wondrous work, came to completion under the orders of the king mentioned.[113]

The extraordinary importance accorded to the construction of churches in this brief picture of a historical moment demonstrates not only an idealized vision of church and state under Visigothic rule but a surprisingly direct interest in building under the Visigoths as a historical act.[114]

The most revealing references to the Visigoths and their buildings appear in Eulogius in the course of arguments concerning where the blame ought to be laid for hardships suffered by the Christians of al-Andalus. The place of Visigothic history in their vision of the future pivoted in fact on such a notion of accountability. If a theological explanation for the invasion could be found in sin, then the invasion could be seen as a transitory punishment, and the time when Christians ruled the peninsula might be regained.[115] Mozarabic authors often blamed their Christian contemporaries. Thus Eulogius contrasts the faith and devotion of his own time with that under the Visigoths, recalling that time when "the happiness of the churches was in full bloom and the high dignity of the priests shone brightly."[116] In answering critics who suggest Christians ought not to attack their Muslim rulers, who allow them to worship, he replies

> "It is not by the favor of this impious people, in whose sway the sceptre of Spain has been transferred by dint of our sins after the destruction and expulsion of the kingdom of the Goths, which long ago was outstanding in the most blessed practice of the Christian faith and blossomed forth with worthy and venerable priests, and was radiant in wonderfully constructed basilicas."[117]

The kingdom of the Visigoths has become here an ideal historical moment, a sort of golden age in which Christians ruled the entire peninsula in "the most blessed practice of the Christian faith." The struggle of the Hispano-Roman church and Visigothic oligarchy is forgotten here in favor of a vision of a unified Christian hegemony. And the two ways in which the author chose to describe that blessed moment were in terms of its "venerable priests" and its "wonderfully constructed basilicas." The constricted frame of the influence of the church had given rise to an idealization of the period of Visigothic rule, while the controls of building and destruction of churches had caused the Mozarabs of Córdoba to scrutinize the ancient buildings in which they worshipped, to evaluate them against the backdrop of a historical moment that loomed large in their cultural memory: that of the invasion. Because the act of building or repair was unusual and tenuous, they understood that the large part of the buildings in which they worshipped were of the Visigothic period, and the association carried with it numerous implications of religious freedom, not the least of which was the freedom to build.

In this way it can be said that Muslim repression gave a new meaning to building for the Mozarabs; it encouraged them to see their churches against the backdrop of the passage of time and to derive a meaning from their own architectural history. It was a meaning shared by the Mozarabic immigrants of the next century, those for whom the life of constricted expression in al-Andalus had become unsupportable. Thus it must have been with not only a highly sensitized notion of the significance of building—as the precious freedom to bear witness to the power of faith and the church—that Abbot Alfonso and his monks constructed Escalada, but also with a strong visual and philosophical vision of the building that would answer their need. In constructing San Miguel de Escalada according to models built in Visigothic times, they created a part of an image meant to link the present with the past; they demonstrated their desire to create in the northern kingdoms an era like that of the Visigoths, when "the happiness of the churches was in full bloom and the high dignity of the priests shone brightly."

III. In the Northern Kingdoms

More important than the historical model chosen as a repository for their message is the meaning the construction of sacred buildings held for the Mozarabs. The identification of a historical style in church building associated with the years of Visigothic rule became the means by which Mozarabic immigrants bore witness to their faith and defiance once settled in the northern kingdoms. Church building had become part of their rhetoric of testimony, their need for palpable, public statements of faith.

It was a rhetoric, however, that could not be fully conceived in a land where building was so limited. Only with the call for repopulation of frontier territories by a series of Christian rulers can we witness, in a number of monasteries of Cordoban Mozarabs—for those who were most intransigent in the south were among those who made their way north[118]—the linking of a literary idea with its architectural manifestation.

The repopulation of the Duero valley was officially begun by the Asturian monarch Ordoño I (850–866), in order to protect newly acquired vulnerable frontier zones that had been substantially depopulated in the early years of the Asturian monarchy.[119] It was carried to completion by his son Alfonso III, "The Great" (866–910). Certainly the early years of the official repopulation coincided with the persecutions in Córdoba, a fact that helps to explain the emigration of entire Cordoban monasteries, abbot and brethren, to the north.[120] Emigration became another means of resisting the implicit complicity of mute obedience to Islamic regulation of Christian life.[121] Inscriptions surviving in the northern kingdoms bear repeated witness to monks, priests, bishops, and abbots "fleeing the land of the moors," "expelled by the moors," or simply *ex Spania* (from Islamic lands)[122]—politicized testimony of their displacement.

For the rulers of the north, there were practical reasons to encourage such emigrations. The resettlement of entire monasteries became key to the repopulation of certain frontier lands, for monastic centers provided administrative and educational centers in areas that had been long deserted. Lands in the repopulated areas were commonly held by *presura*, rights acquired by exploitation of abandoned villas and holdings. Monasteries, in addition, were often granted special royal immunities that gave them a good deal of autonomy, gave them particular authority at the center of such new settlements.[123] As the lands they occupied had often been settlements before the depopulation, houses and even churches often survived on them, in various states of ruin. The particular conditions of *presura* or *apriso* account for much of the language of the documents that record the occupation of land by a group of monks, such as the long list of passages discussed by Bango Torviso.[124] Thus, when an abbot or abbess writes of finding a church "in squalido" or even describes the building as "antiquas" or "ab antiqua constructa," he or she is likely to be referring to the extent of restorations undertaken by the monastic settlers, in fulfillment of the monastery's obligation to develop the land occupied. But in a few of these documents, a fairly specific historical identification is given to the abandoned monument. In 872, two churches given to a deacon, Odoynos by his brother are described in this way: "... he gave to the deacon Odoynos, one manor (or village) ... together with churches built in ancient times, named after Mary always Virgin and Mother of God, and of Saint Columba, virgin and martyr, which were lying abandoned (or in squalid condition) for two hundred years or more."[125] The reference to two hundred years is intended to bring its history specifically before the invasion, and remind us of the passage from Eulogius, complaining of the destruction of churches built "more than three hundred years earlier . . . in the time of peace."[126]

The real force of the testimony of Mozarabic monks is found in the extraordinary change in the style of church building that their emigration created. The ruined churches on the lands they repopulated must indeed have supplied models and materials as Bango Torviso suggests,[127] but I believe the intellectual and emotional bonds between the Mozarabs and their Visigothic past were formed long before their encounters with those vestiges of the ancient Duero; they were the fruit of their suppression and derision in the south. The remains of the Duero's Visigothic past—the "old temple" that remained at a number of sites—were in some cases recognizable to Mozarabic immigrants as constructions from the time of Visigothic rule, and could thus be offered to indigenous masons as technical and stylistic models for a new northern style.[128]

It is not clear to me to what extent the ideas we have been tracing to this point were shared by the Mozarabic monastic community in general, or at what point they were disseminated to the rest of the Asturian-Leonese kingdom. We find their artistic manifestation first, however, at the building that has been at the center of our discussion all along, at a site known to be repopulated by Cordoban monks: San Miguel de Escalada is indeed the earliest building of the repopulation to survive. Its tripartite choir and tall chancel barrier, its consistent use of the horseshoe arch and revival of the column as support, its elegant enclosure of space into compartments, marks the assimilation of plan and elevation characteristic of the Visigothic period into the thin-walled conventions of northern building tradition.

The written dedication of Escalada's Cordoban founders enriches our understanding of the foundation, evoking the importance these Mozarabic monks gave to building and their linking of that act with their own history.[129] Recall that in the inscription the monks recount how the place lay "long in ruin until Abbot Alfonso, coming with his brethren from Córdoba his fatherland," "built up the ruined house" in the time of Alfonso III. The building we see today, then, is the second built by these monks, their first complete creation. Their number increasing, "this temple was built with admirable work," "not by imperial imposition or oppression of the people, but by the insistent vigilance of Abbot Alfonso and the brethren." This last statement occurs in more than one Mozarabic foundation. It has a kind of democratic fervor that is shared by the dedicatory stone of the lost church of San Martín de Castañeda, also the commemoration of a foundation by a group of Mozarabic monks from Córdoba:

> This place, of old dedicated in honor of Saint Martin and with a small building, was for a long time fallen, until Abbot John came from Córdoba and thought of making a church here. The ruined building was constructed from the foundations up, and worked with stone masonry; not by the imposition of authority, but by the insistent vigilance of the monks these works were executed in five months, while Ordoño held the scepter, in 921.[130]

The Castañeda stone is clearly related in its conscious meaning to Escalada's dedication of only eight years earlier. There are enough differences between the two to suggest that the monks of Castañeda explicitly meant to impress upon the reader not only the same formula but the same meanings as are read in the Escalada dedication: the immigrant status of the monks, their Cordoban home, the history of the site that had an old church, abandoned and ruined. Once again at Castañeda the stone was "worked" "not by the imposition of authority," but by the vigilance of the brothers.

Escalada, the earliest surviving church of the repopulation, emerges not only as a highly politicized building but also as part of an influential movement in the north. Its historicism was conceived in a context charged with anger and frustration centered precisely on the issue of architectural expression, and nourished by the physical remains of the site where it was actually constructed. From the manner in which it embraces, both stylistically and typologically, the Visigothic past, we can see the *instante vigilancia* of its immigrant patrons. There was further some level of communication between the Cordoban monasteries in voluntary exile in León, a contact that extended not only to the execution of such inscriptions but to the ideas that lay behind their texts.

Implicit in this conscious attitude toward the patronage of building is an understanding not only of the forms and typology that evoked the Visigothic period in church building but of the architectural style of the culture that must have seemed, in the south, to smother those vestiges of the Christian past. I remarked earlier that San Miguel de Escalada, constructed for monks from Córdoba, contains not one salient form of an Islamic architectural style that flourished lavishly in Córdoba in the ninth century. There is further visual evidence that suggests the monks of Escalada had an identifiable notion of what constituted Islamic architectural style, and that those recognizable architectural qualities carried conscious meaning. In a famous miniature from the *Morgan Beatus* illustrating Baltassar's Feast, the scribe Magius depicts the ill-fated king in a palace described simply by a horseshoe arch. But that horseshoe arch is fashioned of alternating red and white voussoirs, making it an unmistakable reference to the Great Mosque of Córdoba, which was characterized by an entire hall of such arches as early as the mid-eighth century (Pl. 60).[131] Thus, as has been demonstrated elsewhere, Magius clearly aligns the excess and sacrilege of the Old Testament king with Islam, as well as his fate. For the miniature also depicts the writing on the palace wall, which Daniel will interpret as a prophesy of the end of Baltassar's kingdom. The meaning of Magius's architectural allusion is at times diluted in later recensions of the same illustration, suggesting that this heightened consciousness of what constitutes an Islamic style in miniature painting did not, in many cases, survive very long, nor was it shared by all of his contemporaries in the northern kingdoms.[132] But Magius's attitude is of enormous importance to us, for he almost certainly worked at the monastery of San Miguel de Escalada, and so connects for us that church's evocation of a building consciously associated with the Visigoths with a resistance to Islamic architectural form. Such conscious artistic resistance on the part of the Mozarabs has been traced in Cordoban illumination at the end of the tenth century in an important essay by Werckmeister, where it is also allied both to prophesy and political climate.[133] The linkage of resistance to Islam with the conscious revival of Visigothic form in building became for these early tenth-century Mozarabs a means of bearing witness to Christian faith and culture.

It is these qualities that I believe are "Mozarabic" about the tenth-century buildings commonly called by that name. It constitutes an attitude toward building and a historical preoccupation introduced by one set of patrons. The attitude is both unconscious and premeditated, and the style has nothing to do, at this early date, with the transmission of Islamic architectural style to the north. It is rather an example of reactive adaptation to the Mozarabs' experience of Islam.[134] Indeed the argument can be made that the Mozarabs had to attain some distance from Islam before establishing for themselves an identity; the revival of the model perceived as Visigothic is in a way a symbol of the Mozarabs' re-creation of themselves, and their architectural style bore witness to that new definition. The Mozarabic message was also an extremely potent one for the Christians of the north, who, while they did not experience a crisis of identity as Christians within their own society, were struggling for a political inviolability to soothe their own discordant rupture with the Visigothic past. Thus Mozarabic architecture is known today primarily through its entry into both the architectural and ideological world of the northern kingdoms.

Probably the first and most direct means of communication between the artistic worlds of the Mozarabs and the indigenous inhabitants of the northern kingdoms occurred by means of monastic fellowship. Eulogius himself kept a warm correspondence with the northern church, and his famous trip, begun between 848 and 850, to the monasteries of Leyre and Siresa has received much scholarly attention. In Eulogius's letter of thanks to bishop Wilesindus of Pamplona following that trip, Franke has found evidence that he expected more interest and sympathy for his cause outside of Córdoba.[135] For the Cordoban Mozarabs of the repopulation, a key figure must have been Saint Gennadius, a great northern churchman and formidable "repopulator" of monasteries himself. We know Gennadius was present at the consecration of Escalada in 913, and we find him, only six years later, consecrating a foundation of his own in much the same style, producing an inscription with evident Mozarabic influence epigraphically and in content as well.[136]

> The blessed Fructuosus, celebrated for his merits, after founding his *Cenobium Complutense*, also made a little oratory in this place, with the name of Saint Peter. After that, Saint Valerius, not inferior in merits, enlarged the building of that church. In modern times, the priest Gennadius, with twelve brothers, restored it in 895. Once made bishop, he built it from its foundations admirably as can be observed, not through the oppression of the people, but at great cost and with the sweat of the brothers of this monastery.[137]

Both in its formal execution and its content, the consecration stone reflects the impact of the Mozarabic foundations of the repopulation, and Gómez-Moreno believed the church of San Pedro de Montes, now entirely destroyed, must have borne the mark of Gennadius's contact with the Mozarabic immigrants as well.[138] Further, the insistence on the site's history and its privileged Visigothic past draws our attention to the glorification of the theme of the greatness of the church under Visigothic rule, and an attempt on the part of this monastery and its founder to create a concrete and ideological link between those great churchmen and themselves.

The Mozarabs' Visigothicism had been at once historical and contemporary.

For those immigrant patrons, Escalada represented, in addition to the evocation of a potent historical moment, a kind of entrenched conservatism; it was a monument that by its very existence bore witness to the triumph of Christianity, the survival of a tradition of building and worship that was trampled and crumbling in the south. But for Saint Gennadius and his monks, it was the didactic, historical message of the Mozarabs' architecture that held meaning and yielded fruit, for their experience as patrons and their notion of the significance of Islam diverged enormously from those of the Mozarabs. It was the historical vision of a peninsula united under Christian rule—under a state fused to a powerful church—that held the attention of the northern monks.

In a later church, begun by Gennadius and completed by his successors, we can see the architectural expression of the Visigothic theme voiced so carefully in the San Pedro dedication. The monastic church at Santiago de Peñalba embodies, in its compact cross-shaped plan, the sort of compartmentalized central plan seen at Santa Comba de Bande. Peñalba possesses the same horseshoe-arched transitions, alternation of light and dark, and enframing of the sanctuary area that render the effect of its interior space strikingly similar to that of Bande and Nave, despite divergences in decorative style and articulation.[139] We will see further on that Peñalba, with several other Mozarabic foundations, does not entirely resist Islamic architectural vocabulary, yet its Visigothicism remains the most salient aspect of its character and the experience it offers.

It was not long before the style and its message found a place and meaning in the hearts of the ecclesiastical hierarchy, that arm of the church of the northern kingdoms closest to the court. At Santa María de Bamba, a church was built for a bishop, Fruminius, who retired there in the early tenth century (Fig. 26, Pl. 61). The site was potent with a kind of meaning familiar with the Mozarabic preoccupation, but one brought into the realm of secular rule: for Bamba was believed in the tenth century to be Gerticos, the villa where the Visigothic king Recceswinth died in 672, and where Bamba was made his successor.[140] Fruminius's tenth-century church was enlarged and partially remodeled in the twelfth-century Romanesque style of Zamora. What remains of the early period is a tripartite east end, preceded by a three-part choir that was originally separated from the body of the church by means of a high altar barrier like that which exists today at Escalada.[141] This tenth-century east end, each space partitioned and divided catacomblike by wide, robust horseshoe arches falling on piers, guards its character ferociously against the invasively open, light Romanesque nave, with its flat wall and single volume of space. In contrast, one passes into each of the three compartments of the choir from beneath a tall diaphragm wall; only then is the tall, well-like space of the barrel vault or tower above revealed.

The horseshoe arch that dominates the tenth-century portions at Bamba and obscures the square volumes of its apses from the choir is welded here to a pier-type construction. The irregularity of the arch and voussoir shapes, combined with the wild, inventive prolongation of the imposts that resolve them with the piers, suggests that at Bamba a new group of masons—still connected to those of Escalada and Mazote, for instance, in basic tradition—are grappling with the problems of adapting a conventional technique of construction to a desire on the part of patrons for new forms in plan and elevation: in particular, the horseshoe arch. Here the conflation was attempted while preserving the traditional pier-type construction of northern building tradition, and using barrel vaults, which were somewhat common in royal Asturian foundations. It is unclear if columns were simply unavailable as *spolia* or if perhaps the artistic taste of this indigenous patron was brought to bear on the way models were interpreted or transformed, for both the retired bishop and the masons in this case were formed in a context in which fine buildings used piers as a support.

The at times awkward inventiveness of Bamba is our clue that the masons of Escalada were in all probability not performing their first interpretation of the horseshoe-arched building of the Mozarabs. That cool, elegant building, though the earliest conserved, must have profited from other encounters between its masons, Mozarabic patrons, and models from the Visigothic period. Indeed, the repopulation extends, we have seen, back to the time of the persecutions in Córdoba, and though no earlier monuments exist, we know that Cordoban monasteries were part of the emigration from its earliest years. An interest in building according to models from the seventh and eighth centuries proceeds, then, simultaneously at various levels of sophistication, and is embraced by different kinds of patrons for different reasons. The actual buildings of Mozarabs are few, but their influence was enormous.

We should not wonder at the intensity of the Mozarabs' impact on northern culture when we recall their turbulent history. The passion of that politicization emerges, I believe, in one very early and enigmatic manuscript page: the earliest illustrated fragment of Beatus's Commentary on the Apocalypse, commonly called the Silos fragment, believed to have been produced during the reign of Alfonso III (866–910) (Pl. 62).[142] It is an illustration of Revelation 6:9–11, a text that must have held dramatic meaning for churchmen who shared any experience of conviction with Eulogius or Albar: "When he opened the fifth seal, I saw under the altar the souls of those who had been slain for the word of God and for the witness they had borne; they cried out with a loud voice, 'O Sovereign Lord, holy and true, how long before thou will judge and avenge our blood on those who dwell upon the earth?'" The illustration, while cut into two parts, shows one altar, and one moment, as Mezoughi demonstrated; an altar in elevation, and the "under the altar" of the texts, where dwelt the souls of those who had been slain for "the witness they had borne." The martyrs are shown with severed heads, reminding us of the decapitation of the Mozarabic martyrs, an event that must have occurred very few years before the production of the page. The Latin word used to describe their death in the text is a general one, "interfectorum," and it is repeated alongside the miniature, indicating that the miniaturist had no textual compulsion for depicting the martyrs or their souls in that particular manner.[143] There is no demonstrable tradition for the representation of martyrs with severed heads before this period, no compelling evidence that it is the simplification of a more complex, earlier image.[144]

I believe this miniature makes a conscious metaphoric reference to the Mozarabic martyrs of Córdoba. There is a raw, graphic quality to this otherwise simple and schematic painting of martyrs: their necks are long and bare, stained with blood, and the severed heads end with little tails of gore. These are not the whole idealized martyrs of a later illustration of the same passage but an immediate, palpable evocation of a recent event recalled by the Apocalyptic text. It matters little if the miniaturist was a Mozarab or an indigenous monk of the north, for in either case this early manuscript of the northern kingdom reminds us of the extent to which the Mozarabs and their actions brought to traditional religion in the north a new, contemporary, and politicized meaning. The miniature must indeed have been made at a moment not far removed from that January in 884, when Alfonso III received, in great pomp, the relics of the Cordoban martyrs Eulogius and Leocritia, brought from Córdoba by his ambassador, the Mozarabic monk Dulcidius.[145]

When we remember that building was one of the terms by which the Mozarabs' cultural repression or survival was acted out in al-Andalus, we can see the notion of a Visigothic revival in the north as part of the invigoration of Asturian-Leonese building with a religiosity that, like the miniature, had both a traditional and a contemporary meaning.

The meager vestiges of the lost church of San Salvador de Palaz del Rey, in León, would mark the only surviving witness of the penetration of an architectural style into the court itself (Fig. 27). Built by Ramiro II between 931 and 951 next to the royal palace, its vestiges suggest a horseshoe-shaped apse inscribed in a rectangular mass before a vaulted, cruciform crossing, and recent excavations here revealed a western apse as well, like that at Peñalba.[146]. But that ultimate official embrace of an architectural style must have been preceded by the political idea that germinated in the monuments. For the seductive notion of a Visigothic revival, of a link with that time when a strong Christian monarchy ruled the entire peninsula, had already reached the court in the last years of the ninth century as the offering of immigrant Mozarabic churchmen.

IV. Testimony Appropriated: The Meaning of Visigothicism for the Northern Kingdoms

The presence of Mozarabic churchmen, even Cordobans, in court in the late ninth century was established in the beginning of this century by Gómez-Moreno. A "Martinus abba cordovensis" witnessed a donation confirmed by Ordoño II; Alfonso III received Sebastián, the Mozarabic bishop of Ercavica who had been expelled by the Muslims, and made him the bishop of Orense. The same monarch bought the ruined church of Saints Facundus and Primitivus and gave it to an abbot and monks from al-Andalus, thus founding the monastery of Sahagún. A priest with an Arabic name witnessed a sentence before the king in 878, and three more witnessed a document from the court in 898.[147] It was perhaps here that the Mozarabic notion of bearing testimony through the Visigothic past was made a theme of national and political significance by the northern courts.

The Visigothic preoccupations of the Asturian-Leonese monarchy receive their strongest affirmation with the reign of Alfonso III. The passion of that monarch for the Visigothic period was revealed in particular in his interest in the works of Isidore, and for his being the first monarch to style himself in documents as a direct descendant of the Visigothic kings.[148] He was the first monarch "after an eclipse of two centuries," Menéndez Pidal tells us, to renew Isidore's notion that "the Gothic people were worthy of their own history," by means of a revival of the Visigothic historiographical tradition. Indeed the histories written under Alfonso III's rule are the most revealing documents of his fealty to a historical connection with the Visigoths.[149] The Chronicle of Albelda, discussed in chapter 2, was the earliest, composed between 881 and 883, then continued by a scribe named Vigila to the year 976 at the monastery that gave it its name.[150] The main body of the chronicle—its ninth-century parts—is believed to be composed by a Mozarab in Oviedo, some of its materials having been brought from the south.[151] Its creation, however, is also closely connected to royal circles, and its composition is strongly linked to that of the other courtly chronicles.[152] Written very shortly after the Albelda, the first version of the Chronicle of Alfonso III was composed under the careful supervision of the monarch, and he is supposed as well to have directed the embellishments that distinguish the second version.[153]

A large part of the Albelda is devoted to the history of the "Ordo Gentis Gotorum," the "Succession of the Visigoths"—whose history primarily seems to be taken in the Chronicle from Isidore's *History of the Goths*—and the "Ordo Gotorum Obetensium Regum," the "Succession of the Visigothic Rule of Oviedo," the title given to the kings of Asturias. Clearly the main aim of the work is to create a historical and conceptual link by which Alfonso III might be seen as the actual heir to the Visigoths, and a probable restorer of their reign over all of Spain one day. Indeed, not only the Albelda but all three chronicles, according to Menéndez Pidal, "coincide in one basic idea that they all wish to make clear, that of showing the Asturian kingdom to be the immediate continuation of the Kings of Toledo."[154]

The kings of Asturias and León had certainly been familiar with Spain's Visigothic past. One can even say perhaps that the opening up of Asturias at the beginning of the ninth century to an outside tradition—that of the Franks—gave a meaning to that Visigothic past and created a distance that permitted it to be characterized and idealized for adaptation to a new political ideology. But this conscious and purposeful use of history to serve a political idea must have sprung from the symbiotic collaboration of Mozarabic authors and their royal patron, for its focus on the Visigoths is permeated with an intimacy and nostalgia that calls to mind Mozarabic experience and texts.[155]

The only passage of any of the chronicles that might challenge the notion of a Visigothic revival born primarily of the fused interests of Mozarabic churchmen with Alfonso III is the famous passage in the Albelda that describes Alfonso II's creation of a new Toledo at Oviedo: "Omnemque gotorum ordinum sicuti Toleto fuerat, tam in ecclesia quam palatio in Obeto cuncta statuit." The text itself, which was written in a style reminiscent of Isidore,[156] has already been discussed at some length.[157] In light of what we have learned concerning Alfonso II's preoccupations and those of the tenth-century Mozarabs and their northern sovereigns, the passage seems clearly to be the issue of its authors' vision of history, one idealized to serve a tenth-century political idea.[158] The idea of continuity with the Visigoths born in Alfonso III's histories must indeed grow from their Mozarabic authors, for whom connections with the Visigothic past must have seemed continuous and seamless from across two centuries of cultural isolation.

An interest in building of the Visigothic period as a distinct style was clearly a conscious matter of interest for immigrant Mozarabs of the second half of the ninth century; both their monuments and their literature testify to that concern. Indeed, the scholar who remarked that the Chronicle of Albelda possessed something of the character of a "9th-century Baedeker" was not far off the mark.[159] A Mozarab of the late ninth century must have seen such a concentration of grand sacred monuments as existed in Oviedo as testimony to the strength of Christianity in the north—as a glorious and welcome testimony—after experiencing constrictions to patronage and destruction of churches in al-Andalus. It is perhaps to this fresh, exultant interest that we can attribute so many discussions of building in the chronicles of Alfonso III's reign. Buildings and patronage were for the Mozarabs a source of demonstrative faith; their very existence and concentration in a Christian capital merited connection with the myth of Visigothic continuity, not as the faithful reproduction of a historical style but as a robust flourishing of monumental Christian building that paralleled the golden age in Toledo.

Under the influence of the Mozarabs in his court, perhaps even those who wrote the chronicles, a conscious recognition of a historical style associated with the Visigoths must have dawned upon Alfonso III as well. In a curious donation he reveals a pride in the recognition of carvings that he must have believed to be from the Visigothic period, to be the art of the kings of Toledo: "This Holy Cross which was hidden away, is old work in wood, similar to sculpted ivory diptychs that we brought from Toledo."[160]

It seems to me in fact that the exaggeration manifest in the Chronicle of Albelda of Alfonso II's concern with Visigothic culture can be seen as part of the mythology that links all Asturian kings to the Visigoths of Toledo, part of the primary goal of all three chronicles, a goal firmly entrenched in the policies and interests of Alfonso III and the Mozarabic monks who were, at least in part, the authors of the chronicles. The Chronicle of Albelda is a poignant document of the extent to which Mozarabs invigorated the northern monarchy with rich political imagery that nourished a growing sense of national identity and bellicose pride.

The "Prophetic Chronicle," a contemporary to the other two, was also written by a Mozarab in Oviedo. Its date is 883, the year the Albelda was completed, and its earliest copy is incorporated into a surviving manuscript of the Albelda.[161] The author of the Prophetic Chronicle is possibly the Toledan Dulcidius, the ambassador of Alfonso III's court who was sent to Córdoba to bring the bodies of the martyrs Eulogius and Leocritia—bodies heavy with political significance—to Oviedo in 884. A particularly interesting character for our study, Dulcidius is mentioned by the monarch himself in the prologue of the Chronicle of Alfonso III for having given him a copy of Isidore's *History of the Goths*.[162] That the few documents that mention Dulcidius establish both his personal role in the transmission of Visigothic history to the monarch and the seeking out and glorification of the bodies of Cordoban martyrs strongly suggest those twin themes—bearing witness and Visigothic historicism—to be bound to the Mozarabic presence in court.

The text of the Prophetic Chronicle reminds us of Islam's role in the development of this national imagery, and of the link between Visigothic renewal and rejection of Islam. In language brimming with defiant testimony of the greatness of Christ, it predicts the expulsion of the Arabs one year and seven months from the time of its composition, and thus links the Visigothic imagery of both the literature and art of the reign of Alfonso III with the conflict with Islam, with the desire to rid the peninsula of Muslims altogether:

> Declare that God is Omnipotent, so that the church will grow and the audacity of the enemies diminish without cease. Even the same Arabs predict, through certain signals in the stars the proximity of their finish, the restoration of the reign of the Visigoths by our prince; also many Christians, by revelations and apparitions predict that our glorious prince Alfonso will soon reign over all of Spain. . . . As the name of Christ obtains dignity, the enemy's shameful calamity will weaken.[163]

The national and historical identity implicit in a Visigothic renewal is one formed in opposition to Islam. The Mozarabs had brought to the Leonese court a consciousness freshly scarred with the full force of the cultural disequilibrium between Islam and Christianity in Spain. It was just this consciousness that spurred a battle cry in the monarchy of the northern kingdom, one nourished with a historical concept perhaps already familiar and meaningful to the Asturians.

In a codex of the monastery of San Martín de Albelda of 976, we find a miniature that gives a palpable image to the survival, to a later time, of this dream of revival enrobed in the myth of continuity (Pl. 63). On a page divided into nine parts, the reigning Pamplonese family—Kings Sancho (955–957; 960–967) and Ramiro (967–984) and Queen Urraca—occupies the center register.[164] Above them are three late Visigothic kings—Chindaswinth, Recceswinth, and Egica—aligned with the Leonese rulers in an artistic correspondence meant to represent the spurious continuity between the families. Below them are represented Vigila the scribe, his student García to one side, and his assistant to the other. The difference in scale between the clerics and the rulers is so small—it depends really on the hats worn by each monarch, making them appear slightly taller than the scribes—as to make us wonder at the prominence given to those who crafted the manuscript, who appear as lively and colorful as their sovereigns. They emerge indeed from frames that are slightly larger than those which present the six rulers above. All three rows of figures are further arranged identically, with the same hierarchy: a central figure is frontal, and side figures gesture in a more dynamic three-quarter view. In a page generally considered a copy of the *Vigilanus*, dated 992—the *Codex Aemilianensis*, from the scriptorium of San Millán de la Cogolla—the same scheme is repeated, but with a bishop, Sisebus, sitting on a throne in the central panel of the lower register, directing a notary of the same name to write, while a scribe, Velasco, waits to the left.[165]

Churchmen from the monastery of Albelda and San Millán de la Cogolla saw themselves by 976 as the keepers of a historical tradition that was still, nearly a century later, important to the political profile of a northern Christian ruler. They bore witness to the veracity of a lineage fabricated nearly a century before. As in Visigothic days as well, the church saw itself as a primary mover in the secular realm, as the author and preserver of this drama of restoration, as a means by which faith and the authority of the church should also be restored. By 976, of course, the Mozarabic immigrants of the great repopulation of the end of the ninth century were dead, their intellectual progeny absorbed into the Christian culture of the northern kingdoms, but their political message gave a visible image to the emerging identity of the Christian rules of the north, and strengthened and enlivened the place of the church in its growth.

The Mozarabs buttressed their connections with the myth of their own Visigothic past, and nurtured its few physical vestiges as they were threatened by the very repression of rhetorical freedom that cut the power and affective value of the Christian church in al-Andalus. That conservatism became for them conscious and historical, a strident, visual means of bearing witness to the greatness of the church and its culture. The destruction of churches and the suppression of church building in Islam gave the making of architecture special meaning for the Mozarabs, so supercharged it with significance that they created a historical style with conscious meaning. That meaning must have extended, in the first years of the repopulation, to an understanding of what, for the Mozarabs, constituted Islamic style in architecture as well, and a conscious resistance of such forms. The alternating voussoirs of the Feast of Baltassar page from the *Morgan Beatus* give that decorative system a meaning both Islamic and apocalyptic.

The violence of the voluntary martyrs' revolt was verbal, rhetorical. Architecture became, then, a parallel language of expression, of bearing witness to faith, and of differentiation from a stronger culture: a means of creating, in as overt a way possible, an identity for a group that saw its very cultural existence threatened. Through architectural spaces and visual reference that embodied both notions of continuity and nostalgic history, the Mozarabs re-created their own culture, fashioned it around their message of testimony and resistance, encased it in a dream of cohesion of church and state. This same historical paradigm chosen as the vehicle for their message of testimony and resistance would provide a familiar and timely political model for the kingdom of León under the ambitious central rule of Alfonso III: a concern with Spain's Visigothic past that would enjoy a long history. Indeed, that message must have had, for the north, the sound of a deep cultural truth. For it was the same myth of Visigothic unity born in the tentative peace of the sixth and seventh centuries.[166]

The special status accorded the making of architecture would fade with both careful attention to historical style and the resistance to forms identified with Islam. These were the products of a tension born of conflict in the south, meanings evaporated in the dry air of the Christian kingdoms, distilled to one simple political message. Barren and brittle as that message became, it is a trace of the momentary enrichment and vitalization of the Spanish Christian kingdoms through the message of an embattled immigrant population. Building in a style associated with the Visigothic period was the means by which Mozarabs bore witness to their own intransigent faith in the face of an overwhelming Muslim culture; and a revival cloaked in a myth of continuity with the Visigothic past became the means by which northern Spanish Christians first testified to the presence of Islam, and formed a new national identity in opposition to it.

4
Reaction and Absorption

I. In the Northern Kingdoms

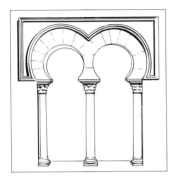

In the year 920, the Mozarab Dulcidius returned to Córdoba in chains.[1] The former ambassador of Alfonso III and author of the Prophetic Chronicle had been taken prisoner by the emir ʿAbd al-Raḥmān III, captured during the battle of Valdejunquera. One wonders how his captive eyes transfigured the capital where, only years before, he had freely sought the Mozarabic martyrs' relics in the service of the king of León. The years that separated his two voyages had brought subtle changes in his adoptive northern home, changes that linked the dynamics of strife to a constantly transforming notion of cultural identity.

Dulcidius had first come to Córdoba on a political mission wedded to a heady and strident resistance to Islam. The relics of Eulogius and Leocritia that he brought back to Oviedo had served to charge the territorial war between the northern kingdoms and the emirate with a vital religious meaning for the Christians and were the means as well by which religiosity in the north was politicized, given palpable contemporary meaning. When the hostilities between Islamic Spain and the northern Christian kingdoms were encased in the natural polarity that exists between a blessed martyr and her enemy, or in a biblical metaphor, as they were in the Prophetic Chronicle, the war necessarily took on cosmic proportions, and its leader's success seemed assured. Such was the attitude, I believe, in the Kingdom of Asturias in the last quarter of the ninth century, the vital, hopeful years in which the Prophetic Chronicle predicted the imminent demise of Islamic rule.

Indeed, during the reign of Alfonso III it seemed for a while as if the small Christian kingdom were rising successfully against the Muslim Goliath to the south. As a young king, Alfonso III took Porto and created in Castile a fortified bulwark to the west. Alfonso supported a Muwallad rebellion that resulted in the Umayyad loss of Badajoz in 875, and delivered into his hands Muḥammad I's chief minister, who was ransomed at great price. The emir sent a large army to Asturias, but Alfonso marched against them for his greatest victory of all, one that culminated in a truce requested by Muḥammad I himself. It was perhaps, as one historian puts it, "the first time that an emir of Córdoba submitted to the will of the king of Asturias."[2]

Muḥammad I was paralyzed, not so much by Alfonso's threat as by cancerous internal unrest, in particular the revolt lead by ʿUmar ibn Ḥafṣūn the Muwallad who led an alliance of Mozarab and Muwallad rebels against the government in Córdoba. Before that crisis was over, Alfonso III cut more deeply into the lands of al-Andalus than had any other Christian monarch before him.

Alfonso III was deposed by his own sons, retired forcibly to Valdediós after a pilgrimage to Santiago de Compostela. García I, Ordoño II, and Fruela II divided the kingdom among themselves, making León its capital, and for some time continued the momentum against Islam begun by their father. Ordoño II defeated the Muslims at Gormaz, a major defensive stronghold, in 917, and began chipping away at the region of Rioja. But the young king faced a new emir in al-Andalus: ʿAbd al-Raḥmān III, who had established internal peace in the south and was determined to paralyze the northern kings. Marching north in the summer of 920, the emir recovered Gormaz, along with the other defensive strongholds, destroyed southern Navarre, and routed the Christian kings at Valdejunquera. When these monarchs assembled to begin new raids, ʿAbd al-Raḥmān III completely destroyed Pamplona in 924. Within a year dynastic crises and chronic internal rebellions seized the north with the death of Ordoño II. Apart from the brilliant victory of Ramiro II at Simancas in 939, the momentum of reconquest was, for the moment, lost. The terms of the Prophetic Chronicle were reversed: the "audacity of the enemy" increased and the heated movement toward the "restoration of the reign of the Goths" was gradually extinguished.[3]

Dulcidius's ignominious entrance into the capital of al-Andalus occurred almost at the moment of that shift in political confidence; his imprisonment emerges, in a way, as a symptom of the changing winds. What is fascinating is that this shift parallels, in a number of specific monuments, a subtle change in the architectural style that had taken hold of the frontier at the end of the ninth and the beginning of the tenth century. Just as the energized message of immigrant monks seeded the frontier with a new, historically focused style of building, which, in some cases, even seemed to resist Islamic forms, the dilution of their message, and the loss of the political momentum that had buttressed it, parallels a marked taste for certain characteristically Islamic forms of articulation and ornamentation in church building. This new admission into northern Christian taste did not relentlessly follow the tide of political submission to Islam, but rather flowed in a slightly more urgent wave, as if propelled by different breezes of the same storm. And it would coexist at times with diverse messages: the notion of artistic resistance would still survive in some quarters, as would the vision of a Visigothic renewal.[4]

At San Miguel de Escalada in 913, we saw a church devoid of any significant Islamic impact, the reflection of an attitude of militant resistance in a "rhetorical war." Escalada embodied an approach to the familiar language of forms of a divergent culture that is parallel in structure to the method by which Albar and Eulogius address Muslim belief and civilization in literature. Millet-Gérard found in their works a deliberate misreading of Islamic texts and beliefs, one that resisted the attractions of Islamic culture by enclosing it within biblical prophesy. Albar's method was

> . . . not a neutral, objective historical study, but an allegorical interpretation which conforms to biblical exegetical tradition. It thus essentially concerns the understanding of the Islamic phenomenon within a Christian vision of the world and of history, an integration which gives it a meaning. Such an

integration can only be negative. . . . It little matters to our author that Islam has its own history, and characteristic traits.[5]

Such cultural myopia was essential to the suppression of an enormously seductive Islamic society. Its effects can be measured not only by the attrition of Christian youth so lamented by Albar, but by a surprising statement of Eulogius himself, who cannot seem to suppress his admiration for the Córdoba of ʿAbd al-Raḥmān II (822–852) in the beginning of his account of the martyrdom of the priest Perfectus. The reign was

> an era in which the Arab people, greater in fortune and importance, submitted almost the entire Iberian Peninsula to his [ʿAbd al-Raḥmān II's] hard rule, but one in which the caliph also elevated to its summit Córdoba, before called "The Patrician," now called the royal city; since his rise to the throne, he has covered it with honor, strewn it with glory, and accumulated riches, multiplied the pouring in of all the pleasures of the world, with an amplitude surpassing the imagination, of a kind which crushes in its radiance all of the royal predecessors of his race in all which touches secular display, while on the other hand the orthodox church trembled beneath his terrible yoke.[6]

The attractions of ʿAbd al-Raḥmān II's court are well known. As a patron he enlarged the prayer hall of the Great Mosque of Córdoba, and built mosques over all al-Andalus for its different communities. An amateur of astronomy and other sciences, the emir also was a patron of poets and satirists, of philosophers and musicians. He brought the poet Yaḥyā al-Ghazāl and the astronomer ʿAbbās ibn Firnās to live at court, along with Ziryāb, a famous singer from the court of Baghdad, who brought with him in turn the fashion for all the refinement of the East: cuisine, dress, and canons of beauty were among the attributes of Islamic culture that were embellished and enriched during the reign of ʿAbd al-Raḥmān II.[7]

Clearly the resistance to Islamic cultural forms was founded to some extent on their vibrancy and attractiveness to Christians. In light of the passages cited here, it would be difficult to suggest ignorance of the brilliance of the court life or of its architectural manifestations. It was instead, I would suggest, their power that sent Mozarabic Christians, in desperation, to link their own past with an exegetical prophesy of the future in a rhetorical drama that vied with the "secular display" of the seductive court. The significance of that architecture, and of the Great Mosque of Córdoba in particular, seems assured by the fact that many of the encounters between prospective martyr and Muslim prefect recorded by Eulogius took place before the mosque or in the antechamber of the mosque itself.

The impact of those forms can be read after the first decades of the tenth century. In particular, it is following the attrition of northern military confidence that the Christian resistance to recognizably Islamic forms relaxed. In surviving buildings of the 930s and 940s—those built after the passing of the first blush of Mozarabic immigration—the visual interest in a Visigothic past is accompanied by a limited but distinct selection of ornamental forms of unmistakably Islamic origin.

Santiago de Peñalba, like most of the buildings in that village, is constructed of long, dark, flat stones quarried from the very mountain on which it sits.[8] It is a tight and organically massed church that clings to its neighbors like the outcrop of a battered, meandering chain of peaks. And yet Santiago's south wall yields a corner of acute refinement, an *aljimez* door—a double-arched door enframed with an *alfiz*—which promises a transformation of experience within (Pl. 64). Twin horseshoe arches, cut sharply from fine ashlar voussoirs, pierce the rough masonry flank. Their profile is radical—in their silhouettes almost an entire circle can be read—and they are bound not only by a shared support, but by a molding course, which defines and enframes them. Though twin-arched windows existed in buildings of the Visigothic period, the prototypes for the door of Peñalba are found in the windows of the Great Mosque of Córdoba, the Toledan mosque of Las Tornerías, and in the mosque of Ibn Ṭūlūn in Cairo.[9] For this *aljimez* reflects the transformation of an indigenous Visigothic form by Islam into something quite different.

Double-arched windows of the Visigothic period, or associated with that tradition, are primarily works of textured ornament revealing occasional hints of plasticity or organic form. In these earlier works, the arches and columns are sculptural; the object of interest to the viewer. Here at Peñalba the double-arched form functions as a sharp profile that frames a negative space and is then itself enframed. It is not the architectural members themselves that are the object of interest but the forms they enframe. The Peñalba *aljimez* is taken from a Spanish Islamic context in which the self-conscious use of exaggerated arch forms and enframing moldings—of the morphemes of architecture—is meant to focus and disperse interest in buildings that contain no figural decoration of any kind. It is the product of this transformation—rather than the double-arched window of Visigothic tradition—that appears at Peñalba before the mid-tenth century, and it appears in a major juncture of the church: its principal entrance.

The capitals that receive Peñalba's *aljimez* also present designs that are defined by shadow, focused on form that is cut away (Pl. 65). The plasticity of other Mozarabic capitals is here almost completely restrained—bound tightly to the basket—and the capitals' two levels are instead transformed into fields of flat, spiny relief carving. The closest prototypes I know are outside the Iberian Peninsula: the capitals at the Umayyad palace of Khirbat al-Mafjar, where sharp, jagged leaves zigzag across the body of the capital. Though various models have been proposed, what is clear is that the aesthetic principles privileged here—the suppression of plastic values for the flat, patterned working of a surface—are found throughout al-Andalus: in the capitals of Madīnat al-Zahrāʾ, or in those from the mosque of Tudela.[10]

In the de-accentuation of that which is plastic and natural in favor of a continuous abstracted design, the capitals belie, with the *aljimez*, the incursion of recognizable Islamic aesthetic values in northern church building in the guise of indigenous forms considered in a different way—transformed by principles of ornament and articulation characteristic of Islamic art in al-Andalus.[11]

Upon passing into the nave of Santiago de Peñalba, the promise of the door is fulfilled. Santiago's gruff exterior obscures a vivid and elegant church composed of four partitioned vessels. Diaphragm horseshoe arches separate the compartments, enframing an apse opening embraced by an *alfiz* used in the manner of the *alfiz* of the earliest doors of the Great Mosque of Córdoba. The *alfiz* at Santiago de Peñalba encases an arch of proportions characteristic of those found at Córdoba (the arch defines four-fifths of a radius more than a semicircle), and it is constructed of uncentered voussoirs,[12] but what frees this borrowing from the intervention of any possible prototype from the Visigothic period that might be shared by both Christian and Islamic monument is its startling decoration and the way in which it originally must have transformed the wall of the sanctuary opening. For the sanctuary opening of Santiago de Peñalba was covered with complex aniconic painting (Pl. 66).[13]

The most prominent of Peñalba's paintings are those that can still be seen on the sanctuary entrance, a double interlace decoration composed of yellow and red ribbons, neatly outlined in black and flanked with interlacing lines to one side, and a row of black toothlike triangles to the other. The vaults are covered with simulated brick, and an occasional string course of frieze is picked out with paint. Several individual motifs of the painting at Peñalba can be found at Valdediós, in the repertory of the Asturian painters from whose ateliers the painters of Peñalba must have come. But the combination of these forms with an even greater number of new ones popular in the relief and minor arts of al-Andalus,[14] in a complex and, most important, completely abstract decorative program, suggests that indigenous artists at Peñalba were interested in recognizably Islamic taste in ornament, and were struggled to incorporate these continuous abstract structures within the highly focused, culminative architectural context of a centrally planned Mozarabic church.

The Great Mosque of Córdoba has lurked at the margins of the past two chapters, emerging to explain some arch construction here or a decorative form there. It has popped up in fragments, which might not be a bad thing, because it is clear that in the first half of the tenth century, Leonese Christian builders and patrons conceived of its contribution to their language of forms in pieces. This derives in part from a need to isolate and defuse the cultural and religious meaning behind a rich and attractive art, but also because, as a mosque constructed to serve a culture that uses architecture and ornament differently than that of the Spanish Christians, the meaning of the Islamic decorative forms in context was largely lost upon the Christians of the north. For a culture for whom religious architecture is designed to reveal an earthly as well as heavenly line of authority, to orchestrate space toward and around an altar (whether revealed or not), the repetitive dispersion of the earliest hypostyle plan at the Great Mosque of Córdoba must have mystified for the refusal of its parts to culminate, to serve a hierarchy in its plan, space, or decoration.

We see at Peñalba the attempt to adapt an entire unit of design, and even to be true to its basic principles; but that bit of wall organized around an arch is made here to serve a principle of architectural space that is wholly Christian and Western in concept: it is the means by which the sanctuary wall takes its prominent place in the carefully orchestrated hierarchy of space and form of the centrally planned church. Once again, the view of Islam is subordinated to a completely Western Christian paradigm as we saw in Paul Albar, yet here the terms of the incorporation are slightly altered. The Christian vision here is not the dramatic apocalyptic one of Albar and Escalada, one that in its most conscious mode linked a Satanic metaphor for Islam to a highly charged notion of the significance of building, creating powerful barriers to the acceptance of the public art of Islam. Sequestered as these foci of Islamic design are within their Christian contexts at Peñalba, the organization of complex aniconic patterning around an enframed arch—that is, the use of the morpheme of architecture itself to orchestrate, and create interest in, a highly ornamented surface—indicates a relaxation at some level of conscious resistance to Islamic cultural forms on the part of northern Christians, a willingness to accept and incorporate.

This new receptiveness makes its way back to Escalada, to which was added in the 940s an extraordinary porch of sharp, enclosed horseshoe arches, enframed by a continuous string course and echoed in its western wall by a tiny *aljimez* window enclosed in an *alfiz* (Pl. 67).[15] And this same receptivity takes an even more startling turn at San Miguel de Celanova and San Cebrián de Mazote. At the tiny chapel of Celanova, the sanctuary wall emerges from a tiny keyhole arch, a careful proportional copy of a door of the Great Mosque of Córdoba, even an exaggeration of the principles that traditionally distinguish the doors of the mosque (Pls. 45, 46, and 53). Its voussoirs are so wide in proportion to the opening and to the sanctuary entrance wall itself that as a stylistic motif they dominate the entire chapel.

At Mazote the distinguishing detail is less prominent but even more referential. A building traditionally related to Escalada, Mazote shares with the earlier foundation both a horseshoe-arched arcade and a tripartite division of choir.[16] Indeed, its relationship to the main part of the church of Escalada, formal and ideological, is a significant one: Mazote shares with all of the Mozarabic-style buildings of the northern kingdoms an ardent attention to forms from the Visigothic period in both plan and elevation. More so even than Escalada, it recalls monuments like San Pedro de la Nave in the "complexity of its volumes, its diverse external heights as well as its ample proportions."[17] But the masons and patrons of Mazote, those monks who signed so many of its stones, also integrated a taste for a different kind of articulation and ornamentation within their handsome, conservative liturgical space, one that betrays close attention to the Great Mosque of Córdoba.

The first indication of such concerns lies in choices that parallel some of the developments noted at Peñalba. Mazote's horseshoe arches surpass the semicircle by three-fifths the radius, to produce a more enclosed arch than occurred in Escalada's interior arcade, or in any constructive context in a monument built under Visigothic rule (Pl. 50). As at the door of Saint Stephen at Córdoba, the radical nature of the horseshoe arch is attained by means of a strongly salient springer, divergent in appearance from the arcade arches of Escalada but almost identical to the blunt, beveled *abaci* of the arcades of the Great Mosque of Córdoba under ʿAbd al-Raḥmān II (Pl. 68). Here are parallels loosed from the Visigothic past, absorptions of an arcade form that evolved under another culture.

What signals the intensity of involvement with Islamic taste, however, is a startling refinement unknown in Christian churches before Mazote: vestiges of painting reveal that Mazote's south transept door was painted over with a design of red and white voussoirs (Pl. 69).[18] It seems to have been accompanied by an ornamental system that is difficult to place in either the Islamic or Christian tradition, except insofar as it links Mazote to Peñalba and Celanova: the walls were white, with the significant exception of bricks in *trompe l'oeil* that patterned the area between the clerestory windows of the nave wall, and three or four rows of such bricks adorned the vaults and the high walls of the crossing just below the vault springers.[19]

Mazote, then, defies any continuity with the potent notion of resistance to Islamic forms suggested for Escalada. Those who decorated Mazote used the same motif for the embellishment of their own place of worship—alternating red and white voussoirs—which declared Islam to be an enemy of the faith in Magius's manuscript. The *Morgan Beatus* illustration had incorporated an Islamic decorative motif into its own prophetic history, giving it a wholly negative meaning within preexisting Christian prophesy. Here, suddenly at Mazote, the form can be comfortably incorporated within a typology that is recognizably Visigothic, one that carries still encased in its forms the myth of continuity and renewal of Christian peninsular rule.

There is, of course, no evidence to support a sudden attraction in this period to Muslim religion or ideology. Such a relaxation of resistance to Islamic cultural forms occurred instead, I think, as northern Christians came to the unconscious recognition of the futility of the polarization of Islam—of setting al-Andalus apart as an other, totally alien. This occurred in part as the momentum of reconquest was spent, and in part as the Mozarabs—the authors of resistance, those for whom impermeability had initially meant cultural survival—were integrated into the northern kingdoms, dispersed and appeased in a Christian world where their message of defiance could not survive a generation, except as a political model for the legitimization of an increasingly confusing number of northern Christian monarchs. But the response is one of interest and admiration that probably had always existed, which was only bridled in the intense resistance movement of the Mozarabs.

Mozarabic immigration, and in particular that of monasteries, began to trail off by the 940s, after three-quarters of a century of movement across the frontier.[20] Indeed, only at Mazote can a foundation that has a substantial connection with monks from Córdoba be linked to an architectural sympathy for Islamic taste. Peñalba was the foundation of the northern abbot Saint Gennadius completed by his followers, and a Galician noble built Celanova.[21]

Though Mozarabs, both secular and religious, continued to move across the frontier, a new rule in Córdoba was changing the Christian experience of Islam. ʿAbd al-Raḥmān III (912–961), the ruler who had so effectively chastised the Christians at Valdejunquera, initiated a moment of great splendor in Córdoba, in which brilliance in culture and learning were matched by an intelligent and liberal attitude toward ethnic and religious minorities. His most significant accomplishment was the assumption of the title of caliph in 929. It was an act that buttressed the independence with which the emirs of Córdoba had always ruled with the public and official rejection of the ʿAbbāsid caliphate in Baghdad.

The infallibility and authority of the new caliph required a cultural setting that defied that of Baghdad, and the emerging Fatimid caliphate in Cairo. As a builder, ʿAbd al-Raḥmān III expended enormous energy and funds in the construction of an entire palatial city, Madīnat al-Zahrāʾ, outside Córdoba.[22] He also embellished the Great Mosque of Córdoba, enlarging the courtyard and framing it with three *riwaq*s, or porticos, and, most significant, constructed a new, larger minaret. A learned man himself, ʿAbd al-Raḥmān III invited philosophers and poets to his court, continuing and intensifying the cultural brilliance of an already worldly and learned capital.

Most significant for the Mozarabs, ʿAbd al-Raḥmān III managed to bring an end both to the Muwallad rebellions and the unrest among Mozarabs with conciliatory social and political policies that soothed the memory of the persecutions of the previous century. The church was livelier than a century before, and there were probably more buildings serving Christian cults.[23] When John of Gorze, ambassador of Otto I, came to Córdoba in 950, he had ample opportunity to record the attitude of the Mozarabs there. ʿAbd al-Raḥmān III had refused to admit John and his entourage to court because of some importunate language in the letter they carried. The bishop of Córdoba, also named John, attempted to explain the most effective way of dealing with the Muslim court:

> We are more condescending with the Muslims. In the midst of the great calamity that we suffered for our sins, we still owe to them the consolation of letting us live under our own laws and of living very closely and diligently the cult of the Christian faith, and they still treat us with respect, and cultivate our acquaintance with affability and pleasure, while, on the contrary, they completely abhor the Jews. In the circumstances in which we find ourselves, our conduct consists in obeying them and pleasing them in all which is not excessive or detrimental to our belief or religion.[24]

The justification offered for compliance—that the Muslims' presence is part of a divine punishment for the sins of Christians, and that they might actually be owed thanks for their tolerance—appeared earlier. But these are the words of the bishop of Córdoba, the position that, a century before, had harbored the greatest official resister to compliance; and, more important, he cites easy social relations with the Muslims as one of the privileges to be gained through accommodation, suggesting an acceptance born of official policy alien to what we know of ninth-century Córdoba.

When the caliph returned the embassy to Otto, he sent a Mozarab, Recemundus, a Christian cleric in charge of the royal chancery, as ambassador, promising to grant him any request once he completed his mission. Sent by the same caliph to Byzantium and Jerusalem, Recemundus clearly attained important status in court, and yet he was well respected in European Christian circles as well.[25] Upon returning to Córdoba, Recemundus composed a work of his own, a *Calendarium* incorporating the feast days of many Mozarabic martyrs whose attitudes to Muslim rules were clearly divergent from his own. ʿAbd al-Raḥmān III had loosened the social and political constraints on Christians just enough to incorporate them within a pacified state. And from the subtly self-congratulatory tone of John of Córdoba's statement, we read the compliment that social acceptance carried. ʿAbd al-Raḥmān III's more gentle posture toward Christians was a policy of seduction quickened by the brilliance of Cordoban culture under the caliphate.

It is not surprising, then, that this reign marks even greater numbers of conversions than the previous centuries; indeed, al-Andalus was well on its way to becoming a Muslim majority.[26] Further, there is greater acculturation among the converts: "bilingualism," Glick tells us, "common in the early centuries, wanes with the fortunes of Christianity" in the mid-tenth century. "The Neo-Muslims," in particular "while retaining certain indigenous and regional customs . . . acculturated massively to Arab norms."[27] The tide of Islamic culture, combined with its military and political ascendancy, was now too forceful for a resistance movement like that initiated by ninth-century Cordoban Mozarabs; and had one sparked, it would have been quenched by the policies of appeasement introduced by the emir who made himself caliph.

Indeed Christians all over Spain succumbed, in the reign of ʿAbd al-Raḥmān III, to the awe Eulogius had barely managed to resist in the reign of ʿAbd al-Raḥmān II.[28] Peñalba, Celanova, and Mazote bear visual witness to a conflicted admiration for Islamic culture that resulted in a selective permeability to its forms. The second half of the tenth century yields a number of traces of this political and cultural vulnerability that leads to adaptation. Sancho I "The Fat," whose obesity prohibited him from mounting his own horse, lost his throne to Ordoño IV after only two years as king of León because of a humiliating defeat at the hands of the Umayyads. Yet when he saw he had to lose weight in order to regain his sovereignty, it was to the caliph he turned for a physician. Seeing the alliance with Córdoba as necessary to his interests in the north, he made a "humiliating" journey to Córdoba with his grandmother, the queen of Navarre, returning in 960, slender, and with a large Muslim army, to regain his own throne.[29] Beginning in 951, the kingdom of León was weakened by almost continual disputes over the throne, to the enormous benefit of Umayyad power. By the 960s, a constant stream of envoys was plying the road from the northern kingdoms to Córdoba with pledges of alliance and fealty to the caliph, as the support of Córdoba was sought even in dynastic disputes between Christians. The presence of Islam had become a fact of life for Spanish Christians; it was part of their functioning political and military structure.

Two buildings of the tenth century emerge as startling documents of high cultural receptivity among northern Christians, an attitude toward Islamic form that might exist simultaneously with these political events or possibly predate them: Santa María de Lebeña and San Baudelio de Berlanga. The first is located in the old kingdom of Asturias, crowned on all sides by the ancient worn peaks of the Picos de Europa, while the second hugs the Islamic frontier deep in the Duero basin. Their appearances are as divergent as their sites and geographic locations, yet I believe they share something fundamental in concept.

Santa María de Lebeña was the private foundation of a new noble, Count Alfonso of Lévana, and his wife, Justa, one that can date anywhere from 924 to the 960s.[30] When one views Lebeña from the exterior, it seems to embody a conflation of Asturian and Mozarabic traditions as well as concerns in building that date from the Visigothic period (Pl. 70). It is constructed of the same frame-and-fill technique that binds Asturian and Mozarabic buildings, including fine ashlar quoining and window frames, and a carnival of richly ornamented roll corbels, like those of Escalada and Peñalba. The exterior volumes mount in a clear, ordered hierarchy. Two low, lateral chambers nestle against the higher roofs of the apse and side arms of a cross plan, from the center of which reaches a fine central tower. Already one perceives a centrally planned church with different ceiling heights, and the corbels suggest a horseshoe-arched interior, perhaps something like Peñalba.

The exterior correctly reflects the details of our expectations concerning Lebeña's interior—the ceiling heights, the plan, and arch shape—but not its space and general appearance (Fig. 28, Pl. 71). For the cross plan and the hierarchy of spaces are all subsumed as Lebeña's lateral spaces are opened up by horseshoe arches of nearly the same height as those that mark the progression to the altar. Low diaphragm walls, supported by compound piers, obscure the variations in ceiling height of the completely vaulted building, giving it a feeling of openness, a lack of direction. Though the building is small and its number of bays limited, it is still difficult at first to orient oneself. "In plan," Gómez-Moreno observed, "the cross often seems to be a primordial organic theme," but here "the elevation robs it of its strength, and the cross plan is consumed."[31]

The structure of Lebeña's interior space defies the hierarchy of volumes that is experienced at Peñalba or Santa Comba de Bande, though these are the monuments with which it would seem most clearly allied. Gómez-Moreno struggled with the paradox of Lebeña: a "perfect crossing of Byzantine type" on one hand, but an elevation that finds parallels in the small, later mosques of Bāb al-Mardūm and las Tornerías, and finally surrenders to a notion of "local aesthetic law."[32] I think it is a good idea to return to those formal contradictions, for their tensions between types and traditions penetrate to the heart of a culturally conflicted time.

Lebeña's traditional, indigenous construction and plan are obscured by the adoption of principles of space and circulation developed in small, private mosques. The earliest example to survive from the Iberian Peninsula is the mosque of Bāb al-Mardūm in Toledo, which dates to the end of the tenth century.[33] This disposition for a smaller, local place of worship must have originated farther east, for we know of examples similar in plan, but divergent in construction and articulation, in Iran and North Africa already in the ninth century (Figs. 29 and 30, Pl. 72).[34] Bāb al-Mardūm is a later example of the kind of building that must have had an impact on the taste of the builders of Lebeña. The open, pavilionlike space, which invites the worshipper to move laterally, is characteristic not just of these two small mosques but of the hypostyle plan in general; of the spatial disposition that is "the most characteristic architectural form of Islam."[35] The tension inherent in Lebeña has to do, I think, with the invasion of an indigenous church type, not just with Islamic decorative forms, but with Islamic ways of using space, of a traditionally Islamic setting for worship.

It would be difficult to assess the level of consciousness with which the patrons and masons of Lebeña embraced the spatial solution employed there. My guess is that it represented a form seen as an attribute of Islamic culture rather than religion; that the ardent resistance Albar had exercised against an entire culture was no longer possible in a Christian state that had incorporated the caliphate into its vision of a practical world. The denizens of the Christian kingdoms could no longer afford an apocalyptic vision that made of everything associated with Islam a Satanic metaphor. A separation was conceived between the political, military, and cultural riches of *Dar al-Islam* and the religion of Muḥammad. It is just such an attitude that John of Córdoba attempted to explain to John of Gorze, the same that permitted Recemundus to serve ʿAbd al-Raḥmān III while paying tribute, in his calendar, to the Cordoban martyrs.

Islam could no longer be isolated, purposefully misunderstood; it could no longer be molded into a corner of a Christian biblical or architectural paradigm. And once this cultural receptivity had occurred, Christian Spain—regardless of the rise and fall of military and political fortunes—could no longer pretend the earlier stance of ignorance and resistance. So by the early eleventh century the Castilian Count

Sancho Garcés (1005–1021), who helped Berber armies defeat caliph Muḥammad II and restore Hishām II to the throne, is recorded as giving audiences reclined on cushions, wearing Arab robes.[36]

Sometime at the end of the tenth or the beginning of the eleventh century, San Baudelio de Berlanga was constructed against the side of a low hill on the wide plain of fortresses and strongholds to the south of the Duero river.[37] It emerges from the hillside, a box or shed in hiding; a tenth-century fallout shelter, opaque and mute to the outer world. Its wonders are within: a simple horseshoe-arched door provides passage to a single space, wide and high, covered by one vast ribbed vault that grows from the center of the room like an enormous palm tree (Pl. 73). To the left is a vaulted apse, and to the right a tribune carried by a little forest of horseshoe-arched arcades. The private sanctuary they hold aloft can be gained by a staircase that hugs the south wall. An opening in that same wall beneath the tribune leads to a small cave, which helps to reinforce the hermetic function usually assigned to Berlanga. The walls now are covered with decoration whose dating is contested, but which might give us a picture of Berlanga as late as the twelfth century.[38]

This "dream architecture," as Fontaine called Berlanga, has, in its unruly brilliance, no conceivable single prototype in Islamic or Christian architectural traditions. Its scholars interpret here a hidden Paradise, one dominated by the palm tree that signifies Paradise in Mozarabic manuscripts. But the vision of Paradise it offers is one that depends on the audacious evolutive manipulation of Islamic forms.

Berlanga's construction, like that of Lebeña, reflects local tradition, and even the rudiments of the arch construction—the manner in which the formerets hug the wall, for instance—suggest some continuity with buildings like Peñalba.[39] But in design and appearance, the central vault also pays a kind of formal homage to the *maqṣūra* of the Great Mosque of Córdoba as it was built by al-Ḥakam II (961–976) in its ribs that are suspended above squinches in each corner.[40] Mosquelike is the space below the tribune, the use of the vault ribs as fields for ornament; and the tiny cupola cradled within the central pier repeats a form in its ribs that mirrors the vaults at Córdoba and those of the mosque of Bāb al-Mardūm. But the building is bold and inventive, and part of that invention depends on the confident manipulation of traditions, both Christian and Islamic, to create something new.

Berlanga's raucous interior is also shaped by its two registers of wall painting, decoration that succeeds in drawing the dialogue with Islam through to the twelfth century. A cycle of bold, simply painted panels of animals, hunt scenes, and a figure occupies the lower architecture of the hermitage, while an intricately painted Christological cycle of monumental figures, at times in architectural settings, covers the upper walls. The upper cycle is a narrative, while the lower cycle is composed of separate images, isolated on deep red grounds, which have defied all attempts to draw from them an iconographic cycle or programmatic meaning.[41] Their juxtaposition as two separate orders is fascinating, and the lower cycle in particular is of interest because of its unique structure and subject matter and because of the parentage of its forms.

Berlanga's lower register cannot in itself be seen as the product of any single Islamic prototype. But it reflects, I believe, an evolution in aesthetic taste related to attitudes toward the cultural products of Islam. Islam serves in some ways as a search for that which is rich and luxurious here, as it always had in the north. During the moments of greatest resistance, and even at times when the frontier seemed most imposing, textiles and objects from al-Andalus carried enormous value. I tend to agree with Camón Aznar and Zozaya that the images here at Berlanga also are derived from Islamic minor arts.[42] Taken selectively from secular objects, the camels, elephants, and hunters of Berlanga were divorced from the jungle of ornamentation that had embraced them in an Islamic artistic context, made easier to see and understand for an audience for whom animate beings are the bearers of meaning in art. The bold ornamental and figural program at Berlanga would then mark, ironically, the incorporation of artistic values associated with al-Andalus, though the motifs appear in a style and context that could not be conceived of in any Islamic religious context.

The images are even farther from carrying the same meanings they had on the Islamic textiles and ivory boxes from which they were gleaned. They evoke, at Berlanga, secular worldly luxury as a metaphor for something that is highly desirable and difficult to attain, and they mark the first entry of such a notion into a monumental context in Spain.[43] It was one, however, that had long been nurtured in the holiest precincts of Christian material culture, in reliquaries whose sacred interiors were lined with Islamic textiles: appropriated swatches of paradise that might press a Koranic inscription up against the relic of a holy martyr. Indeed, reliquaries as important as the Arca Santa in León might themselves display bands of Kufic script, the irresistible display of a material value and level of craftsmanship whose potential to form a metaphor for the power and inaccessibility of the relic overshadowed political or religious associations.

The seeds of this dialogue can be found in Spain by the end of the tenth century, when the Christian kingdoms of the north practiced a kind of selective cultural dependence on Islam, one that paralleled political interpenetration between the two civilizations. Slowly, the resistance to Islamic artistic form had given way as the inevitability of Islamic political predominance and cultural preeminence was accepted in an embattled north, and the likelihood of their apocalyptic end was no longer visible in the muddy waters of the Duero river.

II. In al-Andalus: The Great Mosque of Córdoba

One dark night in the year 750, the head of the ʿAbbāsid family, al-Saffāḥ, is said to have invited all that remained of the Umayyad royal family to a banquet, pretending that he was relenting in his ruthless quest for their downfall. Once seated for the meal, however, the Umayyads and their heirs were slaughtered. A carpet was thrown over the dead and dying, and the banquet continued to the sound of their death cries.[44]

But one Umayyad escaped, the youthful ʿAbd al-Raḥmān, a grandson of the Umayyad caliph Hishām. He flew across the face of North Africa with ʿAbbāsid troops hard on his heels, found allies among his mother's people, and conquered al-Andalus, all in six dramatic and intense years. By the age of twenty-six he had made himself emir of Córdoba.

ʿAbd al-Raḥmān I (756–788) brought the first settled rule to al-Andalus.[45] The extraordinary energy he expended on consolidating Islamic Spain, in suppressing Berber and rebel revolts, never shadowed his vision of an Umayyad state. Though he did not claim the title of caliph, ʿAbd al-Raḥmān never forgot the fate of his family—one he barely escaped himself—and ardently suppressed the pronouncing of the name of the ʿAbbasid caliph in mosques, as was customary, though the effort took a year.

ʿAbd al-Raḥmān I's construction of the Great Mosque of Córdoba must certainly have served not only a growing Muslim population but also part of the creation of an identity for his capital.[46] Built between 786 and 787, it had a simple, conservative hypostyle plan of twelve bays and eleven aisles that ran perpendicular to the *qibla*, like those of the Umayyad mosque of al-Walīd in Jerusalem (Fig. 31).[47] There were no porticos facing the courtyard and only a subtle accentuation of the mihrab aisle, which was less than a meter wider than the other aisles of the prayer hall.[48] Yet in elevation, this unassuming plan exploded into eleven superimposed arcades of horseshoe arches, composed of alternating red and white voussoirs and constructed of bricks and stone (Pls. 47 and 74). The solution is unique, especially on such a large scale and to such strong effect. It is thus often attributed to local developments, in particular to the Roman aqueduct at Mérida, which enlivens two levels of arches with red brick and white stone courses.[49] The adoption of the horseshoe arch shows a clear sensitivity to local tradition, but for that which is most striking in this solution I cannot help but think of one other possibility. Alternating dark and light revetments in the shape of voussoirs appeared in a number of important buildings in Byzantium in the sixth and seventh centuries, and, more important, there is in the archaeological record some suggestion of the same revetment pattern on the arches of Umayyad buildings.[50] In particular some original work has been observed in the largely later revetment of the Dome of the Rock in Jerusalem and at the Great Mosque of Damascus, perhaps two of the most important buildings of the Umayyad caliphate. The appearance of this distinctive decorative form in a totally different, indigenous medium at Córdoba would suggest the attempt to create something of the same appearance without the revetment materials and techniques used at Damascus. It would give meaning to the unusual voussoir arrangement, and suggest as well that ʿAbd al-Raḥmān I's hand as patron affected not a little this carnivalesque solution.

It is known that ʿAbd al-Raḥmān I yearned for his Syrian home. Forever an exile, he named the palace in which he preferred to live outside of Córdoba al-Ruṣāfa, after a summer residence that his grandfather, the Umayyad caliph, had built northeast of Palmyra.[51] It seems likely that ʿAbd al-Raḥmān I constructed a mosque for his nascent emirate that contained lively evocations of an Umayyad Syria that still existed physically and visually even if it were no longer the center of authority for Islam. It was an orientation that voiced political rejection of the Baghdad of the ʿAbbasids, that spoke for the continuation, in this far-off and insular peninsula, of Umayyad Islamic rule.[52]

Of the many meanings encased in the mosque, the notion of the continuity of a basic set of traditional forms survived the whole 250-year Umayyad rule of Córdoba. We know the extent to which the splendor of the reign of ‹Abd al-Raḥmān II (821–852) depended on cultural imports from the East, from the rich cultural center that Baghdad had become, and yet his substantial additions to the mosque—extending it in the direction of the *qibla* eight more bays—follow exactly the plan, elevation, and articulation begun half a century before by ‹Abd al-Raḥmān I (Pl. 68). It is a stylistic dependence that can in no way be linked to a slavish tradition of construction, for the masons of ‹Abd al-Raḥmān II achieved the same effect as his ancestor, in a technique that is at times divergent. ‹Abd al-Raḥmān I had used uniquely *spolia* for the capitals of his prayer hall, and its arches sprang from reused *abaci* of various shapes and widths. Some of the sculpture of ‹Abd al-Raḥmān II's addition is, in contrast, the work of contemporary masons. Many of the capitals are lively, plastic interpretations of Roman originals, and the arches spring from characteristic beveled imposts that thrust like a cool wedge into the space of the arch.[53]

The earliest doors of the Great Mosque of Córdoba reveal the same respect for the continuity of traditional forms. The door of Saint Stephen, begun with the first campaign of the mosque (786–787) and restored in 855, uses a formula of design that survives in the more elaborate doors of the next two centuries: an arch constructed in *tas de charge* with a wide extrados is inscribed in an *alfiz* and originally topped in stepped merlons in relief (Pl. 46).[54] To this basic design can also be added other architectural motifs that serve to enframe and organize, while the whole becomes a field for complex ornament, both geometric and floral.

The notion that the arcades of the Great Mosque of Córdoba still retain in the tenth century an association with a great and continuous Umayyad past is reinforced by additions of ‹Abd al-Raḥmān III (912–961), the tenth-century Umayyad who turned Spain's emirate into a caliphate. It is he who constructed the porticos of the courtyard in an unusual and significant pattern. Though rebuilt, those that survive today retain the alternation of two columns and a pier that mirrors the distinctive and monumental court of the Great Mosque of Damascus as it was constructed by the Umayyad caliph al-Walīd before the ascension of the ‹Abbāsids. To this same courtyard, ‹Abd al-Raḥmān III added a new minaret, to the right of the entrance, just off the axis of the mihrab.[55] The minaret too was in a Syrian style, with its austere, square section.[56]

The new caliph had clearly not forgotton the ancient rights of his family. "By neglecting a title that is due to us," he is recorded as saying, "we would be abandoning a right that belongs to us."[57] While renewing this intimacy with the Umayyad past with new formal and typological connections in his patronage, ‹Abd al-Raḥmān III also brought a new scale of patronage, a new authority and ambition to the Islamic court architecture of al-Andalus. The large part of his patronage was centered on his suburban palace, Madīnat al-Zahrā›,[58] an enormous project managed for some time by his son, al-Ḥakam. It featured a mosque of its own, with five aisles perpendicular to the *qibla*, and a minaret displaced so that the door would align with the mihrab. The most significant structures studied in the ruins of Madīnat al-Zahrā›, however, are its two throne halls: a larger (possibly older) structure and the well-known Salón Rico. Both take the form of three-aisled basilicas with porticos and courts, and they seem to reflect both Umayyad and ‹Abbāsid developments in ceremonial throne rooms.[59]

Upon ascending to the caliphate in 961, al-Ḥakam II turned back to Córdoba, where he began a lavish embellishment of the 180-year-old mosque in 962, a campaign that provides the focus of this study. He enlarged the prayer hall in the direction of the *qibla*, extending the existing arcades twelve bays, always retaining the two levels of horseshoe arches with red and white voussoirs, according to the paradigm provided by his ancestors (Pl. 75).

Al-Ḥakam II diverged from this traditional pattern in the design of his mihrab aisle and in the *maqṣūra*, which forms a grid of three bays in front of the mihrab (Fig. 32). These are set apart because they envelop elaborate domes, three just before the *qibla* and a fourth opposite the mihrab above the first three bays of al-Ḥakam II's addition. The domes, and the space they inscribe, pierce the entire mosque space, for the columns that serve to support them are braced with highly elaborate interlaced lobed arches of carved voussoirs (Pls. 76 and 77).[60]

The twelve bays added to the south of the existing hypostyle structure attenuated it into a longitudinal vessel. Al-Ḥakam's addition directionalized an open hypostyle hall by means of the creation of a strong axis and a hierarchy of forms. On one level, the mosque's design mirrors an interest in spatial focus found in other Islamic monuments, especially in major urban mosques: the creation of *maqṣūras*, or exclusive areas around the mihrab, or the use of domes and accentuated aisles to make an axis or focus attention on the mihrab were developments that had already appeared by the early eighth century in Medina. More recently, they had been accomplished through different designs in the mosque of al-Ḥākim at Cairo and at the Great Mosque of Kairouan.[61] But the means by which this focus, and its accompanying sense of hierarchy, is achieved at the Great Mosque of Córdoba is in many ways distinctive, even unique.

The studies of Ewert in particular have served to trace the often illusive forms axial planning takes in early mosques of the West and the meaning that might have accompanied the development of forms favoring hierarchy. It is possible, as Ewert contends, that on some level the design of the mihrab area of al-Ḥakam II forms part of some such formal dialogue linking it to an Umayyad past.[62] There are, however, unusual variations in the additions of al-Ḥakam II, which suggest that the experience of its interior is tempered by other forces as well.

Where axiality is introduced in mosque plans, it is usually expressed through the widening or heightening of one central aisle, that which aligns with the mihrab, or in the creation of a T-type hypostyle plan, one that accentuates both the mihrab aisle and *qibla* wall. At Córdoba, however, three aisles perpendicular to the *qibla* are accentuated, and their importance as a unit is impressed upon the viewer in a number of ways. First, of course, the design centers on the three domes before the mihrab, concentrating the effect of their brilliant light at the head of the three centered aisles. The same three aisles receive, just before the mihrab, extra columns, between which are threaded the intertwining arches (*tasbīk*: literally interlaced, or embroidered, an inscription tells us),[63] a wild fantasy of architectural members so defiant of architectonic clarity in its design of interwoven forms and continuous, overlapping arcades that it looks like a panel of labyrinthine relief deprived of its ground. The same kind of work marks a square of bays at the beginning of al-Ḥakam II's addition in the mihrab aisle that received a dome as well. Finally, most intriguing and effective in the fusion of the three aisles is the prominence given to those that flank the mihrab: like the mihrab aisle, they culminate at the *qibla*, for the octagonal mihrab is flanked by rooms to either side, two of which are made prominent from the *maqṣūra* because they are gained through smaller doors with decoration that mirrors in diminutive scale the mihrab decoration (Pls. 78–81).

For all that is novel and intriguing in this addition, it still carries several new declarations of a family's ancient heritage. The facade of the mihrab follows the form already established at the mosque, at least with the building of the door of Saint Stephen, and possibly the lost mihrab arch of the *qibla* of ʿAbd al-Raḥmān II, the columns of which are purposefully incorporated and identified in al-Ḥakam II's *qibla* (Pl. 76).[64] The most splendid glance to an Umayyad past surely resides, however, in the mosaics that cover the mihrab entrance, the lateral doors, and the mihrab dome. Entirely aniconic, they are unique in the incorporation of local and Byzantine motifs with mosaic inscriptions to create a complex net of vegetal and geometric forms that combine in an intricate abstract skin for three bays of al-Ḥakam II's *qibla* wall.[65] The story of their execution provided by Ibn ʿIdhārī is a fascinating one:

> Al-Ḥakam had written to the king of the *Rūm* [the Byzantine emperor] on this subject and ordered him to send a capable worker, in imitation of that which al-Walīd ibn ʿAbd al-Malik did at the time of the construction of the mosque of Damascus. The envoys of the caliph brought him back the mosaicist and three hundred twenty five-weights of mosaic cubes that the king of the *Rūm* sent him as a gift.[66]

According to Ibn ʿIdhārī, the assistants assigned to work with the Christian mosaicist soon acquired a talent surpassing that of their teacher, who was then sent home with copious presents.[67] Whatever the actual mechanism by which Byzantine mosaic technique appeared in the Great Mosque of Córdoba, the tradition transmitted by Ibn ʿIdhārī signals for us at least a concern with what Stern calls a "reassertion of Umayyad patronage," by which al-Ḥakam II "doubly legitimized himself."[68]

But there is in the formal structure of the addition, in particular in the basilical plan and space defined by its axial aisle and those adjacent to it, something unprecedented in Islamic religious architecture. Al-Ḥakam II must have been highly familiar with the three-aisled basilical plan in general, for it appears—without, of course, the roomlike mihrab—in his father's palace, culminating in three ornamental blind arches on the end wall.[69] It was hardly surprising to find such a directional, ceremonial space in a royal, secular context, particularly in the palace of the first Umayyad of al-Andalus to declare himself caliph; in adopting such forms, ʿAbd al-Raḥmān III surrounded himself with a visual setting with parallels among those of Umayyad and ʿAbbasid rulers of the center of Islam. However, this particular plan of three privileged aisles is unknown before this time in a congregational mosque, and unknown in any Islamic context when one adds the roomlike mihrab and its smaller dependencies to either side. In the design of the domed *maqṣūra* and the culmination of three privileged aisles of the addition in three rooms, al-Ḥakam II brings to bear upon the mosque new models and new meanings.[70]

It is difficult to ignore the way in which al-Ḥakam II's additions to the Great Mosque of Córdoba mirror, in plan and elevation, Spanish Christian churches. It is a parallel deepened by the mihrab itself, which takes a shape unprecedented before this moment in mosque building. For rather than the traditional form of a niche in the thickness of a wall, the mihrab of the Great Mosque of Córdoba is an elaborate, octagonal room, a space gained through an arch like the apses of Christian churches—the first in the history of mosque architecture to take that form.[71]

The meanings of such forms become more apparent as we consider the closest parallels to the three axial aisles of al-Ḥakam II's additions, those that incorporate not only a three-aisled basilical plan, but one culminating at a short end in three rooms preceded by a partitioned space. Consider the church of San Miguel de Escalada, constructed in 913 (Fig. 18, Pls. 38–43). Its three apses and tripartite choir create a plan identical to those parts of al-Ḥakam II's mosque that hug the *qibla* wall, and the columns and fanciful arches of Córdoba's *maqṣūra* are like wild elaborations of Escalada's elegant altar screen (Fig. 32, Pls. 76–81).

Given the disparity in cultural development, political predominance, and simple financial means between the Christian and Islamic cultures of the tenth-century Iberian Peninsula, there has long been a healthy resistance to viewing al-Andalus as a receiver culture, where appropriation from Christian Spain was concerned, one to which Gómez-Moreno bears elegant testimony: "This surrender of that which is Christian to that which is Moorish does not surprise us. . . . Europe of the tenth century was only in a position to transmit bellicose barbarism."[72] Nevertheless, those aspects of the mosque's plan distinguished here as reflective of a Christian tradition of building are difficult to account for in any other way. They developed far earlier than the invasion, let alone the construction campaigns of al-Ḥakam II. And they are too specific and local in nature to be explained in terms of the common antecedents of mosque and church plans.[73]

Both the liturgy and the architecture of Mozarabic churches belong to an indigenous development: in division of space and disposition of plan, they reflect a design that served the needs of a rite as it evolved over three hundred years. Such formal principles are central to the way church design came about in Spain, so, not surprisingly, they are principles that have been touched upon in a number of these studies. In particular, the tripartite choir preceding three apses responded to the strict separation of clergy and laity and the division of the clergy into three responsorial choirs. The apses and the bays preceding them were bathed in a mystery of sanctity, one that heightened the drama surrounding the priest, as he passed during the liturgy from one world to the other; from the profane world of the nave to the sacred precinct of the choir.

At times the borrowed forms at Córdoba serve a traditional or prosaic function. One of the doors flanking the mihrab leads to the passageway to the caliph's palace, a practical consideration that had existed in many earlier versions of the mosque.[74] But at other times a conflation of uses and meanings can be detected. Thus one of the lateral doors can be related in function so closely to church typology that it may serve to illuminate the function of some flanking chambers in churches built under Visigothic rule. The door to the left of the mihrab served as a treasury, holding, according to Idrīsī, gold and silver chandeliers, vases, lamps, and a precious copy of the Koran that will be of particular interest for this essay.[75] It would seem to have replaced the treasury built by al-Mundhir during his short reign, but unlike the earlier treasury, it is placed in the identical position of a *thesaurus*, which is thought to be the treasury of churches built under Visigothic rule—one of two smaller chambers flanking an apse room—parallel in placement and function to the *diaconicon* of Byzantine architecture.[76]

One means of understanding these appropriations lies in the nature of what is selected. Although we can clearly see the skeleton of a Christian liturgical space in al-Ḥakam II's additions to the Great Mosque of Córdoba, we are still left with a monument that looks nothing like any church ever built. Indeed it is the effect of a basilical space culminating in an oratory—the particular segmented space used in Visigothic-period and Mozarabic churches—that is sought here, not the appearance of a church. And that structure is devoured by the very ornament that sets it apart, a decorative system that, for all of its elaborate newness, strengthens the bond between this section of al-Ḥakam II's addition and the rest of the mosque. Here as elsewhere, the architectural parts create the decoration, arches, columns, and alternating voussoirs. Clearly Christian rite and basilical spatial structure were unacceptable but highly attractive as a focus of religious expression for those who designed al-Ḥakam II's additions to the Great Mosque of Córdoba. They seemed to have entered the architectural and devotional vocabulary of al-Andalus through stimulus diffusion, just as the later Christian military orders can be seen as reinventions of the Muslim *ribāṭs*, stimulated by their existence and yet flushed of all association with the religion it was their goal to destroy.[77]

At Córdoba, then, four domes and complex interlacing arches create a basilical space within the mosque, one that serves to funnel our interest toward the *maqṣūra* and the extraordinary mihrab: that swelling room encased in a double *qibla* wall. The dome at the foot of the additions in the mihrab aisle limits, by virtue of its illuminated bays, the spaces set apart from the rest of the mosque. But for what purpose would such a space be set apart? The original *maqṣūra*, an elaborate wooden enclosure now replaced with an iron railing, only embraced the first two bays immediately facing the three *qibla* doors.[78] Here, clearly, a larger, longitudinal space is set apart by interlacing arches and domes.

What is fascinating is that it must in part have been set apart for a liturgy. The rite, practiced in the mosque at least as early as 1157, centered around a famous Koran about which al-Maqqarī, al-Idrīsī, Ibn-al-ᶜAbbar and Ibn Iyās all speak.[79] Al-Idrīsī describes the ceremony:

> In this room [to the left of the mihrab] there is also a copy of the Koran which, because of its weight, is carried by two men. It includes four leaves of the copy that ᶜUthmān ibn ᶜAffān wrote with his own hand and which is stained with spots of his blood. . . . This Koran is taken [from the room] every Friday morning: two men, who are among the authorities of the mosque, are charged to take it out, preceded by a third, who carries a candle. It is covered with a binding of original work, engraved in the most remarkable fashion, the most delicate and amazing that there is. At the place where one prays

is found a pulpit on which it is posed; the imam gives the customary reading of the *ḥizb* of the Koran, then it is returned to its habitual place.[80]

The three aisles culminating at the *qibla* of al-Ḥakam II's addition to the Great Mosque of Córdoba were set apart not only by their formal properties, but by the procession they harbored. By inhabiting a reserved space in the mosque with a ritual action, a new relationship was created between the *imam* and the rest of the mosque, one defined by architectural form and the exclusionary structure of the procession.

Grabar observed that the ceremony is startling for its resemblance to Christian rite, and he used it to suggest a vision of a tenth-century Islamic community in search of an iconography in local sources.[81] In particular, the procession is identical to one that formed an integral part of the Mozarabic liturgy from at least the sixth through the eleventh centuries. It is described in detail by Isidore of Seville in the sixth century and by Beatus of Liébana in the eighth: the reading of the gospel was preceded by a procession from the altar, where the deacon took the *Liber Sacramentorum* to the lectern, accompanied by a monk with a candle.[82]

It is difficult to accept such a ceremony, performed in an architectural context that so strongly recalls the space of a Christian church, in a mosque that constituted the major architectural centerpiece of the capital of a new caliphate. Al-Andalus, inherited by al-Ḥakam II, was the strongest, most consolidated of all the Muslim rules of Spain. ʿAbd al-Raḥmān III had strengthened its borders against its Christian and Muslim foes and destroyed the last vestige of the shocking Muwallad rebellion led by ʿUmar ibn Ḥafṣūn, which had once threatened the capital itself. Such attention to Christian liturgy and architecture seems out of place in the pomp and splendor of the celebration of a strong new caliphate, especially in the reign of a monarch noted for his particularly pious devotion, one who sought to raise the status of religion in al-Andalus.[83]

What, then, could have been the motive for the adoption of Christian forms and rites? I think a partial answer can be found in the unconscious meaning a number of Christian forms accrued for tenth-century Cordobans. For the conflicts between Christians and their Muslim rulers, while they served at times to polarize certain segments of the population from Islamic authority, also focused new attention on Christian devotion, in particular on its rhetorical nature.

In the century preceding al-Ḥakam II's ascension to the throne, two major revolts had occurred, causing unrest that was only resolved in the reign of al-Ḥakam's father, ʿAbd al-Raḥmān III. Extremely traumatic was that of the Muwallads, who revolted both along the frontiers and in the center of al-Andalus. The most prolonged and threatening revolt came from the fortress of Bobastro, where a kind of guerrilla warfare was maintained by a Muwallad descended from Visigothic aristocracy: ʿUmar ibn Ḥafṣūn.[84] In some ways, the revolt led by Ibn Ḥafṣūn and his sons and their many followers in the countryside was a reaction to the failed promise of their ancestors' conversions, for Islam had not erased for them the social and economic inequality they shared, in the eighth and early ninth centuries, with the "People of the Book." It is not surprising, then, that among their supporters were a large number of Mozarabs as well. Socially and politically their threat was great; at the height of his power, Ibn Ḥafṣūn held all the lands between Algeciras and Tudmir, and at one point he began negotiations with the ʿAbbasid caliph in Baghdad. This Muwallad battle with Córdoba lasted an entire generation, and its culmination was never forgotton by chroniclers. For in an unprecedented and defiant gesture, Ibn Ḥafṣūn reversed the irreversible act of his father, converting publicly to Christianity.

The second revolt was that of the Mozarabs, to which we have already had substantial recourse in this volume.[85] More remote in date from the caliphate than the Muwallad revolts, the acts of the Mozarabic martyrs are important for an understanding of the meaning of this unique building for two reasons: first, because the witnesses of the martyr movement unearth for us a good deal of contemporary opinion concerning building and Christian worship, and second, because the Mozarabs' revolt, and the means by which they accomplished it, had an impact on the rulers of the capital that was not forgotten.

With the Mozarabs, as with the Muwallads, social and economic frustrations were among the sources for the unrest, but it was in both cases the dramatic and rhetorical expression of that frustration that had the most impact on Muslim contemporaries, as it was meant to. The Christians bore witness, accomplishing their goal of martyrdom despite the restraint and horror of Muslim authorities, and a good deal of the church hierarchy as well. Thus it was through the efforts of few that a hitherto relatively sedate community of Christians living under Islamic rule was incited to revolt in a spectacular and dramatic reassertion of their faith. These incidents are interesting to us not only as the general background to the tenth century but because they are part of a dialogue of expression and suppression between Christian subjects and Islamic rulers.

It was noted earlier that when Eulogius complains that Muḥammed I "gave the order to destroy all recently constructed churches and to tear down all new ornaments," he describes the reactivation of traditional laws prohibiting church building.[86] Muḥammad came to power after the lurid and dramatic initiation of the voluntary martyr movement, during which at least twenty-eight Mozarabs had already sought and attained death at the hands of Muslim authorities—all in the last two years of the reign of ʿAbd al-Raḥmān II. Surely his swift act is part of a reaction to the revolt, which must have had a profound effect on everyone in the capital. Eulogius himself alludes to this in a revealing passage concerning Muḥammad's attitude toward the martyrdoms, suggesting his harsh policies were a reaction to them. He says Muḥammad was vexed because many Muslims "fell entirely away [from the faith] piously affirming Christianity, awaiting death with hope of being rescued by Christ."[87]

Muḥammad found himself in the middle of a war fought with rhetoric, and he riposted with strict suppression of the Christians' rhetorical expression. Eulogius and Albar reacted strongly to his acts, for Muḥammad's actions cut to the heart of the problem as they saw it: he constricted the very powers that their violent protest mourned.

In building, the struggle between Christians and Muslims at times resulted in a mutual understanding of the meaning and power of a form. It was not only a matter of the destruction of recently built basilicas, but of those parts of churches that most imposed themselves on the cityscape. Thus, Eulogius recounted how "in the glittering reign of the Arabs the towers of the basilicas of the city were destroyed, the vaults of the temples pulled down, and the pinnacles of the churches cast down."[88] Muḥammad also "pulled down the pinnacles of our temples, even those made in a peaceful and industrious time by our fathers."[89] The reference to towers and the heights of churches is interesting, for it parallels another theme that threads its way through Eulogius and Albar, that of complaints concerning minarets (at times called "idolatrous towers") and the *muezzins* who call from them: "Behold, every day, day and night, in their towers and foggy heights they curse the Lord, when, raising their voice in testimony, they extol their shameless prophet," complains Albar in the beginning of one of the most bitter invectives of his outspoken works. Even more interesting is the manner in which he mirrors this exclamation at the end of the same passage: "But when they hear the sign of the basilica, that is, the sound of ringing bronze, which is struck to bring together the assembly of the church . . . they wail out repeatedly unspeakable things."[90] The reference to towers is not only rhetorical, for Albar continues with one of his complaints concerning the destruction of basilicas. Later Albar complains again that their cries "from their smoky towers" "taint the souls of noble people," and Eulogius tells of how even his grandfather covered his ears to shield them from the cries from the minarets.[91] And yet again, Eulogius speaks of the Muslim repulsion to Christian bell-ringing: "As soon as they hear the sound of clanging metal in their ears, as if beguiled by a false superstition, they begin to exercise their tongues in all kinds of swearing and foulness."[92]

When we recall the restrictions concerning the ringing of bells proposed in the "Covenant of ʿUmar," we see a dialogue emerge whose basic terms concern the power with which towers were invested, especially as the privileged heights from which religious devotion was advertised. It is no wonder Muḥammad made short work of all Christian towers—not just the new ones, for the destruction of which he probably had some legal justification. And surely an earlier part of the same dialogue is the act of ʿAbd al-Raḥmān III, who built a tall minaret as the centerpiece to his additions to the Great Mosque of Córdoba. It is a dialogue continued at least through the thirteenth century in the extraordinary fate of the bells of Santiago de Compostela. Upon sacking the holy center in 997, al-Manṣūr burnt the church but took the bells to Córdoba, where he put them in the mosque. Fernando III, after conquering Córdoba in 1236, sent the bells back to Santiago on the backs of Muslim prisoners.

I believe a similar dialogue developed around two characteristically Christian forms of devotion, modes of expression that find their way to the Great Mosque of Córdoba in the time of al-Ḥakam II: religious procession and the devotion to relics. Recent scholarship concerning al-Andalus and North Africa in the ninth and tenth centuries reveals judgments that remind one of the more traditional laws known to us through the "Covenant of ʿUmar," suggesting they might have been imposed in al-Andalus as well,[93] perhaps at the time of the reimposition of strict limits concerning church building undertaken by Muḥammad I as he came to power. This makes particular sense in light of the view of the "Covenant" as a pattern treaty devised by Islamic schools of law.[94] In particular, the following prohibitions in the "Covenant"—all of which appear to have been repeated and enforced widely in Islam in the ninth and tenth centuries—provide a striking parallel to developments at the Great Mosque of Córdoba: the Christians were prohibited from public processions with crosses, palms, images, or candles in Muslim neighborhoods. In funerals they could not pray out loud or carry candles in processions in the streets occupied by Muslims; they were to recite the divine office in a low voice in church and to ring bells softly.[95]

Clearly the drama and spectacle of Christian worship were recognized by Muslim rulers as having great power. The suppression of processions and towers might have been accomplished not only as a punitive measure toward dissident Christians but as a preventive one, designed to shelter Muslims from these provocative aspects of worship. There is some indication that the impact of Christian ceremony and celebration on the Muslim population was marked. A fascinating judgment recorded in ninth-century Spain prohibits Muslims from taking part in the Christian celebration of the Nativity of Jesus, indeed from accepting an invitation by Christians to join them. This is but one of the official measures that suggests an attraction to Christian observance.[96]

A hint both of the seduction and the danger of Christian ceremony to the Muslims of al-Andalus is voiced in a curious passage of al-Maqqarī, which transmits the reaction of a chancellor of ʿAbd al-Raḥmān V—the poet Ibn Shuhayd—to a Christian liturgy of the beginning of the eleventh century, about a generation after the construction of al-Ḥakam II's additions to the mosque. About the church in Córdoba he said:

> The floor was strewn with green myrtle, and planted with cypress trees; and the tolling of the bells was pleasant to my ears, and the glitter of lamps dazzled my eyes; and then the priest appeared to the worshippers of Christ girded beautifully with belts and sashes. [The worshippers] had abandoned joy and laid aside all luxury. When they sought to drink the water from the vessels, it was done with handful-scoops as if it were wine ponds. [The priest] amid the worshippers sipped long from the cup as if it were a soft-lipped maid, whose fragrance captivated his senses.

> On leaving the church Ibn-Shuhayd extemporized the following verses:

> That which I smelled in the church reminded me of the pleasantness of lost youth. The youth had joy as their symbol, though they prostrated themselves before the Almighty with humility. And the priest, wishing us to stay long among them, began to sing his psalms around us. Offering us new wine, they were like the bat whose safety consists in his hatred for the light. The pleasant youths received it from him, and drank it for their ancestors, and the pork they would eat.[97]

Ibn Shuhayd's attitude, as voiced here, seems that of a tourist seduced by a native ritual—he is moved physically and spiritually but maintains in his account a condescending and critical distance. And it is clear that sensual devices figure prominently in this simultaneous attraction-repulsion: the ringing of bells and drinking of wine; the beautiful vestments of the priests and dazzling candlelight.

The poem suggests to us the lure of the ceremony and spectacle of Christian religion, and acknowledges the power of its ceremonial rites in comparison with the austerity of Islamic ceremonial. But it also shows a high sensitivity to the rite's attractions, one the priest, who aims the splendor of the ceremony at the Muslim observer, seems to acknowledge as well. The content of the rite is disdained, purposefully misunderstood, but the power of the liturgy is nonetheless acknowledged.

Now the relationship between this particular set of documents and the tenth-century additions to the Great Mosque of Córdoba is neither specific nor direct. The sources do provide us, though, with some indication of the unconscious meaning that might have been carried by the forms added to the Great Mosque of Córdoba by al-Ḥakam II and the ceremony practiced there. They tell us first that Christianity was both disdained and admired for its rhetorical qualities, its spectacle. It also seems likely that public displays of Christian religious fervor were suppressed in the ninth and the beginning of the tenth centuries—through the reactivation of traditional laws—just after the Christian outburst that so demonstrated its potency. And yet by the third quarter of the tenth century, a Muslim ruler builds in the Great Mosque of Córdoba an architectural setting that reproduces in many ways that of a church, one that harbored a procession of a strikingly Christian character.

The adoption of both form and rite does not reflect an admiration for or understanding of Christian religious ceremony, but rather it is an acknowledgment of the power of spectacle in religion. In both the rite and the architectural setting in which it is performed, a form disdained as the tool of dissident members of a community is embraced as part of a general acculturation of the values of that now-neutralized group. The rhetorical spectacle and drama that had served the Mozarabic dissidents so well three generations before was now seized upon in reactive adaptation, involving the stimulus diffusion of Christian forms.[98] Now it would appear as the handmaiden of the dignity of the Spanish Umayyads, woven into a hypostyle mosque with interlacing arches, robed in relief and mosaics, in the locus of a traditionally more prosaic rite.

The revolts of the Muwallads and Mozarabs must have provided some unconscious historical motivation for the appropriation of so many non-Muslim forms of expression and display, an adaptation also stimulated perhaps by a recently pacified and rapidly converting indigenous population.[99]

This last supposition is also suggested by the Koranic citations that adorn the lateral door to the right of the mihrab of al-Ḥakam II's addition (the mosaics of the treasury to the left have been lost, probably since the sixteenth century).[100] The Koranic citations of the *qibla* are in general viewed as a curious selection, and have been interpreted by Grabar to suggest a liturgy of prayer, one perhaps linked to the procession of the Koran of ʿUthmān.[101] The specific citations of the lateral door seem to give a particular slant to that program, however.

The texts come from two sūras of the Koran. The first, which is the last āyā of the second sūra, ends with the invocation:

> Pardon us, forgive us our sins, and have mercy on us. You are our only Protector, and give us victory over unbelievers. (II, 286)[102]

The theme of unbelievers is continued in the third sūra, much of which can be said to be a dialogue in which disbelievers are a party. It can be seen also as a prayer to God, in which the Muslim asks God to protect him from becoming as one of the unbelievers. The passage that appears on the side door at Córdoba initiates the theme:

> Lord, do not cause our hearts to go astray after you have guided us. Grant us your own mercy. You are the Munificent Giver. (III, 8)[103]

In the āyā immediately preceding this one is a reminder of the source of Islam's revelation:

> It is He who revealed to you the Koran. Some of its verses are precise in meaning—they are the foundation of the Book—and others ambiguous. Those whose hearts are infected with disbelief follow the ambiguous part, so as to create dissension by seeking to explain it. (III, 7)[104]

The context of the sūra of the inscription—one that concerns the authority of the Koran—contains a hint of the Koran of the processional rite practiced in that part of the mosque, with an assertion of the supremacy and authority of the book of the Muslims to any preferred by nonbelievers.

A parallel with the Gospels is even supported quite clearly in the first āyā of the same sūra, which—with the passage concerning the Koran—is bracketed by the first and second passages actually quoted on the door:

> He has revealed to you the Book with the truth, confirming the scriptures which preceded it; for He has already revealed the Torah and the Gospel for the guidance of men, and the distinction between right and wrong. (III, 3–4)[105]

Read in that distinctive architectural space, in light of the ceremony that took place before it—one that created a metaphor between the Koran and the Gospels—this citation and its Koranic context turn the power of the ceremony and its architectural setting back on a once-dissenting indigenous population. Christian forms here have not only been adapted but subsumed. They function—along with the palatine forms—unconsciously and also on another level: bobbing on the surface of the conscious like a log in the water, enforcing the superiority of one scripture over another, they better the Christians in a language of hierarchy and ceremony borrowed from them.

III. A Muslim Relic

This larger interest in ceremony and pomp followed a general concern with ritual splendor begun by ʿAbd al-Raḥmān III as a natural consequence of the establishment of the caliphate in 929. But the ceremony surrounding the Koran that took place in the Great Mosque of Córdoba was unique, and must have served more specific themes of importance to the caliph as well.

The same passage of Idrīsī that describes the procession in the Great Mosque of Córdoba and those from al-Maqqarī that discuss the mosque transmit a whole series of traditions and arguments concerning the particular Koran that procession honored. Al-Maqqarī cites a passage of a fourteenth-century work of Khaṭīb ibn Marzūq, entitled *Collection of Authenticated Traditions*, which is intended to be a rational accounting of the origins of the volume; a scholarly attempt to appraise what were apparently widespread legends and traditions concerning a Koran that was, Ibn Marzūq tells us, "held in so great veneration by the people of al-Andalus."

He addresses three concerns: that the volume was one of the four famous copies of the Koran sent by the caliph ʿUthmān to Mecca, Basra, Kufa, and Damascus; that it was written by the caliph's own hand; and that "some spots of blood of ʿUthmān are to be seen on it." His analysis admits to its being one of those Korans ordered by ʿUthmān, but he maintains it was requisitioned by him and actually written by others. He contests the notion of Ibn ʿAbd al-Malik that it "cannot be any other than the Syrian one" (that is, the copy ʿUthmān sent to Damascus), opting instead for the Kufa or Basra copy, and he completely rejects the idea that it might have borne drops of ʿUthmān's blood.[106] Those traditions, however, though suspicious as historical fact, are fascinating as meanings that inform this revered object.

First, and most important for our history here, is the association of the Koran with ʿUthmān, a close associate of Muḥammad and caliph from 644 to 656. As only the third caliph in the history of Islam, and the first to introduce the practice of family rule to the caliphate, his prominence was assured, but because some believe he was considered the first Umayyad, ʿUthmān might have occupied a particularly powerful place in history according to the Umayyads of Spain.[107] It seems clear, in any case, that the Umayyad caliphs derived their legitimacy from ʿUthmān, "a legitimate caliph wrongfully killed."[108] The poignancy and emotion of that identification were surely augmented by ʿUthmān's demise, for like the last Umayyads to rule in Syria, ʿUthmān was martyred, slain by mutineers from Egypt in his own home. The Koran then contained political as well as devotional imagery, evoking as it did the Umayyads' past, and their right to openly oppose the ʿAbbāsids in establishing a caliphate in al-Andalus. It is not surprising that some contended it was the particular Koran sent by ʿUthmān to Damascus, for an additional association with the Umayyad capital where ʿAbd al-Raḥmān I's immediate ancestors had governed would have been welcome in such a matrix of meanings.

The notion that the Koran was written by ʿUthmān's hand is an interesting one. It associates the book with the person of the dead caliph in a very personal and graphic manner. That notion appears in a slightly different form in a work of Ibn al-ʿAbbār, who says it was called ʿUthmānī, not because it was written by the old caliph, but because it contained four pages of a Koran that ʿUthmān had pressed against his chest at the moment the daggers of his assailants pierced his body. "Traces of the precious blood of the caliph were still visible in my time," Ibn al-ʿAbbār states, clearly referring to the tradition dismissed by Ibn Marzūq.[109] His observation is corroborated by the geographer Ibn Iyās, and the drops of blood were also mentioned by al-Idrīsī in the midst of his description of the procession of the volume. The key issue here, of course, is not the authenticity of the blood, but that a lively tradition existed that made the revered Koran of the Great Mosque of Córdoba a graphic relic of the death of the Umayyad ʿUthmān. It was a tradition that grew from the dramatic realm of political martyrdom, creating powerful memories and associations that were to be fueled by the relic and sustained in the ceremony that honored it.

There is much in the Mozarabs' movement that could have provided Muslims with a quick and painful education concerning the power and importance of martyrs and relics. Of course, the denunciations and deaths themselves, in their urgent and lugubrious momentum, must have offered the strongest proof of the social and political power of martyrdom, for they created a spirit and cohesion in certain sectors of the Christian community that simply had not existed before. But other details offer a more specific glimpse of attempts on the part of the Islamic authorities to deal, at an uncomfortable proximity, with the creation of martyrs a century before al-Ḥakam II's additions to Córdoba's mosque.

Every martyr's story hints of the cat-and-mouse game between Christians and Muslim authorities, one seeking to preserve the bodies of those killed for solemn processions and excited devotion, and the other hoping to suppress as much as possible the dramatic outburst of piety that seemed to be excited by the martyrs' mortal remains. Already with the earliest martyrdoms, authorities began to burn the bodies of those killed, to keep the Christians from having relics.[110] Muslim authorities next left the bodies of three martyrs unburied for several days by the gates of the palace, to prove they would not be miraculously saved from decomposition, a point their incineration did not serve to clarify.[111] The Christians nevertheless were able to obtain them, and buried them with solemn pomp. Sisenandus's body was left unburied, then thrown into the river; Paul and Theodomirus were also left to decompose, but were stolen by Christians for burial. The truncated bodies of Rudericus and Salomon, "resplendent in beauty," were weighted with stones and thrown into the river, to keep the Christian community from burying them. But Eulogius would have us believe that all of the efforts of Muslim authorities to suppress the martyrs' relics were foiled, and the bodies were found during a miraculous "failing of the sun."[112]

Most striking of all, however, is a passage from Eulogius that describes a martyrdom near the river.

> Some of these from the crowd of people who had come approached the small stones of the river that were sprinkled with the blood of the martyrs. [The Muslims] threw these stones in the water, so that the Christians would not benefit from obtaining relics.[113]

Here, as in ʿUthmān's Koran, a martyr's blood sanctifies an object. While this is a notion neither unique to Spain nor to Christianity, it was clearly of extraordinary sensitivity in the very insular world of al-Andalus, where it was one of the terms of an anguished social and political struggle, one that kept the Umayyad government on the defensive for the reigns of at least two rulers.[114]

Persecution and veneration of the martyrs were cyclical; they created a bloody momentum. By the end of the voluntary martyr movement, Muslim authorities had learned a great deal about the power of the cult of the dead, and of relics: both those of the martyrs' bodies, and those, like the blood-sprinkled rocks, created through association.

Some notion of the political implication of relics was supplied almost immediately, as Cordoban authorities recognized that the creation of martyrs meant the veneration of relics, which in turn served to heat Christian passions. Perhaps this is why Muḥammad I, for all his outrage at the Christians' defiance, abandoned their execution and adopted a more debilitating policy of undermining the church through its own hierarchy.[115] But as early as 858, while the martyrdoms were still occurring, those relics had already attracted international attention to the Mozarabs' cause. In that year two monks from the monastery of Aimoin made a perilous journey to Córdoba to obtain the relics of two of the martyrs.[116] The most striking example of the transcendent power of relics, however, must have been an occasion I have mentioned more than once: Dulcidius's trip to Córdoba in 883 to find the relics of Eulogius and Leocritia for Alfonso III. The official nature of the quest, and the relics' reception in Oviedo, leaves no doubt that they had become the symbol of deliberate Christian distancing from Islam, of political polarization, and the centerpiece for the beginning of the Reconquest.

I believe that the relic of ʿUthmān served a similar purpose, but a parallel one, dissociated from the Christian models it reflects in its conceptual structure. As part of the cultural splendor intended to sanctify and legitimize the new caliphate, it carried in its reminder of the murder of ʿUthmān the later Umayyad martyrdoms as well: the *raison d'être* of the caliphate in al-Andalus. In that highly hierarchical and partitioned space, the solemn procession of that relic directly addressed the problem of legitimacy, religious unity, and devotional fervor in a language of forms learned from Christians but voided of any Christian meaning. Indeed, it was now the language of a rapidly converting population, of socialized Mozarabs, integrated Muwallads and prosperous new Muslims.

Separated from the rest of the Islamic world by geography, history, and the creation of their own authority, the Muslims of Córdoba would turn to indigenous forms of expression to buttress a recently consolidated internal unity and identify their new caliphate, bearing witness to the power those forms radiated by virtue of Spain's heated insularity. First condemned, then acculturated, these roads of expression would be the source of enormous cultural richness in al-Andalus. Far from showing weakness or susceptibility, the reactive adaptation of a liturgical space and a particular kind of devotion served to strengthen the authority of an isolated Islamic caliphate, while weaving it slowly into a fabric of shared cultural meanings.

Conclusion

My heart can take on any form: it is a pasture for gazelles, and a monastery for Christian monks. A temple for idols, and for the Kaaba of the pilgrims, and for the tablets of the Torah, and for the book of the Koran.[1]

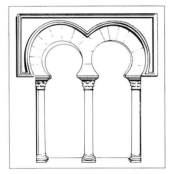 The besieged forms created by the Hispano-Roman church in its slow, subconscious defiance found a constant place in Spanish architecture, remarkably, through the end of the tenth century. These forms can only be called Spanish; nowhere else in Western Europe does such careful partitioning of space combine with the horseshoe arch in elevation. It is no wonder the formula was thought for some time to be originally an Islamic one; it is the means by which the Christian architecture of the Iberian Peninsula is set apart from that of the rest of Europe. But the meaning of this insularity of form goes much deeper than the admission of any apparent exoticism, for at the heart of this separateness is a view of history and the history of architecture that is different from that of early medieval Europe.

The formal system that evolved over the centuries of Visigothic rule became, after the Islamic invasions, first a conscious, then an unconscious historical paradigm for Hispanic Christianity. The Christians' confrontation with a society of economic and political resources that far outweighed its own—one of unparalleled cultural brilliance in the years that form the focus of this book—sent them on a fervent search for self-definition. Their quest was first answered in architecture with a passionate embrace of indigenous historical forms. As early as the tenth century, while the rest of European architecture was engulfed in waves of classical revival, certain Spanish Christians had discovered their own, postclassical history and historical style. It is this self-generated separate identity, this early awkward knowledge born of strife, that sets the Iberian Peninsula—architecturally speaking—apart from Europe, that excludes Spain from the congenial classicizing jumble that forms the core of tenth-century European architecture.

Though Alfonso II lived before this indigenous style was consciously embraced, his choice of classical Carolingian forms for his nascent capital demonstrated a desire to escape the same conflict that would later lead the Christians of al-Andalus to mine their own history for cultural identity. Those forms created a setting emblematic of his independence from the political and cultural impotence of a sequestered church. Alfonso II saw for his new kingdom the possibility not only of an alliance with a stronger power but of the creation of a visual culture that evoked an identification with the world north of the Pyrenees. His gesture was too didactic, too specific, however, to carry meaning very long, and the zealous identification of building with Spain's own lost past would provide the northern kingdoms with a more lasting style that held strong meaning for some and comfortable familiarity for others.

That same indigenous formula would only gradually become permeable to Islamic form, but the significance of that absorption is nevertheless great. It is revealed first in an admission of admiration for the cultural products of Islam—with their separation from apocalyptic history—and next with the embracing of the artistic issue of Islam as part of Christian Spain's architectural image of itself. In the midst of this moment of redefinition, it is crucial that not only the Christians—political dependents—become artistically receptive, but the caliphate as well. The days of the greatest resistance, on the part of southern Christians, to the political and cultural inequality of al-Andalus had spawned rhetorical forms of such power that they inspired not only vigorous suppression on the part of the Muslims but eventual co-option by the empowered culture.

The rupture of Spain's hothouse styles, those intimate architectural dialogues with Islam, began with the fall of the caliphate in 1002. It heralded a series of despotic rules and the disintegration of Islamic unity in Spain. Though strong reformers from North Africa would try twice to unify al-Andalus, the attrition of Islamic grasp on the Iberian Peninsula had begun.

A more complex social and political order arose on the peninsula, one characterized by what Glick has called a "kaleidoscopic shifting of alliances between Islamic and Christian magnates."[2] The *Taifas*, or Party Kingdoms, evolved in lands formerly in the hands of the caliphate, more than twenty of them in the early eleventh century. Their sovereign boundaries, and those of the Christians, were extremely fluid, and the lines of alliance in the many wars and skirmishes that resulted were seldom drawn on the basis of religion.

The Christians of the north experienced other types of changes as well. The eleventh century saw a quick economic enlivening in the northern kingdoms, in part because of the agricultural exploitation of frontier lands, but especially because tribute was now regularly reaching Christian kings in the form of gold, a commodity rarely seen in the north at the height of the caliphate.[3]

The Christian architectural styles traced in this book died with the passing of the tenth century, and with the changes briefly outlined here. Patrons all over Spain would try once again to loose themselves from the bonds of peninsular sequestration through identification with a European community. The architectural expression of this yearning northern gaze was the rush to a new Romanesque vision, one rapidly binding the rest of Europe.

Raoul Glaber tells us in his famous declaration concerning Europe's "white garment of churches" that "every nation of Christiandom rivalled with the other, which should worship in the seemliest buildings," a new proliferation of construction that "befell the world" just after the year 1000, "especially in Italy and Gaul."[4] The embracing of the First Romanesque style in architecture reflected some well-known but nevertheless profound changes in social and economic structure shared by a good deal of Europe.[5] The sheer number of new churches reminds us of the new class of patrons who emerged in this moment. The dissolution of the sovereignty of a number of kings distributed power and wealth to new feudal lords who passed both along to the great monasteries, which became the repository of the old royal prerogatives of pomp and patronage. The enormous amounts of money spent by both lord and monk on building was both a response to and a catalyst for the new, stimulated economy. But in terms of the visual world created by the new buildings, these new patrons abstained, in the earliest years of the eleventh century, from specific reference as a primary motivation for form, away from that use of symbolic typology that made the buildings of their imperial predecessors the reminders of specific ideologies and aspirations.

First Romanesque buildings are bound together instead by their basic adherence to a tradition of construction and the aesthetic system that it spawned, one traced by Armi as the stylistic preoccupation of masons, who in their work became concerned with the abstract expression of the weight-bearing property of support. These are the formal values at the center of Romanesque architecture, and the straight-edged reveals that express them, nascent structures for defining the bay system.[6] As patrons gave priority to the itinerant masons' aesthetic decisions, as they effectively abstained from symbolic intervention, they also stimulated a craftsman's style, which by virtue of the peripatetic nature of the masons' trade and the lively new market for their craft, spread throughout Italy, Switzerland, and southern France irrespective of political boundaries. First Romanesque had become Europe's first international style.

The conditions in Spain were divergent, however, and natural participation in the genesis of First Romanesque on the Iberian Peninsula is limited primarily to Catalonia, where a restive church fought for independence from Islam to the south and feudal interests to the north. There, a land as often as not annexed to France in the early Middle Ages would seize upon First Romanesque masons to rebuild or repair horseshoe-arched churches burnt by al-Manṣūr, or those simply grown small with time.[7] Among numerous buildings constructed in the new style we find strange amalgamations. At San Michel de Cuxa or Santa María de Marquet, vaulted First Romanesque additions in brick-based masonry are grafted unceremoniously to horseshoe-arched churches of the tenth century, leaving the image of a breathless haste to enlarge and rebuild in the new style.[8]

But First Romanesque did not penetrate Spain's interior, where kings actively involved in conquest were the recipients of power and wealth and exercised considerable control over ecclesiastical and monastic affairs. For them, the later acceptance of Romanesque architecture was part of a deliberate, conscious gesture. And so it was that Cluniac reform and Romanesque style invaded the monasteries of the Christian north at the hand of Sancho el Mayor (1000–1035), the first of a series of monarchs who sought for the northern kingdoms an identity bound to that of Europe.[9] The Roman rite soon replaced the Mozarabic rite, despite the resistance at times of Spanish monks who took up arms to defend the liturgy, which, already in Alcuin's time, had been recognized as a Spanish one.[10] Cluniac monks soon presided in the ecclesiastical hierarchy and were presented by monarchs with monasteries along the pilgrimage road to Santiago de Compostela—the most lucrative sources of wealth and power. The alliance between northern Christian monarchs and the Cluniac empire grew both from a desire to codify royal control over the pilgrimage route and

Spain's own church, and also from a fear of the reality of encroaching economic and cultural interdependence with Islam—an ache to bond with the larger European community. The action was the offspring of that early, lonely realization of Spanish identity, and with it, Spanish separateness. "In an anticipation of enlightened despotism," Castro wrote, "Spain for the first time and through the energetic actions of her kings revealed her intention of 'Europeanizing' herself, of assuaging the pains of isolation and self-deprecation."[11]

Only the most insipid hints of a vigorous indigenous style would at first survive the introduction of Romanesque architecture to Spain. Some provincial reminiscence of a basilical style initiated by Alfonso II still clung to Asturias's bland Romanesque buildings, and tiny horseshoe arches are punched into window screens now and then in Aragon and Navarre, like little emblems of a more exotic past. But the distinctive, often didactic styles of early medieval Spain would disappear with the destruction of the caliphate and the internationalization of northern Spain. The very qualities that made Visigothic and Mozarabic churches in particular so effective and powerful—their arresting compartmentalization, their strict, complex liturgical space, which codified the roles of laity and clergy—contributed to their rapid demise. As often specific artistic responses to the fear of identification with an alien culture, the Christian and Islamic typologies and styles explored in these essays held no meaning and lost their *raison d'être* in a still-tumultuous but much more complex world with a less identifiable foe.

The constructional horseshoe arch disappeared with shocking precipitousness in the first decades of the eleventh century. The architectural form that, above all others, had become a Spanish form was studied, nurtured, and revived in the early Middle Ages. In some tenth-century contexts it was understood to be Christian or Islamic in shape and articulation, on the basis of quite subtle differentiations, and yet it seems wildly anachronistic in the context of the buildings of the eleventh century.

Indeed, I think one can say that on the Iberian Peninsula of the early medieval period, the constant overt tension of conflicting cultures possessing divergent formal and architectural systems produced in Spanish Christian patrons a highly sensitized awareness of the structure of their own language of forms, so long as the caliphate provided a single and distinct focus for the identification of Islamic culture. That formal awareness only came with direct and sustained contact with Islam. The Asturians reacted only to the political presence of Islam on the peninsula—few could have known or expressed the artistic presence of al-Andalus at that date—by evoking the architecture of another potent authority. And though the tensions between the Visigoths and Hispano-Romans are acute and have, on both sides, a reactive impact on building, the difference between the artistic contribution of the two groups is based on their relative political and economic positions rather than on strongly perceived, preestablished formal systems that might excite reevaluation on both sides. It is precisely a view of this last kind of entrenched difference in the way a culture uses architecture and its articulation that was provided with the Islamic invasions of the eighth century.

We have seen that the reevaluation that is excited only occasionally results in imitation. The strongest response to the architectural presence of Islam is still the reactive, resistant stance of certain Mozarabs, who identified certain kinds of articulation with Islam but purposefully avoided them at the outset, turning instead to their own architectural history for forms that might hold for them some sort of power or meaning. It need hardly be said that the characterization of Islam that accompanies this stance is a representation, a transformation of the other culture that reasserts its difference, its exteriority.[12] The Mozarabs' meticulous understanding of history and the history of their own architecture is extraordinary. It was born of a care and consciousness that result from cultural suppression—from the hoarding and nurturing of a threatened visual world, and the acknowledgment that that visual context is more than only a metaphor for one's own survival.

The potency and identifiable quality of Islamic architecture, and the conscious association with Islam that it inevitably carries on the Iberian Peninsula, dictated a careful assimilation of Islamic architectural forms. Decorative motifs were first incorporated selectively into the established Christian spatial and decorative structures; then, and only in very selective cases, whole systems for organizing space and worship are incorporated intact. Diverse as these reactions are, they probably represent, along with resistance, a relatively steady state of regard for Islamic architecture as an artistic product. The issue is almost always the extent to which Islamic art, as a direct metaphor for Islamic civilization, might pose a threat to the importance and survival of Christian culture, and vice versa. In that sense, both the moments of Mozarabic resistance and of Islamic absorption can be seen as the strongest reactions to the confrontation of Christian and Islamic artistic culture, while San Baudelio de Berlanga might embody the most passive stance, in its vast inhaling, incorporation, and misunderstanding of the artistic products of Islam.

Where there is sustained contact between the art of two cultures, there must always be change. Rulers—Visigoths and Asturians—made strident and literal statements to support their sovereignty in the face of perceived threats, near or far. Hispano-Romans enclosed themselves unconsciously in a protective space, creating new forms from old ones in defiance of an other. Some sort of impact, be it resistant or receptive, must occur with contact. There is no rule regulating the choices of patrons or masons when confronted with a new, alien form. But I think it can be said that because the Iberian Peninsula housed two cultures that made and used art in such divergent ways, the potential of art and architecture as carriers of meaning and self-definition was underscored, strengthened. With political suppression we saw, more than once, a self-protective entrenchment in form and allusion. With economic and social interdependence came the need, both in the north and in Al-Andalus, to view some aspect of the art of the alien culture as the ideologically neutral product of an acceptable and familiar world, or to flee it.

In both resistance and exchange Christians and Muslims strengthened and enriched their highly distinct visual cultures with shared forms and meanings, and renewed views of their separateness as well. Those tensions and retentions became part of the complex texture of the architectural setting Spanish medieval cultures created for themselves, and also part of a vision they created of themselves. It is clear that Sánchez-Albornoz's notion of an immutable Spanish personality is untenable in the face of such powerful, relentless relationships as those charted in these chapters. But if there is a Spanish experience to be drawn from the monuments of this historical moment, neither is it one that has as its unique terms ethnic, artistic, or religious differences; these become rather the conscious or unconscious terms by which a struggle for cultural hegemony is staged.[13] It is perhaps the creativity born of that shared experience of almost constant struggle that immutably binds the Christian and Islamic buildings of early medieval Spain, and that identifies them both as Spanish.

Notes

Introduction

1. *Ad Opera B. Alcuini, PL,* 101:1333–34.

2. There is only a lively oral tradition among medievalists to attest to Professor Panofsky's having said this. It is, in a way, that tradition, more than Professor Panofsky's authorship, which makes this quote valuable to this Introduction.

3. The methods and goals of this book owe a debt—perhaps not as obvious as great—to Edward Said's *Orientalism* (New York, 1978), to Thomas Glick's *Islamic and Christian Spain in the Early Middle Ages* (Princeton, 1979), and to the works of Meyer Schapiro, especially "From Mozarabic to the Romanesque at Silos" (*Romanesque Art*, New York, 1977, 28–101). Oleg Grabar's *The Formation of Islamic Art* (New Haven, 1973) has also taken quite a toll on the pages that follow.

4. P. E. Russell, "The Nessus-Shirt of Spanish History," *Bulletin of Hispanic Studies* 36 (1959), 219.

5. "[N]uestra moderna inferioridad." *Iglesias mozárabes,* Madrid, 1919, xvi.

6. Castro, *The Spaniards,* Berkeley, 1971, 208.

7. The major works of the polemic are by Castro and Sánchez-Albornoz. Castro's *España en su historia. (Cristianos, moros y judíos.)* (Buenos Aires, 1948) was first. An elaboration of this work appeared in English translation under the title *The Structure of Spanish History* (Princeton, 1954). Sánchez-Albornoz's enormous response is *España: Un enigma histórico* (Buenos Aires, 1956). The polemic is treated in a number of studies, among them: H. Lapeyre, "Deux interpretations de l'histoire d'Espagne: Américo Castro et Claudio Sánchez Albornoz," *Annales* 20:5 (1965), 1015–37; Russell, "The Nessus-Shirt," 219–25; Glick, *Islamic and Christian Spain,* 5–13. In addition, see G. Araya, *Evolución del pensamiento histórico de Américo Castro,* Madrid, 1969; J. L. Gómez-Martínez, *Américo Castro y el origen de los españoles: Historia de una polémica,* Madrid, 1975; J. L. Martín, "El occidente español en la alta edad media según los trabajos de Sánchez-Albornoz," *Anuario de Estudios Medievales* 4 (1967), 599–611.

8. Sánchez-Albornoz, *España,* 1:197–98.

9. Glick, *Islamic and Christian Spain,* 8–9.

10. Russell comments that "in turning from the elucidation of segments of his country's history to an attempt to talk about Spanish history generally, all the frustrations which the subject excites in the Spanish mind have flooded up to submerge Sánchez-Albornoz's professional craft." On his racist stance, see especially Russell's discussion of the treatment Sánchez-Albornoz gives to the Inquisition ("The Nessus-Shirt," 220–21), and the comment in *El drama de la formación de España y los españoles: Otra nueva aventura polémica* (Barcelona, 1973), in which Sánchez-Albornoz suggests that Castro's madness in denying his thesis was due to his "Jewish ancestry" (98, 104; cited by Glick, *Islamic and Christian Spain,* 315–16).

11. Russell, "The Nessus-Shirt," 221; Glick, *Islamic and Christian Spain,* 10.

12. See chapter 1, I.

13. See chapter 2.

14. Or "lo arabizado nuestro," in *A. H.,* 3:357. See also chapter 3.

15. J. Camón Aznar, "Arquitectura española

del siglo X. Mozárabe y de la repoblación," *Goya* 52 (1963), 206–19.

16. Though Gómez-Moreno was simultaneously the premier scholar of medieval Christian and Islamic architecture during the first half of this century, the study of the Islamic architecture of the Iberian Peninsula has been strangely isolated from the study of the architecture of Spain's Christian cultures. For instance, L. Golvin's *L'Art hispano-musulmane* (Paris, 1979) forms part of a multivolume history of Islamic architecture. Recently, however, the studies of Christian Ewert address a number of questions, both against the backdrop of Islam in general and, to some extent, on a peninsular scale as well. (*Spanische-Islamische Systeme sich Kreuzender Bogen*, Berlin, 1968; and with J.-P. Wisshak, *Forschungen zur almohadischen Moschee, Lieferung, 1. Vorstufen. Hierarchische Gliederungen westislamischer Betsäle des 8 bis 11 Jahrhunderts: Die Hauptmoscheen von Qairawān und Córdoba und ihr Bannkreis*, Mainz, 1981).

17. In a recent survey M. Stokstad finishes a discussion of early medieval Spanish art with the comment: "Mozarabic painting, although dazzlingly beautiful as ornament and sometimes persuasive as narrative, exists as an elegant and exotic style outside the mainstream of Western European art" (*Medieval Art*, New York, 1986, 170–73). Beckwith (*Early Medieval Art*, New York, 1964, 206–9) totally excludes Spanish monuments from his textbook, except as a means of showing the transmission of "Islamic influence" (206). Conant judged that a "strong tide of influence from Moorish Spain stunted the promise of Asturian proto-Romanesque" (*Carolingian and Romanesque Architecture, 800–1200*, Baltimore,

1973, 52). In a more specialized study, Jean Hubert assessed the importance of Spanish architecture by the "influence" it exercised on the architecture of other cultures, mentioning major monuments of the Visigothic and Asturian periods briefly and totally ignoring Mozarabic ones: "The Arab conquest put an abrupt end to the art activities of barbarian Spain. . . . the influence of this civilization, whose architecture had been so full of promise in the 7th century, went no further" (*Europe of the Invasions*, New York, 1969, 92–93). See also, for its exclusions, L. Grodecki et al., *Le Siècle de l'an mil*, Paris, 1973, 58, and the response of Bango Torviso quoted above in chapter 3, pages 56–57. Concerning influence in general: M. Baxandall, *Patterns of Intention*, New Haven, 1985, 58–62.

18. In these concerns it is deeply indebted to the works of Meyer Schapiro and Karl Werckmeister in Spanish figural arts in particular, M. Schapiro, "From Mozarabic to Romanesque at Silos"; O. K. Werckmeister, "Islamische Formen in spanischen Miniaturen des 10 Jahrhunderts und das Problem der mozarabischen Buchmalerei," *Spoleto* 12:1 (1965), 933–67. As will become evident in the pages that follow, I have also profited enormously from the research of the late Helmut Schlunk and Manuel Gómez-Moreno, and of my colleagues Jacques Fontaine, John Williams, Peter Klein, and Isidro Bango Torviso.

19. Glick, *Islamic and Christian Spain*, 12.

20. J. Ackerman, "Style," in (with R. Carpenter) *Art History and Archaeology*, Englewood Cliffs, NJ, 1963, 168 and 183.

21. Glick (*Islamic and Christian Spain*, 13–14) contains a valuable explanation of the medieval geographical and political terms for the Iberian Peninsula.

Chapter 1: Visigoths and Romans and Some Problems Concerning Their Architecture

I. Architecture and the Visigothic Rule

1. G. Donini and G. B. Ford, Jr., trans., *Isidore of Seville's History of the Goths, Vandals and Suevi*, Leiden, 1970, 1–2.

2. T. F. Glick, *Islamic and Christian Spain in*

the Early Middle Ages, Princeton, 1979, 28.

3. R. D'Abadal i de Vinyals, "A propos du legs visigothique en Espagne," *Spoleto* 5 (1958), especially 572–85.

4. R. Collins, *Early Medieval Spain*, New York, 1983, 49–50.

5. A popular view is that he hoped to encour-

age with this move the fusion of the two populations. However, Thompson and Glick have convincingly demonstrated that he only repealed a law that was no longer enforceable. Glick, *Islamic and Christian Spain*, 28; E. A. Thompson, *The Goths in Spain*, Oxford, 1969, 58–59.

6. P. de Palol, "Esencia del arte hispánico de época visigoda: Romanismo y germanismo," *Spoleto* 3 (1956), 65–126.

7. Thompson, *The Goths in Spain*, 216–17; Glick, *Islamic and Christian Spain*, 28. D. Abadal too remarks, "il ne faudra pas parler de fusion des races . . ." ("A propos du legs," 556), and cites the survival of laws that carefully maintained the separation between Romans and Goths (573).

8. The dual system of justice was abolished under Recceswinth in 652. However, it is possible that Leovigild's law code applied, to some extent, to Roman and Visigoth alike. See Collins, *Early Medieval Spain*, 124.

9. Glick, *Islamic and Christian Spain*, 29.

10. Donini and Ford, *Isidore of Seville's History of the Goths*, 3.

11. Collins emphasizes the division between local populations and centralized rule (*Early Medieval Spain*, 53). Glick sees the rift as "an intense stratification of society along ethnic lines" (*Islamic and Christian Spain*, 29). Though Goths are often found in the church hierarchy, the struggle for power still often seems to distill into one characterized by Visigoth versus Hispano-Roman.

12. Jacques Fontaine's *Isidore de Séville et la culture classique dans l'Espagne wisigothique*, Paris, 1959, is the most monumental tribute to this theme. Also of interest is his more abbreviated discussion in *L'Art préroman hispanique*, vol. 1, Ste.-Marie de la Pierre-qui-Vire, 1973, 117–24.

13. Particularly from refugees like Saint Donatus, who came to Spain from North Africa. Fontaine, *L'Art préroman hispanique*, 118.

14. I refer to the tradition by which buildings that date before 600 are called Hispano-Roman, and those of the seventh and eighth centuries, Visigothic.

15. Palol, "Esencia." His thesis, which will be the major concern of this section, builds on the studies of Camps Cazorla ("El arte hispano-visigodo," *Historia de España*, ed. R. Menéndez Pidal, vol. 3, Madrid, 1940) and Gómez-Moreno ("Prémices de l'art chrétien espagnol," *L'Information d'histoire de l'art*, 9, fasc. 5, 1964, and studies of individual monuments). Notions of national

unity are also endorsed by Fontaine (*L'Art préroman hispanique*, 126). The formal arguments of Helmut Schlunk (*AH* and with Hauschild in *Die Denkmäler der frühchristlichen und westgotischen Zeit*, Mainz, 1978) are largely parallel, but Schlunk characteristically avoids associating his analysis with cultural or political history except in the most perfunctory chronological sense, even when he treats liturgy ("La iglesia de São Gião cerca de Nazaré: Contribución al estudio de la influencia en la arquitectura de las iglesias prerrománicas de la península ibérica," *Actas do II Congresso Nacional de Arqueología*, Coimbra, 1970, 509–28. There is also a German version: "Die Kirche von São Gião bei Nazaré: Ein Beitrag zur Bedeutung der Liturgie für die Gestaltung des Kirchengebäudes," *MM* 12 [1971], 205–40).

16. See Introduction.

17. Palol ("Esencia," 72–75) relies on the historical notion of social fusion between Hispano-Romans and Visigoths beginning in the years after the conversion of Reccared, and speaks of this fusion creating a new national style: ". . . creemos más justo denominar 'hispanovisigodo' a la concreción nacional del arte 'hispanocristiano' después de la unificación confesional y social, hasta la invasión musulmana . . ." Gómez-Moreno saw in the works of the end of the sixth and seventh centuries an "art neuf qui répond à la puissance wisigothique, si même il ne l'a précédée . . . ; Le qualificatif de wisigothe ou simplement Goth convient à cette nouvelle époque, point de départ de notre Haut Moyen Age, une fois éteinte la tradition classique," and reveals a good bit of competitive national fervor, aimed at France, insisting on "un luxe de structures et de décoration qui élève notre art très au-dessus du mérovingien, comme le prouvent les documents qui exaltent la *manu gotica* au dessus de la *gallicana* en architecture" ("Prémices," 197, 200). Fontaine outlines the "mutation politique et culturelle" which permits one to perceive "en quel sens les arquéologues espagnols parlent volontiers aujourd'hui d'un art hispano-wisigothique, défini comme 'la concrétion nationale de l'art hispano-chrétien.'" He concludes that the many difficulties in documentation, variety, and techniques "n'y doit point exclure la recherche d'une réelle homogénéité," perhaps one that might be linked with his notion of an Isidorian renaissance (*L'Art préroman hispanique*, 126). Only Schlunk avoids the clear identification of the architecture of the

sixth through early eighth centuries with the idea of new nationhood and cultural cohesion, though he seems to endorse such an idea in his discussion of Zeiss and that author's view of the development of Visigothic metalwork (H. Schlunk, "Relaciones entre la península Ibérica y Bizancio durante la época visigoda," *AEArq* 18 [1945], 178–79, n. 4).

18. "Y LA ULTIMA EPOCA—fase isidoriana de paz y fusión étnica y religiosa, de identificación política entre el Estado militar visigodo y la Iglesia hispanorromana—es motivo, también, de la aparición de un arte único donde, en arquitectura y escultura, la tendencia hispanorromana anterior tiene una plena y graciosa evolución y desarrollo." Palol, "Esencia," 75. Author's translation.

19. See note 17. Schlunk, Gómez-Moreno, and Camps Cazorla add to this tradition a strong Byzantine influence in the later period, which Palol also acknowledges. All clearly dissociate that Byzantine impact from the advent of Visigothic power, except for Gómez-Moreno, who is very unclear about the part he sees the Visigoths as having played in the creation of the new style.

20. Thus Palol believes it is best that the national art be called "hispanovisigothic" (see note 17) since "llamar a esta fase artística simplemente 'visigoda' se presta a infinidad de confusiones en especial sobre raíces y parece que implicita, ya, una superioridad germánica que, históricamente, hemos visto no puede probarse, sino que parece más justo pensar que esta supremacía estuvo de parte de los hispanorromanos. El hecho de llamarse visigodo a este arte hispánico tiene sentido, únicamente, por tratarse de un aspecto artístico desarrollado bajo el poder político de este pueblo y que, en el momento de concreción nacional de su Estado, en lo religioso y en lo social, como hemos dicho, se convierte en arte nacional" ("Esencia," 73). It must be observed that this position itself seemed enlightened in view of the Germanic one held by the earliest historians of medieval Spain. For an account of early "Germanism" in historical scholarship, see D' Abadal ("A propos du legs," 542–43). In art-historical literature, Haupt was the main supporter of the Germanic position. See in particular his discussion of San Juan de Baños: *Die älteste Kunst, insbesondere die Baukunst der Germanen*, Berlin and Zurich, 1935, 191.

21. "La era iniciada por Recaredo ... ve aparecer el predominio intelectual y social del grupo hispanorromano sobre la minoría militar visigoda, y la fuerte tutela del Estado visigodo por la iglesia hispanorromana" (Palol, "Esencia," 70). Author's translation.

22. Palol, *Hispanic Art of the Visigothic Period*, Barcelona, 1968, 218.

23. Schlunk from D'Abadal, "A propos du legs," 561. Author's translation.

24. A tradition in which an earlier North African influence has been replaced by the impact of Byzantine models.

25. Camps Cazorla, "El arte hispano-visigodo," 456–57.

26. "... no eran en sí ... un pueblo constructor y arquitecto" (Camps Cazorla, "El arte hispano-visigodo," 456–57). Author's translation. Schlunk, in speaking of monuments of the Visigothic period both in France and Spain, contended that "la evolución de ambos se basa en antecedentes diferentes y se debe no a los godos sino a la población gala e hispanorromana." And, he continues, "faltan, en nuestra opinión a lo menos hasta el momento, monumentos o esculturas que acusen realmente una neta influencia germánica" (*AH*, 228; "Relaciones," 180–81). Palol, as we have seen, excluded the Visigoths from all but an ancillary historical role in the creation of the new art (see note 7), and Fontaine maintains "il est en tout cas bien improbable que les Wisigoths en aient été les médiateurs, et a fortiori les auteurs" (*L'Art préroman hispanique*, 128).

27. J. Vives, *Inscripciones cristianas de la España romana y visigoda*, Barcelona, 1969, no. 303; J. Orlandis, "El reino visigodo, siglos v y vii," *Historia económica y social de España*, ed. L. Vázquez de Parga, vol. 1, Madrid, 1973, 553–60. By the seventh century, churches on the Iberian Peninsula were constructed by workshops of free men who labored for an agreed price. But the use of hereditary servants was also widespread, both in foundations of lay individuals and in monastic foundations. Concerning labor practice, see J. Orlandis, *Historia de España: La España visigótica*, Madrid, 1977; and "El reino visigodo"; T. Hauschild, "Westgotische Quader-bauten des 7. Jahrhunderts auf der Iberischen Halbinsel," *MM* 13 (1972).

28. Author's translation: "no estaría ausente cierta intención política, puesto que había de acrecentar el prestigio de los dominadores a los ojos de la población hispanorromana" (Orlandis, "El reino visigodo," 499). Vives, *Inscripciones*, no. 363.

29. Orlandis, "El reino visigodo," 561; D.

Claude, "Studien zu Reccopolis," *MM* 6 (1965), 178.

Recceswinth's dedication reads: "Precursor D(omi)ni, martiri baptista Johannes / posside constructam in eterno munere sede(m) / quam deuotus ego rex Reccesuinthus amator / nominis ipse tui propio de iure dicaui / tertii post dec(imu)m regni comes inclitus anno / sexcentum decies era nonagesima nobem" (Schlunk, *AH*, 273).

30. Schlunk, *AH*, 280; "Beiträge zur Kunstgeschichtlichen Stellung Toledos im 7 Jahrhundert," *MM* 11 (1970), 182. He urges, however, that it is as North African as Ravennite: "un conjunto insospechado, completamente nuevo" (*AH*, 280). Fontaine makes some fascinating suggestions concerning an aulic iconography at Baños ("Iconographie et spiritualité dans la sculpture chrétienne d'Espagne du IVe au VIIe siècles," *Revue d'histoire de la spiritualité* 50 (1974), 307–8.

31. Restorations were undertaken in 883, when capitals were recut and the vaulting conceivably replaced; in 1523, 1728, and in the twentieth century. What remains that can be dated to the seventh century with some security is the following: the plan in its entirety, including cruciform exterior, three horseshoe-shaped apses, and interior column screens. The original height is undetermined. The western arm of the cross both in plan and elevation is good at least to the springing of the arches, though the arm was shortened by about a third as it was attached to the new church in the eighteenth century. As the western arm was the model for the restored work, its general appearance today cannot diverge significantly from São Frutuoso's original form. For reconstructions and an excellent state of the question, see K. Kingsley, "Visigothic Architecture in Spain and Portugal: A Study in Masonry, Documents and Form" (Ph.D. dissertation, University of California at Berkeley, 1980), 57–75. Dislodged fragments of the capital frieze reveal seventh-century sculpture behind the spiky, sharp acanthus now in place. See Schlunk, *Die Denkmäler*, concerning reconstruction. Kingsley, "Visigothic Architecture," and A. de Azevado, *O Mausoleu de S, Frutuoso de Braga*, Braga, 1965, offer dissenting views as regards function.

32. This comparison has been made by many. See Schlunk (*AH*, 281–83) and Fontaine (*L'Art préroman hispanique*, 163–67, 406) for the best discussion of models. The possible "Byzantinism" of Spanish seventh- and eighth-century architecture has been widely discussed. In particular, Schlunk contended transcendent influence on buildings of the seventh century, through South Italy and Sicily. I am exploring instead a conscious and ideological preoccupation with Byzantine forms in court, of which São Frutuoso is probably the only surviving architectural witness. See Schlunk, "Relaciones," 196, and 191 (where he does address Leovigild's interest in Byzantine ceremony); *AH* 292. Schlunk early established that Byzantine impact on the Iberian Peninsula is unrelated to Byzantine occupation of the peninsula ("Relaciones"). For Galla Placidia, see F. W. Deichmann, *Ravenna: Haupstadt des spätantiken Abendlandes*, Wiesbaden, vol. 2:1, 1958–76, 61–90.

33. Schlunk, *AH*, 282–83. Schlunk, however, explains it as a unique example of direct contact with Byzantium, "distincto del Castellano" (283). Fontaine (*L'Art préroman hispanique*, 166) also favors Justinianic prototypes. On the cross plan with five cupolas, see R. Krautheimer, *Early Christian and Byzantine Architecture*, New York, 1981, especially 252–53. The triple-arched screen, though interpreted by local masons, recalls the more monumental Justinianic examples at San Vitale in Ravenna, H. Sergios and Bakchos in Constantinople, and of course at the H. Sophia. See Krautheimer, chap. 9; E. H. Swift, *Hagia Sophia*, New York, 1940; T. Mathews, *The Byzantine Churches of Istanbul: A Photographic Survey*, University Park, PA, and London, 1971, 42 and 262; Deichmann, *Ravenna*, 226.

34. For an overview of the Spanish masonry tradition, see Hauschild, "Westgotische Quaderbauten."

35. F. C. Nock, *The Vita Sancti Fructuosi*, Washington, D.C., 1946, 86–98; 122–25. He would never realize his voyage east.

36. Claude, "Studien," 178; Fontaine, *L'Art préroman hispanique*, 110; J. N. Hillgarth, "Coins and Chronicles: Propaganda in 6th century Spain and the Byzantine Background," *Visigothic Spain, Byzantium and the Irish*, London, 1985, 482–508; F. Mateu y Llopis, "El arte monetario visigodo," *AEArq* 18 (1945), 34–58.

37. Hillgarth, "Coins and Chronicles"; Mateu y Llopis, "El arte monetario," especially 50–58. Mateu y Llopis believes Recceswinth also adopted Byzantine dress (50–51). See also Hillgarth ("Popular Religion in Visigothic Spain," *Visigothic Spain, Byzantium and the Irish*, 8), who contends that "long before anointing became normal the king had been recognized . . .

as a Byzantine monarch, the successor of Constantine."

38. D'Abadal, "A propos du legs," 584–85. See, in general, 541–85.

39. R. Collins, "Mérida and Toledo: 550–585," *Visigothic Spain: New Approaches*, ed. E. James, Oxford, 1980, 212–19. Collins documents Leovigild's eagerness to "build up the spiritual arsenal of Toledo at the expense of its rivals" (214). In *Vitas Sanctorum Patrum Emeretensium*, building becomes a part of that competition (*Vitas Sanctorum Patrum Emeretensium*, ed. J. Garvin, Washington, D.C., 1946, 199–217).

40. Such an image of kingship might also have protected the ruler from the violent instability attending the notion of transfer of power in Visigothic rule. Both Chindaswinth and his son, Recceswinth, experienced difficulties associated with the transition of royal power. Bishop Braulio of Zaragoza, a friend and correspondent of Fructuosus, urged Chindaswinth to associate Recceswinth with the throne while the old king's reign was still vigorous, a technique practiced by Leovigild as well (Barlow, *The Iberian Fathers*, 2, 83–85; Collins, *Early Medieval Spain*, 36, 115–16).

41. The Visigothic penetration into the church, which began in the second half of the seventh century, existed primarily at the level of church hierarchy and was less common in a monastic context. See Orlandis, "El elemento germánico en la iglesia española del siglo VII," *Anuario de estudios medievales*, 26–64. It is hard to give Fructuosus a political profile. He was clearly not as deferential to the court as Isidore (Hillgarth, "Popular Religion," 41), and his ecclesiastical biographer suggests the topos of an aristocratic convert to the ideals of the Hispano-Roman church—one who is respected by the élite of his own class but can also resist them in the name of the church. However, it is also possible that this account reveals more the wishes of its writer's class than reality. More contentious propagandistic use is made in *Vitas Sanctorum Patrum Emeretensium* of the bishop Masona, a Visigoth who converts to, and sides with, the Hispano-Roman church at the time of the Arian king Leovigild (Garvin, *Vitas Sanctorum Patrum Emeretensium*, 199–217).

42. Demographically it is unlikely that Visigoths were involved in the patronage of the churches discussed in the second part of the chapter, even those, like Fructuosus, who might have dedicated themselves to the church. The in-

filtration of bishops into the episcopate does not seem to be answered by any movement of similar scale on the level of the lower clergy. Even so, it is possible that the developments I discuss in part II of this chapter might have found their way into buildings founded by Visigoths or used by priests who were ethnic Visigoths. The key is that these formal developments to be discussed are the reflection of attitudes toward the liturgy and taste promoted over two centuries by Hispano-Roman patrons and users, concerns that began long before Visigoths made their way into the church structure in the second half of the seventh century. See also Orlandis, "El elemento germánico."

II. Ritual and Resistance in the Hispano-Roman Tradition

43. Schlunk, *AH*, 227. Fontaine has added to this a historical context for the ardent cultural interest in North Africa (*L'Art préroman hispanique*, 36–42).

44. Palol, *Tarraco Hispanovisigoda*, Tarragona, 1953; *Arqueología Cristiana de la España Romana: Siglos IV–VI*, Madrid, 1967, 51–59, with extensive bibliography and a state of the question.

45. Hauschild, "La iglesia martirial de Marialba, León," *BRAH* 163 (1968), 243–349; "Das 'Martyrium' von La Alberca [prov. Murcia], Planaufnahme 1970 und Rekonstruktion versuch," *MM* 12 (1971), 170–94. Hauschild shows that Marialba was transformed into a centrally vaulted martyrium with the addition of four piers and a central vault not long after its original construction.

46. Serra de Rafols, *La villa romana de La Dehesa de la Cocosa*, Badajoz, 1952; Palol, *Arqueología*, 136–45.

47. The appearance in 1906 of Gómez-Moreno's "Una excursión a través del arco de herradura" (*Cultura Española*, vol. 3, 1906, 786–811) set the tone for a careful historical study of the horseshoe arch in Spain and it is to Camps Cazorla that we owe the careful consideration of proportion and technique that has since dominated its study (*Módulo, proporciones y composición en la arquitectura califal cordobesa*, Madrid, 1953). A more recent study of significance is Caballero's "La 'forma en herradura' hasta el siglo VIII, y los arcos de herradura de la iglesia visigoda de Santa María de Melque" (*AEArq*

50–51 [1977–78], 323–64]. Caballero extends the antiquity of the form on the Iberian Peninsula to Celtic funerary monuments (351). Of particular concern is his separation of the decorative and architectural traditions, which are considered together by Gómez-Moreno, and the addition of a large number of monuments that were unknown when Gómez-Moreno wrote his seminal article. Caballero sees the advent of the horseshoe arch in architecture in the fourth century and attributes it to a general wave of Eastern influence. He sees the fifth century as the apogee of the horseshoe arch in plan in Spain, after which certain variations begin. The earliest monuments of Spain to show it in plan are: Clunia, house no. 1, third/fourth century; Arnal, villa (Portugal); Torre Cardera, baths (Portugal); and Marialba. Other horseshoe arches in plan include San Cugat des Valles, perhaps Odrinhas (Palol, *Arqueología*, 144–45), and Brunel near Quesada, the crypt (at least) of the basilica at Segóbriga, Idanha a Velha, Valdecebadar, and São Frutuoso de Montelios. The last two establish continuity of the form through the seventh century. See also Schlunk and Hauschild, *Die Denkmäler*, 12.

48. See an interesting article by Caballero, in which he suggests that the horseshoe arch can be associated in the early period with a funereal function ("Algunas observaciones sobre arquitectura española de 'Epoca de Transición' [Cabeza de Griego y visigoda]," in R. González Ruiz, ed., *Innovación y continuidad en la España visigótica*, Toledo, 1981, 69–103).

49. Inscriptions in the floor mosaic of Santa María de Tarrasa indicated the extent to which the faithful might approach the altar, and where the priests and other notable participants in the liturgy were to sit. The altar was clearly not closed off with a chancel barrier as was characteristic by the seventh century (Schlunk and Hauschild, *Die Denkmäler*, 25). These authors imply that the first evidence of chancel barriers in Spain does not appear until the second half of the sixth century (39–41) at Aljezares, or perhaps the end of the fifth or beginning of the sixth century at Bobalá-Serós (165).

50. This is a difficult issue that remains unaddressed by contemporary scholarship because of the lack of any building of sure Arian patronage in Spain. Outside Spain the Arians co-opted orthodox buildings for their cult initially. Cabrol and Leclercq (*DACL* 1/2:2814–20), who treat Arians in general and do not mention Spain in particular, point out that the Arians tried always to conserve Catholic discipline, customs, and liturgy, and cast doubt on the possibility of the existence of a building typology that diverges significantly from that of Orthodox rulers (2814, 2819). Note, however, Collins's contention that the Arian liturgy was probably conducted in the Gothic language (*Early Medieval Spain*, 30, 40–41). A case in point might be found in the ancient city of Reccopolis—founded in 578 by King Leovigild—and the church commonly associated with it, Zorita de los Canes. We know of Reccopolis from Joannis Biclarensis (*Chronicon*, ES, 6:388). The urban center itself was an ambitious and heady undertaking that exhibited the clear impact of contemporary Byzantine planning (Claude, "Studien zu Reccopolis," 167–94). The church and city are fascinating, particularly as a probable part of the patronage of a Visigothic ruler, one who was Arian, and keenly concerned with the growth of that faith. The church excavated in the ruins of Reccopolis is the only monument that can be viewed as a possible site for Arian cult in Spain. Yet most of the remains of Leovigild's basilica can be understood in the context of the orthodox tradition of building. Beltrán ("Monedas de Leovigildo en el tesorillo de Zorita de los Canes," *Numario Hispánico* 2 [1953], 19–52) doubts this is Reccopolis, but uniquely on the basis of negative evidence. Palol, while not openly endorsing Beltrán's view, seems to take his doubts seriously (*Arqueología*, 90). Schlunk and Hauschild, however, embrace the traditional interpretation of Zorita de los Canes as the church of Reccopolis without reference to Beltrán's dissent, and even present evidence that suggests the church to be a possible palatine chapel (*Die Denkmäler*, 169). Gómez-Moreno accepts Zorita as the church of Reccopolis without question ("Prémices," 199); Fontaine supports the idea with caution (*L'Art préroman hispanique*, 1:412–13).

51. This moment is called "period of transition" by Palol, who parallels it with the period beginning with the first political incursions of the Visigoths in Hispano-Roman Spain, and ending with the architectural "unity" he feels is initiated by the conversion of Reccared (*Arqueología*, 69–70). Caballero comments further on this period in "Algunas observaciones sobre arquitectura."

52. A funerary inscription of 550 provides the terminus for Segóbriga's construction, which might have begun in the second half of the fifth century. Segóbriga is known through the work

of J. Cornide, who published the drawings of Melchor de Prado in the final years of the eighteenth century ("Antigüedades de Cabeza de Griego," *Memorias de la Real Academia de Historia*, vol. 3, 1799, 197–207). Recently Caballero has called for recognition of the drawings of Palomares, in whose plans he places the highest confidence ("Algunas observaciones sobre arquitectura," 75). For Palomares's plan, see R. Puertas Tricas, who also speaks for its preferable reliability: "Notas sobre la iglesia de Cabeza del Griego, Cuenca," *BSAAV* 33 (1967), 49–80. See also H. Losada Gómez and R. Donoso Guerrero, *Excavaciones en Segóbriga*, Madrid, 1965; H. Schlunk "Esculturas visigodas de Segóbriga," *AEArq* 18 [1945], 305, and with Hauschild, *Die Denkmäler*, 43. Caballero sees the foundation as one of two campaigns: a first funereal and commemorative, and a second congregational and liturgical, which develops with the ecclesiastical importance of the site (72–73). Schlunk's identification of Henchir de la Mechta si Salah as the closest prototype for Segóbriga has been generally accepted until recently (*AH*, 229). In "Origins of the Early Christian Architecture," Maloney rejects this parallel, citing no evidence of a crypt, and the possibility that the North African plan might constitute nothing more than an elaboration of a flanking chamber plan, a type unrelated to Segóbriga. She suggests instead the Libyan church of Chafagi Aamer (118).

53. This is the number accepted by scholars, though Fernández's plan suggests nine columns, including those engaged to either side.

54. Vives, *Inscripciones*, 77, 83; Palol, *Arqueología*, 93–97.

55. Schlunk and Hauschild, *Die Denkmäler*, 43. Maloney believes there might have been two levels in the east end: "Origins of Early Christian Architecture," 117.

56. Schlunk and Hauschild, *Die Denkmäler*, 43; Palol, *Arqueología*, 95–96. The apse had both burials and an altar. Palol also cites the opinion of Hubert ("Les églises à rotonde orientale," *Art du Moyen Age: Actes du III Congrès International pour l'Etude du Haut Moyen Age*, Lausanne, 1954, 316 n. 27), who questions if the east end of Segóbriga might not have appeared as a rotunda above ground, a hypothesis that finds no support in other scholarship.

57. Palol places great emphasis on the advent of the crossing in early Spanish architecture: *Arqueología*, 69–70, 87–95; "Esencia," 96.

58. For Fraga, see R. Puertas Tricas, "Trabajos de planimetría y excavación en la 'Villa Fortunatus', Fraga (Huesca)," *Noticiario Arqueológico Hispánico* 1 (1972), 71–81; J. de C. Serra Rafols, "La villa Fortunatus de Fraga," *Ampurias* 5 (1943), 4–35; Palol, *Arqueología*, 88–89. For San Pedro de Mérida, see A. Marcos Pous, "La iglesia visigoda de San Pedro de Mérida," *Beiträge zur Kunstgeschichte und Archäologie des Frühmittelalters*, 1962, 104–30; Palol, *Arqueología*, 97–99.

59. Bobalá-Serós contains the first chancel plaques found *in situ*, dating from the first part of the sixth or the last part of the fifth century (R. Pita and P. de Palol, "La basílica de Bobalá y su mobiliario litúrgico," *Actas VIII Congreso Internacional de Arqueología Cristiana, 1969*, 1972, 383–401). Chancel barriers are recorded at Aljezares, Mérida, Saamasas near Lugo, and Barcelona in the second half of the sixth century and perhaps at Fraga sometime in the sixth century. The eventual dating of the church of Torre de Palma might prove the early existence of a *solea* or protected passageway at an earlier date, a significant but divergent development (Maloney, "Early Christian Double Apsed Churches," 129–43).

60. Schlunk believes Syrian and North African examples "stimulated" the high wall at São Gião once the church established a desire to separate clergy and laity ("La iglesia de São Gião," 526).

61. The term "Visigothic" is traditionally applied to all architecture constructed on the Iberian Peninsula during the later period of Visigothic rule: the seventh and eighth centuries. Because of the obvious pitfalls it poses for a study that seeks to separate the interests of a Visigothic state and a largely Hispano-Roman church, I will try to avoid using it, referring instead to architecture "of the Visigothic period" or "built under Visigothic rule."

62. This is not to say that they do not reflect a general interest in Eastern architecture, which is transformed by a local aesthetic of enclosed and partitioned space. See Schlunk, *AH*, 271.

63. Originally located on the Esla river, San Pedro was moved to accommodate the building of a dam. It is first documented in a donation of Alfonso III of 907, but its date is presently accepted to be in the last part of the seventh or the beginning of the eighth century (M. Gómez-Moreno, *Catálogo monumental de España: Provincia de Zamora*, Madrid, 1927, 66–67). The western nave was reconstructed in the Middle Ages, as the inferior masonry and the irregular

quality of certain aspects of the nave arcade testify. Scholars have found at San Pedro evidence of two earlier campaigns, which are thought to have followed hard upon one another, or simply to represent the intervention of a second master mason (Gómez-Moreno, "San Pedro de la Nave: Iglesia visigoda," *BSCE* 4 [1906], 448–52; Schlunk, *AH*, 289–98; Schlunk and Hauschild, *Die Denkmäler*, 126–38; Palol, *Hispanic Art*, 147–84; Kingsley, "Visigothic Architecture," 39–49; 186–91.

64. Like São Frutuoso de Montelios, Santa Comba de Bande was reconstructed in the course of the ninth-century repopulation. The limits of that reconstruction have been the source of some contention among scholars. Its original date is established by a document of 982 (Archivo Histórico Nacional, Zamora: 986B, folios 97–100), which in turn mentions villages repopulated by Alfonso III in 872 that had been abandoned for about 200 years. They included a manor, "together with churches built in ancient times . . . of Santa Comba, Virgin and Martyr, which were lying abandoned [or in squalid condition] for two hundred years or more." One Odoynos, "as far as he could," "built and held the deed which Lord Odoarius had confirmed to him" (Translation: Kingsley, "Visigothic Architecture," 34). Santa Comba must date, then, sometime in the second half of the seventh century. Kingsley (34–39) includes an excellent review of the document, signaling in particular different meanings for the terms *exqualido*, by which the abandoned state of Santa Comba is established, and *hedificasset*, which can, but not necessarily, indicate some sort of construction. Because of the abundant possible meanings for *aedificare*, and its qualification in the document with the phrase *in quantum ualuisset*, Kingsley concludes that Santa Comba "still stood after 200 years, was in squalid condition, and perhaps, required some renovation" (35). Schlunk and Hauschild (*Die Denkmäler*, 120–23) do not acknowledge any reconstruction, contending that even the vaulting of the crossing and east end is original, citing as substantiation the restored brick vaults of São Frutuoso de Montelios. They fail to cite any dissenting opinion. Such objections are nevertheless widespread. Though the more radical suggestions of Puig i Cadafalch (*L'Art wisigothique et ses survivances*, Paris, 1961, 137–39), who believed it to have been completely rebuilt in the ninth century, have never gained credence, the more moderate reconstruction proposed by Palol—

suggesting the reconstruction of the vaults— seems reasonable (*Hispanic Art*, 91, fig. 67; 160). Caballero and Latorre recently contended that the entire apse was rebuilt by Odoario after 872, in an argument connected with their work concerning Santa María de Melque. In a study that cites recut stones, a turned column in the apse entrance, an *Opus Signinum* floor that they feel corresponds to the period of the Reconquest, and a masonry break at the southwest corner of the apse itself, they assert that none of the actual work of the apse can be dated to the Visigothic period. Caballero and Latorre also suggest that Bande's original apse must have been horseshoe-shaped within, an argument based on proportional and modular comparisons to Melque itself ("Santa María de Melque y la arquitectura visigoda," *IX Symposium de Prehistoria y Arqueología Peninsular*, Barcelona, 1983, 309–12). Caballero's studies of Melque, and in particular his treatment of the history of the horseshoe arch, are of great value, but there is no trace of any horseshoe form in the apse plan of Bande; indeed, there is real reason to believe that the lower courses of the apse were still in place when the building was restored in 872. The southwest masonry break cited by Caballero is really the beginning of the lost wall of the southern sacristy, the foundations of which continue clearly just below it. The apse in fact is firmly coursed into that sacristy wall, suggesting constructional continuity. The turned column of the apse entrance was surely reused even in its Visigothic context, and a new floor does not require a new set of walls. It is rather in the eastern wall of the apse that can be found the real vestiges of reconstruction. Whereas the stones of the lower courses exhibit the eccentric but careful fitting typical of Visigothic masonry, many of those in the upper courses are recut. One very characteristic stone, a large rectangular ashlar with a tiny square cut out of the lower right-hand corner, can be seen reused in the apse at Bande, but not refit carefully with another stone as it would have been in its original, Visigothic context. Rather, the notch is filled in with mortar, a custom unknown in the Visigothic ashlar tradition, and unlikely in view of the aesthetic concerns that accompany it. The masonry break that results is a clear one: it forms a wide triangle, arching steeply over the central window of the apse. It supports the notion that Bande received a new apse vault, accompanied by some rebuilding of the upper courses, and a certain awkwardness in the overlapping of window voussoirs with the new vaults. The studies of Núñez reaffirm this idea, in particular his observation that the use of brick in upper vaults and windows corresponds to an Asturian technique. Núñez's also is the most compelling suggestion for the reconstruction of the blind room above the apse (M. Núñez, *Arquitectura prerrománica*, Madrid, 1978, 86–94). Such a room would provide the most satisfactory explanation for the window that now peeks awkwardly from behind the roof of the apse. If the reconstruction of the upper courses of the apse included an upper room as at San Pedro de la Nave, this would be a dark, interior window, and the alternation of light and dark at Comba de Bande would be identical to that of other monuments constructed under Visigothic rule. Such changes are, in the end, minor, and I thus agree with Núñez and Palol that the reconstructions of the ninth century did not greatly alter the seventh-century monument.

65. Núñez, *Arquitectura prerrománica*, 87–88.

66. Despite suggestions that they served as "refuge rooms," or the sites of secret treasuries, I would rather concur with Schlunk, who sees them as serving aesthetic considerations (*AH*, 294). Such an idea is borne out by the similarly blind spaces above the apses of San Miguel de Escalada, in this case clearly useless from a practical point of view, not only for a lack of entrance, but because it even lacks the window of the pre-invasion monuments.

67. Núñez, *Arquitectura prerrománica*, 87–88.

68. The placement of these screens and those of most known Visigothic period Asturian and Mozarabic churches was studied by Schlunk in "La iglesia de São Gião."

69. Ulbert contests the universality of a three-part liturgical division, because at Valdecebadar near Olivenza there is only evidence of one chancel: an apse chancel. The church is in a very imperfect state of preservation, however. See T. Ulbert, "Die Westgotenzeitliche Kirche von Valdecebadar bei Olivenza," *MM* 14 (1973), 213; *Reallexicon zur byzantinischen Kunst* 3 (1973), 202.

70. The four are San Juan de Baños, Santa María de Quintanilla de la Viñas, São Gião de Nazaré, and São Pedro de Balsemão. San Juan de Baños is dated by an inscription set in the wall over the main church entrance to 661, a date confirmed by excavations of 1956 and 1963. Accord-

ing to tradition, the foundation was made in thanks for King Recceswinth's cure at local mineral baths (Eugenio Muñoz Ramos, "El agua que bebió Recesvinto," *BSCE* 1 [1903–4], 164–65). Restorations of 1865, 1898, and 1903 added a new roof, cornice, and bellgable. Its only original exterior walls are those defining the central apse, the portico, and the exterior of the lateral sacristies: the side-aisle walls, and most of those defining the lateral sacristies, were replaced in the Middle Ages. These now hug the apse in the manner of a tri-apsed church, but the sacristies were originally separated from the sanctuary by arms that stretched to the north and south, like those of the recently discovered church of Alcuéscar (See S. Andrés-Ordax, "La basílica hispanovisigoda de Alcuéscar [Cáceres]," *Norba* 2 [1981], 7–22; and in particular L. Caballero, "Hacia una propuesta tipológica de los elementos de la arquitectura de culto cristiano de época visigoda [Nuevas iglesias de El Gatillo y El Trampal]," *Arqueología Medieval Española*, 1987, 62–97. The porch and the nave arcade are original. Plaques of the chancel barrier were found in excavation, with other seventh-century material. For San Juan de Baños, see P. de Palol, *Excavaciones en la necrópolis de San Juan de Baños [Palencia]*, Madrid, 1964; *La basílica de San Juan de Baños*, Palencia, 1988; Schlunk, *AH*, 273–80; Gómez-Moreno, "Prémices," 185–212. The entire nave of Quintanilla de la Viñas is lost, but excavations have revealed the foundations of a three-aisled basilica, with sacristies projecting to the north and south of the choir. Vestiges of springers indicate that the apse and side aisles were groin vaulted. However, Gómez-Moreno's suggestion that the crossing was covered with a dome can no longer be accepted (Gómez-Moreno, "Prémices," 207). In the west, a three-part porch is interpreted by Schlunk as a tribune like that of São Gião, with lateral rooms. It seems clear that the projecting blocks which form a band around the interior were intended to be carved, binding the interior in the same chain of *rinceau* as the exterior. The idea that they might be rustication or binding (Whitehill and Clapham, "The Church of Quintanilla de las Viñas," *Antiquaries Journal* 17 [1937], 16–27; Camps Cazorla, "El arte hispano-visigodo," 585; Schlunk and Hauschild, *Die Denkmäler*, 230–31) seems unlikely. Attempts to date Quintanilla on the basis of the monograms of the eastern exterior reliefs have proved sterile. A tenth-century date was suggested by the previous generation (Puig i Cadafalch, *L'Art wisigo-*

thique, 133–36; Whitehill, "The Church of Quintanilla de las Viñas," 16–27) on the basis of a document naming a certain Momadona as a benefactress of the church. Kingsley again ("Visigothic Architecture," 49–52) gives the most levelheaded account of the documentary evidence, pointing out that it witnesses a donation, not a foundation. Current opinion favors a seventh- or early eighth-century date on the basis of the sculptural and architectural style (Schlunk and Hauschild, *Die Denkmäler*, 141–52; F. Iñiguez Almech, "Algunos problemas de las viejas iglesias españolas," *Cuadernos de la Escuela Española de Historia y Arqueología en Roma*, vol. 7, 1955, 79–89; Palol, *Hispanic Art*, 178; Camps Cazorla, "El visigotismo de Quintanilla de las Viñas," *BSAAV* 6 [1939–40], 125–34; Kingsley, "Visigothic Architecture," 49–57, 191–93. Fontaine, in *L'Art préroman hispanique*, 1:205–9, suggests it might have been begun before 711 and finished soon after). The small church of São Gião de Nazaré is the only member of the group discussed here which is not built in the fine ashlar masonry typical of seventh-century churches, but is nevertheless in a remarkable state of preservation. São Gião's date is assured by the sculpture and certain aspects of its plan. The apse was probably the only vaulted space. See F. de Almeida and E. Borges Garcia, "Igreja visigótica de São Gião," *Actas del IX Congreso Nacional de Arqueología*, Valladolid, 1965, 460–62; "São Gião, descoberta e estudo arqueológico de un templo cristão-visigótico na região de Nazaré," *Arqueología e Historia*, 8a series, vol. 12, 1966, 339–48; and Schlunk, "La iglesia de São Gião," 509–28. Only the eastern extremities of the nave wall and the apse entrance to São Pedro de Balsemão date from the Visigothic period; its nave arcade and virtually all of its other walls have been reconstructed, in particular in the seventeenth and eighteenth centuries. However, the surviving masonry, its beautiful and eccentric relief fragments, and the apse entrance in both detail and general character serve to date São Pedro to the second half of the seventh century. See J. Pessanha, *Arquitectura pre-románica em Portugal: São Pedro de Balsemão y São Pedro de Lourosa*, Coimbra, 1927; and F. de Almeida, "Arte visigótica em Portugal," 122–30. Of monuments not mentioned here: the church of Vera Cruz de Marmelar was probably also a basilica, but more study is required to demonstrate this (Schlunk and Hauschild, *Die Denkmäler*, 123–24). Only the crypt remains of San Antolín de Palencia, the

martyrium that was probably destined to hold relics brought to Palencia by King Wamba in 672. It can be more easily identified with the persistent Spanish plan of a two-level martyrium (La Alberca, Santa Leocadia in Oviedo) than with three-aisled basilicas (Schlunk, *AH* 283–85). I do not include in this consideration small single-naved chapels like those at Siero and Pedro.

71. Fragments of the springers can still be discerned in the western wall of the choir.

72. The relationship of nave to choir is difficult to document at San Juan de Baños. The main apse is wide and open, because its horseshoe profile does not partition the apse space, but rather defines the edge of its vault. Palol remarks that it is "almost the same dimension as the width of the central nave, that is to say, characteristic of the old paleochristian liturgy." He finds this to be different from most Visigothic churches of the seventh century, "which tended to close the opening to the presbytery, for a liturgy which was not as open as in the first centuries of Christianity" (*La basílica de San Juan de Baños*, 29. Author's translation). But fragments of a chancel barrier were found in excavations at San Juan, and these complement reconstructions of its original east-end plan, suggesting that a lost partition reinforced the transition implied in its stretching sacristy arms. We can mourn with Palol that "in the way in which sanctuary and basilical naves are connected there is a certain rupture in the harmony of structure, which suggests, if not two different building dates, at least an effort to renovate the plan and elevation in order to preserve the basilical tradition" (*Hispanic Art*, 128–30). He urges, however, that the vestiges "do not permit thinking of the existence of an authentic transept . . ." (30). Caballero's work at Alcuéscar opens up the problem substantially ("Hacía una propuesta").

73. Schlunk and Hauschild, *Die Denkmäler*, 160–61; Palol, *Arqueología*, 51–62; Fontaine, *L'Art préroman hispanique*, 1:409).

74. Fontaine offers a fascinating analysis of Quintanilla's decoration: "Iconographie et spiritualité," especially 306–7.

75. Cabrol believes its ultimate roots lie in a primitive Roman liturgy. I would rather concur with Jungmann, who believes it to have grown from the early Ambrosian rite, at a time when the political links between Milan and Spain were strong. Cabrol and Leclerq, *DACL*, 12:390–490; J. Jungmann, *The Early Liturgy*, London, 1959, 227–30. On the rite's expansion, see D. M. Hope,

"The Medieval Western Rites," *The Study of Liturgy*, ed. C. Jones, G. Wainright, and E. Yarnold, New York, 1978, 230.

76. An exception to this might have been made for the movement of the clergy from the first to the second choir in double-apsed churches with *solea*, a practice that seems to have died out by the seventh century (Maloney, "Early Christian Double Apsed Churches," 135–43).

77. Among the other problems of interest are the issue of an entrance and the use of the lateral chambers. On the entrance, see A. de Ceballos, "El reflejo de la liturgia visigótico-mozárabe en el arte español de los siglos VIII al X," *Miscellanea Comillas* 43 (1965), 303. Caballero also speaks briefly and cautiously of architectural provision for the gathering of processions in architecture of the Visigothic period in "Santa María de Melque y la arquitectura visigoda," 330. Gómez-Moreno believes these rooms functioned as cells for monks ("Prémices," 204). More widely discussed in the literature are the very common eastern rooms. At least one of the rooms is provided with a very reduced opening to the aisle or choir of the church, suggesting a need for proximity but excluding them from the actual liturgical space. One of these chambers has been identified with the *Preparatorium*, a place for ornaments and cult objects. The problem was posed first by Iñiguez Almech ("Algunos problemas," 97). It is Ceballos, however, who makes a convincing argument for their association with the *Preparatorium* and *Thesaurus* of liturgical texts ("El reflejo," 309–14). A study in progress by Ms. E. Quevedo promises to dispel some of the confusion surrounding this issue. Puertas Tricas has identified the use of the words *Preparatorium* and *Thesaurus* in the texts. The *Liber Ordinum* describes a small procession the day of the celebration of the office *In Coena Domini* that leaves from the *Preparatorium* and proceeds to the altar for the stripping of its ornaments (*Liber Ordinum*, vol. 82, in M. Ferotin, *Le Liber Ordinum en usage dans l'église wisigothique et mozarabe*, Paris, 1904, cols. 190–91; Puertas Tricas, *Iglesias hispánicas*, 134). A similar ceremony is prescribed after the termination of the Holy Thursday Mass, when the clergy proceeds from the *Preparatorium* to the altar to prepare its austere presentation for Good Friday (Puertas Tricas, *Iglesias hispánicas*, 134). In the *Preparatorium* is kept the cross after the ceremonies and procession to the church of Santa Cruz (*Liber Ordinum*, vol. 84, cols. 199–200; Puertas

Tricas, *Iglesias hispánicas*, 134). The second of these dependencies has been recognized as the *Thesaurus* (Ceballos, "El reflejo," 309–14). This is clearly a treasury in the *Vitas Sanctorum Patrum Emeretensium*, which speaks of King Leovigild seeking the holy tunic of Santa Eulalia there (Garvin, *Vitas Sanctorum Patrum Emeretensium*, 212; Puertas-Tricas, *Iglesias hispánicas*, 143). But it is also in the *Thesaurum* that the clergy secretly light their candles for the Easter vigil, before returning to the darkened sanctuary obscured by curtains with their dramatic, flickering lights (*Liber ordinum*, vol. 86, 208–11; Puertas Tricas, *Iglesias hispánicas*, 143). The *Preparatorium* and *Thesaurum* are clearly associated with similar functions to the *Prothesis* and *Diaconicon* of Syrian liturgy, but I disagree with some scholars that the parallel is exact (Ceballos, "El reflejo," 309–12; and Iñiguez Almech, "Algunos problemas," 95–100, who is more cautious). Perhaps the use of such rooms is associated with the appearance of the *solea*, which Maloney suggests is the result of direct Syrian impact on the Iberian Peninsula (Maloney, "Early Christian Double Apsed Churches," 135–41). Jungmann's contention that the Mozarabic liturgy contained no offertory of the people during Mass suggests the necessity for a dependency where gifts might be received and prepared beforehand, though this issue is yet to be resolved (Jungmann, *The Early Liturgy*, 228–29). The sources further caution us against an ironclad identification, for the function assigned to both rooms by the texts is confusing: in one context the *Preparatorium* serves as a sort of treasury, it is where the ornaments are stored when the altar must be stripped. It is also, however, the origin of the procession to the altar that precedes the removal of the ornaments, evidence perhaps that it is, as its name implies, the site of preparation for the rite. The same confusion exists in the use of the word *Thesaurus*: in one context it also describes a treasury, that in which the relic of Santa Eulalia was kept; but in another, it too serves as the site of liturgical preparations.

78. Schlunk, "La iglesia de São Gião," contains the most complete discussion of this council and its relation to chancel barriers. Caballero ("Monasterios Visigodos: Evidencias Arqueológicas," *Primer Seminario sobre el Monacato. Codex Aquilarensis*, 1988, 41–43) offers some additional questions in a recent publication. It is to Schlunk that we owe our present knowledge of the placement of these barriers in the majority of the

churches mentioned here. Schlunk was not the first to link the barriers to the Fourth Council of Toledo. Ceballos ("El reflejo," 316), in the first comprehensive analysis of the relationship between architecture and liturgy, cited it as well, and Iñiguez Almech ("Algunos problemas," 91–92) understood the liturgical function of the sharp division between choir and nave. The action in Spain is internal, uncharacteristic of currents in other parts of Europe. Canon 4 of the 567 Council of Tours contains a comment on the distribution of the laity and clergy, which, while it limits the movement of the laity during vigils and Masses, makes it clear that they have free access to the sanctuary for prayer, and for receiving communion, as was the custom (C. J. Hefle, *Histoire des conciles*, vol. 3, Paris, 1909, 186. See also H. Beck, *The Pastoral Care of Souls in South-East France During the Sixth Century*, Rome, 1950, 149). Markus sees this canon, and the one immediately preceding it, as an assertion that "the restrictions on the movements of the laity sanctioned by custom are sufficient; there is no need for the complete closing off of the sanctuary space by a screen to conceal the Holy of Holies from the gaze of lay eyes" (R. A. Markus, "The Cult of the Icons in Sixth-Century Gaul," *Journal of Theological Studies* 29 [1978], 155). See also L. Nees, "The Iconographic Program of Decorated Chancel Barriers in the pre-Iconoclastic period," *Zeitschrift für Kunstgeschichte*, 1983, 25–26.

79. Schlunk, "La iglesia de São Gião," 515–16. They might possibly exist at Aljezares as well, and at Bobalá-Serós. See also Maloney, "Early Christian Double Apsed Churches," 135–43. Maloney believes that such passageways were the means by which the distinction between the Mass of the Faithful and the Mass of the Catecumens was accentuated in the intriguing group of double-apsed churches. This might apply also to double-choir churches like Bobalá-Serós. Indeed the use of the barrier to effect a desired separation might at first have been adopted in the moment of Syrian impact suggested by Maloney. Such usage does not seem to survive, however, to the seventh century.

80. In *Die Denkmäler* Schlunk and Hauschild suggest that the earliest Christian architecture in Spain makes little or no use of chancel barriers, and that these come into use in the mid-sixth century. At Tarrasa, they demonstrate that the sanctuary was not closed off and chancels were not used. The next chancels they date are those

of Bobalá-Serós, to the end of the fifth or beginning of the sixth century. This would seem to revise an equally tenuous statement written by Schlunk only five years earlier. In "La iglesia de São Gião," he stated that chancels had existed on the peninsula since the paleochristian period, though he does not hint at what date this might suggest. The only church he cites before the sixth century that might have possessed a chancel is San Fructuosus del Francoli at Tarragona (a different monument from the later monument in Tarragona's amphitheater), which he mentions with the following disclaimer in the text: ". . . si ha de darse crédito a los antiguos planos y dibujos de reconstrucción, hubo incluso un cancel que se extendía transversalmente por las tres naves. Pero este edificio pertenece a otra categoría y no puede compararse con los mencionados anteriormente" (516). Because he includes no reference, one assumes he is referring to the reconstruction of Serra Vilaro, whose reconstructions of San Fructuosus are reviewed by Palol (*Arqueología*, 53–59). Serra Vilaro proposes the existence of a chancel on the basis of a small stringer wall located in front of the apse. As its location is not in keeping with later churches of the Visigothic period with proven chancel barriers, this seems an unlikely explanation in this case, especially since chancels are otherwise undocumented in this period. I do not, on the contrary, oppose the notion that they existed earlier than the sixth century. I wish rather to suggest that their use became important and compulsory at that time. This is amply documented by the archaeological remains.

81. Schlunk, "La iglesia de São Gião," 516; M. Gómez-Moreno, "Exploraciones en Santa Comba de Bande," *Boletín de la Comisión Provincial de Monumentos de Orense* 14 (1943–44), 47–51.

82. Schlunk, "La iglesia de São Gião," 509–15. The nave entrance to the choir at Quintanilla de las Viñas is lost, but the side aisles communicated, as we have seen, through narrow, constricted doors of similar proportions to those at São Gião.

83. It is the appearance of the arcade in conjunction with the low parapet in two divergent building and cultural traditions that suggests for both Escalada and Lena a lost prototype among buildings of the Visigothic period. Schlunk relates this type to the Visigothic buildings that offer the most complete separation: São Gião and Quintanilla de las Viñas, pointing out that they all share a separate access to the choir for the

clergy ("La iglesia de São Gião," 519–20). He associates this formula with monastic, as opposed to parochial churches, but his evidence is very sparse. We do not know if São Gião was monastic or parochial, and Santa Cristina de Lena, a significant member of the group, was not monastic.

84. Schlunk's use of the term *iconastasis* is misleading here. See J. Walter, "The Origins of the Iconastasis," *The Eastern Churches Review* 3 (1971), 251–52. A templon, or open screen of low parapet slabs, occasionally accompanied by colonnettes supporting an architrave or epistyle, existed from the early churches of Constantinople to the time of Justinian (T. Mathews, *The Early Churches of Constantinople: Architecture and Liturgy*, University Park, PA, and London, 1971, 162–71; A. Epstein, "The Middle Byzantine Sanctuary Barrier: Templon or Iconastasis?" *Journal of the British Archaeological Association* 134 [1981], 1–2). There is no evidence for the use of curtains there before the eleventh century (Mathews, *Early Churches*, 162–71), as there is at Escalada, where the total obscuring of the east end from the nave would serve a similar effect as the separation wall at São Gião. The use of curtains might questionably be associated with Syrian liturgical practice (170). Other examples of screens or walls that separate nave from choir can be found in a few dispersed examples in Europe and North Africa. The Merovingian Oratory at Saint Martin at Angers had a triple-arched screen with a larger central arch (G. Forsyth, *The Church of St. Martin at Angers*, Princeton, 1953, 57–58 n. 126); S. Croce in Gerusalemme at Rome (Krautheimer, *Early Christian and Byzantine Architecture*, 51), Cimitile (Chierici, "Di alcuni risultati sui recenti lavori intorno alle basiliche Paoliniane," *Rivista di Archeologia Cristiana* 16 [1939], 69–70); in Italian examples, at least some of which are dependent on Constantinopolitan developments (R. Farioli, "'Pergulae' Paleocristiane del Territorio Ravennate," *Atti del VI Congresso de Archeologia Cristiana*, 1962, 115–21; P. Zovatto, "La Pergola paleocristiana del sacello di S. Prosdocimo de Padova e il ritratto del santo titolare," *Rivista di Archeologia Cristiana* 34 [1958], 137–58); in Kerratin in Syria and Announa in North Africa, where Schlunk has compared separating partitions to that at São Gião ("La iglesia di São Gião," 525–26); and in at least two striking examples in England: Saint Mary's at Reculver (which has a triple-arch screen) and Brixworth (which features a pierced wall similar to that at São Gião). For English examples, see

H. and J. Taylor, *Anglo-Saxon Architecture*, Cambridge, 1965, 1:112–13; 2:506–8; A. Clapham, *English Romanesque Architecture Before the Conquest*, Oxford, 1930, pl. 3. Only on the Iberian Peninsula do we see the consistent separation of the nave from the choir, such an eclectic assortment of high partitions and low barriers, and such a flexible, lively variation in their height and use in conjunction with a wide assortment of plan types. This occurs because their use was mandated in Spain on a peninsular scale, clearly not the case in France, England, or North Africa, where examples are scattered, and often associated with a particular type of plan. See, in general, Schlunk, "La iglesia de São Gião," 521 n. 2; Forsyth, *The Church of St. Martin at Angers*, 57–58 n. 26; T. Mathews, "An Early Roman Chancel Arrangement and Its Liturgical Functions," *Rivista di Archeologia Cristiana* 38/1 (1962), 73–95.

85. For the high chancel screens, there is archaeological evidence of curtain rods in the tenth century at Escalada (Schlunk, "La iglesia de São Gião," 521 n. 2) and of an indeterminate date at Alava and Duratón. The wooden beam that held the curtains at Escalada can still be seen, and holes for such a rod survive at the churches of Alava and Duratón. For these last two, see Iñiguez Almech, "Algunos problemas," 75. The existence of curtain poles at Asturian churches with only low chancel screens suggests that their Visigothic counterparts might also have shared them (Ceballos, "El reflejo," 315). In particular, a fascinating visual document is found in the fragment of a chancel plaque from Córdoba that shows curtains hanging from an arched and columned screen, and later images of curtains blocking a sanctuary entrance, or pulled back from it, abound in the wealth of Mozarabic illuminated manuscripts. Iñiguez Almech ("La liturgia en las miniaturas mozárabes," *Archivos Leoneses* 15 [1961], 51), distinguishes between "cortinas," or curtains, and "velos," or veils, for use in liturgical contexts, and sees the former rather than the latter in Mozarabic miniatures, though he knows both to have existed in pre-Romanesque churches. See Iñiguez Almech's figures 11 and 15, however, which show curtains hanging from a rod before an opening, clearly distinguishable from figure 12, in which curtains before openings revealing altars might well be curtained entranceways, as emblematic of the church in general. Iñiguez Almech also sees shutters or grates in several miniatures, which he relates to the

grates that existed at San Pedro de la Nave and Quintanilla de las Viñas. There the grates served to close the opening from the crossing into the side aisle. The liturgy "continued being mysterious and isolated from the faithful," according to Iñiguez Almech (71). See also Mathews, *Early Churches of Constantinople*, 165. Texts also reveal the use of curtains: consider the curious oration of the *Liber Ordinum* for the blessing of curtains and their frequent mention in liturgical and religious texts. Puertas Tricas (*Iglesias hispánicas*, 147, 288) cites some of these: none suggests where they were hung. A large number of textual references to curtains also appears in donations to parochial churches and monasteries, and in inventories. Gómez-Moreno (*Iglesias mozárabes*, Madrid, 1919, 334) contains a list of the documents. These last also are later in date. See also Caballero, "Monasterios visigodos," 41–43.

86. Ulbert, "Die Westgotenzeitliche Kirche von Valdecebadar bei Olivenza," 202–7.

87. Vives, *Concilios*, 206.

88. As Schlunk observed, a chancel of San Pedro de la Nave must have been in the nave because of the high bases on the crossing columns, and because the side aisles were closed off from the nave to about half its length ("La iglesia de São Gião," 523–24).

89. Schlunk and Hauschild, *Die Denkmäler*, 221–23. San Pedro de la Mata, however, might be an exception: a second altar pedestal in the crossing suggests a double choir or an auxiliary altar for the communion of the people, as Caballero suggests. See "Algunas observaciones sobre arquitectura," 84. His assumption that the tribune at São Gião is an "elevated choir" does not seem the most likely of the various possibilities, and his failure to acknowledge other reasons than double choirs for a tripartite chancel division detracts from his arguments.

90. Excavations at San Juan de Baños revealed the existence of chancel barriers, but their exact placement is unknown. See Schlunk and Hauschild, *Die Denkmäler*, 209 and note 72.

91. The church of Quintanilla de las Viñas would require the same kind of division, but I have some doubts if it held to that rule at all because of its diminutive size. Such three-part choirs that cut across the nave and side aisles of a basilica can be seen at the later churches of San Miguel de Escalada and San Salvador de Valdediós, to name two examples. Concerning the miniature, J. Williams (*Early Spanish Manuscript Illumination*, New York, 1977) discusses the tab-

ernacle as an "allegorical prefiguration of the Christian sanctuary" and points out that the altar was "shaped according to contemporary usage in Spain." He suggests the image was "ultimately based on a Jewish prototype" (60).

92. For text, see Díaz y Díaz, "Los prólogos del 'Antiphonale visigothicum,'" *Archivos Leoneses* 8 (1954), 231. Author's translation. See also J. Vives, "En torno a la datación del Antifonario Legionense," *Hispaniae Sacra* 8 (1955–56), 117–24.

93. Schlunk, "La iglesia de São Gião," 521 n. 2; see note 84 above.

94. "Al comparar la iglesia de São Gião con otros edificios de la Península, creemos haber llegado al convencimiento de que en ella nos encontramos con una iglesia monástica, en la que el santuario hacía el oficio del coro, que en la antigua liturgia 'mozárabe' adquirió una importancia especial por el realce que se había dado al canto polifónico" ("La iglesia de São Gião," 526). Schlunk believes that the low chancel screens, which are generally accompanied by western entrances, occur in parochial churches, while the high ones, with separate entrances for clergy through the transepts, are monastic. For the difficulties with this position, see note 83 above and Caballero, "Monasterios visigodos," 41–43. Mathews and Epstein see an earlier closing off of the choir in monastic contexts than in other churches in Byzantium, but the date is much later than those which concern us in Spain (*Early Churches of Constantinople*, 171; "The Middle Byzantine Sanctuary Barrier").

95. There is a fascinating coincidence, not noted by Schlunk, that links his idea with the suggestions I will make presently. Cabrol speaks of antiphony in the church undergoing a "revolution" in the face of the seductive chanting of the Arians in the east in the fourth century: "On peux donc constater dans le courant du IVème siècle, sur plusieurs points, et précisément là où la lutte contre les ariens fut la plus ardente, que les orthodoxes pour mieux résister aux hérétiques répondirent à leurs chants populaires par d'autres chants populaires" (*DACL*, 1/2:2817). The case, alas, is too remote geographically and chronologically to provide us here with anything more than a bit of pleasant intrigue.

96. Díaz y Díaz, "Literary Aspects of the Visigothic Liturgy," *Visigothic Spain: New Approaches*, ed. E. James, Oxford, 1980, 66, 75. Hillgarth presents a picture of popular religion that includes at once a liturgy of "mystery and transcendence rather than participation," while the

church incorporated the "uneducated mass . . . into its ranks by initiating it into a ritual cycle which covered the whole life of man from baptism to death" ("Popular Religion in Visigothic Spain," in *Visigothic Spain, Byzantium and the Irish*, London, 1985, 22–25 [23, 25]).

97. Jungmann, *The Early Liturgy*, 229. Also see "Die Abwehr des Germanischen Arianismus und der Umbruch der Religiösen Kultur im Frühen Mittelalter," *Zeitschrift für Katholische Theologie* 69 (1947), 53.

98. Jungmann, "Die Abwehr," 74, 37–38; 98–99.

99. Jungmann, "Die Abwehr," 63–65.

100. Jungmann, "Die Abwehr," 63–74; Hope, "The Medieval Western Rites," 230.

101. Díaz y Díaz, "Literary Aspects," 66; Jungmann, *The Early Liturgy*, 229–30; Hope, "The Medieval Western Rites," 230.

102. Vives, *Concilios*, 125: Pro reverentia sanctissimae fidei et propter conrobarandus hominum invalidas mentes consultu piisiimi et gloriosisimi domni Recaredi regis sancta constituit synodus: ut per omnes ecclesias Spaniae, Gallias vel Gallaeciae secundum formam orientalum ecclesiarum, concilii Constantinopolitani hoc est centum quinquaginta episcoporum symbolum fidei recitetur, ut priusquam dominica dicatur oratio voce clara a populo praedicetur, quo et fides vera manifestum testimonium habeat et ad Christi corpus et sanguinem praelibandum pectora populorum fide purificata accedant (See Jungmann, "Die Abwehr," 62: and King, *Liturgies of the Primatial Sees*, 613).

103. Reliefs carved with the *Credo* were even made to hang in the naves, or possibly the baptisteries of churches (Schlunk, "Die Beiträge," 179).

104. It is known similarly that the *Benedicte* was added to the Gallican liturgy after the conversion of Clovis in 496. For the inclusion of the *Benedicte* in the Mozarabic liturgy, see King, *Liturgies of the Primatial Sees*, 580. It was preceded by the lesson.

105. Vives, *Concilios*, 197. Author's translation. It is this reference to a preexisting tradition that leads me to doubt that the hymn was only added in the sixth century, as has been suggested elsewhere. See King, *Liturgies of the Primatial Sees*, 580–81.

106. Hillgarth, "Popular Religion," 10; R. Grégoire, *Les Homéliaires du moyen âge*, Rome, 1966, 208.

107. *Early Medieval Spain*, 51. Indeed, he goes on to say that the "intellectual vigour of the Spanish church in the late 6th and 7th centuries must owe much to the challenge presented to it by Arianism and its final development under Leovigild."

108. Significant in this respect are the suggestions of Collins ("Mérida and Toledo," 189–219), who considers the religious controversy to be only the terms through which a political and social battle was fought between certain members of the Visigothic hierarchy and the indigenous power structures of Hispano-Roman cities. See also Hillgarth, "Coins and Chronicles," "Additional Note," after 508.

109. There are indications that the struggle for power was fought on the grounds of the church long after the conversion of the Visigoths. Thompson links the abolition of Roman law and civil administration by Recceswinth with that monarch's attempt to gain control of the church councils, asking, "did he aim to have not only the state but also the church securely in the hands of the Goths?" (E. A. Thompson, *The Goths in Spain*, 296). See also Hillgarth, "Popular Religion," 9; Orlandis, "El elemento germánico."

110. Interestingly enough, monograms on chancels have been suggested by Schlunk and Hauschild to be possible symbols of the divine nature of Christ, used as a visual reference in the battle against Arianism (*Die Denkmäler*, 69).

111. For the question of remoteness of the sacraments, see Jungmann, "Die Abwehr," 98–99.

Chapter 2: San Julián de los Prados

1. G. Jackson, *The Making of Medieval Spain*, Norwich, 1972, 14.

2. On the question of the cause of the invasion, see E. Lévi-Provençal, *Histoire de l'Espagne Musulmane, 1, La conquête et l'émirat Hispano-Umayade*, Paris and Leiden, 1950, particularly 19–53.

3. For the importance of Toledo and the ecclesiastical consecration of kings, see Collins, *Early Medieval Spain*, New York, 1983, 72.

4. Lévi-Provençal, *Histoire*, 58–59. Though repulsed at the battle of Poitiers in 732, the Islamic presence persisted, for we know they occupied Avignon for four years, from 734 to 738.

5. At the time of the formation of the kingdom of Asturias, there was still an independent Duke of Cantabria. Asturias at that time might have included a minute portion of Galicia, but it was not until the reign of Alfonso I (739–757) that incursions were made into Galicia. Even then, the monarch chose to evacuate the population of such Galician towns as Lugo and Braga, and such centers of the *Meseta* as Zamora, León, and Astorga, feeling that they could not be defended against Islamic forces. Indeed it was not until the reign of Alfonso's son Fruela (757–768) that some of Galicia was repopulated.

6. T. Glick, *Islamic and Christian Spain in the Early Middle Ages*, Princeton, 1979, 42–43. Schlunk called it "historically virgin" (M. Berenguer and H. Schlunk, *La pintura mural asturiana de los siglos IX y X*, Madrid, 1957, 167). See also "El arte asturiano en torno al 800," *Actas del Simposio para el Estudio de los Códices del "Comentario al Apocalipsis" de Beato de Liébana*, vol. 1, Madrid, 1980, 138–39; and F. D. Santos, "De Asturias Sueva y Visigoda," *Asturiensia Medievalia* 3 (1979), 17–59.

7. See discussion in note 101 below.

8. "Nam numquam est auditum ut Libanenses Toletanos docuisset." *ES*, 5:536.

9. "Perspicue clareat hoc templum obutibus sacris. Demonstrans figuraliter signaculum almae crucis . . ." Vigil, *Asturias monumental, epigráfica y diplomática*, vol. 1, Oviedo, 1887, 305. The stone and inscription were lost in the Spanish civil war. In "El arte asturiano en torno al 800," Schlunk demonstrates this to be a reference to a cross plan, rather than to a large cross hung within the church, as Vives supposed ("Características hispanas de las inscripciones visigodas," *Arbor* 1 [1944], 194–95).

10. We know nothing of the technique in which Cangas de Onís was constructed, and it is here perhaps that we might more readily expect to find a divergence from building practice of the Visigothic period. Little of the long-standing ashlar tradition for which the monuments of central Spain are known during the Visigothic period has survived in the mountains of the north. A chancel reused in the ninth-century church of Santa Cristina de Lena suggests that the beveled style was at least imported to Asturias, but few other vestiges of Visigothic period building or sculpture

have been found there. (The sarcophagus of Ithacius provides a possible exception. It is now preserved in the cathedral of Oviedo and dates to the fifth century. It seems to belong more properly within the late Antique tradition, however. See Schlunk, *AH*, 2:240.) This lacuna suggests to some extent a weak artistic tradition, one fostered by general poverty and probably quite poor of monumental endeavors in stone.

11. The church suffered extensive rebuilding in the seventeenth and nineteenth centuries, but recent excavations carried out by Menéndez Pidal have revealed those vestiges that date from the time of King Silo (J. Menéndez Pidal, "La Basílica de Santianes de Pravia [Oviedo]," *Actas del Simposio para el Estudio de los Códices del "Comentario al Apocalipsis" de Beato de Liébana*, vol. 1, Madrid, 1980, 281–97; J. M. González y F. Valles, "Pravia, capital del reino Asturiano," *Asturiensia Medievalia*, 3:87–103).

12. I find it difficult to believe that the arches that remain today are the same that existed in Silos's time, as Menéndez Pidal suggests, when the piers on which they rest were raised with the establishment of the present pavement level ("La Basílica de Santianes," 292).

13. Menéndez Pidal, "La Basílica de Santianes," 291. Santianes also featured a portico, and perhaps a tribune built at a slightly later period. It is reconstructed on the basis of two windows at different levels that appear in the southwestern chapel, added to the basilica of Silos after its original foundation. Menéndez Pidal felt that the irregular placement of the windows indicated that they must have accommodated a staircase, which gave access to a newly built tribune over the primitive portico. He dates the tribune, and the chapel in which the staircase might have been built, with the death of Silo (783) and the conversion of the church's portico into a royal burial place ("La basílica de Santianes," 282).

14. Among the sources that attest to the new diplomatic concerns of Alfonso II is C. Sánchez-Albornoz, *Orígenes de la nación Española: Estudios críticos sobre la historia del reino de Asturias*, vol. 2, Oviedo, 1974, 531–53.

15. For the chronology of the chronicles of Albelda and Alfonso III, see J. Gil Fernández, J. Moralejo, and J. Ruiz de la Peña, *Crónicas Asturianas*, Oviedo, 1985, 33–42; Gómez-Moreno, "Las primeras crónicas de la reconquista," *BRAH* 100 (April–June 1932), 562–623; Sánchez-Albornoz, "La crónica de Albelda y la de Alfonso III," *Bulletin Hispanique* 32 (1930), 305–25; R. Menéndez Pidal, "La historiografía sobre Alfonso

II," *Estudios sobre la monarquía asturiana*, Oviedo (1949), 1971, 11–17. Menéndez Pidal (13) suggests that all three chronicles—the two versions of the Chronicle of Alfonso III and the Chronicle of Albelda—were written about the same time, in the 870s or 880s, during the reign of Alfonso III in Oviedo.

16. "[A]ll in the order": translation by author according to the interpretation of Schlunk, *La pintural mural*, 161–67; "and all the ceremonial": Gil Fernández, Moralejo, and Ruiz de la Peña, *Crónicas Asturianas*, 249. Author's translation from Spanish.

17. Gil Fernández, Moralejo, and Ruiz de la Peña, *Crónicas Asturianas*, 174; 249 (Spanish translation). See also Gómez-Moreno, "Las primeras crónicas," 602.

18. R. Menéndez Pidal, *Historia de España: La España de los siglos VIII al XI*, vol. 7, 1962, 394. He relies heavily on this passage of the Albelda to characterize Alfonso II's reign. See also J. Maravall, *El concepto de España en la edad media*, Madrid, 1964, 299–315, who includes an extensive discussion of the possible implications of this passage; P. Prieto Bances, "La legislación del Rey de Oviedo," *Estudios sobre la monarquía asturiana*, 175–221.

19. Sánchez-Albornoz, *Estudios críticos*, 2:623–39. See also note 101 below.

20. Schlunk, *La pintura mural*, 161–67. Although this interpretation has disappeared from his subsequent publications of the subject, he has never retracted it. A revision, which concentrates on the paintings as palatine in nature, appears in "El arte asturiano en torno al 800" (151–57). Schlunk's position will be discussed at greater length in the text and notes that follow.

21. See note 101 below.

22. Menéndez Pidal, "La historiografía," 11. He states in fact that there was no tradition of historiography in the time of Alfonso II. This runs contrary to the opinion of Sánchez-Albornoz, who believes the chronicles of Alfonso III's time must reflect an earlier one written in the reign of Alfonso II ("¿Una crónica asturiana perdida?" *Revista de Filología Hispánica* 7 [1945], 105–46. Gil Fernández, Moralejo, and Ruiz de la Peña, *Cronicas Asturianas*, 33–34, support this notion). Menéndez Pidal suggests we give credence to the declaration of Alfonso III in the dedicatory letter of the Chronicle of Alfonso III (*ad Sebastianum* or Ovetense), which states that he knows no other history since that of Isidore, which stops with the Visigothic King Wam-

ba (11). A prototype from around the year 800 is also problematic for other reasons (39 n. 5).

23. See Menéndez Pidal, "La historiografía," 13. Alfonso II's "Testament" makes no attempt to link the monarch genealogically with the Visigoths, as do the chronicles written under Alfonso III, but instead identifies his lineage in terms of Alfonso I and his father, Fruela I (Floriano Llorente, *Diplomática española del reino astur*, vol. 1, 1951, 119–21). Though in support of a Visigothic preoccupation on the part of Alfonso II, R. Menéndez Pidal points out that the only two documents preceding Alfonso III that explicitly associate Asturian monarchs with Visigothic antecedents—one allegedly of Alfonso I, and one of Alfonso II, both concerning Lugo—are generally considered to be forged (*El imperio hispánico y los cinco reinos*, Madrid, 1950, 21 and n. 1). Floriano Llorente (*Diplomática*, 1:62, 185) considers both completely false, while Sánchez-Albornoz (*Anuario de la Historia del Derecho*, vol. 2, 1925, 532–33) thinks it is precisely the genealogy that is suspect in the first.

24. See Menéndez Pidal, for instance, for the role of the Mozarab Dulcidius in the amassing of materials for the chronicles ("La historiografía," 13). In 1979 Bango Torviso considered this passage as a witness to Mozarabic ideas: ("El neovisigotismo artístico de los siglos IX y X; La restauración de ciudades y templos," *Revista de ideas estéticas* 148 [1979], 320), but more recently exchanged this for a notion of an indigenous Spanish tradition of monastic art ("L'ordo Gothorum"). See chapter 3 above for Mozarabic preoccupation with the Visigoths.

25. See J. Uría Ríu, "Cuestiones histórico-arqueológicas relativas a la ciudad de Oviedo de los siglos VIII al X," *Simposio sobre la cultura asturiana de la alta edad media*, Oviedo, 1967, 270–91.

26. The Chronicle of Alfonso III (Ovetense or Ad Sebastianum) tells us: "Iste [Alfonso II] prius solium regni Oueto firmabit." Gil Fernández, Moralejo, and Ruiz de la Peña, *Crónicas Asturianas*, 139. See also García Villada, *Crónica de Alfonso III*, 74.

27. Uría Ríu, "Cuestiones," 303–9, 295; The Rotense version of the Chronicle of Alfonso III reads: "Nam et regia palatia balnea promtuaria atque uniuersa stipendia formauit et instruere precepit," Gil Fernández, Moralejo, and Ruiz de la Peña, *Crónicas Asturianas*, 140; M. Gómez-Moreno, "Las primeras crónicas," 61; The Ovetense version of the same chronicle reads:

"Nam et regalia palatia, balnea, triclinia uel domata atque pretoria construxit decora et omnia regni utensilia fabrefecit pulcherrima" (Gil Fernández, Moralejo, and Ruiz de la Peña, 141; García-Villada, *Crónica de Alfonso III*, 76).

28. Uría Ríu, "Cuestiones," 295–96. See also J. Fontaine, *L'Art préroman hispanique*, Ste.-Marie de la Pierre-qui-Vire, 1973, 274–75. The palace of Alfonso II was first identified by Bishop Don Pelayo of Oviedo and Doña Urraca "La Asturiana" on a donation of 1161 (Vigil, *Asturias monumental*, 90–91). The partial excavations were carried out by V. Hevia and J. Fernández in 1942 (*Ruinas del Oviedo primitivo: Historia y secuencias de unas excavaciones*, Oviedo, 1984). There are those who support a date in Fruela I's reign for the palace, though this seems unlikely, for the vestiges of its facade arcade unite it firmly within the construction tradition of Alfonso's patronage. This archaeological evidence would support the testimony of the Chronicle of Alfonso III, which clearly states that only in Alfonso II's time was a royal seat established in the city: "Iste prius solium regni Oueto firmauit" (see note 26 above). Fernández and Hevia also assert (18–36), however, that the surviving tower (Torre de San Miguel) and much of the palace were built by Fruela I because of the use of foundations, customary in Roman and Visigothic period building, but not present in the Cámara Santa. Uría Ríu ("Cuestiones") dates it to the reign of Alfonso II, while recognizing that dating to be somewhat problematical. Particularly compelling is his observation of the relation of the arcade of San Julián de los Prados to that of the palace (298–300). Schlunk ("El arte asturiano en torno al 800," 146) discusses the palace with Alfonso II's work but acknowledges it to be earlier than the Cámara Santa, as Fernández and Hevia suggest. Sánchez-Albornoz wonders if the palace later built in conjunction with San Julián de los Prados might represent Alfonso's main palace, while those in the center of Oviedo correspond to an earlier date. He admits, however, that he has not seen the palace, and so withholds judgment (*Estudios críticos*, 645 n. 15). While clearly of two campaigns, there is not enough documentation to support a palace of Fruela at Oviedo. I would suggest instead two campaigns for Alfonso II's palace: one before his exile, with the addition of the Cámara Santa after 812. This would seem to correspond better to the documentary and historical evidence. See also Fontaine, *L'Art préroman hispanique*, 1:271.

29. Fontaine, *L'Art préroman hispanique*,

1:274. The scheme can be seen in the well-known image of Villa Julius from a North African mosaic. The prototype here too is a Roman one, but it is likely that surviving villas and the continuous use of older monuments transformed such co-opted plans into indigenous ones in the minds of their builders. The same galleried plan, for instance, can be found at the villa of Frades, in Portugal (D. Fernando de Almeida, "Noticia sobre a 'villa' romana de S. Cucufate," *Actas do II Congresso Nacional de Arqueología*, Coimbra, 1970, 475–78; Fontaine, *L'Art préroman hispanique* 1:274). The facade presents a formula that appears in the Roman city gate of Autun, and in a number of Carolingian works contemporary to and later than Alfonso II: two towers embracing an arcaded, multistoried bay appear at Saint Michael of Lorsch (784–91), with stair turrets rather than towers, and at Corvey (873–85), as they once had in earlier Carolingian monuments like St. Riquier (790–99). This same disposition found later expression in twelfth-century monuments like Marmoutier. It is unclear, in an analysis of the palace alone, if the potency of the forms is wrought by a historical notion of Rome, or by a more general meaning subsumed in the greater traditions of Spanish architecture. See C. Heitz, *L'Architecture réligieuse Carolingienne*, Paris, 1980, 45–46, 61–62. See also H. Schaefer, "The Origin of the Two Tower Façade in Romanesque Architecture," *Art Bulletin*, 27 (1945), 85–108. Bango Torviso has recently discussed at some length the problem of Asturian palace architecture in relation to late Roman and Carolingian forms ("El Arte asturiano y el imperio Carolingio," in *Arte prerrománico y románico en Asturias*, Gijón, 1988, 46–65). Barral i Altet suggests parallels between Alfonso's palace and the palace of Charlemagne at Aachen but does not elaborate his idea ("La representación del palacio en la pintura mural asturiana de la alta edad media," *Actas del XXIII Congreso Internacional de Historia del Arte: España entre el Mediterráneo y el Atlántico*, Granada, 1976, 298).

30. Schlunk, "El arte asturiano en torno al 800," 146–47. Though first mention of it is not until the twelfth-century Chronicle of Silos, it would seem likely that, as a palace chapel, it would have merited special mention by chroniclers who do mention the palace of which it was a part (Schlunk, "El arte asturiano en torno al 800," 147). The date is reconfirmed by its excavators (Fernández and Hevia, *Ruinas del Oviedo Primitivo*, 21–23). Much of the upper story was

rebuilt in the twelfth century, but it originally held a wooden-vaulted nave and a curious brick-vaulted sanctuary dedicated to San Miguel. See also A. Bonet Correa, *Spanish Pre-Romanesque Art*, Barcelona, 1967, 94; J. Cuesta, *Crónica del milenario de la Cámara Santa [1942]*, Oviedo, 1947; E. Dyggve, "Le type architectural de la Cámara Santa d'Oviedo et l'architecture asturienne," *Cahiers archéologiques* 6 (1952), 125–33; L. Menéndez Pidal and Hevia, "Notas sobre la reconstrucción de la Cámara Santa," *Revista Nacional de Arquitectura*, vol. 1, 1941, 33–38; Menéndez Pidal, "La Cámara Santa de Oviedo, su destrucción y reconstrucción," *Boletín del Instituto de Estudios Asturianos* 14 (1960). Pita Andrade suggests that the Cámara Santa is the immediate antecedent for Santa María de Naranco (*Arte Asturiano*, Madrid, 1963, 14). F. J. Fernández Conde suggests a later dating (*El Libro de los Testamentos de la catedral de Oviedo*, Rome, 1971, 114–17).

31. Two columns support an arch that enframes a small window against the eastern end, under which is a tabernacle, probably of a later period. This is the contention of Schlunk (*AH*, 2:333); Bonet Correa holds it to be Asturian (*Spanish Pre-Romanesque Art*, 94).

32. Schlunk, "El arte asturiano en torno al 800," 145.

33. Schlunk, *AH*, 2:333–35; T. Hauschild, "Das 'Martyrium' von La Alberca [prov. Murcia]. Planaufname 1970 und Rekonstruktionversuch," *MM* 12 (1971), 170–94.

34. The transverse arches supporting a flat roof are substantiation for believing that San Antolín was the lower story of a two-story structure like La Alberca. It is believed to have been built to house the relics of the martyr San Antolín when they were brought there by King Wamba (672–683). See F. Simón y Nieto, "Descubrimientos arqueológicos en la catedral de Palencia," *BSEE* 14 (1906), 65–82; Fontaine, *L'Art préroman hispanique*, 1:195–97; Schlunk, *AH*, 2:283–85.

35. The testament of 812: Floriano Llorente, *Diplomática*, 121–23; Sánchez-Albornoz, *Estudios críticos*, 643 n. 5, 644. It is presumed to have been rebuilt over time by Alfonso II, completed only after the hostilities that saw him in exile between about 802 and 808 (425–439).

36. There is a reference to a main altar at San Salvador, but it is unclear if this would suggest side apses. For the documentation on San Salvador: Chronicle of Albelda and Chronicle of Alfonso III (Rotense): Gil Fernández, Moralejo, and

Ruiz de la Peña, *Crónicas Asturianas*, 138–41, 174; Gómez-Moreno, *Las primeras crónicas*, 602, 617–18; Chronicle of Alfonso III (Ovetense): García Villada, *Crónica de Alfonso III*, 74–75. See also Fortunato de Selgas, "La basílica del Salvador de Oviedo de los siglos VIII y IX," *BSEE* 16 (1908), 162. The *Testamentum regis Adefonsi* is the source for Tioda, who is listed in the twelfth-century copy and elaboration of that document, the *Liber Testamentorum*, as "Tioda, architect of the same church of San Salvador." The *Liber Testamentorum* is thought to be part of the cathedral's official testament book (Floriano Llorente, "El testamento de Alfonso II el Casto [estudio paleográfico]," *Boletín del Instituto de Estudios Asturianos*, 1975, 593–617). Concerning Tioda, Fontaine calls him Spain's first "urbanist" (*L'Art préroman hispanique*, 1:274), while Azcárate ponders if his "Gothic" name might indicate that he is an architect from Aachen ("Einige Aspekte zum germanische-deutschen Einfluss auf die Kunst des Hochmittelalters in Spanien," *Gesammelte Aufsatze zur Kulturgeschichtes Spaniens*, Münster, 1982, 6).

37. Fontaine, *L'Art préroman hispanique*, 1:272; Gil Fernández, Moralejo, and Ruiz de la Peña, *Crónicas Asturianas*, 138–41, 174; García Villada, *Crónica de Alfonso III*, 75; Gómez-Moreno, *Las primeras crónicas*, 617–18.

38. The ninth-century chronicle of Alfonso III (Ovetense) also describes a room at the west that was designated to receive the king's sarcophagus, and indeed both Morales and Caraballo describe royal burials there. Excavations revealed a chamber with only one access door and columns at its corners, all covered with stucco and some painting. While details of its construction and access are new, the idea of a royal pantheon to the west of a church of royal foundation is not: the same combination appeared as a porch at Santianes de Pravia, under King Silo (A. de Llano, *Bellezas de Asturias*, Oviedo, 1928, 336–40; Gil Fernández, Moralejo, and Ruiz de la Peña, *Crónicas Asturianas*, 139–41; García Villada, *Crónica de Alfonso III*, 75). Schlunk ("El arte asturiano en torno al 800," 145–46) takes special care in distinguishing this pantheon from those of Carolingian and Roman practice. Because it did not serve as a porch as well, it functioned differently from that at Santianes (Fontaine, *L'Art préroman hispanique*, 1:272–73). The pantheon might well have been the prototype for the Pantheon de los Reyes at San Isidoro in León, our clue that, at least by the eleventh century, the form had

strong royal implications.

39. One altar to the right of the main altar was dedicated to Saint Stephen, and the one to the left to Saint Julián (Gil Fernández, Moralejo, and Ruiz de la Peña, *Crónicas Asturianas*, 139–41; García Villada, *Crónica de Alfonso III*, 75).

40. H. Flórez, *Viaje de Ambrosio de Morales per orden del rey . . .*, Madrid, 1765, 87. His contention that there were "marbles" (columns) "to form the vaults in the corners" might suggest a groined vault of the type found at Mazote. See chapter 3 above.

41. Schlunk, *AH*, 2:330; "El arte asturiano en torno al 800," 145; F. Redondo y Cadenas, "La iglesia de San Tirso el Real de Oviedo," *Boletín del Instituto de Estudios Asturianos* 30 (1967), 607–26; Bonet Correa, *Spanish Pre-Romanesque Art*, 98–100; Fontaine, *L'Art préroman hispanique*, 1:272–74. San Tirso was destroyed in 1513. Documents provide illusive data concerning this royal foundation: the Chronicle of Albelda describes a three-aisled church composed "cum multis angulis," which Bonet Correa interprets as referring to side chambers and a porch. The vestiges of San Tirso's apse were discovered in 1912 (98); Gil Fernández, Moralejo, and Ruiz de la Peña, *Crónicas Asturianas*, 174; Gómez-Moreno, "Las primeras crónicas," 602.

I. The Architecture of San Julián

42. This theory was left unquestioned until the discovery of the church of Santa María de Bendones, a construction of the reign (but probably not the patronage) of Alfonso II, which repeats this same motif in its apse window (Schlunk, *AH*, 2:330). Burned in 1936, Santa María de Bendones was not identified until 1954, when it suffered an almost complete reconstruction. It is not a royal foundation; it is not mentioned before a document of Alfonso III in 905. It has an almost identical east end to that of Santullano, but in place of a nave and side aisles, Bendones presents only a series of three rooms, in which Fontaine sees links to a heritage from the Visigothic period (*L'Art préroman hispanique*, 1:404). Rather than a transitional monument between San Tirso and Santullano as he suggests (404), I believe that Bendones reflects the royal monument. Its architect seems to have coped with the tribune porch at San Julián de los Prados—an afterthought which only has meaning for the royal church—by supplying a similar

form to the south. The architect of Santa María chose only to build the three apses and continuous transept of Santullano, that is, the most unique and symbolic part of the monument. See J. M. Pita Andrade, *Arte asturiano*, 16–18; J. Manzanares Rodríguez, *Arte prerománico asturiano*, Oviedo, 1964, 13–16.

43. San Julián de los Prados was discovered and excavated by Don Fortunato de Selgas between 1912 and 1915. He wrote the first studies on the basis of his observations and excavations: "La Basílica de San Julián de los Prados," *BSEE* 24 (1913), 29–51, 97–139. Apart from this preliminary study, by far the most significant work concerning Santullano was undertaken by Helmut Schlunk. In particular, his article "La iglesia de San Julián de los Prados y la arquitectura de Alfonso el Casto," *Estudios sobre la monarquía asturiana*, Oviedo, 1949 (1971), 419–95, contains a complete review of the literature and an intriguing breakdown of the possible sources for Santullano. See also "Las iglesias palatinas de la capital del reino asturiano," discurso en el acto de su investidura como Doctor Honoris Causa por la Universidad de Oviedo, día 14 abril de 1977; "El arte asturiano en torno al 800," 281–97; "La iglesia de São Gião cerca de Nazaré. Contribución al estudio de la influencia de la liturgia en la arquitectura de las iglesias prerománicas de la península ibérica," *Actas do II Congresso Nacional de Arqueología*, Coimbra, 1970; and with Magín Berenguer, *La pintura mural*. Of late, the studies of Bango Torviso have provided fascinating new documentary materials (Bango Torviso, "'L'Ordo Gotorum' et sa survivance dans l'Espagne du Haut Moyen Age," *Revue de l'Art*, no. 70 [1985], 11–12 and "Alfonso II y Santullano," in *Arte prerománico y románico en Asturias*.

44. The Ovetense (Ad Sebastianum) version reads: "Aedificabit etiam a circio, distantem a palatio quasi stadium unum, ecclesiam in memoriam sancti Iuliani martyris, circumpositis hinc inde geminis altaribus mirifica instructione decoris" (Gil Fernández, Moralejo, and Ruiz de la Peña, *Crónicas Asturianas*, 141. See also García Villada, *Crónica de Alfonso III*, 75). The Rotense version reads: "Necon satis procul a palatium edificauit ecclesiam in honorem sancti Iuliani et Baselissa cum uninis altaribus magno opere et mirauili conpositione locauit" (Gil Fernández, Moralejo, and Ruiz de la Peña, 140; See also Gómez-Moreno, "Las primeras crónicas," 618).

45. Schlunk contends that the king watched services from this vantage point (*La pintura*

mural, 8). A royal tribune in the same position existed later at the Capella Palatina in Palermo (E. Kitzinger, "The Mosaics of the Capella Palatina at Palermo," *Art Bulletin* 31 [1949], 283–86), which Schlunk believes might reflect, with Santullano, earlier models.

46. The south porch, which is featured on some plans and in the restoration of Santullano that stands today, is the product of Selgas's rebuilding of the monument at the beginning of the century. Schlunk rejects its authenticity on the basis of the paucity of documentation ("La iglesia de San Julián," 436–37). The northern porch and tribune might have been constructed as an afterthought, though certainly in the same campaign as the rest of the church. A large window, like that which pierces the end wall of the south transept, was originally planned in the north terminal wall, but was subsequently blocked to allow for the construction of the tribune, while the design of the paintings takes the tribune into account.

47. Schlunk, *AH*, 2:339.

48. Pita Andrade believes Tioda was responsible for the revival of Roman construction style at Prados and other monuments of Alfonso II's patronage (*Arte asturiano*, 13).

49. In a lecture given at Columbia University in April 1986, Sabine Noack of the Deutsches Archäologisches Institut in Madrid suggested that *spolia*, when used in Asturian and Mozarabic architecture, carry conscious meaning associated with historical revival.

50. Schlunk first linked Quintanilla with San Julián ("Entwicklungsläufe der Skulptur auf der Iberischen Halbinsel von 8. bis 11. Jahrhundert," *Kolloquium über frühmittelalterliche Skulptur*, vol. 3, Heidelberg, 1974, 123). Bango Torviso, in a fascinating recent study, proposes indigenous models for Santullano, linking the building and its decoration with the personal monastic experiences of Alfonso II. He points to the plan at Quintanilla and that of São Gião de Nazaré, which is divided, as substantiation for this idea ("'L'Ordo Gotorum'"). The question of scale at Quintanilla, and the fact that excavations have left us with no evidence of the transition between nave and choir, makes this single comparison a tenuous one. The small windows piercing the transept wall to either side of the triumphal arch, however, are vestiges of more enclosed east ends of churches of the Visigothic period, like São Gião de Nazaré.

51. Núñez, *Arquitectura prerrománica*, Madrid, 1978, 112.

52. R. Krautheimer, "The Carolingian Revival of Early Christian Architecture," *Studies in Early Christian, Medieval and Renaissance Art*, New York, 1969, 203–56. Helmut Schlunk, San Julián de los Prados's most dedicated scholar, spent much of his book and two major articles concerning that monument resisting the notion that a primary force in its design might have been Carolingian impact: ". . . de la planta de la iglesia de San Julián se ha buscado, siempre erróneamente, paralelismos en el ámbito carolingio" ("Las iglesias palatinas," 6). In a later article concerning San Julián, however, he alluded in passing to the *Libri Carolini* as a possible connection ("El arte asturiano en torno al 800," 156). Bango Torviso offers the most complex argumentation on the subject since Schlunk, in his works concerning the monastic formation of Alfonso II. He attributes allusions to the Carolingian world to the common Spanish background of major Carolingian figures and their influence in the north ("'L'Ordo Gotorum'"; "Alfonso II y Santullano"; and "El Arte asturiano y el imperio carolingio"). Pita Andrade sees in Alfonso's work an emulation of ancient Rome, "con fuertes dosis de orientalismo que fue pensado ya en nuestros monumentos de los primeros siglos" (*Arte asturiano*, 10). Gómez-Moreno linked Santullano with Carolingian forms ("De arqueología mozárabe," *BSCE* 21 [1913], 91; "Prémices de l'art chrétien espagnol," *L'Information d'histoire de l'art* 9/5 [1964], 211). Camps Cazorla and Torres Balbás attributed these motifs to late Roman tradition, perhaps still alive in Asturias, or triggered by developments in France (L. Torres Balbás, in Hauttman and Torres Balbás, *El Arte de la alta Edad Media*, Barcelona, 1934, 163). Significantly, Torres Balbás sees these elements combined with more important aspects of design from the Visigothic period. Thummler was the first after Gómez-Moreno to see in San Julián the impact of Carolingian space and planning ("Carolingian Period: Churches with Latin Cross Plans," *Encyclopedia of World Art*, vol. 3, New York, 1960, 94), a notion Terrasse also considers in passing (*L'Espagne du moyen âge*, 54). This is a notion more recently developed by J.-M. Azcárate, who suggests a "teutonic" connection through the architect Tioda, but he is not sure if this influence—and its architect—come from Toledo or Aachen ("Einige Aspekte zum germanisch-deutschen Einfluss auf die Kunst des Hochmittelalters in Spanien," 6). Crozet, who recognized the typological similarities between the late Car-

olingian church of Saint Généroux and Santullano ("L'église de Saint-Généroux et ses parentés
avec l'architecture asturienne des IXe et Xe siècles," *Simposio sobre cultura asturiana de la alta
edad media*, Oviedo, 1964, 21–25), refrains from
drawing any conclusions, other than intimating
that similar, though unspecified, liturgical requirements are responsible for both. Heitz con-
curs, adding that the east end of San Généroux
must be excavated to determine its original form
(C. Heitz, *L'architecture réligieuse carolingienne*,
Paris, 1980, 193–94). I think it is probably more
likely that Saint Généroux is a late example of
the Carolingian typology that originally made its
impact on the builders or patron of Santullano.
Finally, it is appropriate to make the distinction
here between the position I am taking in this
study: that San Julián reflects the conscious borrowing of certain signifying motifs from Carolingian architecture, and not a transplanted Carolingian atelier as some have contended (F. W.
Deichmann, "Die Entstehungszeit von Salvator-
kirche und Clitumnustempel bei Spoleto," *Römische Mitteilungen*, vol. 58, Rome, 1943, 126
n. 2; P. Verzone, *L'architettura religiosa dell'alto
medio evo nell'Italia settentrionale*, Milan, 1942,
145). A more restricted version of the architectural argument brought forward here appears in
J. Dodds and A. DeForest, "San Julián de los
Prados: Arte, diplomacia y herejía," *Goya* 191
(1986), 258–63.

53. Einhard's basilica at Seligenstadt was
probably begun between 830 and 834 (O. Muller,
Die ehemalige Abtei Seligenstadt, Munich and
Berlin, 1964. For Fulda, see M. F. Fischer and F.
Oswald, "Zur Baugeschichte der Fuldaer Klosterkirchen, Literatur und Ausgrabungen in kriti-
scher Sicht," *Beihefte der Bonner Jahrbücher*,
vol. 28, Cologne and Graz, 1968, 268–80). Fontaine connects "les piles carrées sous la triple ar-
cature des nefs" of Seligenstadt with San Julián
(*L'Art préroman hispanique*, 277).

54. At Hersfeld, excavations of Feldtkeller
and Binding have brought to light a Carolingian
church alongside the present building, confirm-
ing it as the construction begun after 1037 by
Abbot Meginhard (H. Feldtkeller, "Eine bisher
unbekannte karolingische Grosskirche im Hers-
felder Stift," *Deutsche Kunst und Denkmal-
pflege*, 1964, 1).

55. Krautheimer, "The Carolingian Revival,"
223.

56. For apse arcades, see Schlunk, "La iglesia
de San Julián," 1971, 477–78. The sacristies of

Visigothic churches are of course divergent in
both function and form from a tri-apsed east end,
which includes three altars (see chapter 1). There
has been no study to confirm suggestions that
this might have been the case at Las Talmujas in
Toledo (Schlunk, "Entwicklungsläufe," 123).
Schlunk more recently sees tri-apsed east ends as
new to Spain ("El arte asturiano en torno al 800,"
49).

57. A western tribune is reconstructed at San
Pedro de Mérida (Marcos Pous, "La iglesia de San
Pedro de Mérida," *Beiträge zur Kunstgeschichte
und Archäologie des Frühmittelalters, Akten
zum VII Internationalen Kongress für Frühmit-
telalterforschung*, 21–28, 125), and at São Gião de
Nazaré (Schlunk, "La iglesia de São Gião," 513).

58. See Selgas, "La basílica de San Julián," 98;
Schlunk, *AH*, 338, and "La iglesia de São Gião,"
522. Also of interest, though with fragile documentation, is J. and P. Lozinski, "Tradition and
Change in Asturia: The Royal Tribune and the
'Proto Rose' Window," in A. Schmid, ed., *Ri-
forma religiosa e arti nell'epoca carolingia*, Bolo-
gna, 1979, 27–39. The northern portico seems to
be an afterthought to the original architectural
plan, though it predates the paintings. A southern
portico actually reconstructed by Selgas is still
the source of contention among scholars. At
Santa María de Bendones, a building that closely
resembles Santullano, two porches exist, one to
the north and the south of the transept. Was that
the original deposition of San Julián, or a rationa-
lization, in formal terms, of the royal tribune of
Santullano, which could have no meaning for the
small parish church? The date of Bendones is unknown; it is first mentioned in a donation of Alfonso III in 905. See J. M. Pita Andrade, *Arte
asturiano*, 16–18; J. Manzanares Rodríguez, *Arte
prerrománico asturiano*, 13–16. See also note 42
above.

59. For Fulda, see Fischer and Oswald, "Zur
Baugeschichte der Fuldaer Klosterkirchen," 268–
80; for Saint Peter's: Richard Krautheimer, Spen-
cer Corbett, and Alfred Frazer, *Corpus Basilicarum Christianarum Romae*, vol. 5, Rome and
New York, 1977, 253.

60. Bango Torviso sees the transept tribune
as a monastic form: "Dans ce monde carolingien
et même ottonien, ce sont les tribunes monas-
tiques qui se trouvent, normalement, dans le
transept. L'existence d'un transept, le fait que le
roi y occupe une place font de Santullano une
exception dans l'ensemble des églises palatines
asturiennes" (Bango Torviso, "'L'Ordo Goto-

rum,'" 12). He sees the evocation of monastic forms as growing from the personal experiences and connections of the monarch with monastic life.

61. J. Hubert et al., *L'Empire Carolingien*, Paris, 1968, 48.

62. Relations between Charlemagne and Alfonso II were discussed by Defourneaux, who offers careful distinction between legend and documented exchange ("Carlomagno y el reino asturiano," *Estudios sobre la monarquía asturiana*, Oviedo, 1949 [1971], 89–115; "Charlemagne et la monarchie asturienne," *Mélanges d'histoire du moyen âge Louis Halphen*, Paris, 1951, 174–84). Sánchez-Albornoz (*Estudios críticos*, 416–17, 435, 537–43) sees the consequences of Alfonso II's exchanges with Charlemagne as highly significant ones for the Asturian monarchy. Of great interest is the fascinating study of R. D'Abadal y Vinyals (*La batalla del adopcionismo en la desintegración de la iglesia visigoda*, Barcelona, 1949, 165–71). Also of interest are A. Prieto Prieto, "¿Establecimientos francos en el reino de Asturias? Sus posibles ecos: Toponimia y epopeya," *Asturiensia Medievalia*, 4:61–92; R. Lapesa Melgar, "Los 'francos' en la Asturias medieval y su influencia lingüística," *Simposio sobre cultura Asturiana en la alta edad media*, Oviedo, 1964, 341–54; J. M. Lacarra, "La projección cultural del mundo carolingio sobre la cristianidad hispánica," *Mélanges de la Bibliothèque espagnole*, Paris, 1977–78, 15–24.

63. "Annales regni Francorum," *MGH*, 798; *Vita Hludowici*, in Bouquet, *Recueil des historiens des Gauls et de la France*, vol. 6, Paris, 1870, 90; D'Abadal, *La batalla*, 165–71.

64. Jonas of Orleans visited the Asturian court before 799. His interest in the image controversy makes this visit especially significant for the argument that follows (Sánchez-Albornoz, *Estudios críticos*, 539).

65. Alfonso is known to have adopted titles taken by Visigothic monarchs, and is sometimes called the restorer of the Visigothic palatine office, because of the citation from the Chronicle of Albelda discussed in this chapter. But Sánchez-Albornoz, who believes the Albelda reflects an earlier, Asturian history, expresses dismay that the actual palace organization, while showing some continuity from Visigothic times, seems rather to reflect Carolingian custom (Sánchez-Albornoz, *Estudios críticos*, 625). He concludes that the reference to the establishment of a "Visigothic order" must reflect Alfonso's new bishop-

ric and council at Oviedo. Barrau-Dihigo in particular supports the notion that the *Comes palatii* appears in Asturias because of Frankish influence ("Recherches sur l'histoire politique du royaume Asturien," *Revue Hispanique* 52 [1921], 226 and n. 4). Alfonso also adopted the silver standard on the model of the Carolingian empire (Sánchez-Albornoz, "Moneda de cambio y moneda de cuenta en el reino Astur-leonés," *Cuadernos de Historia Española* [1960], 15). Menéndez Pidal takes issue with any non-Visigothic source for these political and economic conventions (*Historia de España*, 394). See also note 18 above.

66. Einhard, *The Life of Charlemagne*, trans. L. Thorpe, Bungay Suffolk, 1980, 70. This quote is also interesting for revealing a correspondence between Alfonso and Charlemagne.

II. The Paintings of San Julián and the Problem of Asturian Aniconism

67. Schlunk, "El arte asturiano en torno al 800," 156–57; Barral i Altet, "La representación del palacio."

68. Schlunk and Berenguer, *La pintura mural*, 95–105. His idea is buttressed by the fact that the notion of Holy Jerusalem, as well as that of the Holy Cross, was important to the Spanish rite. A particularly sensitive interpretation of the 812 testament of Alfonso II is given by Bango Torviso, in which he notes the mention of the Celestial Jerusalem by that monarch, and equates it with the paintings at Santullano ("'L'Ordo Gotorum,'" 16–17).

69. Schlunk and Berenguer, *La pintura mural*, 46. Núñez (*Arquitectura prerrománica*, 131–38), however, considers the paintings of Santa Eulalia de Bóveda to be part of an Asturian reconstruction of the Roman monument. See also note 84.

70. See notes 81 and 85 below.

71. References to San Julián de los Prados appear in both versions of the Chronicle of Alfonso III, while the quote associating Alfonso II's buildings in Oviedo with Toledo appears only in the Chronicle of Albelda (Gil Fernández, Moralejo, and Ruiz de la Peña, *Crónicas asturianas*; Gómez-Moreno, "Las primeras crónicas," 602, 618; García Villada, *Crónica de Alfonso III*, 75–76). On the relationship of these documents, see Menéndez Pidal, "La historiografía," 11–13.

72. Schlunk, *La pintura mural*, 57–60; F. Wirth, *Die römische Wandmalerei*, Berlin, 1934, pl. 7.

73. G. Becatti, *Scavi di Ostia, VI, Edificio con Opus Sectile fuori Porta Marina*, Rome, 1969, pl. 65.

74. Barral i Altet, "La representación del palacio," 295. Schlunk's concern can be seen in *La pintura mural*, 161, and "Las iglesias palatinas," 6, among other places.

75. Schlunk ("El arte asturiano en torno al 800," 159) recognizes it as an Asturian capital type.

76. Hubert, *L'Empire Carolingien*, 11.

77. Schlunk used this image as part of an argument that links the Santullano paintings, through shared Late Antique and eastern Roman prototypes, to models from the Visigothic period (*La pintura mural*, 95–105). For a more recent revision of his stance that does not use the Soissons miniature, see "El arte asturiano en torno al 800," 152–54. Barral i Altet sees the miniature, as do I, as witness to cultural contact with the Carolingian empire ("La representación del palacio," 293–303. See also N. Duval, "La representation du palais dans l'art du Bas-empire et du Haut Moyen Age d'après le psautier d'Utrecht," *Cahiers Arquéologiques*, 1965, 207–54).

78. F. Mutherich and J. Gaehde, *Carolingian Painting*, New York, 1976, 39.

79. C. Heitz (*Recherches sur les rapports entre l'architecture et liturgie carolingiennes*, Paris, 1963) suggested various manifestations of the Celestial Jerusalem in Carolingian architecture and liturgy. The Carolingian notion of Celestial Jerusalem was bound to the evocation of the Constantinian empire. The actual city of Jerusalem that Constantine had constructed was converted into the emblem of the celestial city of Saint John's apocalyptic vision. Also of interest is R. Krautheimer, "An Introduction to the Iconography of Medieval Architecture," *Journal of the Warburg and Courtauld Institutes* 5 [1942], 1–33.

80. Schnitzler, "Das Kuppelmosaik der Aachener Pfalzkapelle," *Aachener Kunstblätter* 29 [1964], 17–44. For a refutation, see H. Schrade, "Zum Kuppelmosaik der Pfalzkapelle und zum Theoderich-Denkmal in Aachen," *Aachener Kunstblätter* 30 [1965], 25–37.

81. J. Vives, ed., *Concilios visigóticos*, Madrid, 1963, 8. Among those who feel that the thirty-sixth canon of the Council of Elvira had an important impact on early medieval Spanish art is: Gómez-Moreno, *Iglesias mozárabes*, Ma-drid, 1919, 323. It is a difficult position to maintain in the face of the lavish figural programs of San Pedro de la Nave, Quintanilla de las Viñas, the Córdoba column, and later Asturian paintings at San Miguel de Lillo, San Salvador de Valdediós, and San Salvador de Priesca. See Schlunk and Berenguer, *La pintura mural*, 164, 109–15, 126–37, 150–58. I support instead the view of the impact of the Council of Elvira offered by P. de Palol ("Esencia del arte hispánico de la época visigoda: romanismo y germanismo," *Spoleto* 3 [1956], 104– 12). Palol allows for a certain restraint in the Spanish tradition, but points to surviving art of the Visigothic period as the obvious means of rejecting the notion of a systematic suspicion toward images. J. Fontaine offers finally an intriguing and stimulating argument for the meaning of certain nonfigural forms in the Paleochristian and Visigothic periods ("Iconographie et spiritualité dans la sculpture chrétienne d'Espagne du IVe au VIIe siècles," *Revue d'histoire de la spiritualité* 50 [1974], 285–318). In terms of monumental art in particular, it must be remembered that, in addition to the impressive figural remains noted above, a large number must have been destroyed or defaced by Muslim iconoclasts (the heads of the Córdoba capital, for instance, have been defaced). Isidore of Seville (560–636), the great Spanish father who lived three centuries after the Council of Elvira, devotes chapters 16 and 17 of book 19 of his *Etymologies* to painting and color, and mentions in his *Versus in Biblioteca* painted portraits of famous authors in his library (Isidore of Seville, *Etimologías. Edición bilingüe*, ed. J. Oroz Reta and M. A. Marcos Casquero, vol. 2, Madrid, 1982, 451–57; "Versus in Biblioteca," *PL*, 81:574; J. Williams, *Early Spanish Manuscript Painting*, New York, 1977, 10). Of interest is the argument that lost manuscript painting on the Iberian Peninsula might have had a connection to the Bibles of Theodulf (see note 85). See, however, Nees, *The Gundohinus Gospels*, Cambridge, 1986, 43–46; and "Image and Text: Excerpts from Jerome's 'De Trinitate' and the Maiestas Domini Miniature of the Gundohinus Gospels," *Viator* 18 (1987), 1–21.

82. Vives, *Concilios visigóticos*, 1–2.

83. Vives, *Concilios visigóticos*, 398–99; 498–500.

84. The lack of wall painting from the years of Visigothic rule is to some extent due to the prominent place of the thick-walled ashlar tradition of construction, an expensive technique in

which the masonry most often remained exposed, and decoration took the form of carved moldings and capitals. San Pedro de la Nave and Quintanilla de las Viñas are the two primary examples. More likely candidates for a painting tradition might be buildings excavated in the south that are constructed of rubblework—a tradition more suited to interior wall painting—but these are without evidence of painting, (for instance, Casa Herrera, the double-apsed church (Schlunk and Hauschild, *Die Denkmäler*, 145). There was certainly painting in the Late Antique period, however, and this had some impact on the ornamental registers and San Julián. Santa Eulalia de Bóveda (see note 69) reveals decorative paintings in lozenge patterns identical to those of the apse vaults of Santullano, as Schlunk and Berenguer have shown (*La pintura mural*, 46). The fragments are so close that Núñez suggests them to be part of an Asturian reconstruction of the building (Núñez, *Arquitectura prerrománica*, 136). Details of the *trompe l'oeil* decoration can also be seen in Late Antique sites like Troia, in Portugal (fourth century) (P. de Palol, *Arqueología cristiana de la España romana*, Madrid, 1967, 235–39). Asturian wall painting abounds in the years following San Julián. Fragments of stucco covered with red painting have also been discovered at Santianes de Pravia and at Alfonso's church of Santa María, but there is no evidence of a tradition of the scale of San Julián (Menéndez Pidal, "La Basílica," 287; Schlunk, "El arte asturiano en torno al 800," 145). The Cámara Santa was covered with stucco "prepared like that used for fresco" (Fernández and Hevia, *Ruinas del Oviedo primitivo*, 102).

85. It is a problem complicated by the paucity of manuscripts from that period. Vieillard-Troiekouroff has suggested aniconic Spanish sources for Theodulf's Bibles (M. Vieillard-Troiekouroff, "Les bibles de Théodulfe et leur décor aniconique," *Etudes ligériennes d'histoire et d'archéologie médiévales*, Saint-Benoît-sur-Loire, France, 1975, 345–60; "Les bibles de Théodulfe et la bible wisigothique de la Cava dei Tirreni," *Synthronon*, 1968, 153–66). Note Nees's objections in *The Gundohinus Gospels*, 43–46; and especially in "Image and Text: Excerpts from Jerome's 'De Trinitate' and the Maiestas Domini Miniature of the Gundohinus Gospels." J. Williams (*Early Spanish Manuscript Illumination*, 10–11) discusses a single illuminated page from around 700 in a manuscript now in Verona that affirms, in part, his contention that "Spain's cul-

ture was based upon developments in more cosmopolitan centers of the Mediterranean" (10). Elsewhere, in discussing the Evangelist frontispieces of the Morgan Beatus and the Bible of San Millán, he states that "there is no reason to think that they too did not go back to an illustrated Spanish Bible of the sixth century" ("The Beatus Commentaries and Spanish Bible Illustration," *Actas del Simposio para el Estudio de los Códices del "Comentario al Apocalipsis" de Beato de Liébana*, 1, Madrid, 1980, 210).

Schlunk has suggested a tradition of Visigothic miniatures related to the later *Beatus* manuscripts, which were the models for the sculptural program of San Pedro de la Nave ("Observaciones en torno al problema de la miniatura visigoda," *AEArte* 71 [1945], 241–65). On later manuscripts as echoes of lost art of the Visigothic period, see O. K. Werkmeister, "Die Bilder der drei Propheten in der Biblia Hispalense," *MM* 4, (1963), 141–88. A Spanish attribution for the Ashburnham Pentateuch has been suggested (W. Neuss, "Probleme der Christlichen Kunst im Maurischen Spanien des 10. Jahrhunderts," *Frühmittelalterliche Kunst*, 1954, 253, 261, 271) but rejected by Vieillard-Troiekouroff ("Les bibles de Théodulfe et la Bible wisigothique de la Cava dei Tirreni," note 10). See notes 81 and 84.

86. See note 84.

87. The notion of Adoptionism as one of the motives for the aniconic program of Prados was first advanced in a more restricted argument written by myself and A. DeForest, "San Julián de los Prados: Arte, diplomacia, y herejía," 258–63.

88. Concerning Adoptionism, see E. Amann, *L'Epoque carolingienne*, Strasbourg, 1937, 129–52; W. Heil, "Der Adoptionismus, Alkuin und Spanien," *Karl der Grosse*, 2:166–68, 95–155; D'Abadal, *La batalla*. Though there is considerable evidence that a pictorial tradition can be associated from the beginning with the Commentary of the Apocalypse written by Beatus of Liébana, I do not think that provides contradictory evidence to the association of Adoptionism and San Julián in this single case. I am arguing for an isolated association of the doctrinal and artistic issues, one which springs from the court, not from Liébana. In the course of this essay, I hope to demonstrate that it grows from concerns peculiar to Alfonso II, not from those necessarily of Beatus. On the pictorial tradition of the Beatus manuscripts, see P. Klein, "La tradición pictórica de los Beatos," *Actas del Simposio para el Estudio de los Códices del "Comentario al Apocalip-

sis" de Beato de Liébana, vol. 1, Madrid, 1980, 85–115; *Die ältere Beatus-Kodex Vitr. 14–1 der Biblioteca Nacional zu Madrid, Hildesheim*, vol. 1, 1976, especially 157–74; O. K. Werckmeister, "Pain and Death in the Beatus of Saint-Sever," *Studi Medievali* 14 (1973), 565–626. One does not expect, of course, that every reaction to Adoptionism will take the same form. See D. Guinta, "I mosaici dell'arco absidiale della basilica dei SS. Nereo e Achileo e l'eresia adozionista dell Sec. VIII," in *Roma e l'età carolingia*, Rome, 1976, 195–200.

89. D'Abadal, *La batalla*, 41. Concerning Carolingian-Asturian relations, see Amann, *L'Epoque carolingienne*, 133; Heil, "Der Adoptionismus."

90. Amann, *L'Epoque carolingienne*, 133.

91. Ibid.; D'Abadal, *La batalla*, 53.

92. "Heterii et Beati ad Elipandum," *PL*, 96: 893–1030.

93. Amann, *L'Epoque carolingienne*, 134.

94. See page 28.

95. *ES*, 5:536.

96. Sánchez-Albornoz, *Estudios críticos*, 433.

97. E. Ewig, "The Age of Charles the Great, 768–814," *The Church in the Age of Feudalism*, New York, 1969, 80. See also, for this issue, Amann, *L'Epoque carolingienne*, 132–33; D'Abadal, *La batalla*, 65–66; and Defourneaux, "Carlomagno y el reino Asturiano," 94. Collins disagrees with this position (*Early Medieval Spain*, 212).

98. Barrau-Dihigo, "Recherches sur l'histoire politique du royaume Asturien," *Revue Hispanique* 52 (1921), 159 n. 1.

99. Sánchez-Albornoz, "El 'Asturorum Regnum' en los días de Beatus de Liébana," *Actas del Simposio para el Estudio de los Códices del "Comentario al Apocalipsis" de Beato de Liébana*, 1:30–31.

100. Ewig, "The Age of Charles the Great," 81–82. Only Teudila of Seville failed to stand behind Elipandus. Here again Adoptionism was condemned in a detailed refutation by Charlemagne and his court.

101. Demetrio Mansilla, "La supuesta metrópoli de Oviedo," *Hispaniae Sacra* 8 (1955), 259–74. It is clear that only a bishopric, and not an archbishopric, was established during Alfonso's reign, despite Ewig's assertion that an archepiscopal see was established in 811 as the logical culmination to the Adoptionist controversy ("The Age of Charles the Great," 83). At the heart of the problem are the apparently falsified

documents of Bishop Pelayo of Oviedo (1101–29), who hoped to establish a long history for an archbishopric at Oviedo, in order to resist the authority of Bernard, archbishop of Toledo. Defourneaux, who is cautious in his assessment of these documents, feels it is likely that a council of Asturian bishops was held around this time, an act that points to consolidation and "political and religious reconstruction" ("Carlomagno y el reino Asturiano," 97–98). Sánchez-Albornoz, (*Estudios críticos*, 2:433–35) sees the bishopric and council as part of the "restoration of the Gothic order" spoken of in the Chronicle of Albelda. He views the new organization as part of a conscious projection of the "proud intent of the little monarchy to elevate its integral rank" (433). He further mentions that he does not think the rupture was ordered specifically to cut ties with "Toledan heterodoxy." I would agree, for it seems clear that the quarrel over Adoptionism was used as the justification for a rupture that was surely effected for reasons close to those offered by Sánchez-Albornoz.

102. Falsified eleventh-century documents recount that Theodulf might have attended the council as *missus* of the Carolingian court (Fernández Conde, *El Libro de los testamentos de la catedral de Oviedo*, 130–36). It is impossible to know if any truth is encased in this account, which was intended to increase the power of Oviedo as a see. One wonders, however, how its twelfth-century authors knew, over two centuries after Alfonso II, of Theodulf at all and of the appropriateness of injecting him into that particular political context (Sánchez-Albornoz, *Estudios críticos*, 2:435, 638–39). Defourneaux vacillates concerning this issue ("Charlemagne et la monarchie asturienne," 178–84), offering arguments both for the acceptance and rejection of Carolingian participation in this early council.

103. The issues are the same, if one accepts the representation of Adoptionism offered by Beatus and Etherius: whether Christ's humanity precludes his divinity. The *Apologeticus* (864) of Abbot Samson of Córdoba, the abbot's defense against the Anthropomorphists, who were his enemies, "bears a likeness to the treatise of Beatus and Eterius against Elipandus of Toledo, which occupies the first half of the manuscript in which the *Apologeticus* is found" (E. Colbert, *The Martyrs of Córdoba*, Washington, D.C., 1962, 370). Their association in the same manuscript, combined with the similarities in structure and style and the similar nature of the dogmatic digres-

sions alleged, would suggest some association in the ninth century.

104. On the *Libri Carolini*, see A. Freeman, "Theodulf of Orleans and the *Libri Carolini*," *Speculum* 32 (1957), 663–705; E. Dahlhaus-Berg, *Nova Antiquitas et Antiqua Novitas: Typologische Exegese und isidorianisches Geschichtsbild bei Theodulf von Orleans*, Vienna, 1975. Barral i Altet suggested that Santullano reflected "La misma actitud que dirigió el iconoclasmo bizantino" ("La representación del palacio," 299), an idea seconded briefly by Schlunk in "El arte asturiano en torno al 800," 156.

105. Amann, *L'Epoque carolingienne*, 129; Ewig, "The Age of Charles the Great," 78.

106. Schnitzler would take issue with this, in particular as regards the mosaics from Aachen ("Das Kuppelmosaik der Aachener Pfalzkapelle." For a refutation, see H. Schrade, "Zum Kuppelmosaik der Pfalzkapelle und zum Theoderich-Denkmal in Aachen"). The surviving painting programs at Mustair (B. Brenk, *Tradition und Neuerung in der Christlichen Kunst des Ersten Jahrtausends: Studien zur Geschichte des Weltgesichtsbildes*, Vienna, 1966, 107–18) and later at Ingelheim (W. Lammers, "Ein karolingisches Bildprogramm in der Aula Regia von Ingelheim," *Festschrift fur Herman Heipel* 3 [1972], 226–89) suggest none of the aniconic ideas voiced in the *Libri Carolini*. Further, a poem of Theodulf himself describes a figural fresco of the Seven Liberal Arts, which Esmeijer sees as a propagandistic device for furthering educational reform (A. Esmeijer, "De VII liberalibus artibus in quadam pictura depictis: Een reconstructie van de arbor philosophiae van Theodulf van Orleans," ed. J. Bruyn et al. *Album Amicorum J. Van Gelder Martinus Nijhoff*, The Hague, 1973, 102–13).

107. F. Mutherich, "I Libri Carolini," 286. There are also some manuscripts that might, for their rejection of images, reflect the impact of the *Libri* (288). See also note 85 above.

108. Theodulf's birthplace is based on a passage from one of his poems, in which he states: ". . . a happy crowd met me, the remnant of the Gothic people; and a crown of Spaniards also, who were happy that I, an official, was of their blood" (N. Alexandrenko, "The Poetry of Theodulf of Orleans: A Translation and Critical Study" [Ph.D. dissertation, Tulane University, 1970], 164). See also Dahlhaus-Berg, *Nova Antiquitas et Antiqua Novitas*, 7. For Germigny des Prés, dedicated in 806, see P. Bloch, "Das Apsis-mosaik von Germigny-des-Prés, Karl der Grosse und der Alte Bund," *Karl der Grosse*, 3:234–61; Vieillard-Troiekouroff, "Nouvelles études sur les mosaïques de Germigny des Prés," *Cahiers Archéologiques* 17 (1967), 103–12; "A propos de Germigny des Prés," *Cahiers Archéologiques* 13, 1962, 267–68.

109. A. Freeman has made a strong case for Theodulf's authorship of the *Libri Carolini* ("Theodulf of Orleans and the *Libri Carolini*"). Though her contention is strongly opposed by Wallach ("Theodulf of Orleans; Alleged Authorship of the *Libri Carolini*: On Fictions and Facts," *Diplomatic Studies in Latin and Greek Documents from the Carolingian Age*, Ithaca, NY, 1977, pt. 3), the consensus is with P. Meyvaert, who contends that Ms. Freeman has proved Theodulf's authorship of the *Libri Carolini* "beyond any reasonable doubt" ("The Authorship of the *Libri Carolini*: Observations Prompted by a Recent Book," *Revue Bénédictine* 89/1–2 [1979], 29–57). Concerning Théodulfe and aniconism, see Vieillard-Troiekouroff, "Les bibles de Theodulf et leur décor aniconique," 345; Dahlhaus-Berg, *Nova Antiquitas et Antiqua Novitas*, 190–201; Freeman, "Theodulf of Orleans and the *Libri Carolini*," especially 699–701. See, however, Nees's objections, in *Gundohenis Gospels*, 43–46; "Image and Text: Excerpts from Jerome's 'De Trinitate' and the Maiestas Domini Miniature of the Gundohinus Gospels." Vieillard-Troiekouroff (349) establishes a number of Carolingian bishops who were of Spanish origin, and identifies them as having similar attitudes as Theodulf toward the cult of the images. Bango Torviso follows her argument in his treatment of San Julián de los Prados, proposing a Carolingian aniconic tradition inspired largely by Hispanic ecclesiastical and monastic traditions (Bango Torviso, "'L'Ordo Gotorum,'" 16–17).

110. A. L. Kroeber, "Stimulus Diffusion," *American Anthropologist* 42/1 (1940), 1–20. Stimulus diffusion, according to Kroeber, "occurs in situations where a system or pattern as such encounters no resistance to its spread, but there are difficulties in regard to the transmission of the concrete content of the system. In this case it is the idea of the complex or system which is accepted, but it remains for the receiving culture to develop a new content" (1).

111. "Libri Carolini," *MGH*, Legum sectio III, Concilia 2, supplementum 1.

112. Theodulf of Orleans, *De ordine baptismi; De spiritu sancto, PL*, 105:223–76.

113. Jonas of Orleans, *De Cultu Imaginum*, *PL*, 106:308. Sánchez-Albornoz suggests he went as *missus* of Charlemagne's court (*Estudios críticos*, 539).

114. A. Freeman, "Carolingian Orthodoxy and the Fate of the Libri Carolini," *Viator* 16 (1985), 64–108.

115. W. Heil, "Der Adoptionismus, Alkuin und Spanien," 149–50.

116. Heil, "Der Adoptionismus, Alkuin und Spanien," 150.

117. "Libri Carolini," 5.

118. Ewig, "The Age of Charles the Great," 82.

119. Schlunk's date is widely accepted: *La pin-tura mural*, 5 n. 4. See also Floriano Llorente, *Diplomática*, 127. Concerning the authenticity of the document, see Floriano Llorente, "El testa-mento de Alfonso II el Casto," 593–617; Sánchez-Albornoz, *Estudios críticos*, 567–75.

120. He compares his misfortunes with those of Jacob (Sánchez-Albornoz, *Estudios críticos*, 555–56).

121. Bango Torviso, "'L'Ordo Gotorum,'" 17; Floriano Llorente, *Diplomática*, 2:118–31. Con-cerning the authenticity of the document, see Floriano Llorente, "El testamento de Alfonso II el Casto," 593–617; Sánchez-Albornoz, *Estudios críticos*, 567–75.

Chapter 3: Bearing Witness

1. The continuity of the architectural space distinguishes Valdediós from those monu-ments in which the spaces set apart by church furniture, such as chancel screens, are reas-serted in architectural space, such as Visigothic and Mozarabic foundations. On Valdediós, see Helmut Schlunk, *AH*, 2:377–81, 388; M. Gómez-Moreno, *Iglesias mozárabes*, Madrid, 1919 (reprint, Granada, 1975), 76–81; J. Pita An-drade, *Arte asturiano*, Madrid, 1963, 31–33. On the paintings of Valdediós, see Helmut Schlunk and Magín Berenguer, *La pintura mural asturiana de los siglos IX y X*, Madrid, 1957, 126–49. Schlunk argued for considerable Is-lamic influence in the ornamentation of Astu-rian churches (window screens, pinnacles, a kind of fillet at the neck of capitals). With the exception of the pinnacles, the impact he sees is in tiny details that find a common foundation in Visigothic period and Late Antique proto-types (for example, the decorated windows carved from one or a number of stones, orna-mented with abstract motives. See page 33). Any actual evidence of formal appropriation of Islamic ornamentation is so limited and ab-sorbed into the local tradition that it is difficult to see with Schlunk "Mitarbeit" with Islamic artists ("Die Auseinandersetzung der Christ-lichen und der Islamischen Kunst auf dem Ge-biete der Iberischen Halbinsel bis zum Jahre 1000," *Spoleto*, 1965, 1:912).

2. For example, as at San Julián de los Prados. See chapter 2.

3. For San Salvador de Priesca, see Schlunk, *AH*, 384–88; Gómez-Moreno, *Iglesias mozárabes*, 86–88; Schlunk and Berenguer, *La pintura mural*, 150–60. Valdediós does contain motifs not found at San Julián, notably a human figure. These of course are far from the paintings that will appear in Mozara-bic buildings, and which are discussed in chap-ter 4.

4. García Lobo supposes the monks settled there at Alfonso III's direction, and possibly even lent them masons for the first, now-destroyed church (*Las inscripciones de San Miguel de Escalada: Estudio crítico*, Barcelona, 1982, 44). For Escalada, see also Gómez-Moreno, *Iglesias mozárabes*, 141–62; and Schlunk, "Die Auseinandersetzung," 914–15, 921–25. Certain parts of the church now standing are not contemporary with the 913 dedication. The tower and several truncated walls extending from it are Romanesque in construction and dec-oration. They must date to 1040, when one Sabarico reconstructed and inscribed a south door. The porch, with its arcade of radical horse-shoe arches, betrays two campaigns: the seven westernmost surely date near 940, for in details of construction they are extremely close to Santi-ago de Peñalba, dated to the end of the third de-cade of the tenth century, when it received the relics of its founder San Genedio (*Iglesias mozá-rabes*, 227). In particular the arch form and its construction, the use of a cyma and monolithic jambs, are evidence of this connection (Gómez-Moreno, *Iglesias mozárabes*, 154). The balance of the porch (five eastern arches) includes capitals

of the Peñalba style as well, but these are the *spolia* of the ruined monastery of Eslonza, destroyed by al-Manṣūr in 988. That section of the portico, then, must date with the Romanesque tower. Finally, Escalada's central apse is encased in ashlar that recalls the section of the portico dating to the 940s: the apse's exterior, and possibly also its vault, was reconstructed during this period.

5. The panels of this barrier, now partially reconstructed, can be found at Escalada in the church itself, reused in the portal of the Romanesque tower, and in the Museo Arqueológico Provincial in León.

6. Gómez-Moreno cites some of these similarities, calling them "Asturian influence" (*Iglesias mozárabes*, 148). Some of the examples cited here have also been noted by José Camón Aznar in an article discussed in note 16 ("Arquitectura española del siglo X; Mozárabe y de la repoblación," *Goya* 52 [1963], 206–19).

7. Gómez-Moreno, *Iglesias mozárabes*, ix–xvi; xxi.

8. Gómez-Moreno, *Iglesias mozárabes*, ix–xxiv.

9. Gómez-Moreno, *Iglesias mozárabes*, xviii.

10. Camón Aznar, "Arquitectura española del siglo X." On the question of Asturian and Mozarabic architecture, see also Schlunk, "Die Auseinandersetzung." Manuscript illumination must, of course, be considered separately. The idea that northern styles of illumination associated with the repopulation must not be defined in terms of Islamic content is discussed by J. Williams, "A Contribution to the History of the Castilian Monastery of Valeranica and the Scribe Florentius," *MM* 11 (1970), 247. He notes that the manuscript tradition cannot be said to be the work of Mozarabic monks in particular, and that it is steeped in a number of diverse artistic traditions, including those of Carolingian France.

11. Camón Aznar, "Arquitectura española del siglo X," 207. He calls it "una continuación sin fisuras" (212).

12. I. Bango Torviso, "Arquitectura de la décima centuria. ¿Repoblación o Mozárabe?" *Goya* 122 (1974), 75. Pita Andrade calls it "Arte fronterizo" (*Castilla la Vieja, León*, Madrid, 1975, 104).

13. Author's translation. "Hic locus antiquitus Michaelis archangeli honore dicatus, brevi opere instructus, post ruinis abolitus, diu mansit dirutus, donec Adefonsus abba cum sociis adveniens a Corduvensi patria edis ruinam erexit sub valente seren(issim)o Adefonso principe. Monachorum numero crescente demum hoc templum decorum miro opere a fundamine exundique amplificatum erigitur. Non iussu imperiali vel oppresione vulgi sed abbatis Adefonsi et fratrum instante vigilantia duodenis mensibus peracta sunt haec opera, Garsea sceptra regni paragerens Mumadona cum regina Era DCCCCLI Sacratumque templum ab episcopum Iennadium XII kal. decembrium." Transcription, Gómez-Moreno, *Iglesias mozárabes*, 141. See also García Lobo, *Las inscripciones de San Miguel de Escalada*, 41–47, 64–65.

14. Those who interpret this passage through such social intention are: M. de Escalada, *San Miguel de Escalada*, Gijón, 1954, 14; A. Calvo, *San Pedro de Eslonza*, Madrid, 1957, García Lobo interprets this passage as indicating the monks completed the work themselves (*Las inscripciones de San Miguel de Escalada*, 46).

15. Bango Torviso argues for an understanding that the Mozarabs themselves did not construct their own buildings for the most part ("Arquitectura de la décima centuria," 74–75). Documents that refer to Mozarabic architects do not in any way contradict the notion that the Mozarabic monks of Escalada and other foundations were not the masons of their own monuments. First, of course, the existence of architects among Christians from the south does not imply that all were architects. More specifically, the Cordoban architect Zacarías, who went to work at the monastery of Lorban, near Coimbra, in the mid-tenth century, is recorded as doing general work, including bridges and windmills (Gómez-Moreno, *Iglesias mozárabes*, 7; F. J. Simonet, *Historia de los mozárabes*, Madrid, 1903, 633). There is no reason to suppose these activities were excluded to Christians under Islamic rule, but there is also no suggestion that Zacarías was a monk. Indeed, the fact he was called in from the outside suggests that monasteries—indigenous or immigrant—were not filled with monks who, in addition to their regular duties, also doubled as masons or architects. We can suppose the existence of, at the most, an odd brother skilled in architectural design or used to serving in the capacity of construction supervision, such as the *Aedificium* mentioned in Visigothic documents.

16. Bango Torviso came the closest with his

analysis of Visigothic documents, which led him to interpret Asturian-Leonese interest in Visigothic culture in general as initiated by their contact with ruined Visigothic churches during the repopulation ("El neovisigotismo artístico de los siglos IX y X: La restauración de ciudades y templos," *Revista de Ideas Estéticas* 148 [1979], 35–54). In "Arquitectura de la décima centuria," he says, "in the tenth century there is a 'Renaissance' of Hispano-Visigothic forms, with an Asturian parenthesis" (73). However, he does not connect the notion to the Mozarabs themselves, or to any ideological interest in the Visigoths, which is my primary aim in this work. Puig i Cadafalch considered many Mozarabic buildings to represent survival of forms from the Visigothic period (*L'Art wisigothique et ses survivances*, Paris, 1961). Gómez-Moreno saw some retention of seventh- and eighth-century forms as well as many characteristics from the Visigothic period that he believed were absorbed first in Islamic building, then passed to Mozarabic architecture (*Iglesias mozárabes*, xviii–xx). This attitude is basically accepted and extended by Fontaine (*L'Art préroman hispanique*, vol. 2, Ste.-Marie de la Pierre-qui-Vire, 1977, 49–60), who stresses that opening up to al-Andalus reacquainted the Mozarabs with motives from the Visigothic period shared by them both. Camón Aznar explains the strong relationship that exists between architecture of the Visigothic period and Mozarabic architecture through the notion of continuity of tradition ("Arquitectura española del Siglo X," 207). Also of interest is the work of S. Noack, who sees in Mozarabic monuments the conscious use of *spolia* from the Visigothic period ("Typologische Untersuchungen zur den mozarabischen Kapitellen von San Cebrián de Mazote [Prov. Valladolid]," *MM* 26 [1985], 314–45; also an unpublished lecture given at Columbia University, April 1986). Werckmeister found significant attention to Visigothic style in manuscripts produced by Christians in al-Andalus, but at the end of the tenth century: "Die Bilder der Drei Propheten in der *Biblia Hispalense*," *MM* 4 (1963), 141–88.

17. On the whole, this means of distinguishing an arch of the Visigothic period from an Islamic arch presents difficulties, since the Islamic examples are derived from seventh- and eighth-century prototypes. Decorative arches of the Visigothic period—though rarely constructive ones—sometimes surpass the one-third to one-half radius normally assigned to pre-Islamic arches, and some Islamic arches retain the more subtle profile traditionally associated with the Visigothic period. In particular, the horseshoe arches of the Great Mosque of Córdoba before the caliphate seem to maintain similar proportions to those built before the invasion, from which they ultimately derive. Such proportions are important for establishing a general trend of taste within the two periods, especially after the mid-tenth century, but ought not to be used as an airtight means of attribution. See J. Fontaine, *L'Art préroman hispanique*, vol. 1, Ste.-Marie de la Pierre-qui-Vire, 1973, 127–28; L. Caballero, "La forma en herradura hasta el siglo VIII, y los arcos de herradura de la iglesia visigoda de Santa María de Melque," *AEArq* 50–51 [1977–78], 323–37; and E. Camps Cazorla (*Módulo, proporciones y composición en la arquitectura califal cordobesa*, Madrid, 1953), who gave us much of the technical language in which we discuss horseshoe arches today. Camón Aznar attempts to assign the horseshoe arches of the churches commonly called Mozarabic to indigenous Asturian tradition. He thus calls "repopulation" (those we call Mozarabic here) arches of the type generally associated with the Visigothic period, but claims that they are all filtered through Asturian examples. One of his examples, however, is constructed in an ashlar tradition, and is also dated to the Visigothic period by some (San Félix at Oca, see J. Uranga Galdiano and F. Iñiguez Almech, *Arte medieval navarro. I. Arte prerrománico*, Pamplona, 1971, 40). Another is known through a description of the sixteenth-century text only (Santa María at Oviedo). Those at Nora and Priesca are incredibly timid and on piers, and are further thought by Gómez-Moreno to reflect the influence of the Mozarabic churches because of their late date (Gómez-Moreno, *Iglesias mozárabes*, 86–88). The horseshoe arches of Lena, Salas, Sariego, and Valdediós are tiny decorative ones carved in window shapes from a single stone, and the remains of Santiago only offer similar decorative examples of stone carving ("Arquitectura española del siglo X," 211). None of the examples offered by Camón Aznar addresses the new appearance, at Escalada, of the consistent use of constructive horseshoe arches fashioned with voussoirs and received by columns.

18. For instance, San Pedro de la Nave, where the arches range from +1/3 to +1/2; +1/3 to +2/5 at San Juan de Baños. For a his-

tory of the constructive horseshoe arch in Spain, see Caballero, "La forma en herradura," 332–37. Concerning the later dating claims for some of the monuments of the Visigothic period discussed here, see Palol, who in excavations dates the nave of Baños and excludes the possibility of Mozarabic reconstruction: *Excavaciones en la necrópolis de San Juan de Baños*, Madrid, 1964, 22. For a review of the reconstructed parts of Santa Comba de Bande, see chapter 1, II, note 64; for São Frutuoso de Montelios, chapter 1, I. Concerning San Pedro de la Nave, I favor a late seventh- or early eighth-century date (see chapter 1, II, note 63). This seems especially likely since the 907 document—the first mention of the church—refers in no way to its construction or foundation, though these events are usually spelled out clearly in repopulation texts (see chapter 1, note 63). Quintanilla de las Viñas, like San Pedro de la Nave, is very much a part of the masonry and sculpture tradition developed under Visigothic rule, so that I see its ninth-century patrons as having completed, at most, a building cut and largely built the century before (see chapter 1, section II, note 70).

19. Nonradial voussoirs are found in Islamic arches, for instance, at the Great Mosque of Córdoba, in the reconstructed patio entrance to the mosque built by ʿAbd al-Raḥmān III in 958 (F. Hernández Giménez, *El alminar de ʿAbd al-Raḥmān III en la Mezquita Mayor de Córdoba*, Granada, 1972, 273, fig. 56).

20. This occurs in Islamic doors at the Great Mosque of Córdoba, but in arches with much wider extrados.

21. L. Caballero, "La forma en herradura," 351–64; "Algunas observaciones sobre arquitectura española de 'Epoca de Transición' [Cabeza de Griego y Visigoda]," in R. González Ruiz, ed., *Innovación y continuidad en la España visigoda*, Toledo, 1981, 69–79.

22. See chapter 1, II and III.

23. Fontaine, *L'Art préroman hispanique*, 2:17.

24. Escalada is probably not the first monument of the repopulation to copy a horseshoe-arched arcade—though it is the earliest to survive—but it is clearly a place in which not only the consultation of models from the Visigothic period but also the masons' experimentation was still key to the realization of its patrons' vision. We cannot know whether these details of construction were first introduced in

the south or the north, or exactly when. They may well be the tenuous technical contribution of the Cordoban monks, whether through a brother who was himself a mason, or through contacts with an immigrant Mozarabic mason or two within indigenous Asturian ateliers. The presence of one or even a few such masons, it need not be said, cannot be seen as the impetus for such an enormous change in typology and formal tradition as appears in the north with the spread of Mozarabic architecture, especially since the main force of the atelier seems to have been Asturian by training. The presence of a diverse atelier, hypothetical at this point, forms for us perhaps a more complex and textured vision of the circumstances under which Mozarabic patrons might be seen as having achieved the creation of a specific novel style in the north through the agency of local masons.

25. The most authoritative work for the construction of the Great Mosque of Córdoba is to be found in the work of C. Ewert and J.-P. Wisshak, *Forschungen zur almohadischen Moschee, 1. Hierarchische Gliederungen westislamischer Betsäle des 8. bis 11. Jahrhunderts: Die Hauptmoscheen von Qairawan und Córdoba und ihr Bannkreis*, Mainz, 1981. For the chronology and construction of the eighth- and ninth-century arches of the Great Mosque of Córdoba, see also Gómez-Moreno, *AH*, 3:41–59; E. Camps Cazorla, *Módulo proporciones y composición*; E. Lambert, "Las ampliaciones de la Mezquita de Córdoba en el siglo IX," *Al Andalus* 4 (1935), 391–92; H. Terrasse, "La portada de San Esteban en la Mezquita de Córdoba," *Al Andalus* 12 (1974), 127–44; F. Hernández Giménez, *El alminar de ʿAbd al-Raḥmān III*. The "Puerta de Deanes" is known from its interior and thought by Hernández Giménez to date from the foundation of the mosque (147), while Gómez-Moreno dates it to the enlargements of ʿAbd al-Raḥmān II (822–852) (56). The Door of Saint Stephen was primarily constructed in two campaigns: one in the eighth century (tripartite organization and perhaps lateral reliefs) and one in the ninth century (arch form). Aspects that probably must be dated later are the mosaic tile work and the ornamentation found at high levels, among the windows, which is probably twelfth century (Gómez-Moreno, *AH*, 3:41–42). The "Portal of Saint Michael" is dated by Gómez-Moreno to the reign of ʿAbd al-Raḥmān II (*AH*, 3:56–59) and by Hernández Giménez to the reign of ʿAbd 'Allah (888–912) (*El alminar*, 147–50).

Both hypotheses present a door that would predate Mozarabic buildings.

26. A later arch with uncentered voussoirs like that at Escalada demonstrates the significant aspects of design which distinguish it as Islamic, but which are missing at the Mozarabic monument; the entrance arch from the patio of the Great Mosque of Córdoba into the hypostyle hall, though restored, is reconstructed with red and white polychromy on alternating voussoirs, and an enframing *alfiz*. See Hernández Giménez, *El alminar de ʿAbd al-Raḥmān III*, 273, fig. 56.

The arches of the altar screen at Escalada are more radical in proportion, exceeding the semicircle by three-fifths of the radius. They were traced on the basis of an equilateral triangle (Gómez-Moreno, *AH*, 3:369). Though this is unlike most Visigothic prototypes, it does not provide a strong recollection of surviving Islamic prototypes either.

27. This section dates to ʿAbd al-Raḥmān I (756–788). See Gómez-Moreno, *AH*, 3:28–44.

28. The groins at Escalada are consonant with traditions of the Visigothic period in technique (Santa Comba de Bande probably had a groin originally, and Santa María de Quintanilla de las Viñas certainly did), though the domical shape evokes no surviving indigenous examples either in Christian or Islamic architecture. The oldest example of the vault type can be found at Saints Sergios and Bakchos in Constantinople (Gómez-Moreno, *Iglesias mozárabes*, 149), and a more recent example exists at Saint Laurent, Grenoble (Gómez-Moreno, *AH*, 3:372). Camón Aznar sees the vault types as responding to Byzantine and Carolingian influences ("Arquitectura española del siglo X," 211). See also Bango Torviso, "Arquitectura de la décima centuria," 71–72.

29. See Bango Torviso, "Arquitectura de la décima centuria," 71–72. Camón Aznar ("Arquitectura española del siglo X," 211) relates the roll corbels to Visigothic "zapatas." There are no modillions in Islamic or Visigothic architecture that provide convincing prototypes for Escalada's (see also L. Torres Balbás, "Los modillones de lóbulos," *AEArteArq*, 12:1–113). Gómez-Moreno points to Sassanian and Achaemenid prototypes for the first Islamic modillions, those with rolls that seem closest to those at Escalada, but sees later examples with only one roll or disk as deriving from Visigothic prototypes *AH*, 3:41; *Iglesias mozárabes*, 149–50. See also Schlunk, "Die Aus-

einandersetzung," 926–27. For the chancel barriers, see H. Schlunk, "Die Entwicklungsläufe der Skulptur auf der Iberischen Halbinsel vom 8. bis 11. Jahrhundert," *Kolloquium über frühmittelalterliche Skulptur*, Mainz, 1972, 128–32, 137; "Die Auseinandersetzung," 921–25. These reliefs bear vestiges of polychromy.

30. Lena is generally believed to have been built under Ramiro I, because of its striking affinities in decoration and construction technique with Santa María de Naranco and San Miguel de Lillo: buttresses on a plinth push against the transverse arches of an interior barrel, capitals carved in a distinctive relief style, and other details of a textured type of articulation. (Schlunk, *AH*, 2:69–74); Camón Aznar tries to suggest a later date on the basis of its enclosed spaces, and because it does not appear in a 905 donation of Alfonso III. Disregarding as it does the strong links between Lena and other buildings of Ramiro I, his attempt is not convincing ("Arquitectura española del siglo X," 212). Pita Andrade, *Arte asturiano*, 28–30; J. B. Lázaro, *Ermita Santa Cristina de Lena, reseña de las obras hechas para su restauración*, Madrid, 1894.

31. See chapter 2, page 28.

32. Schlunk separates these plan types on a functional rather than chronological basis, claiming a monastic, and so more ardently private, function for churches with high barriers like São Gião de Nazaré, and parochial, public functions for those with low barriers like Valdediós and Priesca (Schlunk, "Die Kirche von S. Gião bei Nazaré [Portugal]. Ein Beitrag zur Bedeutung der Liturgie für die Gestaltung des Kirchengebäudes," *MM* 12 [1971], 225–30). The difficulties with this interpretation lie in the total lack of documentation for São Gião (see chapter 1, note 83). The total lack of such barriers and—more important—of the architectural reinforcement of the spaces they define sets Asturian architecture apart in intent and influence. The lack of Asturian monastic churches cannot really answer the whole question, since it is not only the absence of the high altar screen but the supporting enclosed aesthetic in architecture that suggests a loosening of the visual separation of clergy and laity in Asturias.

33. Gómez-Moreno, *Iglesias mozárabes*, 84–85; Schlunk, *AH*, 2:371–72.

34. See chapter 1, II.

35. Fontaine, *L'Art préroman hispanique*,

2:39–48. The description of the clergy separated into the three choirs from the Antiphonary of León becomes a "nostalgic evocation of the golden age of Spanish liturgy" (46). D. Millet-Gérard, *Chrétiens mozarabes et culture islamique*, Paris, 1984, 86. See also chapter 1, note 92.

36. A privilege in favor of the monastery of San Martín of Castañeda, dated 952, mentions that its monks lived first at Mazote, with their abbot, Martín. (For the text, see Gómez-Moreno, *Iglesias mozárabes*, 173–74 n. 3.) Gómez-Moreno interprets the documentation as showing that these monks left Mazote in 915 because of the drought, epidemics, and hunger mentioned by one Arab author almost immediately upon completing their work (since he dates it "estrechamente" with Escalada) (*Iglesias mozárabes*, 173–74). A less tortured hypothesis lies in the possibility that the church was constructed in a wider time frame, perhaps by Abbot Martín, perhaps by the community members who must certainly have been left behind to administrate a monastery whose church is the largest and most beautiful of the repopulation foundations that survive. Both Nave and Quintanilla feature the same mix of vaulted and wooden-roofed spaces. The two-apsed plan is related to Paleochristian prototypes, while the triconched aspect of the east end recalls, in general, the disposition of La Cocosa and Marialba, the former Early Christian and the latter with both Early Christian and Visigothic campaigns. Núñez, in the spirit of Bango Torviso, believes the "neovisigotismo" of the plan must derive from the large number of reconstructions of seventh-century monuments being conducted at this time (*Arquitectura prerrománica*, Madrid, 1978, 189). Recently it has been suggested that the nave was restored too high (J. M. Pita Andrade, *Castilla la Vieja, León*, vol. 1, Madrid, 1975). Almost all vaults were destroyed in a fire; all but one that appear now are reconstructions based on springers surviving above the cornice level. The decoration of Mazote and Peñalba revealed in the course of reconstructions are treated in chapter 4. See also Noack, "Typologische Untersuchungen"; Schlunk, "Die Auseinandersetzung;" Fontaine, *L'Art préroman hispanique*, 2:160–63, 197–99, 411; Universidad de Valladolid, Facultad de Historia, "La reconstrucción de San Cebrián de Mazote," *BSAAV* 4 [1933–34], 95–99; chapter 4, note 16.

37. Gómez-Moreno, *AH*, 3:371.

38. The Mozarabic style here must in part be due to Alfonso II's advances into Portugal. Lourosa's east end was destroyed by al-Manṣur in 987. The building was restored in 1930. See Gómez-Moreno, *Iglesias mozárabes*, 100–104; *AH*, 3:363. J. Pessanha, *Arquitectura pre-románica em Portugal: S. Pedro de Balsemão e S. Pedro de Lourosa*, Coimbra, 1927, believed it to be the reconstruction of a church built before the invasion. Gómez-Moreno posits an east end very characteristic of building of the Visigothic period (103).

39. Its exterior blocking too resembles that of Nave and Bande, and its lateral chambers, like those of Quintanilla and Lena, suggest an attention to a liturgical space long since ignored in Asturias. The twin apses reflect a Paleochristian tradition, the second apse dedicated to the burial of Saint Gennadius himself. Gómez-Moreno places its date with donations of Ramiro II in 937, most of the work achieved after the death of Gennadius in 936. Some windows of the western apse are dated 1170 by inscription. See Fontaine, *L'Art préroman hispanique*, 2:138–43; Gómez-Moreno, *Iglesias mozárabes*, 224–38; *AH*, 3:380–81; Pita Andrade, *Castilla la Vieja, León*, 106–10.

40. Gómez-Moreno calls Celanova an imitation of Peñalba, but in miniature (*AH*, 3:381). Founded by Froila, the brother of Saint Rosendo, between 936 and 940, it is dated by a commemorative poem recommending the founder, inscribed over its lateral door. Saint Rosendo was a familiar of the Asturian-Leonese monarchy. Celanova's extraordinary ashlar masonry is clearly executed in imitation of Visigothic masonry. See Gómez-Moreno, *Iglesias mozárabes*, 239–50; Núñez, *Arquitectura prerrománica*, 256–73. Santa María de Vilanova originally had horseshoe arches in elevation, which are now lost. Its ashlar walls relate it to Celanova and Pazo, and its capitals are rough imitations of Peñalba. The monastery for women was founded by Iladura, who retired there before her death in 958. See Núñez, *Arquitectura prerrománica*, 251–55; Gómez-Moreno, *Iglesias mozárabes*, 250–52. Williams has also brought to light the remains of a monastic building at Valeranica, which originally possessed an apse with a horseshoe-shaped interior as well as reused Visigothic reliefs ("A Contribution to the History of the Castilian Monastery of Valeranica," 239–44). Though Williams cites the evidence cautiously, it seems clear

that he is correct in his identification of a tenth-century church at the site. Of interest is the brick construction, which Williams equates with the use of brick in the clerestory of Escalada.

41. The origins of San Pedro de Rocas are lost, but there remains a legend of a double foundation, and a number of tenth-century documents associating monastic foundations and caves. Gómez-Moreno supports the notion of a hermetic monastery founded here under Alfonso III, and an altar table with elegant horseshoe-arched reliefs is dated by him to the end of the ninth century. There is Romanesque reconstruction in reinforcing arches and the entrance arch. (Gómez-Moreno, *Iglesias mozárabes*, 94–95). The other rupestral churches offer more difficult problems in dating. Pita Andrade believes there was a high degree of survival of monasticism in the Ebro region during the depopulation, which leads him to date many of the cave churches that survive to the Visigothic period (*Castilla la Vieja, León*, 100). For examples in the Visigothic and Mozarabic periods, see R. Vano Silvestre, "Oratorio rupestre visigodo del Cortijo de Valdecanales, Rus (Jaén)," *MM* 11 [1970], 213–22; T. Hauschild and H. Schlunk, "Die Hohenkirche beim Cortijo de Valdecanales," *MM* 11 [1970], 223–30; Uranga Galdiano and Iñiguez Almech, *Arte medieval navarro*, 45–53. The little church of San Esteban de Viguera presents a different problem. Its disproportionately wide apse is clearly added to the body of the nave, cutting off the chancel wall and suggesting, perhaps, its disuse at a late period. The curious Islamicizing paintings are twelfth century. See Uranga Galdiano and Iñiguez Almech, *Arte medieval navarro*, 44–45; Fontaine, *L'Art préroman hispanique*, 2:253, 424. Durliat sees Viguera as eleventh century in its totality (review of Fontaine, *Bulletin Monumental* 136 [1978], 92), a position I find difficult for two reasons. The first is the presence of the chancel wall, which is simply unknown after the tenth century. There is also a clear break in campaigns, and the second of these—the apse—is in proportion and design characteristically eleventh century. Other chapels simply feature the horseshoe-shaped apse entrance supported on adossed columns, as in Hermedes de Cerrato.

42. R. Collins, *Early Medieval Spain, Unity in Diversity*, New York, 1983, 216. See also M. Díaz y Díaz, "La circulation des manuscrits dans la peninsule ibérique du VIII au XI siècles," *Cahiers de Civilisation Médiévale* 12 (1969), 219–41; V. Cantarino, *Entre monjes y musulmanes: El conflicto que fue España*, Madrid, 1978, 112–15; G. Menéndez Pidal, "Le rayonnement de la Culture Isidorienne: Les Mozarabes;" *Cahiers d'Histoire Mondiale* 6, 1960–61, 160–61, 714–31; and H. Grassotti, "Lo mozárabe en el norte cristiano como proyección de la cultura hispano-goda," *Cuadernos de Historia de España* 33–34 (1961), 336–44. The political use of the Visigoths as a historical ideal will be treated later. The most important discussion is to be found in J. A. Maravall, *El concepto de España en la edad media*, Madrid, 1964. See also Werckmeister, "Die Bilder der drei Propheten in der *Biblia Hispalense*."

43. Author's translation: H. Focillion, *L'an mil*, 1952, 26.

44. Bango Torviso, "Arquitectura de la décima centuria," 69.

45. L. Grodecki et al., *Le Siècle de l'an mil*, Paris, 1973, 58.

46. Author's translation. Gómez-Moreno, *Iglesias mozárabes*, xvi.

47. Author's translation. Gómez-Moreno, *AH*, 3:357.

48. "Arquitectura española del siglo X."

49. Madrid, 1955, 132–33.

50. G. Gailliard, "Cluny et l'Espagne dans l'art roman du XIème siècle," *Bulletin Hispanique* 63 (1961), 153–60.

51. The sculptural style traced by Gailliard hardly seems central to the conception or formation of Romanesque sculpture or architecture. The most interesting parallels are made with Asturian, not Mozarabic, architecture, but these also seem unlikely prototypes for the development of Romanesque: the compound piers that appear at Valdediós and Escalada have a simultaneous development in the north, where they first develop in a Romanesque context. The transverse ribs of Naranco (Oviedo) are decorative, not constructive like the Romanesque ones, and are isolated; they are without issue so that the connection with early Romanesque buildings seems remote. The decorative motifs that might have derived from contact with Mozarabic buildings, in which Mozarabic buildings might actually have provided transmission of Islamic impact, are really trivial. Corbel types and ribbed arches such as those found in Mozarabic churches after Escalada appear occasionally but cannot be considered part of the

formation of the Romanesque style. Fontaine reviews the arguments (*L'Art préroman hispanique*, 2:89). See also Gailliard, *Premiers essais de sculpture monumentale en Catalogne aux Xème et XIème siècles* (Paris, 1938), "Cluny et l'Espagne dans l'art roman du XIème siècle" (153–60), and "La Catalogne entre l'art de Cordoue et l'art roman" (*Studia Islamica* 6 [1956], 19–35, where he argues unconvincingly for the presence at San Michel de Cuxa of Islamic masons who thereby bring the header and stretcher masonry of Córdoba to the north. The masonry at Cuxa, however, is only faced rubblework. Further, the suggestion does not take into account all the formal properties that truly compose Romanesque architecture, properties developed before ashlar became one of the primary media of the architectural style. See E. Armi ("Orders and Continuous Orders in Romanesque Architecture," *JSAH* 34/3, [1975], 173–88) for a definition of the properties of early Romanesque architecture and its development. See also E. Lambert, *Etudes Médiévales*, vol. 3, Paris, 1956; K. J. Conant, *Cluny: Les églises et la maison du chef d'ordre* (Mâcon, 1968, 81).

I. Christians and Building in al-Andalus

52. For a survey of the military campaigns and early rule of al-Andalus in the eighth century, see Evariste Lévi-Provençal, *Histoire de l'Espagne Musulmane: La conquête et l'Émirat Hispano-Omaiyade*, Paris and Leiden, 1950, 19–89.

53. T. Glick, *Islamic and Christian Spain in the Early Middle Ages*, Princeton, 1979, 168.

54. Z. García-Villada, *Historia eclesiástica*, vol. 3, Madrid, 1929–36, 31. Concerning the first treaties between Christians and Muslims in al-Andalus, see A. M. Howell, "Some Notes on Early Treaties Between Muslims and the Visigothic Rulers of al-Andalus," *Actas del 1 Congreso de historia de Andalucía*, Córdoba, 1978, 3–14; K. B. Wolf, *Christian Martyrs in Muslim Spain*, Cambridge, 1988, 2–15; Edward Colbert, *The Martyrs of Córdoba [850–859]: A Study of Their Sources*, Washington, D.C., 1962, 26. The treaty of Theodomirus, however, is a treaty for the capitulation of a rural province; we will have to search farther afield for one that addresses more mixed, urban societies like Córdoba or Toledo.

55. Glick, *Islamic and Christian Spain*, 169.

56. For studies of Christian status under Muslim rule, see Glick, *Islamic and Christian Spain*, 165–69; Wolf, *Christian Martyrs in Muslim Spain*, 1–35; N. A. Stillman, *The Jews of Arab Lands*, Philadelphia, 1979, 157–58; Colbert, *The Martyrs of Córdoba*, 25–33.

57. The so-called Covenant of ʿUmar is preserved in a number of sources, none before the eighth century. Fattal believes it to date to the reign of ʿUmar II (717–720). Many of the traditions from the earliest period in Islam are much more lax, one even encouraging Arabs to help Christians rebuild ruined churches. It is possible that the covenant was a sort of model for one used in Spain, though clearly this is not necessary for its ideas to have entered the legal climate. It contains notions concerning the treatment and status of the "People of the Book" that pervade the Fertile Crescent, North Africa, and Spain before the year 1000. Indeed it seems to be a pattern treaty created by Islamic schools of law. This explains the pervasiveness of its tenants. See A. Fattal, *Le statut légal des non-Musulman en pays d'Islam*, Beirut, 1958, 69, and 174–211; A. S. Tritton, *The Caliphs and Their Non-Muslim Subjects*, London, 1930, 5–17; C. E. Bosworth, "The Concept of *Dhimma* in Early Islam," in B. Broude and B. Lewis, eds., *Christians and Jews in the Ottoman Empire*, vol. 1, New York, 1982, 46–47. For the application of such restrictions in Spain, see Wolf, *Christian Martyrs in Muslim Spain*, 9–15.

58. H. A. Hamaker, *Incerti autoris liber de expugnatione Memphidis et Alexandriae*, Lugduni Batavorum, 1825, 165–66. See also J. F. Rivera Recio, "Formas de Convivencia y Heterodoxias en el primer siglo mozárabe," in *Instituto de Estudios Visigótico-Mozárabes de San Eugenio, Toledo: Historia mozárabe*, Toledo, 1975, 6–8.

59. Serrano, "*De habitu clericorum*, obra inédita del presbítero cordobés Leovigildo," *BRAH* 54 (1909), 496–517. Wolf cites Leovigildus's criticism of a "lack of ardor" and a "fatuity among some of the clerics" caused by "Ishmaelite oppression" (*Christian Martyrs in Muslim Spain*, 12). On the imposed difference of the dress of non-Muslims, see also I. Lichtenstadter, "The Distinctive Dress of Non-Muslims in Islamic Countries," *Historica Judaica* 5 (1943), 33–52.

60. A. al-Maqqarī. *The History of the Mo-hammedan Dynasties in Spain*, vol. 1, New York, 1840, 217; Ibn ʿIdhārī al-Marrākushī, *Histoire de l'Afrique et de l'Espagne intitulée Al-bayano'l-Mogrib*, vol. 2, trans. E. Fagnan, Algiers, 1901–4, 378–79. If this tradition is correct, it would affirm a treaty the terms of which correspond to the "Covenant of ʿUmar" (Wolf, *Christian Martyrs in Muslim Spain*, 6). The Spanish tradition, however, is regarded with some suspicion because of its closeness to the story of the founding of the Great Mosque of Damascus (Terrasse, *L'Art hispano-mauresque*, Paris, 1932, 59 n. 2). Whether, however, it reflects the actual means of the founding of Córdoba, or a literary tradition based on practice, it contributes equally to the notion of the importance of expropriating the church space. See C. Creswell, *Early Muslim Architecture*, New York, 1979, vol. 1, part 1, 187–96; vol. 2, 138–39; Gómez-Moreno, *AH*, 3:24–29. M. Ocaña Jiménez accepts the tradition literally ("La basílica de San Vicente y la Gran Mezquita de Córdoba," *AA* 7 [1942]: 347–66). See also Lévi-Provençal, *Histoire de l'Espagne Musulmane*, 134. For the Great Mosque of Damascus, see Tritton, *The Caliphs and Their Non-Muslim Subjects*, 9–10, 39, 40–42; Creswell, *Early Muslim Architecture*, vol. 1, pt. 1, 151–205; O. Grabar, *The Formation of Islamic Art*, New Haven, 1973, 110–15; "La Mosquée Omeyyade de Damas," *Synthronon*, 1968, 107–14.

61. The custom of sharing churches with Christians is still accepted by most scholars. If the case of Córdoba is an apocryphal one, it reflects a desire on the part of the Umayyads of Córdoba to create a tradition that might associate them with the custom of their earlier ancestors. Creswell accepts it (*Early Muslim Architecture*, vol. 2, New York, 1979, 138–39), as does Ocaña Jiménez ("La basílica de San Vicente y la Gran Mezquita de Córdoba"). Fattal records a number of passages in which Muslims are mentioned praying in churches, both those appropriated from Christian communities and those used primarily by Christians. He also produces a number of cases of informal sharing—as opposed to the contractual type recorded at Córdoba. See A. Fattal, *Le statut légal des non-Musulman en pays d'Islam*, 178–211. The exception is Jerusalem, where such a total co-opting could not take place. Grabar, *The Formation of Islamic Art*, 49–67, and in general Creswell, vol. 1, pt. 1, *Early Muslim Architecture*, 65–131.

62. J. Pérez de Urbel, *San Eulogio de Córdoba y la vida andaluza en el siglo IX*, Madrid, 1942, 61. There could of course have been many others not mentioned in documents. On textual sources and the survival of churches, see Wolf, *Christian Martyrs in Muslim Spain*, 13 nn. 37–40.

63. Gómez-Moreno, *AH*, 3:29–44. Not only are *spolia* from churches built under Visigothic rule to be found at the mosque, but the use of arch types and proportions that are our witness of the buildings of the Visigothic period whose remains were lost to the mosque.

64. Al-Maqqarī, *The History of the Moham-medan Dynasties in Spain*, 1:217; Gómez-Moreno, *Iglesias mozárabes*, 3–4.

65. Camón Aznar believes them to date from the Mozarabic period ("Arquitectura española del siglo X," 209). Fontaine speaks for a formal parentage in Visigothic or Mozarabic basilicas in the earlier period (*L'Art préroman hispanique*, 2:79–80).

66. It was first only in the cities that mixed populations were found, which might expose Muslims to the propaganda of a new, attractive monument. The Mozarabic communities of the countryside by all appearances continued the pace and structure of their lives much as they had before the invasion. We know, for instance, that the father of the renegade Ibn Ḥafṣūn had built a church as well (Ibn Hayyān, *al-Muktabis*, trans. Guarieb, in *Cuadernos de Historia de Islam*, 28, 172). See also Colbert (*The Martyrs of Córdoba*, 115) for the identification of Ibn Ḥafṣūn's father as a Christian.

67. For the chancel screens of both Melque and São Gião, see Schlunk, "Die Kirche von São Gião," especially 223.

68. Melque possesses the vestiges of decorative stuccos that ornamented its arch intrados at least. They are of indeterminate date, perhaps Mozarabic. See Fontaine, *L'Art préroman hispanique*, 2:78.

69. See chapter 1. Gómez-Moreno (*Iglesias mozárabes*, 14–27) feels the lack of stone ornamentation is the one indication of a later date for Melque. Schlunk ("Die Auseinandersetzung," 910–11) places Melque after the invasion because of stucco decoration that indicates to him Islamic influence. L. Caballero Zoreda and J. I. Latorre Macarrón, "Santa María de Melque y la arquitectura visigoda," *IX Symposium de Prehistoria Peninsular i Arqueología Peninsular*, Montserrat, 1978, present the argument for the earliest date.

70. Caballero Zoreda and Latorre Macarrón, "Santa María de Melque," and Caballero Zoreda, "La forma en herradura."

71. Ibn Hayyān, *al-Muktabis*, 28, 172. See also note 66.

72. C. de Mergelina, "De arquitectura mozárabe, la iglesia rupestre de Bobastro," *AEArq* 1 (1925), 159–76.

73. J. Vallve, "De nuevo sobre Bobastro," *AA* 30 (1965), 139–75; "Bobastro," *Andalucía Medieval: Actas del I Congreso de Historia de Andalucía*, Córdoba, 1978, 112–14; C. Torres Delgado, "Excavaciones en los montes de Málaga: Poblados mozárabes," ibid., 105–11; M. Ríu Ríu, "Primera campaña de excavaciones en el cerro de Marmuyas y prospecciones previas en la zona de los montes de Málaga," ibid., 115–18.

74. See chapter 1, II.

75. See note 41.

76. Two of the arcade arches are only half voided, and one other is only inscribed in the stone, awaiting the chisel. The southwest corner is marked out on the stone but was never excavated.

77. See chapter 2.

78. Eulogius, *Memoriale Sanctorum* 3:iii, in *PL*, 115:801. Wolf sees lax enforcement in the early years, with a sudden, strict interpretation of the treaties under Muḥammad I, in reaction to the Mozarabic civil disobedience (*Christian Martyrs in Muslim Spain*, 14–17). The enforcement seems to have applied only to Christians, and not to the Jews, who were also subject to the *dhimma* restrictions.

79. Author's translation. Eulogius, *Memoriale Sanctorum* 3:iii. Fontaine interprets this as a comment on caliphal art, which does not seem to me to be consonant with the rest of the text. *L'Art préroman hispanique*, 2:62.

80. Gómez-Moreno, *Iglesias Mozárabes*, xxx–xxxi. Though Mozarabic architects are mentioned in this period, they are cited for civil work, never church building (7).

81. Author's translation. Eulogius, *Memoriale Sanctorum* 3:iii and x.

82. Eulogius, *Memoriale Sanctorum* 1:21.

83. Eulogius, *Memoriale Sanctorum* 1:30. Translation: Colbert, *The Martyrs of Córdoba*, 222.

84. Eulogius, *Apologeticus Martyrum* 19, in *PL*, 115:862.

85. Paul Albar, *Indiculus Luminosus* 7, in *PL*, 121:522.

86. See J. Williams, *Early Spanish Manuscript Illumination*, New York, 1977, 16, for a list of the extraordinary number of signatures and portraits of scribes and miniaturists that appear in tenth-century Spanish manuscripts. One might consider these as part of the tradition of bearing witness. Consider as well the signatures found in manuscripts that came north with immigrant monks: "Samuel Librum ex Spania veni" on a compendium including Visigothic fathers and illustrious Toledan bishops. See Díaz y Díaz, "La circulación," 224–26.

II. Texts of the Martyr Movement

87. Colbert, *The Martyrs of Córdoba*, 25.

88. Millet-Gérard, *Chrétiens mozarabes et culture islamique*, 59–61. On Cordoban monasteries as the generators of the resistance movement, see also F. R. Franke, "Die Freiwilligen Martyrer von Cordova und das Verhältnis der Mozaraber zum Islam (Nach den Schriften des Speraindo, Eulogius und Alvar)," *Gesammelte Aufsätze zur Kulturgeschichte Spaniens*, vol. 13, Münster, 1953, 18 (he describes the monastery of Tábanos as the center of the rebellion); and Wolf, *Christian Martyrs in Islamic Spain*, especially 109–19.

89. Glick, *Islamic and Christian Spain*, 168. For Christians in posts of authority in al-Andalus, see Wolf, *Christian Martyrs in Muslim Spain*, 13–14.

90. Colbert, *The Martyrs of Córdoba*, 169. See also C. J. Halperin, "The Ideology of Silence: Prejudice and Pragmatism on the Medieval Religious Frontier," *Comparative Studies in Society and History* 26/2 (1984), 442–66.

91. *Indiculus Luminosus*, 6. Translation: Colbert, *The Martyrs of Córdoba*, 274.

92. *Indiculus Luminosus*, 10. Translation: Colbert, *The Martyrs of Córdoba*, 267.

93. See note 58 above.

94. *Indiculus Luminosus*, 6. Translation: Colbert, *The Martyrs of Córdoba*, 275–76.

95. Eulogius, *Documentum Martyriale*, 11. Author's translation with reference to translation of Millet-Gérard, *Chrétiens mozarabes et culture islamique*, 23.

96. R. Bulliet, *Conversion to Islam in the Medieval Period*, Cambridge, 1979, 117–26; Glick, *Islamic and Christian Spain*, 34.

97. Glick, *Islamic and Christian Spain*, 176.

98. *Indiculus Luminosus*, 35, translation:

R. W. Southern, *Western Views of Islam*, 21; R. Dozy, *Histoire des Musulman d'Espagne*, vol. 1, 1932, 317. Concerning the actions of the Mozarabs as the result of anxiety concerning an eroding culture, see J. Waltz, "The Significance of the Martyrs of 9th Century Córdoba," *The Muslim World* 60/2–3 (1970): 143–59, 226–36; and N. Daniel, *The Arabs and Medieval Europe*, London, 1975, 23–48.

99. Cantarino, *Entre monjes y musulmanes*, 59.

100. Cantarino, *Entre monjes y musulmanes*, 108–9. Though I agree with Cantarino, I will continue to use the traditional word "Mozarab" as meaning a Christian who lived or had at one time lived under Muslim domination.

101. *Vita Eulogii* 4, in Carleton Sage, trans., *Paul Albar of Córdoba*, Washington, D.C., 1943, 194.

102. Colbert, *The Martyrs of Córdoba*, 276, 281.

103. Colbert, *The Martyrs of Córdoba*, 106; Wolf, *Christian Martyrs in Muslim Spain*, 13–14. On conversion, see Bulliet, *Conversion to Islam*, 117–26.

104. I see this as being a major impetus for the voluntary martyr movement. Very influential to my thinking is Fontaine's article concerning the Mozarabs' apologetic literature: "La literatura mozárabe 'Extremadura' de la latinidad cristiana antigua" (*Arte y cultura mozárabe*, Toledo, 1979, 101–38), in which he speaks of the importance of the notion of bearing witness to the Mozarabic writers. This will be pursued at greater length later in this chapter. An excellent review of the literature can be found in Millet-Gérard, *Chrétiens mozarabes et culture islamique*, 28–34. Earlier studies cite similar points stressing on the whole other themes of cause. Lévi-Provençal sees the origin in taxation, and presented the martyrdom as the result of Spanish nationalism, led by apostates from Islam and other malcontents who allied themselves with rebels (*Histoire*, 225–39; Colbert, *The Martyrs of Córdoba*, 8). I. Cagigas also saw therein a Spanish nationalist movement (I. de las Cagigas, *Los mozárabes*, vol. 5, Madrid, 1947, 1–2). Colbert offers an elegant Christian *Apologia* for the martyrs, in his conclusion of a scholarly consideration of their texts (*The Martyrs of Córdoba*). Franke contrasts the spiritual motives of the Mozarabs with subjected Christians of the east (F. R. Franke, "Die Freiwilligen Martyrer von Cordova und das Verhältnis der Mozaraber zum Islam [Nach den Schriften des Speraindeo, Eulogius und Alvar]". Recently Kenneth Wolf expanded the spiritual role of the Mozarabs' movement, citing "spiritual anxiety" and "obsessive concerns about personal salvation and the need to reject Islam" as sources of the martyr movement (*Christian Martyrs in Muslim Spain*, 116–17). James Waltz and Norman Daniel offer interpretations that are particularly important for this study, for each sees the threat to Latin Christian culture as a major catalyst for the Mozarabs' revolt. Waltz sees cultural erosion and assimilation as causing a need on the part of the Mozarabs to "sharpen the outlines of each culture," to make "explicit and obvious previously implicit and muted culture conflicts" ("The Significance of the Voluntary Martyrs," 226). Daniel shows that death and the rejection of Islam were the means by which the Mozarabs established "for their own assurance a clear communal identity" (*The Arabs and Medieval Europe*, 37). For the Mozarabs, assimilation was unacceptable. "The theory was simple: Christianity cannot live side by side with any other religion; and the martyrs practiced the theory with a logic untempered by common sense" (48).

105. Eulogius, *Memoriale Sanctorum* 2:i,4; Translation: Colbert, *The Martyrs of Córdoba*, 196.

106. Eulogius, *Memoriale Sanctorum*, preface to 1, 2–3. Translation: Colbert, *The Martyrs of Córdoba*, 203.

107. Millet-Gérard, *Chrétiens mozarabes et culture islamique*, 30; Daniel, *The Arabs and Medieval Europe*, 45–46; Wolf, *Christian Martyrs in Muslim Spain*, 96–104.

108. Fontaine, in "La literatura mozárabe," shows that Eulogius identified the position of the Mozarabic martyrs with that of the martyrs of the early church, "una vuelta violenta y entusiasmante a la era antigua de los mártires, a la iglesia del siglo III" (105).

109. Fontaine, "La literatura," 123–25, Millet-Gérard, *Chrétiens mozarabes et culture islamique*, 85–123; Daniel, *The Arabs and Medieval Europe*, 34–35.

110. Fontaine, "La literatura," 136. See also Daniel, *The Arabs and Medieval Europe*, 45–48; Waltz, in "The Significance of the Voluntary Martyrs," calls the movement "the crystalization and exemplification of an ideology" (229). Halperin ("The Ideology of Silence") is also significant in this context.

111. Fontaine, "La literatura," 124 n. 25. He calls it a revival based on "interior experience"

rather than an intellectual revival of the sort practiced earlier in the Carolingian empire (133–36).

112. Author's translation. *Memoriale Sanctorum*, 3:iii. See also Colbert, *The Martyrs of Córdoba*, 252.

113. *Apologeticus Martyrum*, 16. Translation: Colbert, *The Martyrs of Córdoba*, 336.

114. It is possible that this information was gleaned from a chronicle Eulogius had at hand, a fact that in no way diminishes the importance of the material he chose to repeat in his short evocation of the early seventh century. See Colbert, *The Martyrs of Córdoba*, 333–36. We know of Eulogius's interest in texts from the Visigothic period through the analysis of his own writings, as well as his attention to Isidore. Indeed, Eulogius completed his own copy of the *De Natura Rerum* (G. Menéndez Pidal, "Le rayonnement de la culture Isidorienne," 724).

115. Cantarino, *Entre monjes y musulmanes*, 120.

116. *Documentum Martyriale*, 18. Translation: Colbert, *The Martyrs of Córdoba*, 231.

117. *Memoriale Sanctorum*, 1:30. Translation: Colbert, *The Martyrs of Córdoba*, 221–22.

III. In the Northern Kingdoms

118. Cantarino, *Entre monjes y musulmanes*, 115.

119. There is disagreement concerning the extent of the depopulation. See C. Sánchez-Albornoz, *Despoblación y repoblación del valle del Duero*, Buenos Aires, 1966; R. Menéndez Pidal, "Repoblación y tradición de la cuenca del Duero," *Enciclopedia Lingüística Hispánica*, 1:xxx. Glick, who sees the resulting population as extremely low but not completely depopulated, suggests the depopulation had a great deal to do with drought (*Islamic and Christian Spain*, 45, 88). Opponents to depopulation are less convincing: M. Á. García Guinea, *Excavaciones en Monte Cilda [Olleros de Pisuerga-Palencia]*, Palencia, 1966; L. Caballero Zoreda, *La necrópolis tardorromana de Fuentespreadas [Zamora]: Un asentamiento en el valle del Duero*, Madrid, 1974, 215. Concerning repoblación, see Sánchez-Albornoz, *Despoblacíon y repoblacíon*; "Repoblacíon del Reino asturoleonés: Proceso, dinámica, y proyecciones," *Cuadernos de Historia de España* 53–54 (1971), 236–459. Some private repopulation had occurred earlier, but it is

with Ordoño I that the monarchy takes control of the process, encourages it, and establishes jurisdictions and lines of authority.

120. C. Sánchez-Albornoz, *Estudios críticos sobre la historia del reino de Asturias*, vol. 3, Oviedo, 1975, 351; Glick, *Islamic and Christian Spain*, 89–90.

121. Gómez-Moreno (*Iglesias mozárabes*, xiii) speaks of the Mozarabs moving north in protest. A fascinating paper by Rosa Guerreiro Golay contends that the Mozarabs' "monachisme héroïque engendrera une spiritualité particulière, tournée vers un ascetisme démesuré, vers des préoccupations eschatologiques" ("Rupture de la coexistence et quelques causes à l'émigration mozarabe," unpublished paper, 2).

122. Gómez-Moreno, *Iglesias mozárabes*, 107.

123. Sánchez-Albornoz, "Repoblación del Reino asturoleonés," 295, 440.

124. I. Bango Torviso, "El neovisigotismo artístico de los siglos IX y X: La restauración de ciudades y templos," *Revista de Ideas Estéticas*, 148, 1979. Bango Torviso brings together a highly valuable group of passages concerning monastic repopulation to support his argument that Visigothic preoccupations of the tenth century grow from contact with the abandoned monuments found on the land settled. He says that "al restaurar estos edificios, asimilaban técnicas olvidadas y, por encima de todo, los motivos tradicionalmente visigodos eran vueltos a interpretar por los artistas-repobladores" (321).

125. Trans. K. Kingsley, "Visigothic Architecture," 34. See also A. López Ferreiro, *Historia de la S.A.M. Iglesia de Santiago*, Santiago, vol. 2, 1911, 2, 176; Bango Torviso, "El neovisigotismo artístico," 39.

126. Eulogius, *Memoriale Sanctorum*, 3:iii; Translation: Colbert, *The Martyrs of Córdoba*, 252.

127. Bango Torviso, "El neovisigotismo artístico," 321.

128. There is still the possibility of some limited intervention in the actual building on the part of the monks.

129. For full text, see page 50; note 13.

130. The text, with its abbreviations resolved by Gómez-Moreno, reads: "Hic locus antiquitus—Martinus sanctus honore dicatus brevi opere instructus—diu mansit dirutus donec Iohannes abba Cordoba venit—et hic templus litavit edis ruginam a fundamine erexit—et acte saxe exarabit non imperialibus iussus—et fratrum vigilantia instantibus duo et tribus men-

sibus—peracti sunt hec operibus Hordonius peragens sceptra—era nobies et semis centena nona" (*Iglesias mozárabes*, 169–70).

131. G. Menéndez Pidal, *Sobre miniatura española en la Alta Edad Media; corrientes culturales que revela*, Madrid, 1958, 30. The most complete discussion of the minature, however, is found in J. Williams, "The Beatus Commentaries and Spanish Bible Illustration," *Actas del Simposio para el Estudio de los Códices del "Comentario al Apocalipsis" de Beato de Liébana*, vol. 1, Madrid, 1980, 212–13, 217–19, with discussion 221–27. In the conclusion to a wide-ranging article, Williams contends that "in the course of the ninth century . . . the malevolent forces of Daniel and the Apocalypse came to be explicitly identified with the Muslims, as may be seen in the writings of Alvarus of Córdoba, and in the Life of Muḥammad which circulated in the Peninsula" (219). Williams does not think it likely, however, that Magius himself was one of the monks who came from Córdoba ("Introducción," *Actas del Simposio para el Estudio de los Códices del "Comentario al Apocalipsis" de Beato de Liébana*, 12–13), since he questions, with reason, the cipher date and places the illustrations nearer to mid-century. See also *Early Spanish Manuscript Illumination*, New York, 1977, 20–21, 77. On the *Morgan Beatus*, see also the important work of P. Klein, *Der ältere Beatus-Kodex Vitr. 14–1 der Biblioteca Nacional zu Madrid*, Hildesheim, 1976, 280–86, and "La tradición pictórica de los Beatos," *Actas del Simposio para el Estudio de los Códices*, 1, 97–98. O. K. Werckmeister has studied the extent to which Islamic forms in "Mozarabic" miniatures can be seen as conscious statements of a political position ("Islamische Formen in Spanischen Miniaturen des 10. Jahrhunderts und das Problem der Mozarabischen Buchmalerei," *Spoleto*, 12:1, [1965], 933–67). He found that a figure type probably associated by Christian artists with Islam aided in the creation of a parallel between the Israelites and the Spanish Christian martyrs (960). In general, Werckmeister concludes that such associations are specific cases, and that the meaning of stylistic or formulaic appropriations must be discovered and studied as separate phenomena (967). A. Grabar's article ("Eléments sassanides et islamiques dans les enluminures des manuscrits espagnols du haut Moyen Age," *Arte del primo millènnio, Atti del II Convegno per lo studio dell'alto medioevo*, Turin, 1953, 312–19) is somewhat outworn today.

132. The scene appears in the *Gerona Beatus*, but the voussoirs no longer alternate in the same manner as the Great Mosque and instead have become decorative design. This miniature was executed by Emeterius, who might have been a student of Magius (W. Neuss, "The Miniatures of the Gerona Codex in Light of Other Illuminated Manuscripts of the Beatus Apocalypse," *Sancti Beati A Liébana in Apocalipsin. Codex Gerundensis*, Oltun and Lausanne, 1962, 47). In the *Beatus* manuscript of the eleventh century now in Seo de Urgel, the voussoirs have disappeared altogether from the arch, though this is an illustration from the same *stemma*, according to Neuss, as the Gerona page (W. Neuss, *Die Apokalypse des Hl. Johannes in der altspanischen und altchristlichen Bibel-Illustration*, Münster, 1931, 31). I am indebted to Ms. Janice Mann for these observations. The *Beatus of Saint-Sever*, however, though it changes the arch to a semicircular one, retains the alternating voussoirs, and also, Williams contends, their meaning ("The Beatus Commentaries and Spanish Bible Illustration," 20). See also Klein, "La tradición pictórica de los Beatus," 114–15.

133. O. K. Werckmeister, "Die Bilder der drei Propheten in der *Biblia Hispalense*." The notion that the Mozarabic style might contain a political message of resistance was introduced, of course, by Schapiro, "From Mozarabic to Romanesque at Silos," in *Romanesque Art*, New York, 1977, 28–101.

134. Later, however it will. See chapter 4, I. See, on reactive adaptation, T. Glick and O. Pi-Sunyer, "Acculturation as an Explanatory Concept in Spanish History," *Studies in Society and History* 11 (1969), 152.

135. Franke, "Die Freiwilligen Martyrer" 104. On his trip north: E. Lambert, "Le voyage de Saint Euloge dans les Pyrénées en 848," *Estudios dedicados a Menéndez Pidal*, vol. 4, Madrid, 1953; C. Sánchez-Albornoz, "La epístola de San Eulogio y el Muqtabis de Ibn Ḥayyan," *Príncipe de Viana* 19 (1958), 265–66; Colbert, *The Martyrs of Córdoba*, 181–90; C. Sage, *Paul Albar of Córdoba*, 16–18; Franke, "Die Freiwilligen Martyrer," 38.

136. Gómez-Moreno, *Iglesias mozárabes*, 214–16.

137. Insigne meritis beatus Fructuosus, postquam Complutense condidit cenobium, et nomine sancti Petri, brebi opere in hoc loco fecit oratorium; post quem non inpar meritis Valerius sanctus opus aeclesie dilatabit. Nobissime Gen-

nadius prebiter cum XII fratribus restaurabit, era DCCCCXXXIII; pontifex effectus a fundamentis mirifice ut cernitur dennuo erexit, non oppresione vulgi, sed largitate pretii et sudore fratrum huius monasteri. Consacratum est hoc templum ab episcopis IIIIor, Gennadio Astoricense, Sabarico Dumiense, Fruminio Legionense, et Dulcidio Salamanticense; sub era nobies centena, decies quina, terna, et quaterna, VIIII kalendarum nobembrum" (Gómez-Moreno, *Iglesias mozárabes*, 214–16).

138. Gómez-Moreno, *Iglesias mozárabes*, 215.

139. It is in this context—of indigenous monastic and ecclesiastical traditions that adopt forms like those found to be Visigothic in character at Peñalba—that the church discovered by Williams at Valeranica must be considered ("A Contribution to the History of the Castilian Monastery of Valeranica," 239–44); see also note 40 above. As a later church, Peñalba exhibits many details of Islamic influence resisted at Escalada. See chapter 4.

140. Gómez-Moreno, *Iglesias mozárabes*, 193–94. Some building of the Visigothic period did indeed exist there before the depopulation, for fragments of seventh-century sculpture, now preserved at the Museo Arqueológico Provincial at Valladolid, have been uncovered at the site.

141. Gómez-Moreno, *Iglesias mozárabes*, 198– 99. It is not yet clear to me which sort of western resolution existed at Bamba. Gómez-Moreno reconstructs a nine-bay church, much like a pier-type version of Santa María de Lebeña, a later church with Mozarabic influence in Asturias (*Iglesias mozárabes*, 193–99). However, since no scars are evident that might suggest an impost on the south wall such as that reconstructed by Gómez-Moreno (194), and that must exist for his reconstructed plan, I think it is wise to suppose that a pier-type nave might also have been the resolution to Bamba's western portions. See also "Pintura mural de la iglesia de Santa María de Wamba (Valladolid)," *BSAAV* 32 (1966), 435–36.

142. Monastery of Santo Domingo de Silos, frag. 4:b.n 19. Neuss, *Die Apokalypse*, 55–56; J. Williams, "Introducción" and Díaz y Díaz and others, "Consideraciónes en torno al fragmento de Silos" (recorded discussion), *Actas del Simposio para el Estudio de los Códices del "Comentario al Apocalipsis" de Beato de Liébana*, vol. 2, Madrid, 1980, 12, 15, 315–28. An important consideration, including an excellent state of the question concerning the fragment and its bibliography, can be found in two publications of my dear and painfully missed friend Noureddine Mezoughi: "Le fragment de Beatus illustré conservé a Silos," *Cahiers de Saint Michel de Cuxà* 13 (1982), 125–51, and "Le fragment de Beatus conservé à Silos (Intermezzo)," ibid., 14 (1983), np. Klein discusses the fragment's style in relario to the early development of *Beatus* pictoral tradition ("La tradición pictórica de los Beatos," 98).

143. Mezoughi pointed out that a Vulgate text describes the souls under the altar as having been "decollatorum," decapitated in particular. There is no indication the text was known to the Spanish miniaturist, however, and no known visual tradition that might have grown from it to influence our painter in this detail ("Le fragment de Beatus," 1983).

144. Mezoughi, "Le fragment de Beatus," 1983; The same author was able to produce a number of images in which heads appeared to be dismembered, and in general reviews the possible visual prototypes and their meanings ("Le fragment de Beatus," 1982).

145. C. Sánchez-Albornoz, "Dulcidio," *Estudios críticos sobre la historia del reino de Asturias*, vol. 3, Oviedo, 1975, 729–40. The incident is mentioned in a page of a lectionary of the Cathedral of Oviedo: *ES*, 37:226. Werckmeister argues for a conscious allusion to the Cordoban martyrs in an Old Testament image from the Bible of San Isidoro, of around 960 ("Islamische Formen in Spanischen Miniaturen," 960).

146. Gómez-Moreno, *Iglesias mozárabes*, 253–59.

IV. Testimony Appropriated: The Meaning of Visigothicism for the Northern Kingdoms

147. Gómez-Moreno, *Iglesias mozárabes*, 107.

148. R. Menéndez Pidal, *El Imperio hispánico y los cinco reinos*, Madrid, 1950, 21–23. Concerning the continuity created between the Visigoths and Alfonso III's reign, see Maravall, *El concepto de España en la edad media*, especially 157–90; 299–337. The notion of survival and revival of the Visigothic monarchy as a political myth is central to Maravall's work, and it has informed many of the more recent works cited in this essay as well. His argument concerning art is outdated (168–74). He points out that the only documents linking Alfonso II with a Visigothic past are forg-

eries (21 n. 1). See also G. Menéndez Pidal, "Le rayonnement de la culture Isidorienne," 723; Gómez-Moreno, *Iglesias mozárabes*, 130–31.

149. Menéndez Pidal, "Le rayonnement de la culture Isidorienne," 723; Waltz, "The Significance of the Voluntary Martyrs," 233.

150. J. Gil Fernández, J. Moralejo, and J. Ruiz de la Peña, *Crónicas asturianas*, Oviedo, 1985. The same chronicles are also traditionally cited from the following publications: the Chronicle of Albelda and of Alfonso III, Rotense version: M. Gómez-Moreno, ed., "Las primeras crónicas de la reconquista," *Boletín de la Real Academia de Historia* (Madrid) 100/2, (1932); the Ovetense version: Z. García Villada, ed., *Crónica de Alfonso III*, Madrid, 1918; R. Menéndez Pidal, "La historiografía," 11–13.

151. Gil Fernández, Moralejo, and Ruiz de la Peña, *Crónicas asturianas*, 33.

152. Díaz y Díaz, "Isidoro en la edad media hispana" and "La historiografía hispana desde la invasión árabe hasta el año 1000," in *De Isidoro al siglo XI*, Barcelona, 1976, 179, 218; Menéndez Pidal, "La historiografía," 13. Gómez-Moreno's notion that the author came from Monte Latruce is seldom followed today (*Las primeras crónicas*).

153. C. Sánchez-Albornoz ("¿Una crónica asturiana perdida?" *Revista de Filología Hispánica*, vol. 7, Buenos Aires, 1945, 105–46) believed one of the sources for the Albelda might have been a lost chronicle from the time of Alfonso II, a notion supported enthusiastically by Ruiz de la Peña ("Estudio preliminar," 33–36). I concur instead with Menéndez Pidal, who takes Alfonso III at his word when he states that he knows of no other history since Isidore: ". . . doy crédito a la epístola dedicatoria a Sebastián, en lacual el rey cronista declara no conocer otra historia escrita anterior a la suya, sino atribuida a San Isidoro, que llegaba hasta el rey Vamba" ("La historiografía," 13). See also Sánchez-Albornoz, "La redacción original de la Crónica de Alfonso III," *Orígenes de la nación española*, 3:755.

154. Author's translation. Menéndez Pidal, "La historiografía," 15.

155. V. Cantarino has also come to this conclusion: "las primeras crónicas de la Reconquista, de las que son autores, además, monjes y mozárabes . . . al escribir sobre la caída del reino visigodo ante el ataque sarraceno y los comienzos de la resistencia contra el invasor, van a demonstrar, más o menos claramente, un prejuicio cris-

tiano, mozárabe y visigodo . . . a crear una continuidad histórica artificial, al proyectar al pasado su propia interpretación de los acontecimientos que están narrando" (*Entre monjes y musulmanes*, 119).

156. J. M. Lacarra, "La península ibérica del siglo VII al X," *Estudios de la alta edad media española*, Valencia, 1971, 156. He still interprets the texts literally, however.

157. Sánchez-Albornoz (*Estudios críticos*, 2: 623–39) associates the reform of the church in Oviedo, the establishment of a capital that rivaled Toledo in authority, and the holding of a church council there in 821 as the events characterized in this passage. Schlunk saw the passage as a reference to the actual copying of Visigothic monuments (*La pintura mural*, 161–67). See also chapter 2 above.

158. See chapter 2: similarly, there is no evidence of a revival of art from the Visigothic period in Alfonso II's reign, though numerous examples of his patronage survive.

159. R. Menéndez Pidal, "La historiografía," 21.

160. Author's translation: "vetusto opere, ubi reconditum est lignum Sancte Crucis tue, pariter cum dipticeis sculptos eburneos que utrumque de Toledo adduximus." Published in Lacarra, *La península ibérica*, 162.

161. On the Prophetic Chronicle, see Gil Fernández, Moralejo, and Ruiz de la Peña, *Crónicas asturianas*, 36; Díaz y Díaz, "La historiografía hispana," 226; Sánchez-Albornoz, "Dulcidio," *Estudios críticos sobre la historia del reino de Asturias*, vol. 3, Oviedo, 1975, 729–40.

162. See Sánchez-Albornoz, "Dulcidio."

163. Quod prestet omnipotens Deus, ut inimicorum crebro deficiente audacia in melius semper crescat eclesia. Quod etiam ipsi Sarrazeni quosdam prodigiis uel a[u]strorum signis interitum suum adpropinquare predicunt et Gotorum regnum restaurari per hunc nostrum principem dicunt; etiam et multrum Xpianorum reuelationibus atque ostensionibus hic princeps noster gloriosus domnus Adefonsus proximiori tempore in omni Spania predicetur regnaturus. Sicque pretegente diunia clementia inimicorum terminus quoddiie defecit et ecclesia Domini in maius et melius crescit. Et quantum perficit Xpi nominis dignitas, tantum inimicorum tabescit ludibriosa calamitas" (Gil Fernández, Moralejo, and Ruiz de la Peña, *Crónicas asturianas*, 187–88).

164. See the fascinating study of O. K. Werckmeister, "Das Bild zur Liste der Bistümer Spa-

niens im 'Codex Aemilianensis,'" *MM* 9 (1968), 399–421. The most complete discussion of this manuscript is in S. de Silva y Verástegui, *Iconografía del siglo X en el Reino de Pamplona-Nájera*, Pamplona, 1984. She suggests the association of the six kings might relate to the interests of the kings of Pamplona with the *Liber Iudicorum* and the copying of Visigothic legislation (419). See also M. Díaz y Díaz, *Libros y librerías en la Rioja altomedieval*, Logroño, 1979, 66; de Silva y Verástegui, "Neovisigotismo iconográfico del siglo X: Ordo de celebrando concilio," *Goya* (1981), 70–75, 164–65; and a recent intriguing analysis of the *Codex Aemilianensis* and the *Codex Vigilanus* in terms of the councils and rites they depict: R. Reynolds, "Rites and Signs of Conciliar Decisions in the Early Middle Ages," *Spoleto* 33 (1987), 207–49. Both illustrate the Visigothic *Collectio canonum Hispana* of Julian of Toledo.

165. For example, de Silva y Verástegui, *Iconografía del Siglo X*, 69; Reynolds, ("Rites and Signs," 225–49) points out, however, that for the text, "studies of the ... *Collectio Hispania* within these manuscripts indicate that there were older related but separate models" (227). He believes that parts of the full-page illustration of Toledo in the *Codex Aemilianensis* exhibit "Visigothic echoes" (243).

166. R. D'Abadal i de Vinyals, "A propos du legs visigothique en Espagne," *Spoleto* 5 (1958), 584.

Chapter 4: Reaction and Absorption

I. In the Northern Kingdoms

1. C. Sánchez-Albornoz, "Dulcidio," *Estudios críticos sobre la historia del reino de Asturias*, vol. 3, Oviedo, 1975, 729–40.

2. J. O'Callaghan, *A History of Medieval Spain*, Ithaca, 1975, 113.

3. For the full text of this passage from the Prophetic Chronicle and a translation, see chapter 3, page 80 and note 163.

4. O. K. Werckmeister, "Die Bilder der drei Propheten in der Biblia Hispalense," *MM* 4 (1963), 141–88. J. Williams has noted that an increase in Islamic influence in manuscript illumination in the north also takes place in the second half of the century, rather than in the first years of the Mozarabic emigrations ("Introducción," *Actas del Simposio para el Estudio de los Códices del "Comentario al Apocalipsis" de Beato de Liébana*, vol. 1, Madrid, 1980, 13.

5. Millet-Gérard, *Chrétiens mozarabes et culture islamique*, Paris, 1984, 111.

6. *Memoriale sanctorum*, 2:1. Author's translation with reference to Millet-Gérard, *Chrétiens mozarabes et culture islamique*, 54.

7. E. Lévi-Provençal, *La civilisation arabe en Espagne*, Paris, 1953, 68; *L'Histoire de l'Espagne Musulman*, vol. 1, Paris and Leiden, 1950, 239–79; L. Golvin, *Essai sur l'architecture réligieuse musulmane*, vol. 4, *L'Art hispano-musulman*, Paris, 1979, 20, 48–50, 80. We know the Mozarabic martyrs were familiar with the architecture at least: Colbert, *The Martyrs of Córdoba [850–859]: A Study of Their Sources*, Washington, D.C., 1962, 124. Servus Dei and Rogellius are said to have dared to preach in the mosque (204, 243).

8. For the bibliography concerning Peñalba, see chapter 3, note 39.

9. Gómez-Moreno, *Iglesias mozárabes*, Madrid, 1919, 233. See chapter 3, note 36, and chapter 4, note 16.

10. In a recent unpublished lecture, Sabine Noack of the Deutsches Archäologisches Institut in Madrid revealed a number of capitals from the Fertile Crescent that also bore strong similarities with this style. See also H. Schlunk, "Byzantinische Bauplastik aus Spanien," *MM* 5 (1964), 234–54. He relates these to several Byzantine prototypes found on the peninsula. Even if Byzantine capitals served from time to time as models, the key here is the privileging of Islamic taste.

11. This local characterization of Islamic and Christian taste, is based entirely on contemporary Spanish monuments. For a more general discussion of the formation of an "Islamic style" of ornament, see O. Grabar, *The Formation of Is-*

lamic Art, New Haven, 1973, 188–205; T. Allen, *Five Essays on Islamic Art*, Sebastopol, 1988, especially 1–15.

12. Gómez-Moreno, *Iglesias mozárabes*, 231.

13. L. Torres Balbás ("La pintura mural en las iglesias mozárabes," *Al Andalus* 23 [1958], 417–24) and J. Menéndez Pidal ("La pinturas prerománicas de la iglesia de Santiago de Peñalba," *AEArte* 29 [1956], 291–95) identify the paintings as contemporary with the original construction. See also Gómez-Moreno, *AH*, 3:375.

14. Torres Balbás, "La pintura mural," 419–22, 424. It appears, for instance, above the *alfiz* of an arch now in the cloister of Tarragona cathedral (see Gómez-Moreno, *AH*, 3:88) and on bases at Madīnat al-Zahrā› (Fig. 115).

15. Gómez-Moreno, *Iglesias mozárabes* 161–62.

16. Though it was originally presumed to be a near contemporary of Escalada because of typological similarities between the two buildings, Mazote clearly dates, at the earliest, to the 940s, both because of its documentation and its use of Islamic forms. There is no reason to suppose that because it is a basilica it must be dated closely with Escalada, the only other surviving basilica of the Mozarabic group. Basilicas are common both before and after Escalada, and so provide a precarious basis for chronological grouping. Instead, Mazote bears in its decoration the marks of stylistic preoccupations similar to those of Peñalba and Celanova. In particular, the close attention to the part of the Great Mosque of Córdoba built by ‹Abd al-Raḥmān II suggests a particularly Islamic orientation in the construction of horseshoe arches, an attention not found at Escalada. Furthermore, there is nothing in the documents that countenances an early date for Mazote. The 952 privilege of San Martín de Castañeda, which is the sole source for the church's dating, states that Castañeda's monks lived first at Mazote, with Abbot Martín. It is not reasonable to believe, with Gómez-Moreno, that all the monks of the monastery left immediately after completing their church, a hypothesis necessary to sustain his notion of an early date. We must instead see a wider time frame for the construction of Mazote, one that embraces a good part of the tenth century. The famine suggested by Gómez-Moreno as their reason for leaving is not very specific geographically, and would better account for a general delay in the building. Stylistically, Mazote falls more easily among the

other islamicizing Mozarabic churches: Peñalba, Celanova, and the porch of Escalada—in the late 930s and 940s. See chapter 3, note 36; Gómez-Moreno, *Iglesias mozárabes*, 173–74; J. Fontaine, *L'Art préroman hispanique*, vol. 2, Ste.-Marie de la Pierre-qui-Vire, 1977, 160–61.

17. Fontaine, *L'Art préroman hispanique*, 2:160.

18. Since such painting certainly finds no more comfortable chronological resting place than the tenth century, where it can join the decorative systems of Peñalba and Celanova, this clear evocation of the Great Mosque of Córdoba is best seen as part of the original design at Mazote. The paintings at Bamba (J. J. Martín González, "Pintura mural en la iglesia de Santa María de Wamba (Valladolid)," *BSAAV* 32 (1966), 435) are quite different, suggesting textiles instead, and perhaps the impact of Santullano. An archaeological study of Santa María de Peñalba at Arnedillo will determine if the modern alternating voussoirs of that building reflect its original disposition (J. A. Sopranis, "Nuestra Señora de Peñalba, Una iglesia mozárabe en la Rioja," *Arte Español* 15 [1944–45], 70–74; J. E. Uranga Galdiano and F. Iñíguez Almech, *Arte prerománico*, Pamplona, 1971, 110–13). The nave, organized around a central pillar, as at Berlanga, and the presence of the *alfiz* suggest a context sympathetic to Islamic form in any case.

19. Gómez-Moreno, *AH*, 3:372–75. Fontaine does not mention the paintings, despite the fact that the photos in his volume show the nave paintings clearly (*L'Art préroman hispanique*, 2:160–63, 197–99).

20. R. Collins, *Early Medieval Spain*, New York, 1983, 219.

21. See note 16 above and chapter 3, notes 36 and 40.

22. See note 58.

23. Colbert, *The Martyrs of Córdoba*, 386; P. B. Gams, *Kirchengeschichte von Spanien*, 2/2, Regensburg, 1869, 455–56.

24. *Vita B. Joannis Gorziensis*, in *ES*, 12:171. Author's translation with reference to D. Simonet, *Historia de los mozárabes*, Madrid, 1903, 608, and I. de Cagigas, *Los mozárabes*, Madrid, 1947, 331–32.

25. Liutprand of Cremona stated that he wrote his *Antapodosis* at Recemundus's suggestion, and the work is dedicated to the Mozarabic cleric. See Colbert, *The Martyrs of Córdoba*, 384.

26. T. Glick, *Islamic and Christian Spain in*

the Early Middle Ages, Princeton, 1979, 34–35, 41.

27. Glick, *Islamic and Christian Spain*, 187.

28. See page 85.

29. O'Callaghan, *A History of Medieval Spain*, 124.

30. For documentation, see Gómez-Moreno, *Iglesias mozárabes*, 267–69. Lebeña must date after 924, and is often placed in the late 920s because of connections with Bamba and Peñalba. Since there are no other buildings dated later than the 940s, and the connections between Peñalba and Bamba bind a century of Spanish architecture, the later years of Alfonso's life (the 960s) ought also to be considered. But at Lebeña, dating is less important than the attitude toward form that the church embodies. See also *Iglesias mozárabes*, 267–71; Fontaine, *L'Art préroman hispanique*, 149–58.

31. Gómez-Moreno, *Iglesias mozárabes*, 271.

32. Gómez-Moreno, *Iglesias mozárabes*, 271.

33. See Christian Ewert, "Die Moschee am Bāb al-Mardūm in Toledo—ein 'Kopie' der Moschee von Córdoba," *MM* 18 (1977), 287–354; G. King, "The Mosque of Bāb Mardūm in Toledo and the Influences Acting upon It," *AARP* 2 (1972), 29–57; Gómez-Moreno, *AH*, 3:201–7, followed by a later discussion of the small nine-bay oratory called "Las Tornerías."

34. The Nūḥ Gunbād mosque in Balkh, constructed of baked and mud brick, was originally vaulted with nine domes and its columns, capitals, and arches covered with stucco decoration. It was built in the ʿAbbāsid period. See L. Golombek, "ʿAbbāsid Mosque at Balkh," *Oriental Art* 15 (1969), 173–89. The Bū Fatātā mosque in Sūsa also has a nine-bay plan, but vaulted with barrel vaults. It is dated by inscription to 838–41. See L. Golvin, *Essai sur l'architecture religieuse musulmane. 3. L'Architecture religieuse des "Grands ʿAbbāsides": La mosquée de Ibn Tulun, L'architecture religieuse des Aghlabides*, Paris, 1974, 210–12. Terry Allen has identified more than twenty nine-bay mosques and interprets their pan-Islamic function as serving "the full ceremonial needs of local congregations and their religious leaders, whom we know to have had their own mosques." He identifies the form of the earliest examples (Balkh and Sūsa) with the nine bays just before the mihrab at the Umayyad mosque at Wasit—an area privileged decoratively and most probably in elevation as well. The small mosques become like disembodied *maqṣūras*,

"functionally and visually parallel to the spaces used for official ceremonial" (unpublished manuscript for the article "Early Nine Bay Mosques," cited with the kind permission of Professor Allen). See also Golombek, 188–89; Allen, *Five Essays*, 79–83; and O. Grabar, "The Earliest Islamic Commemorative Structures: Notes and Documents," *Ars Orientalis* 6 (1966), 10–11.

35. O. Grabar, *The Formation of Islamic Art*, 118. Some of the similarities between Bāb al-Mardūm have to do with later Christian incursions into Islamic tradition, for instance, the multi-leveled vaulted ceiling; these will be discussed in the second part of this chapter. The plan and use of space are not among these incursions, however.

36. *Anales Complutenses*, in *ES* 23:312; Gómez-Moreno, *Iglesias mozárabes*, 265.

37. Concerning the architecture of San Baudelio, see Gómez-Moreno, *Iglesias Mozárabes*, 309–90; P. Banks and J. Zozaya, "Excavaciones en San Baudelio de Casillas de Berlanga (Soria)," *Noticiario Arqueológico Hispanico* 16 (1983), 383–440; J. Zozaya, "Algunas observaciones en torno a la ermita de San Baudelio de Casillas de Berlanga," *AEArq* (1977), 307–31; J. Alvarez Villar, "Precisiones sobre San Baudel de Berlanga," *Actas del XXIII Congreso Internacional de historia del arte*, 1, Granada, 1975, 275–79.

38. The dating of the lower register of the paintings of San Baudelio is presently unresolved. A long tradition favors the contemporaneity of the registers, based on striking similarities in details of execution and drawing. However, the excavators of the monument offer archaeological evidence that suggests some separation of the registers. See J. Sureda (*La pintura románica en España*, Madrid, 1985, 68–73, 319–27) for a review of the question and a complete bibliography, especially as regards a twelfth-century dating for the paintings of the lower register. In particular, the work of M. Guardia Pons (*Las pinturas bajas de la ermita de San Baudelio de Berlanga (Soria)*, Soria, 1984) is of interest. Zozaya heads those who argue for an early dating ("Algunas observaciones," 321 and note 18), with Álvarez Villar ("Precisiones"). The most recent works outside Spain take the late dating for granted (C. Gilbert, "A Statement of the Aesthetic Attitude Around 1230," *Hebrew University Studies in Literature and the Arts* 13/2 [1985], 125–52; M. S. Frinta, "The Frescos from San Baudelio de Berlanga," *Gesta* 1 [1964], 9–13).

39. Fontaine, *L'Art préroman hispanique*, 2:242.

40. For the *maqṣūra*, see above, II. The undated church of Santa Maria de la Peñalba at Arnedillio would suggest, in its reduced plan organized around a single pillar, that Berlanga's formula was not unique. The presence there of the *alfiz* further associates the type with Islamic taste. See note 18 above.

41. It has been suggested that the paintings conceal a devout imagery, contain reference to palatine themes, and act as a subordinate foil to the christological cycle of the upper register. See Guardia Pons, *Las pinturas bajas*; Frinta, "The Frescos from San Baudelio"; and Gilbert, "A Statement of the Aesthetic Attitude."

42. J. Zozaya ("Algunas observaciones") suggests that the forms borrowed from Islamic contexts relate to paradisiacal imagery, an idea expanded somewhat by Fontaine (*L'Art préroman hispanique*, 227–46). See also J. Camón Aznar, "Las pinturas murales de San Baudelio de Berlanga," *Goya* 26 (1958), 76–80.

43. The choice of a figurative imagery springing from al-Andalus is fascinating. A century and a half before, the Cordoban writers equated worldly learning and sensual life with Islam. Albar's complaint concerning the passion of young Christians for Arabic poetry is only one example. Again and again he speaks against rhetoric and style—even in Latin—as vain and worldly pursuits, as if polarizing all stylistic embellishment, emphasizing his own austerity in defiance of an exaggerated picture of a Muslim world of unbridled materiality and sensuality. That association would be the residue of a time when Islam was part of Christians' "apocalyptic reading of their own history" (Millet-Gérard, *Chrétiens mozarabes et culture islamique*, 142). Indeed, asceticism was often one of the means by which Mozarabic clerics or entire monasteries recorded their defiance of Islamic domination. I wonder if the austerity of Escalada, a church of cool ashlar profiles, can be seen as part of the resistance to Islam that crumbled as early as Bamba and Peñalba? The emphasis of stone carving over wall painting is characteristic of the close examination of traditions of the Visigothic period that we know to have been exercised there, just as the ornamental wall paintings at Peñalba accompanied the use of an *alfiz* and radical arches in *tas de charge*.

II. In al-Andalus: The Great Mosque of Córdoba

44. See J. Wellhausen, *The Arab Kingdom and Its Fall*, Beirut, 1963, 552–53; Ibn al-athīr, *ʿIzz al-Dīn ʿAli Al-Kāmil fī al-tārīkh*, Beirut, 1965–67.

45. For the early history of his reign, see Lévi-Provençal, *Histoire de l'Espagne Musulmane*, vol. 1.

46. The most current treatments of the Great Mosque of Córdoba are to be found in: C. Ewert and J.-P. Wisshak, *Forschungen zur almohadischen Moschee, Lieferung, 1. Vorstufen. Hierarchische Gliederungen westislamischer Betsäle des 8. bis 11. Jahrhunderts: Die Hauptmoscheen von Qairawān und Córdoba und ihr Bannkreis*, Mainz, 1981, and Golvin, *L'Art hispano-musulmane*. Less current but still excellent and complete is the treatment of K. A. C. Creswell, *Early Muslim Architecture*, vol. 2, New York, 1979, 138–66. Also of value are Gómez-Moreno, *AH*, 3:19–40, 45–59, 77–82, and 91–165; G. Marçais, *L'Architecture musulmane d'occident*, Paris, 1954, 135–82; H. Terrasse, *L'Art hispano-mauresque*, Paris, 1932, 53–76, 104–51; Grabar, *The Formation of Islamic Art*, 111–15, 119–23, 126, and 130–34; as well as F. Hernández Giménez, "Die Elle in der arabischen Geschichtsschreibung über die Hauptmoschee von Córdoba," *MM* 1 (1960), 182–223; E. Lambert, "Histoire de la grande mosquée de Cordoue au VIIIe et IXe siècles, d'après des textes inédits," *Annales de l'Institut d'Etudes Orientales* 2 (1936), 165. More specialized studies will be mentioned in the course of this essay. See also the extensive bibliography in Golvin, 21–27. Concerning the possibility that the original mosque was a Christian church shared with the Christians of the community, see chapter 3, note 61. Whether or not the mosque was actually shared, the transmission of that tradition indicates a keen attention to the history of the Umayyad Great Mosque of Damascus, one that follows a thematic preoccupation that saturates the Great Mosque of Córdoba throughout its history before the year 1000.

47. On the relationship between the Aqṣā mosque and the Great Mosque of Córdoba during various stages in its development, see Ewert and Wisshak, *Forschungen zur almohadischen Moschee*, 1:8–29. On the controversy concerning the number of aisles of ʿAbd al-Raḥmān I's mosque, see Golvin, *L'Art hispano-musulman*, 45–48. Concerning the Aqṣā mosque, see R. W. Hamil-

ton, *The Structural History of the Aqsa Mosque*, Jerusalem, 1947; H. Stern, "Recherches sur la mosquée el-Aqsa," *Ars Orientalis* 5 (1963), 28–48. Al-Walīd's mosque was rebuilt and enlarged under the ʿAbbāsid al-Mahdī (775–785) after repairs by al-Manṣūr. He enlarged the building and added a dome before the mihrab, a form absent from the Great Mosque of Córdoba. It is possible that to al-Mahdī's reconstruction as well is due the enlargement of the mihrab aisle.

48. The mihrab aisle is 7.85 meters wide, while most of the other aisles measure 6.86 meters wide. The exception is the outermost aisles, those against the east and west walls of the mosque, which are 5.35 meters wide. Golvin (*L'Art hispano-musulman*, 48) suggests that ʿAbd al-Raḥmān I's mosque might have been a T-type hypostyle plan, an idea that must remain conjecture for lack of formal or archaeological evidence.

49. G. Marçais, *Manuel d'Art Musulman*, Paris, 1926, 231; Gómez-Moreno, *AH*, 3:36. Golvin also posits local tradition, though a Byzantine origin for the practice (*L'Art hispano-musulman*, 79). Creswell illustrates Marçais's parallel with the Augustinian aqueduct of Mérida, but finishes by calling the architectural use at Córdoba "a novelty" (*Early Muslim Architecture*, 2:157). The best technical analysis is found in Ewert, (*Spanisch-Islamische Systeme sich Kreuzender Bogen*, vol. 1, Berlin, 1968, 12–14). Heinrich Gerhard Franz ("Die ehemalige Moschee in Córdoba und die zweigeschossige Bogenordnung in der Maurischen Architektur," *Spanische Forschungen der Görresgesellschaft Erste Reihe, Gesammelte Aufsätze zur Kulturgeschichte Spaniens* 13 [1958], 171–87) relates superposed arches to the false clerestory at the Great Mosque of Damascus, and in particular to double arcades in earlier Christian basilicas, like that at Tebessa. He believes it reflects not a structural goal but the desire to produce a "transcendental world surpassing the earthly" (178).

50. Sauvaget assumes that alternating voussoirs formed part of Umayyad architecture, at least insofar as marble revetment is concerned, and accepts the originality of the alternation at Damascus. About Córdoba he remarks: "Il faut sans doute tenir plus largement compte de ces faits syriens dans la recherche des origines du décor—briques et pierre—des arcs de la Grande Mosquée de Cordoue" (*La mosquée Omeyyade de Medine*, Paris, 1947, 105 and n. 3). The notion that the alternating voussoirs of the Great Mosque of Damascus might constitute part of the original work of Walīd I (705–715) was advanced earlier by Hitchcock ("Banded Arches before the Year 1000," *Art Studies* 6 [1928], 186). Creswell illustrates them but does not discuss them in particular, though he shows the revetment of the western portico, where they occur, to be original in general (*Early Muslim Architecture*, 1/2, pls. 51a–b, 51a, 54a). They appear in the doorway integrated with the marble revetment around them very much in the way the earlier, original revetment alternating voussoirs of the Hagia Sophia in Istanbul fit into its revetment program (see below). Sauvaget also reconstructs alternating masonry voussoirs as part of the Umayyad mosque of Hama, finding them in surviving vestiges of the old covered portico (104–5). Creswell, who dates this section to the ninth century, takes exception. In a testy exchange with Sauvaget, he maintains that "the south part of the present east *riwāq* (where the alternating masonry occurs) is part of the ancient *riwāq*s which ran around three sides of the *ṣaḥn*, but we are not bound to believe *they go back to the beginning* for it is quite possible that there were no *riwāq*s at first" ("The Great Mosque of Hama," *Aus der Welt der Islamischen Kunst, Festschrift für Ernst Kuhnel*, Berlin, 1959, 53). Sauvaget also mentions the marble and basalt voussoirs at Quṣayr el-Ḥallābāt (105 n. 3; "Remarques sur les monuments omeyyades," *Journal Asiatique* 221 [1939], 20–22). Once again, Creswell contests the date, relating the work to a preexisting Byzantine building (*Early Muslim Architecture*, 1:502–5). I believe, however, there is enough evidence to support the view that Umayyad mosques with marble revetment might often have featured voussoir-shaped revetment in alternating colors on their arches. Professor Estelle Whelan pointed out to me that though Creswell contends all of the revetment in the ambulatory of the Dome of the Rock to be replacement, some panels—including panels that compose some of its alternating voussoirs—are quartered, and so must be original. Creswell himself asserts that only in the Umayyad period was that technique known to Islamic artists. Speaking of a section of revetment at Damascus, he says: "This I am convinced is a fragment of the original decoration because quartered marble paneling, although such a beautiful and effective treatment, is never found, as far as my knowledge goes, in any Muslim monument after the Umayyad period" (Creswell, *Early Muslim Architecture*, 1/2:174). The use of alter-

nating voussoirs in the revetment of Christian buildings in Byzantine territories also suggests that part of the Mediterranean as a likely place for its development in Islamic architecture: in particular, the revetment voussoirs of Hagia Demetrios of Salonika of the seventh century (G. and M. Soteriou, *Hi basiliki tou Hagiou Dimitriou tis Thessalonikis*, Athens, 1952, 159–62 and pl. 7), and alternating voussoirs in revetments existed originally in the doorways to vaulted passages at the Hagia Sophia in Constantinople (E. H. Swift, *Hagia Sophia*, New York, 1940, 75, pl. XXVI; H. Kahler, *Hagia Sophia*, New York, 1967, pls. 40, 55). For the restoration of the revetment, see C. Mango, *Manual for the Study of the Mosaics of Saint Sophia at Istanbul*, Washington, D.C., 1962, 13. Alternating voussoirs thus appear as a form of architectural decoration that might very well have been characteristic of Umayyad building in Syria. Clearly they are used at Córdoba to a greater extent and effect than in any surviving building in the Fertile Crescent, but I believe there exists a healthy possibility of a reference to Umayyad building.

51. Lévi-Provençal, *Histoire de L'Espagne Musulmane*, 1:135; *Espagne Musulmane au Xème siècle: Institutions et vie sociale*, Paris, 1932, 224. About the Ruṣāfa of Hishām, see Sauvaget, "Remarques sur les monuments omeyyades," 1–13. Lévi-Provençal points out that according to al-Fatḥ ibn Khāqān one Umayyad palace of Córdoba was named al-Dimashq, or "Damascus" (*Histoire de l'Espagne Musulmane*, 136 n. 1).

52. Al-ʿAynī states this quite openly. See G. Marçais, *L'architecture musulmane d'Occident*, Paris, 1954, 137. See also Golvin, who declares ʿAbd al-Raḥmān I's mosque to be built in "bonne tradition Syrienne" (*L'Art hispano-musulman*, 45). Ewert argues a complex evocation of Umayyad architectural tradition throughout the history of the mosque (Ewert and Wisshak, *Forschungen zur almohadischen Moschee*, vol. 1).

53. See Golvin, *L'Art hispano-musulman*, 48–50, 80; Gómez-Moreno, *AH*, 3:47–51. Ewert suggests that variations among capitals become the means by which a multilayered, intersecting design is drawn with the architectural members of the Great Mosque of Córdoba, one that centers on the mihrab (Ewert and Wisshak, *Forschungen zur almohadischen Moschee*, 1:155–90). See also P. Cressier, "Les chapiteaux de la Grande Mosquée de Cordoue (oratoires d'ʿAbd Ar-Raḥmān I et d'ʿAbd Ar-Raḥmān II) et la sculpture de chapiteaux à l'époque émirale," *MM* 25 (1984), 216–81; *MM* 26 (1985), 257–313.

54. On the Door of Saint Stephen, see, in particular, K. Brisch, "Zum Bāb al-Wuzarāʾ (Puerta de San Esteban)," *Studies in Islamic Art and Architecture in Honour of Professor K. A. C. Creswell*, Cairo, 1965, 30–48; Creswell, *Early Muslim Architecture*, 2:153. The earliest disposition of the portal is revealed in its interior facade. The form is similar to that of the slightly earlier mihrab of the great mosque of Kairouan. On the early doors of the Great Mosque of Córdoba, see also Gómez-Moreno *AH*, 3:56–59.

55. Golvin, *L'Art hispano-musulman*, 55, 70–75. F. Hernández, *El Alminar de ʿAbd al-Rahman III de la Mezquita Mayor de Córdoba, su génesis y sus repercusiones*, Granada, 1975.

56. The upper portions were converted into a belltower after the Reconquest. See Hernández for reconstruction and history: *El Alminar de ʿAbd al-Rahman III de la Mezquita Mayor de Córdoba*.

57. *Crónica anónima de ʿAbd al-Rahman III*, 59. O'Callaghan, trans., *A History of Medieval Spain*, 118.

58. L. Torres Balbas, *La Mezquita de Córdoba y las ruinas de Madinat al-Zahra*, Madrid, 1960; R. Velázquez Bosco, *Arte del Califato de Córdoba: Medina Azzahra y Alamiriya*, Madrid, 1912; B. Pavón Maldonado, *Memoria de la excavación de la mezquita de Medīnat al-Zahrāʾ*, Madrid, 1966; S. López Cuervo, *Medina Az-Zahra*, Madrid, 1983; R. Castejón, "Nuevas excavaciones en Madinat al-Zahra: El Salón de ʿAbd al-Rahman III," *Al Andalus* 10 (1945), 147–54; K. Brisch, "Madīnat az-Zahrāʾ in der Modernen Archäologischen Literatur Spaniens," *Kunst des Orient*, 4, 1963, and F. Hernández Giménez, *Madīnat al-Zahrā, arquitectura y decoración*, Granada, 1985, lamentably published without illustrations.

59. Torres Balbas related the plan of the Salón Rico to Khirbat al-Minya and asks if it might not reflect some lost palatial prototype in Constantinople (*La Mezquita de Córdoba y las ruinas de Madinat al-Zahra*, 152). Hoag notes that "the form seems to have evolved from a blend of Umayyad throne halls found at ʿAnjar and the ʿAbbāsid *bayt* in its most evolved form—the throne complex of the Jawsaq al Kharqānī at Samarra" (*Islamic Architecture*, 82). See also Hernández Giménez, *Madīnat al-Zahrāʾ, arquitectura y decoración*; C. Ewert, "Elementos de-

corativos en los tableros parietales del Salón Rico de Madīnat al-Zahrāʾ (1)," *Cuadernos de Madīnat al-Zahrāʾ* 1 (1987), 27–60.

60. The extraordinary plan and elevation of the mihrab and *maqṣūra* of al-Ḥakam II at the Great Mosque of Córdoba have excited a number of studies. Foremost are the works of Ewert and Wisshak (*Forschungen zur almohadischen Moschee*, vol. 1) and Golvin (*L'Art hispano-musulman*). Among the more specific studies are Christian Ewert's analysis of the interlacing arches (*Spanisch-Islamische Systeme*), Klaus Brisch's consideration of the window screens (*Die Fenstergritter und Verwandte Ornamente der Hauptmoschee von Córdoba: Eine Untersuchung zur Spanische-Islamischen Ornamentik*, Madrid, 1966), and Henri Stern's study of the mosaics (*Les mosaïques de la Grande Mosquée de Cordoue*, Berlin, 1976). Ibn ʿIdhārī gives the most complete historical account: Ibn ʿIdhārī al-Marrākushī, *Histoire de l'Afrique et de l'Espagne intitulée Al-bayano' I-Mogrib*, trans. E. Fagnan, 2:385.

Ewert contends a steady, conservative development toward hierarchy in the prayer hall at Córdoba, which begins as early as the mosque of ʿAbd al-Raḥmān I. Through the coupling of capital types and the color of shafts, first a central nave and then a transverse direction are articulated, according to Ewert. In the addition of al-Ḥakam II he sees these coded subtle patterns corresponding with the more obvious typology of the plan, with its axial scheme. In addition, a pattern of capitals in the prayer hall to either side can be seen to point diagonally to the mihrab axis. Ewert sees this formal dialogue with the T-type plan as part of a conscious dialogue with traditional Umayyad form as a sacred model (Ewert and Wisshak, *Forschungen zuralmohadischen Moschee*, vol. 1, especially 57–80; 155–90).

61. O. Grabar, *The Formation of Islamic Art*, 125.

62. Ewert and Wisshak, *Forschungen zur almohadischen Moschee*, vol. 1. See also note 60 and Grabar's discussion in *The Formation of Islamic Art*, 124–25. Ewert sees the primary sacred model for Córdoba in the Aqṣā mosque in Jerusalem, and he sees subtler, coded patterns created by capital types and shaft color. Though the models and meanings I propose are different, they do not form part of the conscious meaning ascribed to the mosque forms and are compatible with such political connections.

63. E. Lévi-Provençal, *Inscriptions Arabes d'Espagne*, Paris and Leiden, 1931, 15–16. See also Golvin, *L'Art hispano-musulman*, 38.

64. On the mihrab, see N. B. Le Plaideur, "Analyse esthétique et symbolique du mihrâb de Cordoue"; O. Grabar, "Notes sur le mihrab de la grande mosquée de Cordoue"; M. Lillo, "Le mihrāb dans l'al-Andalus," in A. Papadopoulo, ed., *Le Miḥrāb dans l'architecture et la religion musulmanes*, Leiden, 1988, 129–35; 115–22; 123–28. An inscription on the imposts of the mihrab identifies the reuse of the columns. See Lévi-Provençal, *Inscriptions*, 13; Golvin, *L'Art hispano-musulman*, 37, 61, 80. Sauvaget found a similar mentality at Medina, where bits of the past were incorporated into new restorations (*La mosquée Omeyyade de Medine*, 120).

65. Stern, *Les mosaïques de la Grande Mosquée de Cordoue*, 46.

66. Ibn ʿIdhārī al-Marrākushī, *Histoire de l'Afrique et de l'Espagne*, 2:392.

67. Ibid. Author's translation after Fagnan.

68. Stern, *Les mosaïques de la Grande Mosquée de Cordoue*, 47.

69. There was clearly a separate and more immediate relationship with Christian models at the mosque to serve an entirely separate goal. The intermingling of the two projects nevertheless must have been extensive. It is quite possible that the original design for al-Ḥakam II's addition was conceived in the reign of his father. Ibn ʿIdhārī tells us that the additions to the mosque were the first order he gave upon assuming the title of caliph (Ibn ʿIdhārī, *Histoire de l'Afrique et de l'Espagne*, 385). Golvin believes, on the other hand, that, as ʿAbd al-Raḥmān III's son and superintendent of works, al-Ḥakam II must be seen as one of the principal authors of the works of his father's reign, including Madīnat al-Zahrāʾ (*L'Art hispano-musulman*, 20). Concerning the interchange of secular and religious architectural form in western Islam, see also C. Ewert, "The Mosque of Tinmal (Morocco) and Some New Aspects of Islamic Architectural Typology," *Proceedings of the British Academy* 72 (1986), 125–35.

70. See Golvin, *L'Art hispano-musulman*, 52. Excavations have revealed that the mihrab of ʿAbd al-Raḥmān II had foundations: its form cannot, however, be understood from those foundations, and is still described as a niche. Gómez-Moreno nevertheless hypothesizes one that is horseshoe-shaped (*AH*, 3:49), but Golvin

does not believe it can be considered a room like the mihrab of the additions of al-Ḥakam II (*L'Art hispano-musulman*, 80).

71. Grabar, *The Formation of Islamic Art*, 121.

72. Gómez-Moreno, *Iglesias mozárabes*, xiv. Author's translation.

73. Concerning the general development of the Umayyad basilical hall in Syria, including the impact of Christian forms, see Sauvaget, *La mosquée Omeyyade*, 158–85; Grabar, *The Formation of Islamic Art*, 139–60; Ewert and Wisshak, *Forschungen zur almohadischen Moschee*, 1:1–20.

74. See Golvin, *L'Art hispano-musulman*, 63–66.

75. Ash-Sharīf al-Idrīsī, *Waçf al-Masjid al-Jāmi bi-Qurṭuba. Description de la Grande Mosquée de Cordoue*, trans. A. Dessus Lamare, Algiers, 1949, 8–11.

76. For a brief discussion of the lateral chambers in architecture of the Visigothic period and pertinent bibliography, see chapter 1, note 77. The closest parallel to the east end of the Great Mosque of Córdoba is the church of Son Bou, in Menorca.

77. See T. Glick and O. Pi-Sunyer, "Acculturation as an Explanatory Concept in Spanish History," *Studies in Society and History* 11 (1969), 152; A. L. Kroeber, "Stimulus Diffusion," *American Anthropologist* 42 (1940), 1–20.

78. Golvin, *L'Art hispano-musulman*, 83; al-Idrīsī, *Waçf al-Masjid*, 8–9.

79. See A. Dessus Lamare, "Le Muṣḥaf de la Mosquée de Cordoue et son mobilier mécanique," *Journal Asiatique* 230 (1938), 551–75. A. al-Maqqarī, *The History of the Mohammedan Dynasties in Spain*, ed. P. de Gayangos, vol. 1, 1840, reprint New York, 1964, 222–23 and 498 n. 31.

80. Al-Idrīsī, *Waçf al-Masjid*, 8–11; See also Dessus Lamare, "Le Muṣḥaf de la Mosquée de Cordoue," 551–56.

81. Grabar was the first to signal the significance of this text to the mosque and to relate it to Christian liturgy: "Notes sur le mihrab de la Grande Mosquée de Cordoue," 115–22, including discussion. Even apart from its clear relationship to Christian rite, the procession diverges significantly from Umayyad ceremonial. While acknowledging the existence of official processions in which the caliph played a major role, Grabar concluded elsewhere: "It would seem more likely that there were few processions and that Umayyad ceremonial was essentially a static one" (Grabar, "Ceremonial and Art in the Umayyad Court," Ph.D. dissertation, Princeton University, 1955, 70). See also K. Lech, *Geschichte des islamischen Kulturs*, Wiesbaden, 1979. For other Umayyad ceremonies, see Sauvaget, *La mosquée Omeyyade de Medine*, especially 129–53. For Fatimid ceremony, which includes much procession, see M. Canard, "Le cérémonial Fatimite et le cérémonial Byzantin: Essai de Comparaison," *Byzantion* 21 (1951), especially 384, 396–420, and J. Bloom, who suggests interesting relationships between Byzantine ceremonial and Fatimid mosque design ("The Mosque of al-Hākim in Cairo," *Muqarnas*, vol. 1, New Haven, 15–36).

82. "Heterii et Beati ad Elipandum," in *PL*, 96:935.

83. Lévi-Provençal, *Histoire de l'Espagne Musulmane*, 2:168–69.

84. Lévi-Provençal offers an overview of the development and culmination of the revolt of Ibn Hafṣūn. See the pertinent parts of *Histoire de l'Espagne Musulmane*, vol. 1, chap. 4; vol. 2, chap. 5, pt. 1.

85. See chapter 3, II.

86. See chapter 3 pages 59–61, 63–64, and notes 57, 58, and 78. The "Covenant of ʿUmar" was probably not itself written until the caliphate of ʿUmar II (717–720). There is evidence that its terms were taken up and systematically developed in Iraq in the mid-ninth century as well. See A. Fattal, *Le statut légal des non-Musulman en pays d'Islam*, Beirut, 1958, 69; A. S. Tritton, *The Caliphs and Their Non-Muslim Subjects*, London, 1930, 5–17; C. E. Bosworth, "The Concept of *Dhimma* in Early Islam," in B. Braude and B. Lewis, eds., *Christians and Jews in the Ottoman Empire*, vol. 1, New York, 1982, 46–47.

87. *Memoriale Sanctorum*, 3:iv, in *PL*, 115:802. See also Colbert, *The Martyrs of Córdoba*, 253.

88. Author's translation: "nunc autem florentissimam regni Arabici urbem basilicarum turres everteret, templorum arces dirueret, et excelsa pinnaculorum proterneret . . ." *Apologeticus Martyrum*, 22, in *PL*, 115:863.

89. Author's translation: "etiam ea templorum culmina subruunt, quae a tempore pacis studio et industria patrum erecta, pene trecentorum a diebus conditionis suae numerorum excedebant anorum." *Memoriale Sanctorum*, 3:iii.

90. *Indiculus*, 6. Translation: Colbert, *The Martyrs of Córdoba*, 275.

91. Author's translation: "Quod iste in fumosis turribus quotidie barritu inormi ... spiritu nobilium animas inficit." *Indiculus Luminasus*, verse 25, in *PL*, 121:539–40. Eulogius, *Apologeticus Martyrum*, verse 20 in *PL*, 115:863.

92. Author's translation: "Mox ut illectum superstitione mendaci vulgus clangorem tinnientis metalii aure captaverit, in omnem maledictionem et spurcitiam linguam admovere non differt." *Memoriale Sanctorum*, 1:21.

93. H. R. Idris ("Les tributaires en occident musulman médiéval d'après le "Mi‹yār" d'al-Wansarīsī," *Mélanges d'Islamologie*, Leiden, 1974, 172–95) brings to light a number of judgments in cases concerning Christians and Jews that indicate the same attitudes concerning ceremony, building, and dress outlined in the "Covenant of ‹Umar." In particular in the ninth century: a Jew who dresses in the same clothing as a Muslim is jailed and beaten; Christians and Jews are ordered to wear their belts so they can be distinguished easily from Muslims; they are to be beaten and imprisoned if they mount on horseback (a Muslim is even prohibited from wearing a Christian garment while praying); Christians in North Africa are prohibited from raising their churches, from completing unfinished building, or from replacing brick work with stone masonry. They can only repair that which is already constructed, raise the door in case the ground below it is eroded, or work on the interiors of the churches. A synagogue built in Córdoba is demolished because it was built in a Muslim city. See also C.-E. Dufourcq, *La vie quotidienne dans l'Europe médiévale sous domination arabe*, Biarritz, 1978, 72–77; Simonet, *Historia de los mozárabes*, 84. Fattal speaks of prohibitions against processing with candles in other parts of the Muslim world, also in the ninth century (*Le statut légal des non-Musulman en pays d'Islam*, 207).

94. Tritton, *The Caliphs and Their Non-Muslim Subjects*, 60–69; Bosworth, "The Concept of Dhimma," 46–47. See also Fattal, *Le statut légal des non-Musulman en pays d'Islam*, 17–18.

95. There is even a hint of the prohibition against the staging of highly dramatic display, especially that involving processions and candles, in Eulogius's account of the discovery of the body of Rudericus. In it, he takes pains to tell us the martyr was buried in a magnificent secret ceremony with a procession (*tripudiis*), in which the whole church was lighted up, and the faithful sang hymns and psalms (*Apologeticus Martyrum*, 33). Colbert (*The Martyrs of Córdoba*, 341 n. 21) suggests bishop Saul, who attended the ceremony, might have been in hiding, and offers that as an explanation for the secrecy.

96. Idris, "Les tributaires en occident," 173; Dufourcq, *La vie quotidienne dans l'Europe médiévale sous domination arabe*, 72–77.

97. Translation: Tayeb El-Hibri. Aḥmad ibn Moḥammed al-Maqqarī, *Kitāb Nafḥ al-tīb min ghuṣn al-Andalus al-raṭīb wa-dhikr wazīriha Lisān-al-Dīn ibn al-Khaṭīb*, ed. M. Abdul Ḥamīd, Cairo, 1949.

98. See T. Glick, *Islamic and Christian Spain*, 290–99; Glick and Pi-Sunyer, "Acculturation as an Explanatory Concept in Spanish History"; A. L. Kroeber, "Stimulus Diffusion."

99. R. Bulliet, *Conversion to Islam in the Medieval Period*, Cambridge, 1979, 117–26; Glick, *Islamic and Christian Spain*, 34.

100. Stern, *Les mosaïques de la Grande Mosquée de Cordoue*, 4–5.

101. Grabar, "Notes sur le *mihrab* de la grande mosquée de Cordoue," 116–17." For a transcription of the inscriptions, see Lévi-Provençal, *Inscriptions*, 9–20; *Répertoire Chronologique d'Epigraphie Arabe*, vol. 4, Cairo, 1933, 192–93. Neither translates Koranic passages; the *Répertoire* gives citations but does not transcribe Koranic text.

102. Lévi-Provençal, *Inscriptions Arabes d'Espagne*, 17; Translation: N. J. Dawood, *The Koran*, New York, 1974, 365.

103. Lévi-Provençal, *Inscriptions*, 17; translation: Dawood, *The Koran*, 409.

104. Translation: Dawood, *The Koran*, 408.

105. Ibid.

III. A Muslim Relic

106. Al-Maqqarī, *The History of the Mohammedan Dynasties in Spain*, trans. P. de Gayangos, vol. 1, 1840, reprint New York, 1964, 222–24.

107. P. Crone and M. Hinds offer an even more radical position (*God's Caliph*, Cambridge, 1986, 31–32): "It is clear from this that, as far as the Umayyads were concerned, the Umayyad period began with ‹Uthmān, not with Mu‹āwiya, and this makes sense, given that they never regarded ‹Alī as anything but a pretender" (32).

108. Crone and Hinds, *God's Caliph*, 32.

109. Al-Maqqarī, *History of the Mohammed-an Dynasties in Spain*, 1:222. For comments on the opinions of Ibn Baṭṭūṭa, al-Idrīsī, Ibn Iyās, and Ibn-al-ʿAbbār concerning the Koran, see 498 n. 31. Grabar notes a reaction to the gifts of one Umayyad caliph similar to the adoration of relics ("Ceremonial," 51).

110. *Memoriale Sanctorum*, 2:iv; Colbert, *The Martyrs of Córdoba*, 206.

111. Colbert, *The Martyrs of Córdoba*, 206.

112. *Apologeticus Martyrum*, 33. Translation: Colbert, *The Martyrs of Córdoba*, 341.

113. Author's translation: "Nonnulli etiam e turba gentilium venientes, sumebant lapillos fluminis, qui cruore martyrum erant aspersi, et lymphis abluentes projiciebent in pelago, ne Christianis in emolumentum existerent lipsanorum." *Indiculus Luminosus*, 32.

114. The fear of the Spanish Muslim toward Christian relics is recorded by one of the latest of the Mozarabic writers, Samson, who wrote his *Apologeticus* in 864. See *Apologeticus*, preface to Book 2, 5.

115. Colbert, *The Martyrs of Córdoba*, 357–58.

116. Their story, written at Aimoin, is also mentioned in the *Annales Bertiniani PL*, 115: 939–60; *Annales Bertiniani*, ed. Waitz, *MGH*, "Scriptores . . . in usum scholarum," Hanover, 1883; Colbert, *The Martyrs of Córdoba*, 345. It contains, of course, numerous references to the sanctity of the relics, but most interesting is the account of the monks' reception in Córdoba. Though Cordoban monks did not want to lose them, church officials were anxious to see the relics make their way to other lands, partly perhaps because the French monks insisted their veneration would be greater there. But the task of leaving with the relics was the most difficult of all, for this was accomplished in secrecy and fear since the Muslims strictly prohibited the worship of the relics of those they had slain.

Conclusion

1. Ibn ʿArabi (1164–1240), *The Tarjuman al-Ashwaq*, trans. R. A. Nicholson, London, 1911, 67.

2. Glick, *Islamic and Christian Spain*, Princeton, 1979, 127.

3. Ibid.

4. From the *Chronicle* of Raoul Glaber: trans. C. Davis-Weyer, *Early Medieval Art, 300–1150: Sources and Documents*, Englewood Cliffs, NJ, 1971, 124.

5. The works that address this topic are many and distinguished. Particularly valuable for the general issues touched upon here are: M. Bloch, *Feudal Society*, vols. 1 and 2, Chicago, 1968; R. Fossier, *Histoire sociale de l'occident médiéval*, Paris, 1970, especially pts. 2 and 5; and G. Duby, *Age of the Cathedrals*, Chicago, 1981.

6. Armi's article, "Orders and Continuous Orders" (*Journal of the Society of Architectural Historians* 34/3 [1975], 173–88), revolutionized the study of First Romanesque architecture, and went a long way as well toward defining mature Romanesque as a style. It also contains a bibliography of the problems surrounding First Romanesque architecture. A very general perspective is offered by Durliat in the introductory article:
"Les maçons du premier art roman méridional," *Monuments historiques* 127 (1983), 20–27.

7. I am indebted to Sheila McTigh for the notion that the Catalan church might have intended a conscious gesture of independence in choosing masons it understood to be Italian. It is important to note that in Catalonia, the horseshoe-arched style that was replaced with First Romanesque buildings constituted the continuation of architecture from Early Christian and Visigothic times. See the excellent survey: X. Barral i Altet, *L'Art pre-romànic a Catalunya segles IX–X*, Barcelona, 1981.

8. The best illustrated survey is still that of Puig i Cadafalch, *La géographie et les origines du premier art roman*, Paris, 1935. On Cuxà and Marquet, see also Puig i Cadafalch, "L'église de Saint Michel de Cuxà," *Bulletin Monumental* 94 (1935), and "La frontière septentrionale de l'art mozarabe," *Compte-rendu des séances de l'Académie des Inscriptions et Belles Lettres*, Paris, 1943–44; S. Stym-Popper, "L'église de Saint Michel de Cuxà," *Congrès Archéologique*, 1959. See also J. Fontaine, *L'Art préroman hispanique*, vol. 2, Ste.-Marie de la Pierre-qui-Vire, 1977; Barral i Altet, *L'Art pre-romànic*; M. Durliat, *L'Art*

Catalan, Paris, 1963; and numerous articles in the *Cahiers de Saint Michel de Cuxà*.

9. For an overview of French intervention in Spanish political and economic life in the eleventh century, see J. M. Lacarra, "La repoblación de las ciudades en el camino de Santiago: Su transcendencia social, cultural y económica," in *Peregrinaciones a Santiago*, ed. Vázquez de Parga, 1:465; M. Desfourneaux, *Les Français en Espagne au XIe et XIIe siècles*, Paris, 1949; A. Castro, *The Spaniards*, Berkeley, 1971, chap. 11.

10. *DACL*, 12:395–96.

11. Castro, *The Spaniards*, 425.

12. See E. Said, *Orientalism*, New York, 1978, 21.

13. Concerning ethnic identity in general, see P. Geary, "Ethnic Identity as a Situational Construct in the Early Middle Ages," *Mitteilungen der anthropologischen Gesellschaft in Wien* 113, (1983), 15–26, in which the author observes that the issue of ethnicity is usually encased in the context of politics (16). On cultural creativity and internal constraint, see Said, *Orientalism*, 14.

Index

ILLUSTRATIONS

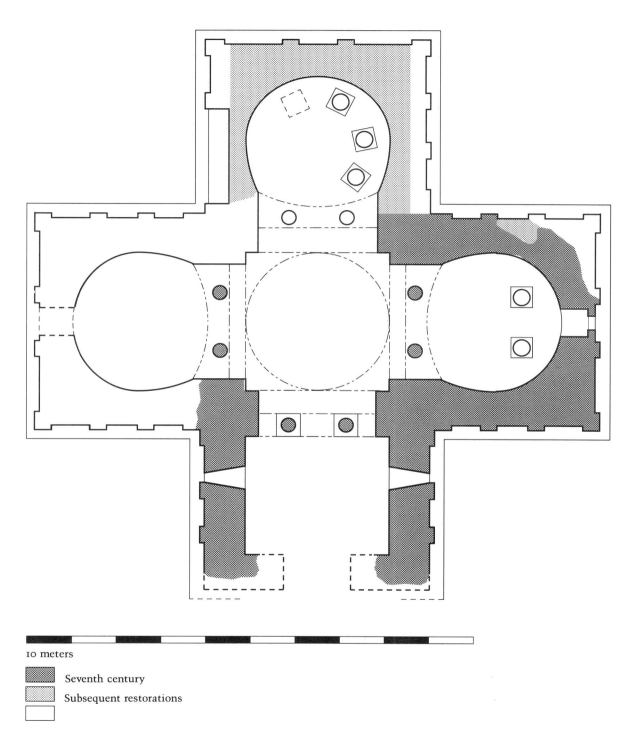

10 meters

Seventh century

Subsequent restorations

Fig. 1. São Frutuoso de Montelios, plan

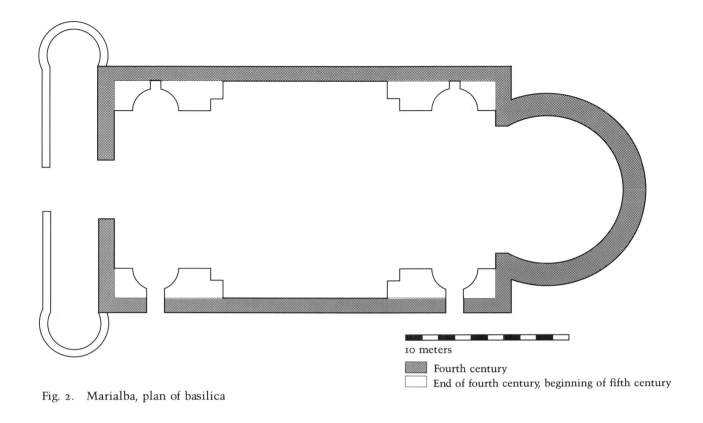

10 meters

▨ Fourth century
☐ End of fourth century, beginning of fifth century

Fig. 2.   Marialba, plan of basilica

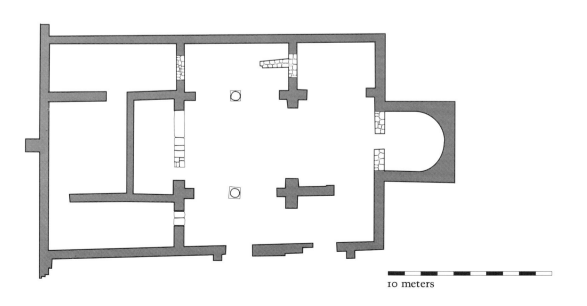

10 meters

Fig. 3.   Villa Fortunatus near Fraga, plan of basilica

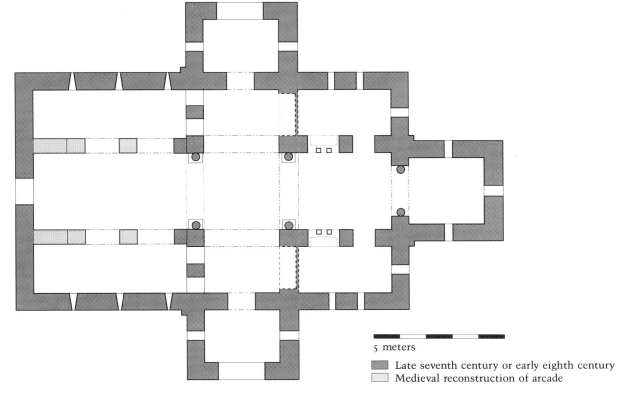

5 meters

■ Late seventh century or early eighth century
▨ Medieval reconstruction of arcade

Fig. 4.   San Pedro de la Nave, plan

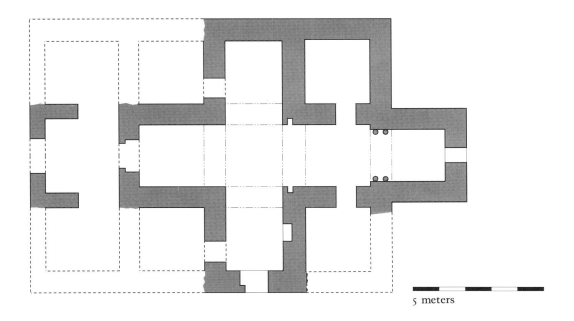

5 meters

Fig. 5.   Santa Comba de Bande, plan

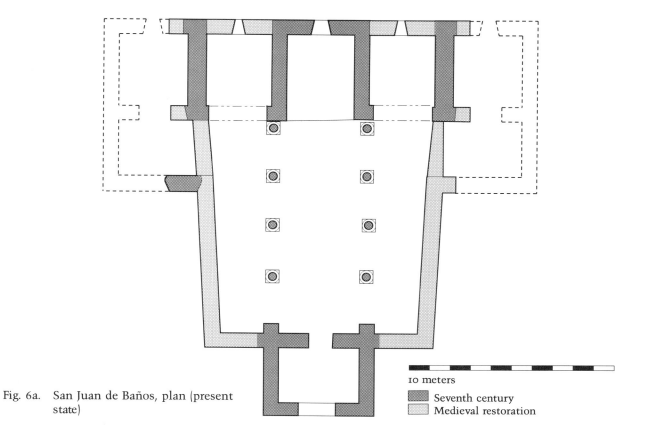

Fig. 6a. San Juan de Baños, plan (present
state)

10 meters

Seventh century
Medieval restoration

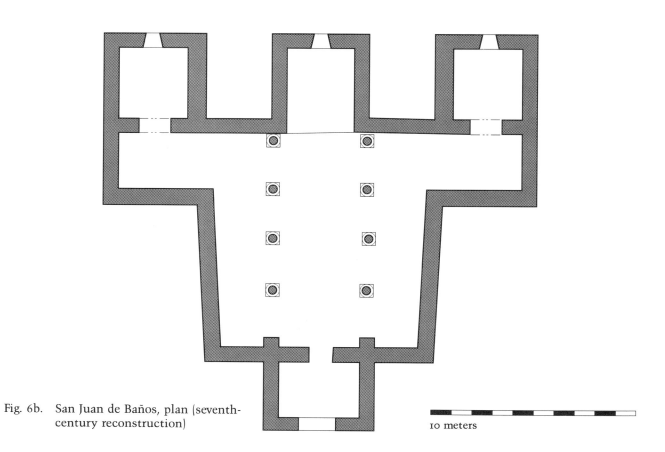

Fig. 6b. San Juan de Baños, plan (seventh-
century reconstruction)

10 meters

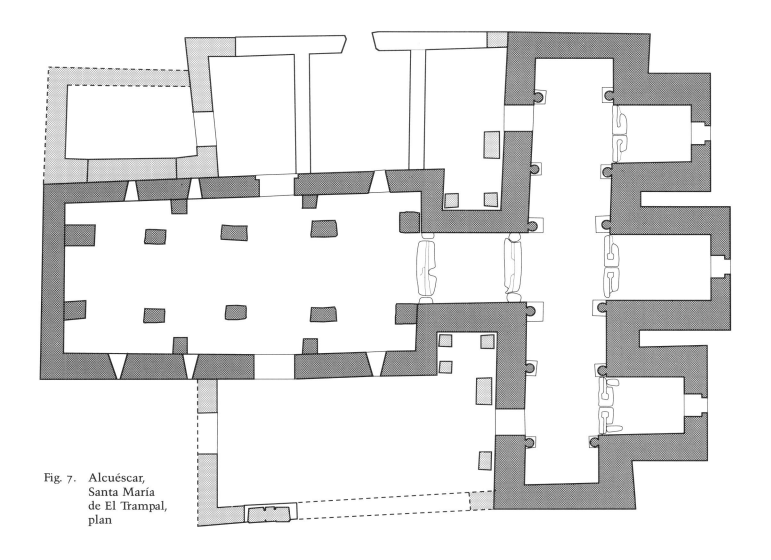

Fig. 7. Alcuéscar,
Santa María
de El Trampal,
plan

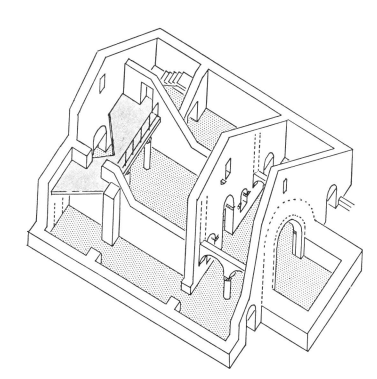

Fig. 8. São Gião de Nazaré, axonometric

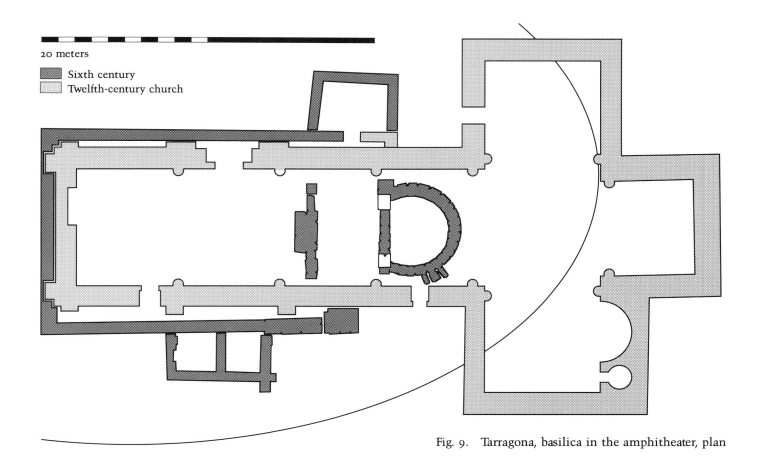

20 meters

Sixth century
Twelfth-century church

Fig. 9.   Tarragona, basilica in the amphitheater, plan

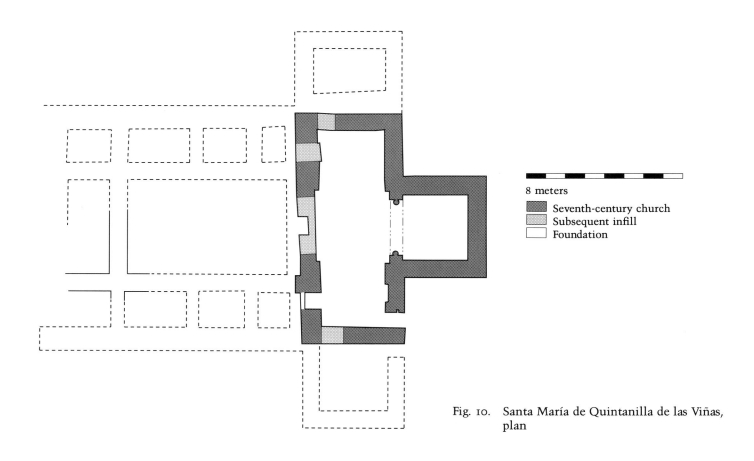

8 meters

Seventh-century church
Subsequent infill
Foundation

Fig. 10.   Santa María de Quintanilla de las Viñas, plan

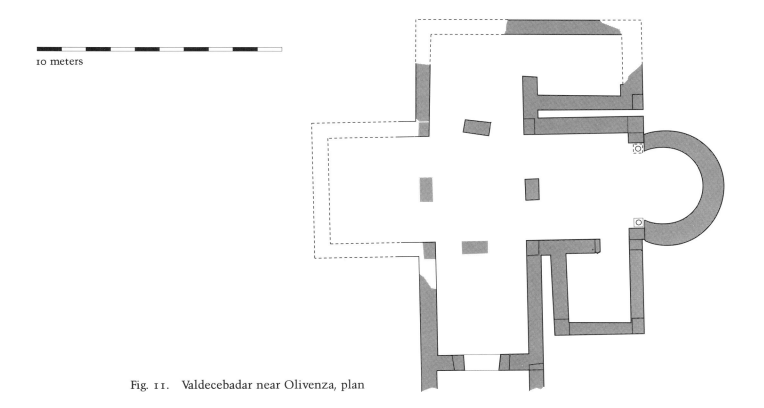

10 meters

Fig. 11. Valdecebadar near Olivenza, plan

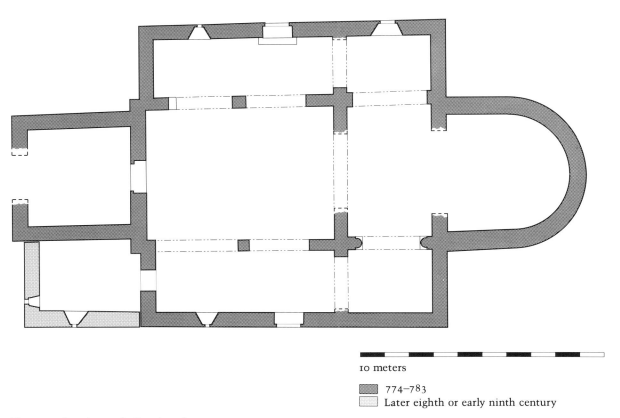

10 meters

■ 774–783
□ Later eighth or early ninth century

Fig. 12. Santianes de Pravia, plan

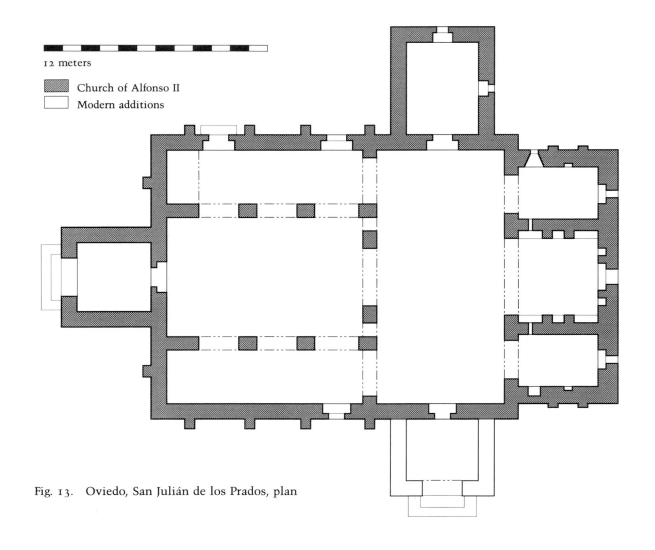

12 meters

Church of Alfonso II

Modern additions

Fig. 13. Oviedo, San Julián de los Prados, plan

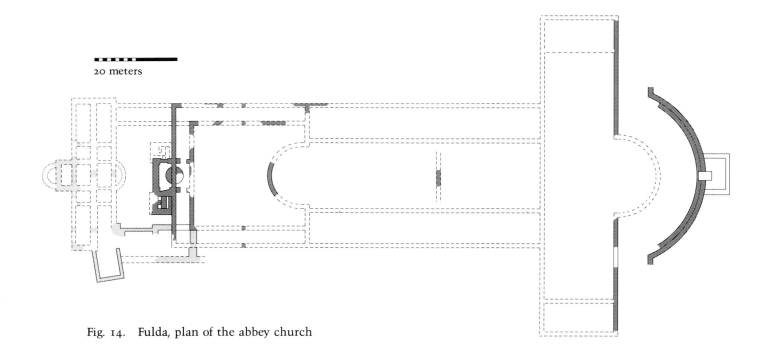

20 meters

Fig. 14. Fulda, plan of the abbey church

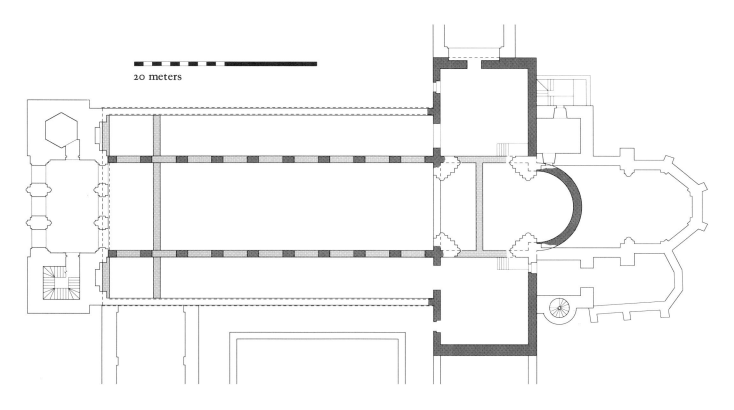

Fig. 15. Seligenstadt, plan of the abbey church

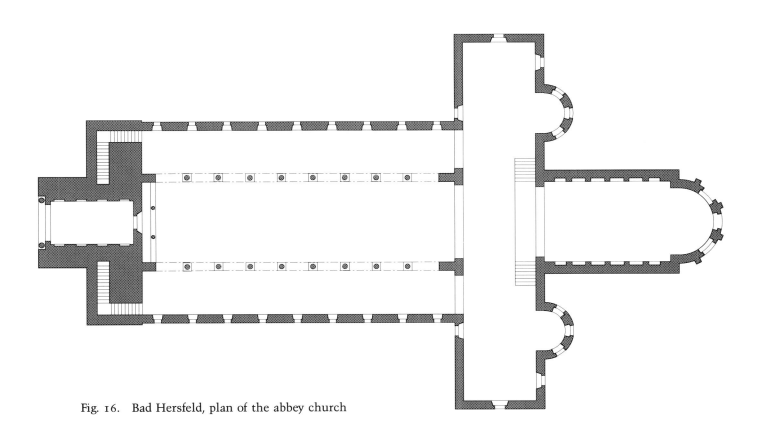

Fig. 16. Bad Hersfeld, plan of the abbey church

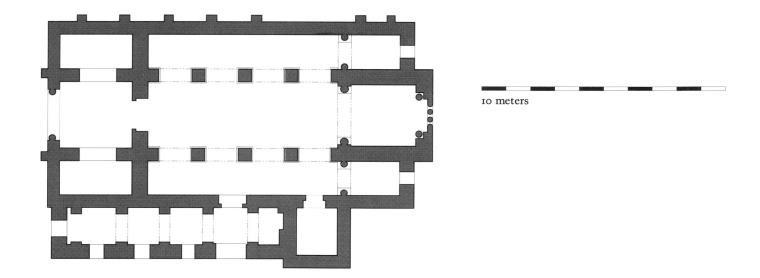

Fig. 17.   San Salvador de Valdediós, plan

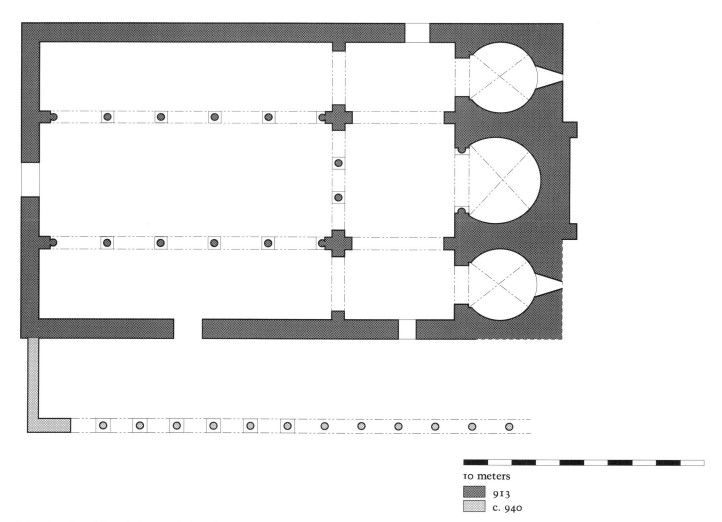

10 meters

913

c. 940

Fig. 18.   San Miguel de Escalada, plan

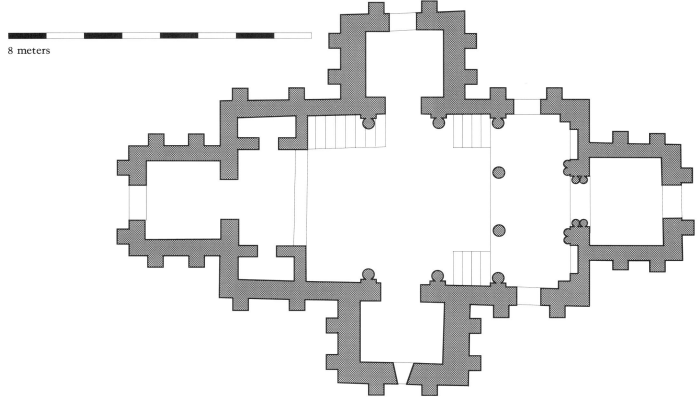

8 meters

Fig. 19.   Santa Cristina de Lena, plan

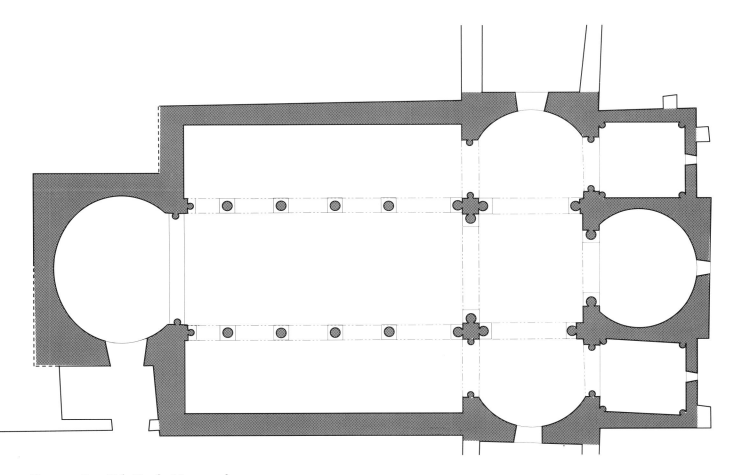

Fig. 20.   San Cebrián de Mazote, plan

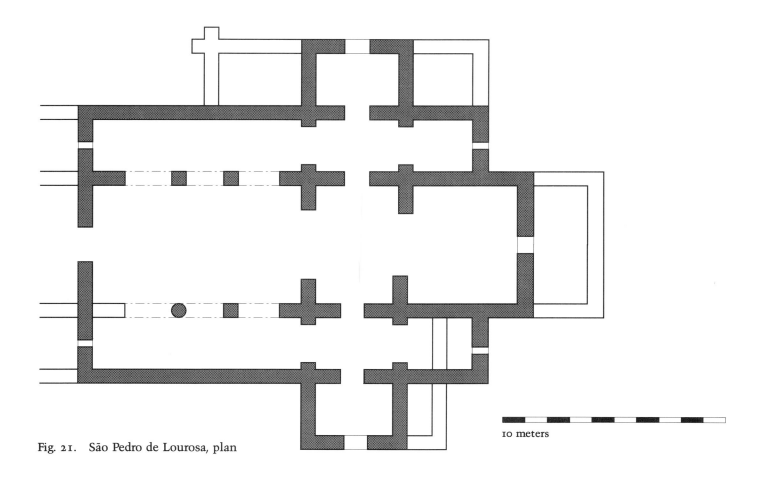

Fig. 21. São Pedro de Lourosa, plan

10 meters

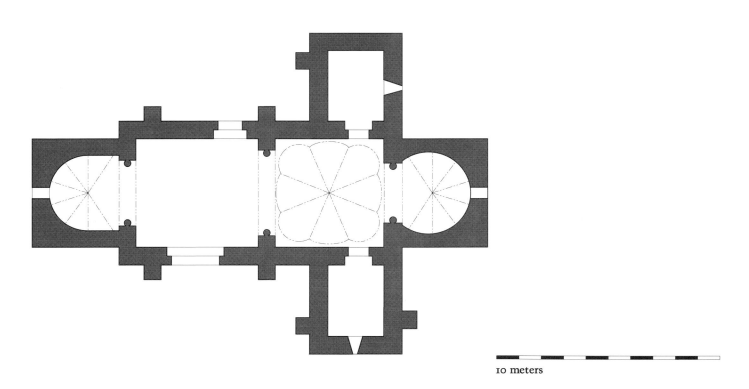

10 meters

Fig. 22. Santiago de Peñalba, plan

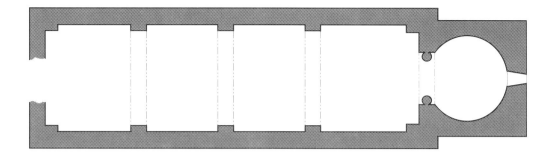

Fig. 23.   Santa María de Vilanova, plan

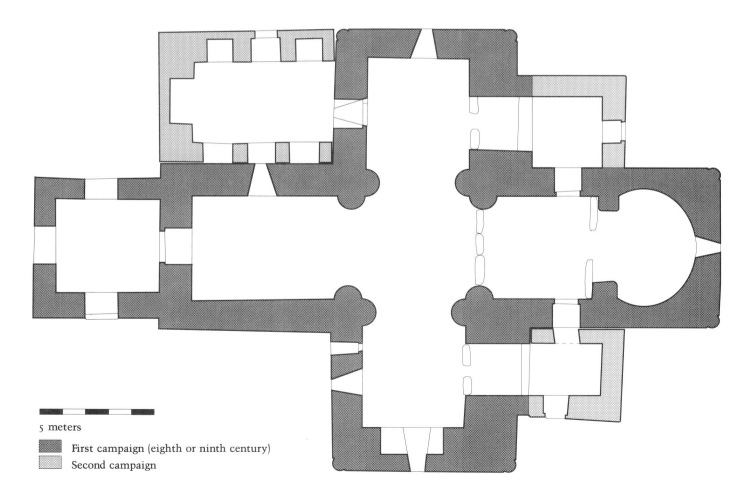

6 meters

5 meters

First campaign (eighth or ninth century)
Second campaign

Fig. 24.   Santa María de Melque, plan

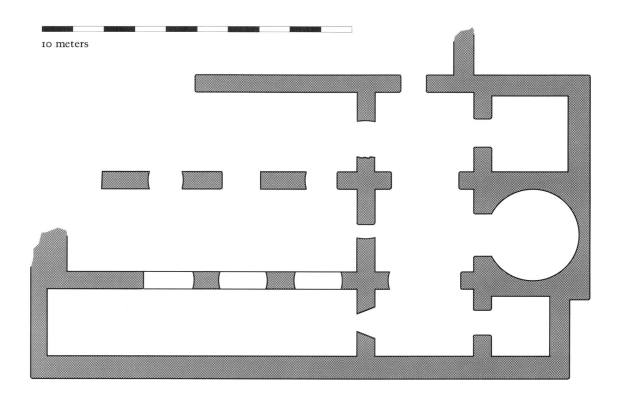

Fig. 25. Mesas de Villaverde ("Bobastro"), plan of church

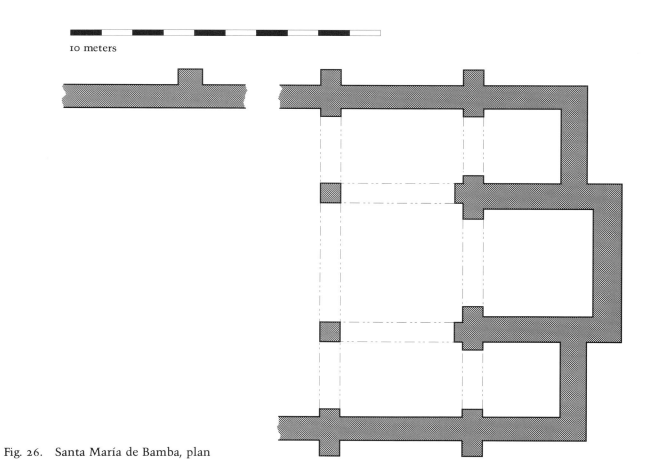

Fig. 26. Santa María de Bamba, plan

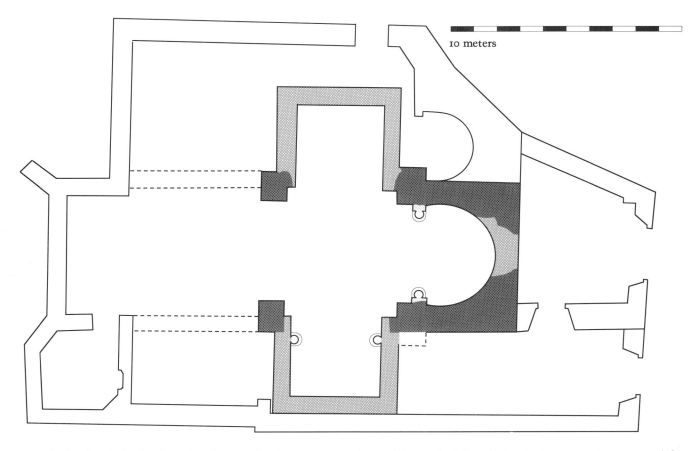

Fig. 27.   León, San Salvador de Palaz de Rey, plan (recent excavations of Fernando Miguel Hernández suggest some modifi-
cations, including a western apse)

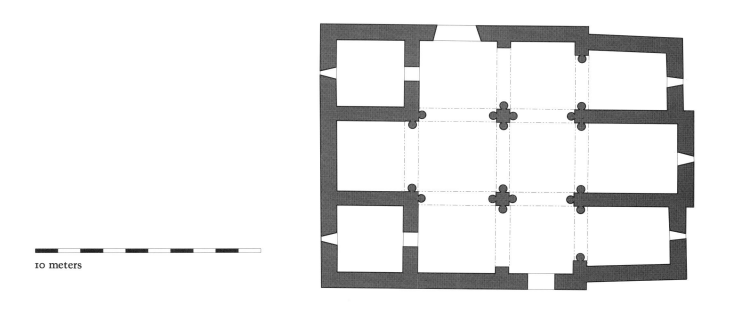

10 meters

Fig. 28.   Santa María de Lebeña,
plan

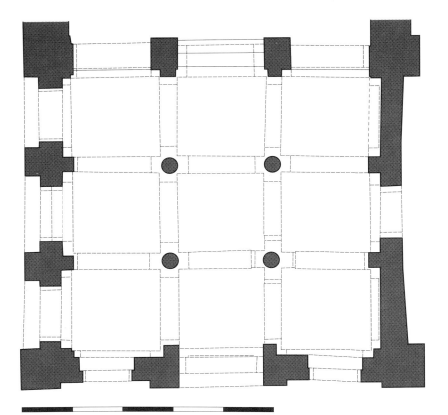

Fig. 29.   Mosque of Bāb al-Mardūm, plan

5 meters

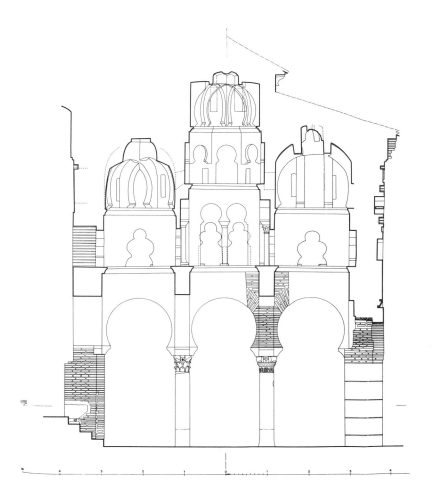

Fig. 30.   Mosque of Bāb al-Mardūm, elevation

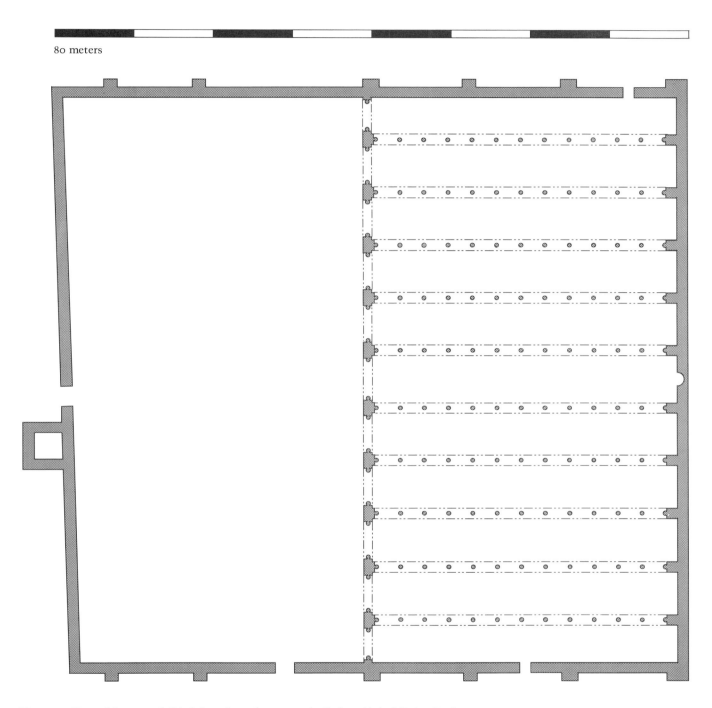

80 meters

Fig. 31. Great Mosque of Córdoba, plan of mosque built by ʿAbd al-Raḥmān I

80 meters

░░░ ʿAbd al-Raḥmān I

▒▒▒ ʿAbd al-Raḥmān II

███ ʿAbd al-Raḥmān III

☐ al-Ḥakam II

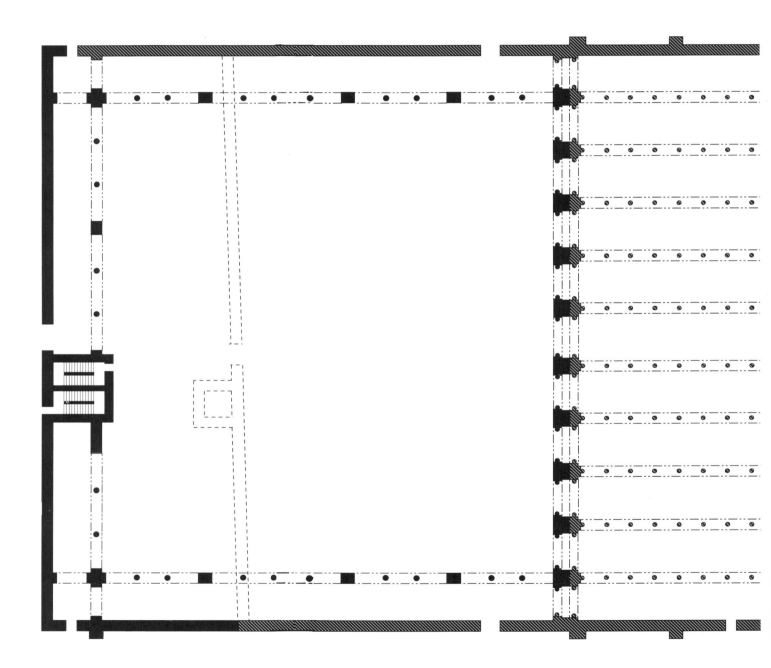

Fig. 32.   Great Mosque of Córdoba, plan after additions of al-Ḥakam II

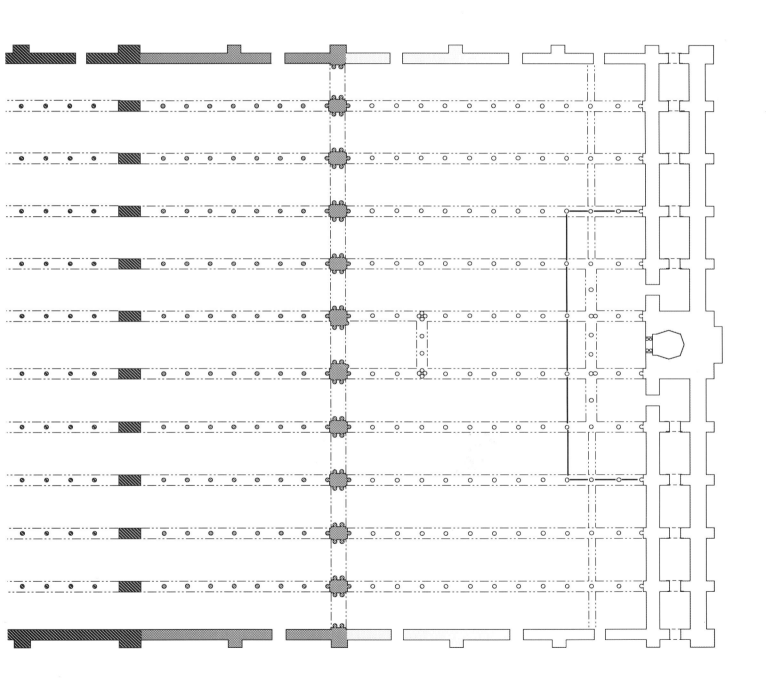

Plate 1.   São Frutuoso de Montelios, exterior

Plate 2.   Ravenna, so-called mausoleum of Galla Placidia, exterior

Plate 3.   São Frutuoso de Montelios, interior

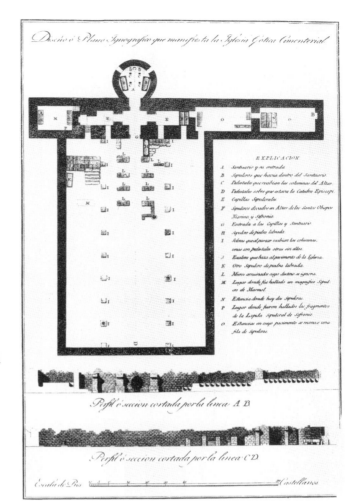

Plate 4. Segóbriga (Cabeza del Griego), plan and elevations of the basilica by J. Cornide

Plate 5. San Pedro de la Nave, exterior

Plate 6. San Pedro de la Nave, interior looking east

Plate 7. Santa Comba de Bande, interior looking east

Plate 8. San Juan de Baños, nave arcade

Plate 9.   São Gião de Nazaré, wall separating choir from nave

Plate 10.   Santa María de Quintanilla de las Viñas, communication between side aisle and crossing

Plate 11.   São Pedro de Balsemão, apse entrance

Plate 12.   San Pedro de la Nave, window from exterior

Plate 13.   Quintanilla de las Viñas, apse entrance

Plate 14a.   Quintanilla de las Viñas, impost block

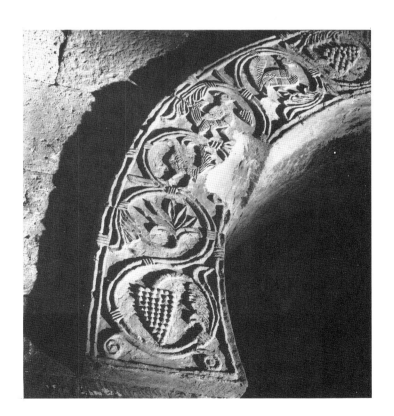

Plate 14b.   Quintanilla de las Viñas, triumphal
arch

Plate 15. León Bible of 960: Aaron at the Tabernacle

Plate 16. Santianes de Pravia, window fragment found in excavations

Plate 17. Oviedo, Cámara Santa, exterior

Plate 18. Oviedo, San Tirso, surviving eastern apse wall

Plate 19. Mérida, Museo Arqueológico Provincial, window

Plate 20. Oviedo, San Julián de los Prados (Santullano), interior looking east

Plate 21. San Julián de los Prados, interior of transept

Plate 22. San Julián de los Prados, exterior

Plate 23. Bad Hersfeld, remains of abbey church

Plate 24. San Julián de los Prados, paintings of nave elevation (rendered by Magín Berenguer)

Plate 25. San Julián de los Prados, detail, nave painting (rendered by Magín Berenguer)

Plate 26. San Julián de los Prados, paintings of transept elevation (rendered by Magín Berenguer)

Plate 27. Istanbul, Hagia Sophia, *opus sectile* panel

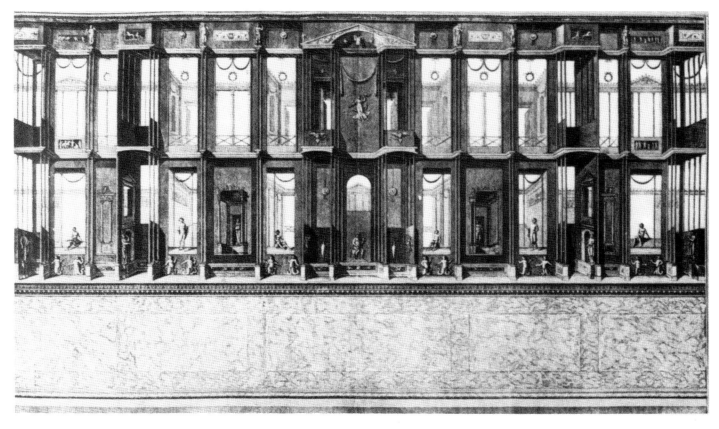

Plate 28.   Rome, Domus Aurea (rendering of wall paintings by Smugliwicz)

Plate 29.   Ostia, Corporation House, *opus sectile* panel

Plate 30. San Julián de los Prados, painted capital

Plate 31. Saint Germain d'Auxerre, painted capital

Plate 32.   Gospel of Saint Médard of Soissons: Adoration of the Lamb

Plate 33. San Salvador de Valdediós, exterior

Plate 34. San Salvador de Valdediós, interior looking east

Plate 35.   San Salvador de Valdediós, window from exterior

Plate 36.   San Salvador de Priesca, interior

Plate 37. San Miguel de Escalada, interior looking east

Plate 38.   San Miguel de Escalada, nave arcade

Plate 39.   San Miguel de Escalada, choir looking west

Plate 40. San Miguel de Escalada, view from side aisle

Plate 41. San Miguel de Escalada, arches of nave arcade

Plate 42. San Miguel de Escalada, side apse
entrance

Plate 43. San Miguel de Escalada, central apse
entrance

Plate 44. San Juan de Baños, entrance arch

Plate 45. Great Mosque of Córdoba, door of ʿAbd Allāh

Plate 46. Great Mosque of Córdoba, door of Saint Stephen

Plate 47. Great Mosque of Córdoba, prayer hall of ʿAbd al-Raḥmān I

Plate 48.   Santa Cristina de Lena, interior

Plate 49.   San Cebrián de Mazote, interior looking east

Plate 50. San Cebrián de Mazote, nave arcade

Plate 51. São Pedro de Lourosa, nave arcade

Plate 52. Santiago de Peñalba, interior looking east

Plate 53.   San Miguel de Celanova, interior looking east

Plate 54.   Viguera, San Estebán, wall separating choir area

Plate 55.   Santa María de Melque, exterior

Plate 56.   Santa María de Melque, interior looking east

Plate 57.   Santa María de Melque, window from exterior

Plate 58.   Mesas de Villaverde ("Bobastro"), ruins of choir
entrance

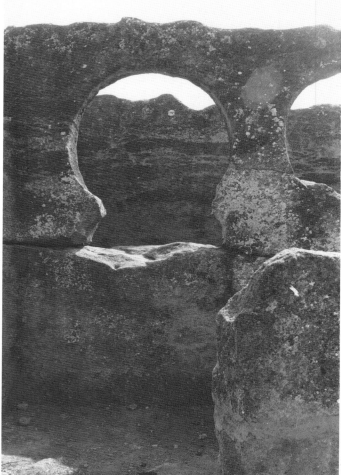

Plate 59.   Mesas de Villaverde, ruins of nave arcade

Plate 60. *Morgan Beatus,* The Feast of Baltassar

Plate 61. Santa María de Bamba, interior

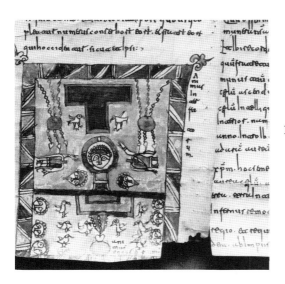

Plate 62. *Silos Beatus* page, The Souls of the Martyrs Under the Altar

Plate 63. *Codex Vigilanus* of 976, Visigothic and Leonese kings, the scribe Vigila and his assistants

Plate 64. Santiago de Peñalba, south entrance

Plate 65. Santiago de Peñalba, capital

Plate 66. Santiago de Peñalba, paintings on apse entrance (drawing by J. Menéndez Pidal)

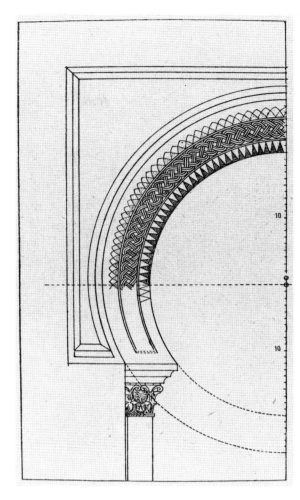

Plate 67. San Miguel de Escalada, exterior with south porch

Plate 68.   Great Mosque of Córdoba, prayer hall of ʿAbd al-Raḥmān II

Plate 69.   San Cebrián de Mazote, door in north transept end

Plate 70.   Santa María de Lebeña, exterior

Plate 71.   Santa María de Lebeña, interior

Plate 72.   Mosque of Bāb al-Mardūm, interior

Plate 73.   San Baudelio de Berlanga, interior before re-
            moval of paintings

Plate 74. Great Mosque of Córdoba, prayer hall of ʿAbd al-Raḥmān I

Plate 75. Great Mosque of Córdoba, prayer hall of al-Ḥakam II

Plate 76.   Great Mosque of Córdoba, mihrab aisle of al-Ḥakam II

Plate 77.   Great Mosque of Córdoba, mihrab aisle of al-Ḥakam II

Plate 78. Great Mosque of Córdoba, mihrab aisle of al-Ḥakam II

Plate 79. Great Mosque of Córdoba, aisle to the right of the mihrab aisle of al-Ḥakam II

Plate 80.   Great Mosque of Córdoba, *maqṣūra* of al-Ḥakam II

Plate 81.   Great Mosque of Córdoba, mihrab of al-Ḥakam II